WELCOME TO THE JUNGLE

NAVIGATING THE MUSIC BUSINESS IN AUSTRALIA

4th Edition

ANDREW WATT

Copyright © Andrew Watt 2013-2017

First Published 2014 by Ravens Nest Consulting Pty Ltd
Second Edition 2015 published by Ravens Nest Consulting Pty Ltd
Third Edition 2016 published by Ravens Nest Consulting Pty Ltd
Fourth Edition 2017 published by Music Business Education Pty Ltd

All rights reserved. No part of this book may be reproduced in any form by any mechanical or electronic means including information storage or retrieval systems, without permission in writing from the publisher, except by a reviewer who may quote brief passages.

The Australian Copyright Act 1968 allows a maximum of one chapter or 10 per cent of this book, whichever is the greater, to be photocopied by any educational institution for its educational purposes provided the educational institution has given a remuneration notice to Copyright Agency Limited (CAL) under the above Act.

www.musicbusinesseducation.com.au

www.facebook.com/musicbusinesseducation/

National Library of Australia
Cataloguing-in-Publication entry:

Author:	Watt, Andrew, 1962 - author.
Title:	Welcome to the Jungle: Navigating the Music Business in Australia / Andrew Watt.
ISBN:	978-0-9924203-1-4 (paperback)
Notes:	Includes bibliographical references.
Subjects:	Music trade--Australia.
	Music publishers--Australia.
	Music publishing--Australia.
	Popular music--Writing and publishing--Australia.

Dewey Number: 070.5794
ISBN 13: 9780992420307
ISBN 10: 099242030X

Dedicated to Kate Bentley, John Bromell, Aaron Chugg, Ed Nimmervoll, Ian Smith and Gary Rabin– who all worked in the Australian music business but gave so much more than just their time.

Contents

Acknowledgments · vii
Preface · ix
Part 1   **Overview of the Music Industries** · · · · · · · · · · · · · · · · · 1
Chapter 1   The Music Business in Perspective · · · · · · · · · · · · · 3
Chapter 2   A Short History of the Recorded Music Business · · · · 21
Chapter 3   Copyright, Contracts and the Recording Industry · · · 61
Chapter 4   The Live Music Industry · 89
Chapter 5   The Relationship Between the Live and
                  the Recorded Music Businesses · · · · · · · · · · · · · · · · 131
Chapter 6   New Models and Changing Times · · · · · · · · · · · · · · 147
Chapter 7   International Ambitions · 175
Part 2   **Roles in the Music Industries** · · · · · · · · · · · · · · · · · · 189
Chapter 8   Major Record Companies · · · · · · · · · · · · · · · · · · · 195
Chapter 9   Independent Record Companies and Distributors · · · 207
Chapter 10   Publishing, Synchronisation and
                  Music Supervision · 233
Chapter 11   A&R ·251
Chapter 12   Management · 265
Chapter 13   Venue Operation and Band Booking · · · · · · · · · · · 293
Chapter 14   The Agent · 309
Chapter 15   Promoters · 323
Chapter 16   Festivals · 335
Chapter 17   Publicity and Promotion · 353
Chapter 18   Digital Marketing ·375
Chapter 19   Branded Entertainment · 389
Chapter 20   Merchandise · 403
Chapter 21   Industry Bodies and Government · · · · · · · · · · · · · ·413
Chapter 22   Entreprenuerism in the Music Industries · · · · · · · · 435

WELCOME TO THE JUNGLE

Part 3	**Breaking into the Music Industries** · · · · · · · · · · · ·	449
Chapter 23	Music Business Education ·	453
Chapter 24	Internships & Work Experience · · · · · · · · · · · · · · · ·	477
Chapter 25	Industry Events ·	495
Chapter 26	Music Media ·	503
Chapter 27	Mentors ·	511
Chapter 28	Conclusion ·	519
Interviewees ·		533
Index ·		547
About the Author ·		555

Acknowledgments

As with the previous editions of this book, I offer my heartfelt appreciation to the now almost 100 music industry professionals who shared their time, thoughts, experience and energy, doing the interviews that form its backbone. My words simply fill the gaps between their generous and wise contributions.

The contributions of those people who assisted in the creation, development and publication of the first edition - Brett Murrihy, Simon Moor, Colin Daniels, Jo Roberts, Al Kennedy, Stuart Gibson, Simon Smith, Phil Leahy, Leanne Menard and Sam Gowing remain important and appreciated.

I also acknowledge the support of various media outlets who assisted in promoting earlier editions, and especially those students and industry people who have used the previous editions and graciously commented on its usefulness and value. Without those responses there would be no reason for further editions.

Finally I acknowledge the support of Andrew Rutter and David Cochran, the team at Creative Victoria, Mark Hodgetts and all those who have contributed to the development of the Music Business Education on-line platform.

Preface

So you want a career in the music business? Naturally you're a music fan, but you are *more* than just a fan, right? You've always been interested in the stories behind the scenes, the moves and machinations of those you don't see on stage.

You've always wanted to have a job where you can wear sneakers to work.

As a music fan, you've possibly read biographies of famous rockstars and were engaged by the behind-the-scenes mayhem. Perhaps someone gave you the Michael Gudinski biography for Christmas. If you are really up to speed, the names Martin Mills, Troy Carter, Guy Oseary, Coran Capshaw or Scooter Braun might mean something to you. You've imagined yourself on a tour bus, or working your mobile phone in the first class lounge of an international airport. But how do you turn those daydreams into a reality? Is that even a reality?

Rather than attempt to answer that question right away, let's consider one of the live touring industry's most essential tools.

The Tour Itinerary

This is the bible for all participants of a major concert tour. Handed out by the tour manager at the start of a tour, the Tour Itinerary tells the touring party everything they need to know to make the tour run smoothly. It details how the tour party will get from Point A to Point B, whether on a plane, bus, airport transfer or taxi, and who the vital contact person might be every step of the way. It will detail the hotel accommodation and whether it has a gym, Wi-Fi, a restaurant, laundry

WELCOME TO THE JUNGLE

service and how close it is to the venue or festival site. The Tour Itinerary will let the touring party know what late-night food delivery is available (and if it is edible), who the trusted local doctor is, what newspapers and street press the city has, and any 'must-see' local attractions, or places to avoid. Of course, it will have all the details of the show itself – soundcheck and show times, other artists performing, sponsors and local media and any special guest that might be in the audience. And once the show is over, the Tour Itinerary will provide details of the exit from the venue, after-show commitments/options/parties and the next morning's wake-up call and travel. And it will do this every day until the tour is finished. The Tour Itinerary never sleeps and very rarely lies.

Every member of the touring party is expected to treat the Tour Itinerary as gospel. Ignore the sacred document at your peril. The Tour Manager creates the Tour Itinerary for a reason and it's not for his or her own amusement. In the random, sometimes wildly unpredictable world of live music the Tour Itinerary stands as a beacon of solidarity and certainty.

Once the tour is over and the participants have all gone back to their respective homes, families, share houses and bedsits, the Tour Itinerary becomes no more than a souvenir. Tour party members are left to organise their own lives, pay their own bills, meet their own responsibilities and find their next gig. When they wake up, in their own bed, and have to decide what they are going to do with their day, they won't have that trusty spiral-bound document to make their decisions for them.

Wouldn't it be great if your entire working life in the music business came equipped with a Tour Itinerary?

Unfortunately it's not that simple. Your career in the music business doesn't have such a factory-fitted roadmap. Your career plan won't give you departure and arrival times; it won't tell you what bus to catch, what time to be in the hotel lobby, who your key contact person is, who to call in an emergency. It doesn't have GPS. It doesn't even have an operating manual. All that you get as standard equipment is (hopefully) a love of music, some street smarts, a willingness to take a chance and a fair degree of lifestyle flexibility.

This book is not the Tour Itinerary for your career in the music business. It doesn't even attempt to be.

For a start, the whole point of a Tour Itinerary is that there is a bunch of people, sometimes in the hundreds, all of whom are on the same tour and so it makes sense that they have some commonality of purpose and methodology of achieving it. Some might travel in first class and others in economy, but at the end of the day they are all likely to be at the same destination, with a pre-arranged job to do. Like any project that involves teamwork, a certain degree of duplicated and regimented activity is inevitable.

Your career isn't like that. Sure, there will be some people you work with time and again; in some cases you will form a working relationship so close and trusted that it's like a marriage or family. That's not unique to the music business, of course, but it's a business that does lend itself to career-long friendships and relationships. But even in the closest of partnerships, individuals have their own career paths. They may have had different entry points, their 'big break' may have been different, their passions, motivations, strengths and weaknesses may be divergent, but often complementary.

No two stories are the same. You can model your career on someone you admire that has gone before you – and this book provides plenty of examples of likely candidates – but eventually you'll have to carve

WELCOME TO THE JUNGLE

your own path through the jungle. You can learn from those pioneers, but be aware that the terrain they leave behind has already changed the moment they pass through.

Each career that is observed through this book is unique and remarkable in its own way. They could be role models for you, or they may have nothing in common with your goals; either way there is much to be learned from their experiences.

So this book is neither a Tour Itinerary for your career, nor a step-by-step guide on how to make it in the music business. But if it helps you crystallise your own thoughts, look at your career in a different way, speak the language of the industry or de-mystify those people whose names you see in the liner notes of albums, then it's done its job.

Well over 100 people are interviewed in this book, and each gave of their thoughts and experience freely and openly. That fact alone probably makes it the most comprehensive survey of the Australian contemporary music business ever undertaken. Each of them had a story to tell, and each of them could probably write their own book. In fact, a couple of them already have. Other than their willingness to share their knowledge and practical experiences what united them was a belief that they were working in one of the most exciting industries you could find. Presumably, if you are reading this book, you may already suspect that.

Michael Newton is the director of Roundhouse Entertainment, the concert promoter and producer behind the hugely successful *A Day On The Green* concert series. For Newton, it's the unpredictable and ever-changing nature of the music business that has kept him excited to go to work in the morning after more than two decades in the industry.

ANDREW WATT

[**MICHAEL NEWTON**] "The exciting thing about the music business is that a lot of it is about the next thing – the next big artists, the next tour, the next way of promoting, the latest in production, the latest in social media, the latest way to purchase music.

I always think that right now there is an act playing in a local pub, or in their lounge room, that in five years are going to be massive. And how many people will be involved in making that happen? There's always another chapter to be written in the music business and so from that point of view it's always exciting for somebody getting into the business or trying to. It's just a matter of getting yourself involved at some level and being ready for that moment or that time when the opportunity presents itself. Doing something will get you somewhere and doing nothing will get you nowhere."

This book provides an insight into the stories of a lot of people who did something and got somewhere.

Who should read this book?

Many of the people interviewed for this book were once professional musicians. Many of them still play music because its something they love to do. Some of them even play music rather well. But the book is not about that.

This book won't help you be a better musician. This book isn't a self-help guide for young bands; there are plenty of those books around and some of them are very good.

It also isn't a legal guide to the music industry, even though the author is an entertainment lawyer, and sometimes can't help but give a legal

WELCOME TO THE JUNGLE

perspective on the issues confronting the industry and the people working in it.

The book isn't an A-Z of the business either, although by the end of it you should be familiar with most of the terminology that will help you to sound like you know what you are talking about, even when you are still learning. Everyone featured in this book is still learning <u>and that's part of the reason they are still successful</u>.

This book is aimed at people who want to work in the music business, but not necessarily as musicians. It's not exclusively aimed at people who want to be the next big mover and shaker in the business, although there is plenty of good advice in here from people who are at the top of the tree. It's for anyone who wants to get a foot in the door, to see what's on the other side and where it may lead. There are hundreds of people working successfully in the music business who will never be described as "music mogul."

However, working and aspiring musicians <u>should</u> read this book. If you are a musician you are going to have to deal with a lot of people who don't know a G string from a g-string. Among them, could be some of the most important people in your career. You need to understand what these people do and, more importantly, how and why they do it. Your music might be your business card, but you are in the minority. The motivations and passions of the people you work with *outside* your band are what will make the difference between you being a successful artist and another weekend hobby musician. They say it takes a village to raise a child; it certainly takes a whole host of diversely talented and motivated people to create a hit record or a sell-out tour. Musicians reading this book will learn a lot about the mysteries of "the business."

Paul Gildea is a successful musician (25 years as the touring guitarist for iconic Australian band Icehouse will attest to that) but he's also

ANDREW WATT

been a manager of artists such as Motor Ace, Michael Paynter and Stonefield, and is a program head for the Melbourne Campus of the Australian Institute of Music. He takes the view that musicians cannot avoid understanding how their business operates.

> **[PAUL GILDEA]:** "There is a far greater emphasis on DIY and self reliance than ever before. Without a more developed understanding of the processes of business I can't see how it is possible to achieve what you set out to do without both educating yourself, developing and establishing a network and reading as much as possible about the almost daily but certainly weekly changes in the way the music model is being transformed – often by forces outside the industry. This is the most commercially reactive arts model in the world."

Those that are already working in a part of the business could also benefit from reading this book. It's a big and diverse industry and it attracts a wide variety of people with vastly different backgrounds and skill sets. The various right hands don't always know what the various left hands are doing, or how they are doing it. There isn't anyone already working in the industry that couldn't benefit from learning more about their contemporaries and the details of the jobs they do.

Who else should read this book?

Speaking of raising a child, the music industry hasn't always been the first business of choice for parents seeking a career path for their offspring!

The business has often been in need of some positive PR to counteract some negative perceptions. Add to that the grim suggestion around the turn of the century and beyond that the music business was in its death throes and that the onset of various threats such as illegal

WELCOME TO THE JUNGLE

downloading, piracy, urban gentrification and competition for the leisure dollar were colluding to kill off the industry. Why would any parent encourage their kid to work in the music business?

Parents of teenagers, school leavers or university students who are showing an interest in the music industry should read this book. It will undoubtedly change some perceptions of what the business is, who populates it, and open eyes to the diversity of skills and passions that it welcomes. Hopefully is dispels the myth that it's all about sex, drugs and rock n' roll because, well, it isn't!

Who shouldn't read this book?

If you love music but couldn't care less about the people behind the scenes who are responsible for its reproduction, marketing, distribution, staging and promotion, then this book probably won't greatly interest you. That's fine. Some of the most passionate and connected music fans have never, ever wanted to work in the music industry. Two friends immediately come to mind. One has the best music collection of any of his peers and the second goes to more gigs than he has any right to! The first is a project manager for major construction companies and the other works in the high end of the financial services industry. Neither of them would find this book of benefit to their careers or even to their appreciation of great music.

Consider this comparison. There are lots of people that play golf. They love golf; they play most weekends, they spend exorbitant sums of money on club memberships and equipment and they talk about the intricacies of the game until all around them are driven to distraction. But none of them work in the golf industry; they are much happier being customers and consumers of the industry rather than participants in the industry.

ANDREW WATT

The point is – you need to be more than simply a passionate music fan to want to work in the music business. Some might say that you also need to be slightly mad, but that's a disingenuous observation that's only partly true. There's a certain attitude to life and work that makes some people suited to the music industry and others not. It's hard to put a finger on exactly what it is, but most industry people instinctively recognise it - and just about everyone interviewed for this book has it.

If you already know that you'd rather be a music fan than a music industry participant, then you may want to stop reading now. If you are not sure, hopefully this book will help you decide.

How to read this book

The book can be read cover to cover or selectively, depending on your areas of interest. It is recommended, however, that you read all of **Part One**, the first seven chapters. Here, the landscape of the music business is surveyed and some of the essential historical, legal and structural concepts that form the foundations of the business are introduced. **Part One** also gets you up to speed with some of the current issues, drawing on the experience of the key industry players who are living it every day. There is no substitute for gaining your own experience, but by the time you consume **Part One** you will be capable of holding your own in a conversation with anyone in the industry and leave them impressed by the depth of your understanding.

Without the knowledge you'll gain in **Part One,** the value of the rest of the book is reduced as you'll find yourself assuming things about the various industry roles and participants – and you won't always be right.

Part Two focuses on some of the roles and participants in the industry. This is where you will start to identify what areas of the business most interest you, best suit you or are likely to impact on your career if you

WELCOME TO THE JUNGLE

are an artist. You'll probably be surprised just how diverse the skill sets of those in the industry are. This is also where the most interview material is found. There's a simple reason for that. These industry players know more about what they do and how they do it than the author could ever know, and their comments, observations and opinions about their specialist field are particularly useful in these chapters.

Martin Elbourne is an important figure in the music business. In 2014, the Glastonbury Festival booker and co-founder of WOMAD authored a report titled *The Future of Live Music In South Australia*, but the report's content is relevant far beyond the SA borders. It's considered in detail later in this book, but Elbourne's introduction to the section titled "Development of Industry Professions" provides a succinct insight into the importance of industry participants supporting the creative artists.

"The music industry starts with the artist, but is not only about the artist. An infrastructure and network of people grows around an artist and furthers their career. The flow-on effect from the creation of music keeps millions of people employed worldwide. A robust industry creates employment in all areas of music from its creation to its performance, and to the distribution and promotion of music. The types of employment and/or businesses include; music publishers; producers; recording studios; sound engineers; record labels; retail and online music stores; performance rights organisations; booking agents; promoters; music venues; road crew; artists; managers; business managers; entertainment lawyers; journalists; educators; musical instrument makers and the myriad of new opportunities and businesses being forged in the ever developing music industry technology. All of these play a role in an active, healthy industry. A healthy industry in turn supports and nurtures the musical vision of the artist and can provide the framework for all parties to gain maximum benefit."

Elbourne's words summarise the content and importance of **Part Two** of this book.

Part Three looks at ways of breaking into the industry and suggests steps you can take to get noticed and get a foot in the door. This is where you'll be reminded of Michael Newton's words from this introduction – "doing something will get you somewhere, doing nothing will get you nowhere."

You'll be exposed to the thoughts of many great industry professionals throughout the book and the material they provided in hours of interviews is used with much gratitude.

The people interviewed for the book are credited whenever they are directly quoted and some of their comments are used to illustrate points being made. Every interviewee and their credentials are listed at the end of the book. It's always a good idea to refer to their biographic information when considering their comments to give those comments some context and enhance their meaning. Many of them are names well known to even the most casual observer; others are less familiar, but no less important. All have fascinating insights and anecdotes to offer.

Hopefully the book provides an insight into not only the skills and knowledge that these people possess, but also the attitude they bring to work every day. As longtime Mushroom Group employee Ann Gibson says, "I haven't had a career, I've had a social life that I've been paid for". The music business is like that, much to the joy of the people that work in it.

Their story could be your story.

PART 1

OVERVIEW OF THE MUSIC INDUSTRIES

My Path into the Industry

CHARLES CALDAS

"I was at uni back in the days when you could take a very long time to do a very short course. I was much more interested in working at the radio station, doing radio shows and trying to play in a band. The band got signed to Rampant Records, which was an old Melbourne underground label. I finally got my BA after five years, and I was still playing in the band. Rampant was distributed by a company called Musicland, which was run out of a little house in Ripponlea and they would import and distribute all sorts of weird music. On holidays I'd go in there and pack boxes and send them to record shops. One day the sales manager walked out and the guy who ran Musicland, who was a real character called Jeremy, came into the warehouse, and said, "There's the list, there's the phone, start selling records". So I sold records on the phone to people who didn't want them for about six to eight months until I started going mad.

Then I travelled for a little while. The band was on and off and we were fairly lazy as people and never really took it seriously enough. I came back from travelling and I was living at my Dad's house thinking, "Oh shit, now what do I do?" I was working as a waiter at the Arts Centre. Shock had just started and I got a phone call from David who ran Shock asking me to do a two-month stint in sales. I went in and sold records and packed boxes and I was there really from the very beginning of Shock; I was the fifth or sixth employee. It went from there – as the company grew those of us who understood the business instinctively stayed at the centre of it and it ended up getting to the point of being a serious and significant part of the market and next thing I knew I was the CEO trying to work out what that meant and what I was supposed to do! It was an accidental but happy path."

CHAPTER 1
THE MUSIC BUSINESS IN PERSPECTIVE

Having decided that you actually want to work in the music business, as opposed to simply being a rusted-on music fan, the next step is to understand exactly what the music industry is. It isn't as obvious as it sounds. If you are just starting out you probably don't realise the massive generational change the Australian music industry has seen. Music has always been an in-demand commodity, but the industry that supplies it hasn't always been as sophisticated as it is today.

Michael Gudinski, is the founder of the Mushroom Group of Companies, arguably the most important collection of businesses in the Australian music industry. He's been in the business around 40 years and there's very little he hasn't seen or done. A biography (written by Stuart Coupe and published in 2015) details Gudinski's remarkable history. Many of the people in this book owe their career to him, and for many in the corporate world, in government and the general public, he is the face of the Australian music industry. Gudinski is perfectly placed to put some perspective around the industry as we know it.

> **[MICHAEL GUDINSKI]:** "I was there when it was a backyard business, and in fact, 'business' is a pretty loose word to use. There were a lot of fly-by-nighters and it wasn't looked at as a business at all both from within and certainly from the outside looking in. I never thought about being 60 and being in this business. It

WELCOME TO THE JUNGLE

was about living for tomorrow. I didn't have a big plan, but I saw something that I thought was shaped all the wrong way.

Australian music was regarded as second rate, and it wasn't just music, it was the same with clothes and cars. The people who were doing it for art were very non-commercial. There wasn't an industry as such devoted to getting those people heard.

The reason I started Mushroom Records wasn't because I thought it was some big business idea and that it would turn out to be what it did. It was purely out of the frustration of being a young manager and seeing my two or three acts told what to record, who to record with, and what their album cover would be. The Australian record labels that existed then were mainly doing cover versions of overseas pop tunes.

As time went on, it obviously became a big business. It became a big business before government and before the general business community really accepted it."

These days the Michael's son Matt takes a very prominent role in running the Mushroom Group and he can see how the new generation of music industry professionals are shaping the business.

[MATT GUDINSKI]: "There was a time when a lot of change was needed at a local level and a worldwide level. It was necessary for the industry to take the next step. It is much more corporatized now and the biggest brands and biggest entities worldwide want to have an involvement in music. I'm thinking of Apple and Google and companies like that. So the music industry has definitely grown as a whole."

Where Does the Music Business Begin?

Nobody would deny that for nearly half a century Ian "Molly" Meldrum has been an iconic figure in the Australian music industry and the

ANDREW WATT

2015 television series made about his life confirmed this. Yet, putting aside for one moment his significant work as a record producer and a label owner, he has spent most of his career working in television, radio and print media. It's arguable that the man synonymous with Australian music actually works in another industry completely! Does highly influential Triple J music programmer Richard Kingsmill also work in the media, or does he actually work in the music industry? And what of the numerous journalists, television producers and radio personalities who regularly attend music industry events? There are still hundreds of people employed at a retail level, whose job involves selling music. To which industry do they belong? Does a business that sells band T-shirts work in the music or apparel industry? The significance of the cross-over between the music and technology industries is a lengthy, complicated and very important discussion.

Clearly the lines are fuzzy and will continue to blur.

If you ask the proprietors of many of the most prominent music venues in Australia what industry they work in, the answer could be "hospitality". Music is just a means to attract patrons to buy beverages. In some respects that doesn't make them that much different to a hairdresser or clothing retailer that uses music to generate the atmosphere to encourage sales of their goods or services.

As former CEO of the Hi-Fi Group, the operator of three eponymously-named live venues in Melbourne, Sydney and Brisbane (since rebranded as Max Watts), Luke O'Sullivan understands the different aspects of the business.

> **[LUKE O'SULLIVAN]:** "There's a bit of a divide in the live venue business. Is it the entertainment business, the hospitality business or the music business? It's probably a bit of all three. On the operations side you need to have an understanding of

WELCOME TO THE JUNGLE

the beverage business, so those people would probably come from a hospitality background.

But even on the music side of the business – and strangely enough, there are a number of positions where people do not have a background in music or have not been in the music industry – they just have good commercial sense and they are savvy and they are engaged by it and they just 'get it.' To me that's more important than knowing who the drummer of the Black Keys might be."

The Impact of Technology

In recent years the biggest talking points in the recorded music industry have been around streaming and internet radio services such as Apple Music, Spotify, and Pandora. There has been a great deal of debate around the impact they have on the way music fans consume music. Yet, arguably, these companies are not even operating in the music industry! Rather, they would be defined as technology, media or communications companies.

This may seem like a semantic argument, but it's actually very significant and has repercussions for those already working in the business as well as those planning to.

Colin Daniels is the managing director of Inertia, one of Australia's leading music companies. Blessed with a very forward thinking approach to his industry, he relates a story from the 2011 SXSW (South by South West), a music industry convention held annually in the Texas capital, Austin.

[COLIN DANIELS]: "What worries me about the music industry the most is the lack of passion for music from the technology sector of the business. There are a lot of people with a desire to work in the technology section of the industry, inventing new models and all of that, but their thinking is about exit strategies and making money very quickly, rather than the long-term benefit of the industry…and that scares me. I was at a big dinner in Austin a few years ago, with all the people working in the technology side of the business. There were 2500 bands playing that week and I'm at this dinner with 20 people working in the digital side of the industry and none of them were talking about music. Not one person was going to see a band after dinner. That scared the shit out of me."

Charles Caldas is the CEO of Merlin, a digital rights organisation representing many of the world's biggest and most influential independent labels. He came to that role after being a long-time executive at Shock, an Australian music distributor. He has seen similar scenarios to that described by Daniels.

[CHARLES CALDAS]: "I can absolutely relate to that. If you don't like shoes, why open a shoe shop? In the digital world there's a lot of venture capital money around looking to make quick returns. There will be people like that in the digital world. There was this mad period of all this investment and there was all these people telling me in meetings that they were going to succeed because they had the best technology. It was like meeting a retailer who said they were going to succeed in selling music because they had the best cash register and the shop looked great. It's taken a while for that mentality to seep in, but the services that are succeeding are putting music people right at the centre of their business. Spotify hired from the independent sector and from majors to try and get the essence of what those people are passionate about into their business. They are thinking about what the consumer might want and music people know that."

WELCOME TO THE JUNGLE

[MATT GUDINSKI]: "I probably don't have as in depth knowledge of technology as some other people around me but, of course, for us to be successful and for us to be at the forefront of our game we have to be across all the latest technologies. Six or seven years ago Interactive and Music parts of SxSW were quite far apart and in the last few years they have almost merged. It's an indication that there is a huge importance and reliance on being across the latest technology and how people are going to consume and discover music."

What Business Is This Anyway?

Clearly, music is not simply just one industry. The core of the music business is, of course, the artists who create the music, and the reason an industry exists is to connect that music to an audience, whether that be in a live environment, through recordings, or some other process.

Colin Daniels provides some perspective about what makes the music industry unique – the inherent qualities of music.

[COLIN DANIELS]: "What is different with music to so many other forms of entertainment is that it's theatre of the mind. You can be lost in music still and dream and love and be emotionally touched by music that can mean something completely different to you than it means to someone else.
What keeps me engaged is the change. I've been in the music industry for well over 20 years and in that time it's completely changed. When I first started out we had telex machines and were selling vinyl to record stores. That constant change of technology and business practices and change in the thought processes of how you break artists is what actually keeps me

interested. If that had stayed the same, I'd have to go looking for another industry that was in change."

Sophie Miles co-founder of record label and touring company Mistletone, has a similar fascination that drives her work.

> **[SOPHIE MILES]:** "It's all about helping the music to find its audience. Not that I really know how that happens; it is still quite a magical and mysterious process, how people find the music they love. But it's exciting to watch it happen. Of course there is a difference between going to a show and listening to an album at home, but I think the love that you feel is the same love. It's just a different experience. Live music is exciting to me because of the shared transcendent experience that is possible when a group of people share in something that's beyond words."

In a changing environment, the music business draws together skills, disciplines and technologies from many and varied industries. Together, they fulfil the overall objective of connecting music makers to music consumers. Some of these businesses deal in music as a commodity to be bought and sold, while others seek to be paid for the provision of services.

In his book *Free Ride – How the Internet is Destroying the Culture Business and How the Culture Business Can Fight Back*, Robert Levine, a former features editor at technology magazine *Wired*, summarises the challenges faced by the record companies in the online environment.

"To understand why the music industry has had so much trouble operating online, it helps to understand that "the music industry" is only a general term for several interrelated businesses that co-exist in the same world, but run very differently. When a label releases an album, it only controls the right to the recording. Separate copyrights cover

WELCOME TO THE JUNGLE

the songs as compositions, which are usually owned or administered by publishers; they collect money when songs are played on the radio, recorded on albums or licensed to movies or television. And the concert and merchandise businesses have their own approaches to making money and hence their own priorities."

By the time you complete this book you'll have a thorough understanding of Levine's description.

Clearly there are many doors into the industry via many skill sets; skills that may have been acquired through different academic environments and/or from practical experience in vastly divergent industries. In the modern era the music industry is not just made up of traditional music industry people.

As the long-time head of Mushroom Marketing, Carl Gardiner, who now works as an industry consultant, puts it in a broader perspective.

> **[CARL GARDINER]**: "Mobile phone companies are as big a player in the music industry as any record company these days. The definition of what businesses are related to music is so much broader than what it was. I even say to some kids, 'go and study copyright law as it applies to digital technology and I reckon you can make a lot of money in the music industry'".

After spending time with Nokia and T-Mobile in the '90s, Vanessa Picken is now a leading digital strategist in the music business operating a business called *Comes With Fries*. After Nokia, she found herself working in the banking sector, a field not normally regarded as a breeding ground for music industry tyros.

> **[VANESSA PICKEN]**: "I was working on corporate online activities and working with small businesses, but I was spending my

nights going to gigs and listening to as much music as possible. There was a role going at Capital Records as a label manager and I had no idea what a label manager was. I knew at the end of the day the skills and pre-requisites for that were marketing, but the product just happened to be music rather than a corporate online solution or a mobile phone plan. I thought I had nothing to lose. I asked them to give me a go so I could show them what I could bring to the table. When I got the job I was shocked that it was all people [who had come through] the music industry and they had developed their staff internally. I walked in there knowing how to write a marketing plan and understanding consumer segmentation and those other basic principles of marketing, having marketed so many other products before."

Mark Poston has been a leading executive in the recorded music business Australia, with experience at the head of several major labels. In these roles he saw the emergence of a new breed of music industry workers.

[**MARK POSTON**]: "I definitely saw a change in people coming in. They need to be younger, more tech-savvy, more switched on. The industry has a pretty sophisticated model of measuring artist success; having to be across all of the stats and how they are growing week to week – whether it be the traditional radio play, social media, You Tube hits, fan base etc. When people come in to interview for jobs, we saw a huge shift in the level of expertise and passion and also the work ethic. You have to be always on, and it's really good to have young people coming into the business and young people working with you because they have new ideas and I'm pretty much blown away that they are always working 24/7."

Perhaps the evolution of the industry in the digital age is still only in its early stages. As the industry recovers from the initial 'shock of the

WELCOME TO THE JUNGLE

new', some of the smartest players are cautiously optimistic about its short and medium term future.

> **[CHARLES CALDAS]:** "I see cause for optimism. Markets are returning to growth again and Australia is one of them. To me the caution comes from asking who is going to come into the space and what are their incentives going to be? Are we really going to be in a world that is controlled by Apple, Amazon and Google and if so are those companies really in the business of maximising the value of the music industry? I think we know the answer to that!"

Music as a Service Business

Perhaps the most important notion to establish early in your understanding of the music industries (either live or recorded) is that the industries are 'service' businesses. In theory artists and audiences could connect directly and in some cases they do – even more so in the era of social media connectivity. However there are some services that third parties can provide that help facilitate that connection and that is how an "industry" evolves; through the provision of those services.

Wherever you see yourself fitting into these industries – other than as an artist or an audience member – you will probably find yourself in a services role. Perhaps it will involve your business taking ownership of assets, either tangible or intangible, or perhaps you will simply be paid in one form or another for your services without taking ownership of rights.

> **[COLIN DANIELS]:** "We do four things. We do what an artist doesn't want to do, what an artist doesn't know how to do, what an artist doesn't have the time to do or what an artist doesn't think of doing. I'm in the service business. I serve the artist.
> We used to be a distribution company, now we are a service company. We help them with making music, with touring, with merchandise. We'll do their accounts for them if that's what

they need. It's about what the artists need. It's our job to do what they need us to do and that will constantly change. There will always be content creators and there will always be a content business and in reality that is about the artist. You have people that create content and then you have a servicing industry built around that. I'm not in a circle of creating content, I'm in a circle of servicing content."

Jaddan Comerford operates UNFD, a Melbourne-based collection of music businesses including a record company, a booking agency, a merchandising business and an event and touring company, working with artists such as The Amity Affliction, Vance Joy and Violent Soho, amongst many others. Comerford sees the business in a similar way to Colin Daniels.

[JADDAN COMERFORD]: "We see them as services, and within those services there are rights. Sometimes we acquire those rights, sometimes we license those rights and sometimes we just provide a service around those rights. It really is about looking at how we can provide a service to our clients rather than how we can acquire those rights.
It's definitely what I think is the future. I'd be lying to say that we didn't own rights – we own lots of rights, but I think, in the past, a lot of rights have been taken from artists in situations where artists haven't completely understood what they are signing. I strive to ensure that we never put an artist or an employee in a position like that."

Internationally, Sat Bisla's Los Angeles based business A&R Worldwide takes a similar approach but not as a label or management company but in a consultancy and artist development sense. A&R Worldwide as its name suggests provides an artist development service to independent artists or small labels looking to break into the US and other important territories.

WELCOME TO THE JUNGLE

[SAT BISLA]: "We provide access and opportunity. Initially it was passion built. I was helping out artists all over the world as a fan, providing access and opportunity and not charging anything. I was helping other people make lots of money and not charging a penny, so that made no sense. So that's when it became a service business. A&R Worldwide stands for three things – Artist & Repertoire, Artist & Relationships and Artist & Revenue. The revenue part is essential for the artist to sustain a livelihood."

Size of the Australian Business

Here's a key perspective. While everyone interviewed in these pages brings an enthusiasm and passion for their business to their daily work, most of them won't become multi-millionaires doing it. There are some exceptions, of course, and most of these are people working at least partially on the world stage.

Most people reading this book will want to start their careers in Australia, and many may not ever want to leave. There are lots of really good reasons for that! However it does mean constantly dealing with the same issue – the Australian music market, while important, is small compared to those in entertainment epicentres such as America, Europe and India.

John Watson is one of Australia's leading artist managers, with the likes of silverchair, Gotye, Wolfmother and Missy Higgins on his resume. He also operates a successful record label, Eleven. Watson is better placed than just about anyone to offer this important perspective.

[JOHN WATSON]: "The economics of the Australian music business all flow from one simple fact ... Australia is a small market so most artists earn below-average weekly earnings. Local managers and labels have to try and run a business based on receiving a percentage of those already insufficient revenue streams. Unless you're lucky enough to have one of the handful of big-name artists who can help cover your overheads, you're either a sole trader trying to manage half a dozen artists out of your bedroom, or you're managing a couple of artists part-time while juggling a day job. This has been a fundamental problem of the Australian industry for 40 years and it's not going to change any time soon. The country's simply not big enough to sustain more than a handful of indie labels and management companies who have proper resources ... and they will typically be the ones who were lucky enough to get one or two of the five to 10 local artists who are earning reasonable money in any given year.

Managers, by definition, have access to multiple revenue streams. Labels probably *need* to have access to more than one stream. However, the main problem is that due to the size of the country they're streams rather than rivers. In America a mid-level artist earns a comfortable living and so do the labels and managers around them. In Australia that same level of success means that the artist probably has to work a part-time job or such, and their support people are cottage industries at best."

According to live performance peak body, Live Performance Australia, in 2015, 18.38 million tickets were issued to live performance events in 2015, generating total ticket sales revenue of $1.41 billion. As they point out hat's more than the combined attendances at AFL, NRL, Soccer, Super Rugby and Cricket in 2015. $447 million of that revenue was generated by contemporary music events.

The following excerpt from their 2016 Report gives further information:

"In 2015, the Contemporary Music category experienced a decline in gross revenue, falling by 21% from $604.96 million to $447.90 million. The fall in gross revenue can be explained by the 13% fall in attendance

WELCOME TO THE JUNGLE

and 10.4% decrease in the average ticket price. Despite the generally weak result, the Contemporary Music category continues to be the biggest in the Live Performance Industry, commanding 34.0% of revenue and 30.2% of attendance of the live performance industry's share. Comparatively, in 2010 Contemporary Music commanded 49.6% of revenue and 40.8% of attendance of the live performance industry's share. However, the annual variability of this category strongly reflects the number of big-name international artists which tour in any given year, particularly the number of stadium tours. These figures do not include music festivals, which are categorised under Festivals (Single-Category). Successful tours by Fleetwood Mac, AC/DC, Ed Sheeran, and the Foo Fighters contributed significantly to the revenue and attendance in this category. However, there were significant declines in the Contemporary Music category, with performances in 2015 unable to match the growth recorded in the previous two years. Major international acts, such as Katy Perry, Bruce Springsteen, Eminem and Bruno Mars, whose successful national tours were a contributing factor to the high revenue and attendance results recorded in 2014, did not return in 2015".

A 2011 study by Ernst & Young that was commissioned by APRA/AMCOS (the Australasian Performing Right Association and the Australian Mechanical Copyright Owners Society) and the Australia Council showed there were more than 3900 licensed live music venues in Australia. These included hotels, bars, clubs, restaurants, cafes and nightclubs. It was estimated that these venues hosted about 328,000 live shows in the 2009-10 financial year, equating to around 6300 performances weekly.

Live music in smaller venues such as hotels, clubs, cafes and restaurants had previously been estimated by Live Performance Australia to generate 41.97 million attendances, and generate $1.21 billion in revenue through audience spending in venues. With 6300 such gigs each week across the country, live music also helps to sustain almost 15,000 jobs.

ANDREW WATT

Hotels and bars represented the biggest portion of the venue-based live music sector – estimated to attract more than 24 million attendances per year.

Later chapters will look at the revenue that is generated by public performance of live and recorded music and the roles played by APRA/AMCOS and the PPCA (Phonographic Performance Company of Australia), an organisation providing licences to Australian businesses to play recorded music in public places such as clubs, hotels, bars, restaurants, fitness centres, shops, halls and dance studios and also on radio and television. Chapter 3 will explain the importance and legal basis of these organisations but for the purposes of this introduction though, let's consider some key figures.

In 2015-16 APRA/AMCOS issued licenses to 142,000 businesses across Australia that consume music through broadcasting, performance and other uses. On behalf of 89,000 members, composers and publishers, and representing over a million unique songs, it collected over $333 million from licensees.

The PPCA have licences in place with more than 60,000 venues Australia-wide. On behalf of rights holders, in 2014-15 it collected almost $46 million from licensees - up 7.2% from the previous year. The PPCA distribution for the 2014-15 financial year was paid in December 2015, and saw just over $31.3 million distributed to licensor labels and registered Australian artists.

On the recorded music side, statistics provide impressive economic impacts. Artfacts states that almost all Australians (99%) listen to recorded music, and 92% do so weekly or more. On average, Australians listen to recorded music every one to two days (222 times a year). Recorded music is consumed significantly more often by people under 44 than those over 45 years. In 2009-10 each Australian household

WELCOME TO THE JUNGLE

spent an estimated $380 on music related goods and services, totally over $2 billion economy wide. The majority of this expenditure was on concert tickets, recorded music and audio-visual equipment.

International Perceptions of the Australian Music Business

By international standards, Australia is a big music market. Half the world's recorded music consumption occurs in the USA and Japan combined, but after that Australia ranks sixth behind Germany, UK and France and ahead of Canada and Brazil.

However a large slice of our music consumption is from international artists. Local acts comprised only 35 of the national top 100 albums in 2015, and many of these were compilations of heritage artists, television compilations and Christmas albums. This was a lower percentage than in France, Germany and Japan where local acts account for around half of the top albums. Of course the fact that we speak English and are thus a big market for American and British music has a lot to do with that.

Australia ranks 34th in a list of 48 markets in terms of the proportion of local products in our recorded music market, with just 25% of physical products sold originating in Australia. This places us slightly behind our most comparable market, Canada.

It's easy to become infatuated by the success of music on local charts or in local venues, but the reality is that the rest of the world music business doesn't have the same pre-occupation with the Australian market. However, there is a healthy respect for our industry.

International artist manager Peter Leak, who has managed or co-managed artists such as Cowboy Junkies, Grant Lee Buffalo, 10,000 Maniacs, Avril Lavigne and Dido, and is now part of the mega-powerful Red Light Management Group, knows the Australian market well.

ANDREW WATT

> **[PETER LEAK]**: "I think Australia is thought of as a really good touring market if you can get your artists going there. That's the hardest part for a developing artist - getting the artist promoted and marketed effectively. I think most people would think Australia is an important market if you can get it and often if you have had success in the UK or the US, or ideally both, then Australia is one of the next markets you should be getting. In terms of actual touring potential, Australia is at least as good as Canada. I've got a lot of respect for it as a market, but it can be hard to break in to."

The Song

That may seem like a strange little sub-heading to include at this point but it's something that anyone reading this book shouldn't forget. For all the machinations and theories about the music industries that will be explored throughout these pages one factor will always remain – it all starts with a song (or preferably a whole bunch of them!)

Sat Bisla has had great success working with Australian artists such as The Temper Trap and Sheppard on the international stage. He's never lost sight of where it begins.

> **[SAT BISLA]**: "The song is what attracts audience. The song is what connects business to the artist. The song is the creative nucleus of the artist. Without the song you don't have the live show, you don't have airplay on the radio, you don't have music for television or advertising, you don't have music streaming. How music is packaged, consumed, experienced or distributed will change but it is still about the song."

My Path Into The Industry

CRAIG HAWKER

"I had an obsession with Australian music in the mid to late "90s while I was still in high school and I would go and see as many all-ages gigs as possibly could. That passion led me to teach myself how to build a website so I could set up an unofficial band website to post my gig photos for the then-upcoming rock band, Grinspoon. That turned into running the official website for the band and put me in touch with management, label and the band directly. It opened up my understanding of some of the mechanics of the industry and this cemented my desire to pursue a job in the music industry. I moved to Sydney and my foot in the door started with a week's work experience at Murmur music (a subsidiary of Sony Music) - home of silverchair, Something For Kate, Jebediah etc. I was meant to do a week and stayed for 2 months working for nothing. I loved it though, and it gave me an opportunity to try a bit of everything and get an understanding of all the important elements of what make a successful artist and record. It was also my first contact with one of the best A&R guys Australia has ever had - John O'Donnell, who was the boss of Murmur at the time and he remains a great mentor of mine. Once I had some experience under my belt I was able to apply for a job as an A&R scout for EMI Music Australia and was hired by the then-head of A&R Colin Daniels (now Inertia Music managing director) who really taught me what it took to be a good A&R person."

Chapter 2

A Short History Of The Recorded Music Business

In order to understand what the music business actually is and to determine whether you want to be a part of it, it's important to see how that business evolved from its most rudimentary form. There have been hundreds of books and scholarly articles written on this subject and at the risk of simply adding to that information, the next couple of chapters of this book will briefly introduce this historical perspective. This will be as close as this gets to being a traditional textbook, but the history is worth knowing.

From Troubadours To Recording Artists

From the earliest times, musicians sought out audiences and audiences wanted to hear music. That was the founding principle of the music business and it remains true today. Initially the connection between musicians and artists was immediate; both needed to be in the same place at the same time to make that connection.

This led to the earliest forms of venues, which were really any suitable places for large numbers of people to congregate to hear musicians play. Equally, musicians realised that anywhere people could gather in large numbers were going to be preferred places to play their music and have it appreciated. It's not all that different to the thinking that drives music festivals today.

Inevitably some form of organisation became necessary for these meetings between audiences and musicians. Travelling musicians were

WELCOME TO THE JUNGLE

seeking suitable places to play and audiences wanted to know when and where the travelling musicians could be heard. This exchange of information created a need for intermediaries. Once an organisational structure was imposed on the relationship between musicians and their audiences, an industry - or rather several industries - was born.

Today's live touring industry is really no different to this, albeit the methods and systems used to connect audiences to musicians have become more complex and sophisticated.

People came to realise that once the musicians had moved on to the next town, their subsequent absence left a void in their lives. Wouldn't it be nice to still be able to hear the music after the musicians had gone?

A solution to this problem wasn't too far away and it came in the form of a historic technological advancement.

This is a Journey Into Sound

It was famed American inventor, Thomas Edison, who originally developed the means to make recordings of sound, as the following extract from the American Library of Congress explains:

> "Of all his inventions, Thomas A. Edison was most fond of the phonograph. As a result of his work on two other inventions, the telegraph and the telephone, Edison happened upon a way to record sound on tinfoil-coated cylinders in 1877. Edison set aside this invention in 1878 to work on the incandescent light bulb, and others moved forward to improve on his invention, including Chichester A. Bell and Charles Sumner Tainter, who developed a wax cylinder for the phonograph. In 1887,

Edison resumed work on his phonograph, using wax cylinders. Although initially used as a dictating machine for offices, the phonograph proved to be a popular form of entertainment, and Edison eventually offered a variety of recording selections to the public through his National Phonograph Company. Edison introduced improved phonograph models and cylinders over the years, ending with the Blue Amberol Record, an unbreakable cylinder with superior sound. In 1910, the company was reorganized into Thomas A. Edison, Inc. The Edison Disc Phonograph was developed in 1912 with the aim of competing in the popular disc market. The Edison Diamond Discs offered excellent sound, but were not compatible with other disc players. The advent of radio caused business to sour in the 1920s. Edison gave in to the popular trend and offered lateral-cut records and accompanying portable players in the summer of 1929, before recording production at Edison ceased forever in October 1929."

The first gramophone was manufactured in 1906. In 1909, new provisions were enacted in US copyright law and by 1914 the American Society of Composers, Authors and Publishers (ASCAP) was formed to collect those fees that were now payable to their members. This organisation serves a similar purpose to the Australian collection society APRA.

By 1930 a company called Electrical and Musical Industries was formed from the merger of two gramophone companies. Who would have predicted the remarkable path that company, beter known as "EMI" would take?

When technology evolved to enable a musician's performance to be recorded, some significant legal and philosophical issues arose. While a live performance was an experience of a transient moment in time, a recording was permanent, and with that, came a perception of value. It was something that could be "owned".

WELCOME TO THE JUNGLE

So naturally, the first question to be addressed was, "Who owns those recordings?" Was it the musicians who performed the music, or the owner of the technology that allowed the performance to be recorded? Could one exist without the other?

The related questions included: "Were the recordings a product in their own right, that had a value and a meaning for those who wanted to hear them, or were the recordings simply an early form of advertising that alerted people to what they might see or hear when a particular musician played at a place that they could attend? Could, or should, these recordings be given away, and by whom?"

These underlying questions should sound familiar to anyone whose first exposure to the music industry was in the 21st century, when discussions regarding whether recorded music was something to be sold or given away took on a whole new meaning, in the digital age.

The Changing Recorded Music Industry

From the time sound and music recording was invented, an eternal theme in the music business has been the ownership and the use of those sound recordings. It is these questions that continue to fuel the on-going debate about copyright ownership and sale of music today, with the only difference being that the technology has changed dramatically from when these questions first arose.

The changes in technology emphasise the **four** essential services provided by the recording industry;

- the creation of sound recordings;

- the reproduction of those sound recordings and manufacture of devices embodying those reproductions;

- the marketing of those reproductions of sound recordings to create a demand for those products, and;

- the distribution of those sound recordings to consumers, so that the demand created by the marketing can be fulfilled.

We need to consider the evolution of these four functions.

Recording

Due to technological advancements, the means of recording have become markedly more accessible and simple to operate. Rather than having to pay for an expensive and technically complex recording studio to make a commercially viable recording, artists are able to own and operate the technology themselves for the price they once had to pay for a reel of tape. This isn't to say that recording studios are completely redundant – they certainly are not – but it does mean that low-cost alternatives exist for artists. Further issues arise from this relating to the viability and sustainability of the recording studio business and the roles of record producers and recording engineers.

As a record producer Todd Rundgren has been responsible for some of the most important albums in contemporary music, such as Meatloaf's *Bat Out of Hell* and the New York Dolls' self-titled debut, and he's widely known as one of the more far-sighted artisans in contemporary music.

> **[TODD RUNDGREN]:** "Even I forget how short a time it was since...you would have to spend thousands and thousands of dollars to get into recording your own music. The sophistication of the software and the power of a laptop have brought it down to something that is accessible to anyone. There is no excuse why people can't get into the game at this point.

WELCOME TO THE JUNGLE

> Things have changed a lot; there are a lot of extremes. I don't think that music has become monolithic, even though a lot of the styles cross over from genre to genre. In the strictly pop – Katy Perry and Lady Gaga – world, if you look at the production credits there are five songwriters and three producers on every song and it's not the same bunch of people on every song. It becomes a real 'by committee' production. And then you've got someone like Skrillex who is just in his room with his laptop, doing it all by himself. There is a broad range of ways to do it and a lot of different ways to collaborate, or not. I think it's a great time and I think it's the technologies that have enabled music to break out of whatever it is that pop music is supposed to be at any one time."

Artist manager Gregg Donovan, whose company Wonderlick Entertainment has worked with artists such as Grinspoon, The Paper Kites, Boy & Bear, Airbourne and Josh Pyke, among others, also makes interesting observations on the recording process:

> **[GREGG DONOVAN]:** "It's really lucky that recording costs have dramatically come down at the exact same time that recording income has dramatically come down. Those two things have probably balanced each other out - to a point. Making records is cheaper these days. Often a lot of recording can be done in the demo and writing phase because home studios are so good. When the artist goes to a studio with a producer they already have a palette of things recorded that they are able to use. It saves a lot of time and a lot of money."

Manufacturing

Previously once a recording was made, it required a suitably equipped factory to manufacture reproductions of that sound recording, in the form of vinyl records, cassettes or CDs. Factories require buildings and machinery, and a labor force skilled in the operation of that machinery. In the digital age the reproduction of a sound recording is as simple as "Save As" on a drop-down menu. The process is remarkably – some would say "dangerously" – simple. Again this is a simplification of the situation; there is still a significant demand for hard copies of recordings (and indeed the demand for vinyl format is growing for some releases), but it's undeniable that digital reproduction is the dominant form of "manufacturing". And anyone can do it. When a person can carry tens of thousands of songs in their pocket, there are obviously issues confronting businesses based around the manufacture of physical products.

Marketing

Once a sound recording was manufactured into a saleable form, the next step in the traditional model was to create a demand for that recording by a series of actions grouped under the heading "marketing and promotion". Whether it was through paid advertising, promotional media appearances or more complex methods involving radio play, retail promotions and the like, it was a specialised set of skills, with a budget and people to execute the strategies. The point of the exercise was to create awareness of the sound recording to a group of consumers that would hopefully respond so favorably that they were moved to purchase one (or more) of those carefully manufactured reproductions. Of course that was before the internet! This book will go into far greater detail about the jobs that the internet has created in the music marketing world, but for now it's sufficient to acknowledge that the online environment has broken down the barriers between the creators or sound recordings and their potential customers. Whether it is social media platforms such as Facebook, Instagram, Twitter and You Tube or the blogosphere, the means of access are available and cost comparatively little. It has created a whole new set of functions while making others virtually redundant.

WELCOME TO THE JUNGLE

Distribution

The final step of the process was the distribution of those now "in-demand" reproductions of sound recordings into the hands of those now-eager customers. This previously involved a sales team convincing music retailers that the demand was genuine and, once this was done, loading up trucks at the factory with boxes full of those products and shipping them as quickly and efficiently as possible (that usually meant one to two weeks) into the hands of those retailers who in turn would have them on the shelves a few days later. The process wasn't exactly instantaneous! Now, once demand is created it can be fulfilled as quickly as it takes to hit "send" on an email, or can even be automated. And that's before we even consider the massive change that "consumption" via streaming has bought to the industry!

Traditional music retail still exists and there is definitely a consumer base who would prefer to buy their music in physical form, from a traditional retail environment, but equally there is a generation or two for whom this sounds like ancient history.

Artfacts provides some interesting, yet hardly surprising, information on this:

"The number of retail music stores has declined in the past decade. In the early 2000's the number of stores contributing data to the ARIA charts included around 1100 stores. In early 2013 there were closer to 600 specialty music stores. Over that time there has been a significant reduction in the number of chain locations, while some smaller specialist retailers have sustained their businesses servicing a small but committed customer base away from high traffic shopping centres." According to the Australian Music Retailers Association (AMRA), some of the key factors affecting the business include: declining average unit prices, rise of digital downloads, unauthorised file sharing, international online retailers and increased cost of rental spaces."

None of which probably comes as any surprise to anyone reading this book!

Adopting to Change

There's an element of exaggeration in the analysis put forward to explain the differences in the four elements of the recorded music sales process – recording, manufacturing, marketing and distribution – but it isn't a great exaggeration. Ask anyone under the age of 25 about the traditional model they would genuinely find it laughable and rightly so. Such is the speed of technological advancement that what seemed incomprehensible 20 years ago is commonplace now.

With change occurring at every point in the recorded music food chain, the onus is on those working within it to move rapidly with the times.

> **[JOHN WATSON]**: "Of course there have been a thousand changes. Most arise from new technology and media fragmentation. The overarching consequence is that there are a lot fewer intermediaries between artist and fan. If you were an artist 20 years ago you typically needed to find a manager who could get you a record contract. The record label had relationships with the programmers of the big radio stations, newspapers and TV shows and at the manager's urging they would then hopefully use those relationships to expose your music through those channels. If you got that mass media exposure then the public often bought your albums and concert tickets as they were only exposed to that limited playlist, so then you were on your way. These days there's still a role for traditional

WELCOME TO THE JUNGLE

media, but it's likely that at least the first few steps of an artist's career won't involve big labels or commercial radio. They'll involve direct communication with fans online and the creation of a genuine community around the music.

Lots of other changes flow from that reorientation. One particularly interesting one is that most of the 'gatekeepers' (ie: managers, labels, radio programmers etc) no longer need to trust their own eyes and ears in picking which projects to support. These days A&R people can pick which bands to sign based on their YouTube views or Twitter followers, radio programmers can add the song that's getting the most searches on Shazam, managers can take on the band that's already got lots of Facebook friends and so forth.

In short, the music business has always been about 'build it and they will come', but in today's media environment that's more true than it's ever been. Therefore people who understand how to help artists build a genuine fan community online are more important than ever, because that's really the core of everything these days."

Joel Connolly, a partner in management and communications company Umbrella (working with The Rubens, Cloud Control, Urthboy, Saskwatch among others) has taken a different approach to his company's label dealings.

> **[JOEL CONNOLLY]:** "We don't necessarily need a label in the same way we used to. We do deals where we would just release one song on a label and we have open-ended plans with that label. You are not necessarily looking for the same things that you were."

Another partner in Umbrella, Greg Carey suggests that the change of label relationships has also altered the role of the manager in the recording process.

ANDREW WATT

[GREG CAREY]: "Managers have now taken the place of a lot of things that labels used to do, and one of the main ones is A&R. Typically there was a guy at a label that would do that job and help the artist make a record. He'd help them find a direction, get a sound, figure out the songs. Record labels don't have time or money to invest in that kind of development, so now managers typically take on a band long before a label is going to be interested and the managers develop the act so that the labels have less to invest. So that is non-traditional but I think it's the way things have to be done these days."

Matt Gudinski is adamant that there is still an essential role for labels in the new environment.

[MATT GUDINSKI]: "The best and smartest artists out there realise that they have to use all the available resources around them to be able to stand above the millions of songs out there. That might be label A&R or it might be collaborating with other songwriters or producers, which a label can facilitate. We approach artists at a very early stage now which means we need to have a lot more patience and dedication and investment to get them to a level. We are putting faith in our own abilities to work with the artist and their extended team to get them to that point."

One of the beneficiaries of the change in technology has been the Electronic Dance Music genre. Richie McNeill, a former DJ and a founder of Totem One Love, the promoter of major EDM festivals, sees his genre of music as being early adapters of the technological revolution.

[RICHIE MCNEILL]: "I think the reason that electronic music has really boomed is its affinity to technology. You look at all the electronic music and the way the bands dismiss it as

WELCOME TO THE JUNGLE

being just done on keyboards, but the fact that it is done that way is what gives it that affinity with technology. The producers and the people writing the music are tech-savvy and that's why electronic music has spread so rapidly and exploded."

McNeill's erstwhile business partner Dror Erez sees that EDM benefited from another source.

[DROR EREZ]: "Where it is different now is that a few years back, radio stations made a decision to start playing electronic music, or at least pop electronic music – not just in this country. So artists start to write and record more dance-infused music and now that's what the kids hear on the radio. They hear it much more than rock n' roll. When we were doing electronic dance music back then, it was a bit like blues or jazz, it was something in the corner."

As managing director of Sony Music Asia Pacific, and one of the most celebrated Australian record company executives ever, Denis Handlin has seen it all and can attest to the rapid evolution of modern times.

[DENIS HANDLIN]: "The industry had to and indeed has revolutionised and very much leads the way amongst content industries in new business models with over 500 digital retail services licensed worldwide featuring over 30 million tracks for consumers to enjoy. At the same time we continue to support our physical retailers strongly with service levels and campaigns to generate demand. The growth in digital services will continue in Australia, providing consumers with even more choice and value. The industry has also diversified and in Sony Music's case we have significant revenues in touring, brand alliance, artist management and other initiatives."

ANDREW WATT

Simon Moor heads up the Australian operation of Kobalt Music Group, an international music company founded by noted industry disruptor Willard Ahditz. Kobalt Music Group began life as a music publishing company with a different business model to most others and more recently launched both label services and a neighbouring rights company. Kobalt is a company that has made significant waves internationally.

Moor has an insightful view on the impact of the changes of technology on the recorded music business.

> **[SIMON MOOR]**: "It's re-addressed the balance of power and shifted the power back to the people who are creating the music and the people who are closest to them - their managers. That shift away from the record companies has created a shift in the paradigm, where to be successful and have a career you no longer have to give up your copyright, and have someone else own that copyright for them to be able to help you. Now the power is sitting with the artists, the songwriters and their managers and that has led to a situation where the services part of the market has become a lot more prevalent. That's the biggest change."

Since the first recordings were made, businesses existed to own, manufacture and exploit those recordings. This inevitably meant that these businesses would find themselves interacting with the musicians they sought to own and exploit.

Agreements needed to be negotiated and made about the terms and conditions that would govern these relationships and the cornerstone of these agreements was the law of contract. And just like any other business, a number of standard terms and conditions evolved driven

WELCOME TO THE JUNGLE

by the nature of the relationships between the parties, the balance of power and the ownership of the means of production.

Marianna Annas is a music industry lawyer with corporate experience in the major label system. She now heads prominent music publisher ABC Music.

> **[MARIANNA ANNAS]:** "You now have a lot more incantations of recording agreements. You have your direct signings, you have your label deal, you have your master license deal, you have your distribution deal and then you have your multiple rights deal. This means that managers are having to orchestrate where they go in terms of a recording arrangement more than they have had to in the past and I guess the onus is more on the manager to make a commercially savvy decision, and I'm not convinced that a lot of managers are doing that. First of all you need to look at the options and you need to make a decision based on informed commercial knowledge. I think the mentality that you can do wonders without a label is very naïve. For every Jezabels and Gotye, there are two million stories that don't work out like that."

The former managing director of distributor Shock, David Williams, who now is a prominent tour promoter, supports the view that record labels still have an important role in the new world order.

> **[DAVID WILLIAMS]:** "I don't know if the question of ownership of copyright is the main driving principle. It is if you build a business around owning the copyright and you won't work any product unless you own the copyright. For all the talk of artists going to market themselves, from where I look at it, a lot of it is still being driven out of record labels. Whatever a record label might end up being in the future, there's still some

things that apply. No one wants to tour a new act unless it's on the radio somewhere. Radio doesn't go out and find music. Someone has to deliver the music to them. Someone has to do that work. A manager can do that, but at the moment it's still record companies that are doing that and I would expect that to continue for a while. And you have to consider that there are not that many managers – really good, smart managers – who can do that."

Dan Rosen is the CEO of ARIA. ARIA has over 100 members, being record companies, and of these only three are the major labels: Warner, Sony and Universal. Rosen is acutely aware of the changes in his industry.

[DAN ROSEN]: "It's interesting when you meet the younger members of the industry, and I'll put myself in there as well, all they have known is dealing with the digital world so they are not pining for the days where the CD ruled or vinyl ruled and so they just get on with it. I think it's nice to be born digital, so you accept this is the way it is and you understand how consumers engage in music and you understand how bands can promote themselves and you understand the way that online, social and community works. I think it's a distinct advantage and I think it's a great time to get into the music business because there is so much innovation and opportunity."

Overlaying the collision between emerging technologies and traditional business models is the law of copyright, which provide some principles about ownership of creative works like compositions and sound recordings. The recorded music industry is based around the ownership of copyright and the way the various parties deal with their rights under copyright laws, which are examined in greater detail in the next chapter.

WELCOME TO THE JUNGLE

False Sense of Security

From their inception, record companies were devoted to the pursuit of ownership of copyrights in sound recordings. It was an industry based on the control and exploitation of these valuable assets, and it was made so by the ability to reproduce those recordings by the thousands or even millions. Owning the original sound recording of Frank Sinatra singing *My Way* would certainly be a lovely experience (and would undoubtedly be worth a lot of money as a collectible), but having the right to reproduce that recording and sell it millions of times over a number of decades was definitely more financially rewarding. The ownership of this intangible 'right' outweighed the value of tangible possession, almost the opposite to what happens in the fine art world, where originals are paramount and reproductions virtually worthless.

Over the decades, those companies accumulated literally thousands of sound recordings and many of these became integral to the lives of music fans around the world. Many of these recordings passed through generations on successive formats, from 78s to vinyl albums, eight-track cartridges and cassettes. All of these formats had their advantages and each time a new format was introduced, it led to a new surge of sales in copies of the same sound recording, as music fans sought to replace or supplement their old format, with something that promised a better experience – better sound, greater durability, amazing portability or additional content. The same sound recordings that had already paid for themselves many times over would be responsible for new sales with minimal further investment. Economists would understand this in terms of an initial investment in the creation of the recording as a fixed cost and then a low marginal cost for each new reproduction of that recording.

The advent of the compact disc was the high watermark of that process, at least up until that time. Here was a format that was small, lightweight, extremely cheap to manufacture, resilient to scratching or breakage (at least compared to vinyl albums or cassettes), capable of holding large amounts of information and came with a promise of never-before-heard sound quality. Before long, cash registers worldwide were chiming as consumers rushed to replace their old music collections with shiny new discs containing the music that had been accumulated over decades by the record companies. It was like the goldmines had been refilled with gold and the labels had exclusive prospecting rights. Consumers were besotted by this new format – they were happy to pay close to $30 for a piece of plastic that had probably cost a couple of dollars to manufacture. The profit margins on this back catalogue product (with its low marginal cost per unit) were astronomical.

On the back of this new format, music companies enjoyed cashflow like never before and, to their credit, they chose to re-invest these rivers of gold into the creation of more and more sound recordings. They could easily see the value of owning sound recordings and they, understandably, wanted to own as many as possible. The 1990's saw a frenzy of new signings and recordings, and major labels aggressively acquired smaller labels that may have been able to contribute to this cache of copyright.

Not all of these signings were successful; in fact, only a tiny percentage of them even came close to breaking even. Huge recording budgets and even bigger video and promotion budgets meant that quite often artists would be over a million dollars "in the red" before their album was even released. It was the equivalent of betting a million dollars on a horse that was a very small chance of even running a place. A label's solution was to bet another million dollars on a bunch of other horses in the same race in the hope that maybe one would come home a winner. The earnings from the rare winners were supposed to pay for the hundreds of losers that had been backed. It was clearly an unsustainable practice, but one that persisted because of the streams of cash coming into these businesses from the sales of back-catalogue CDs.

WELCOME TO THE JUNGLE

In retrospect, labels would have been much better off banking the profits from their back catalogue sales and re-investing much more conservatively, but that's only obvious in hindsight. Most of those companies were driven by the need to maximize market share and it became what is now known, in modern business terminology, as a "race to the bottom". It wasn't all disaster, of course. There were numerous example of new 1990's sound recordings that were hugely successful and are now in the perennially selling back-catalogue, whether it be the likes of Guns N' Roses or Mariah Carey or Nirvana. (for example Fleetwood Mac's Greatest Hits came in at No. 61 on the 2015 ARIA Chart, six spots ahead of Troye Sivan). The problem lay with the hundreds of poor imitations signed in the hope of replicating those success stories and having money thrown at them like confetti.

The public's love affair with the CD hasn't completely faded, and there are still many consumers re-discovering and re-purchasing back catalogue in that format and even (increasingly) in vinyl format. Now, however, the price of most of those CDs is down to under $10. That next step in the evolution of music consumption became obvious as the last millennium drew to a close.

> **[COLIN DANIELS]:** "What has remained constant, and I think this is really important, is that we need great artists and we need great teams of people working with those artists. What the team does might change, who that team works for might change, but you still need a great team. An artist can't do it on their own, and a great team can't do anything without a great artist."

Recorded Music Business Since 2000

It's been said that the seismic changes in the music industry began in May 2000 when Metallica drummer Lars Ulrich symbolically delivered to the offices of Napster a list of 335,000 people who had illegally downloaded Metallica songs from the file sharing service. The gesture was intended to be a display of a musician standing up to the tide of technology that was robbing him and his peers of income that was rightfully theirs.

For a time around the turn of the millennium, the single word "Napster" probably was debated more than any other business enterprise in the history of the music industry. It requires some further examination.

Napster had been founded by Shawn Fanning, a 19-year-old computer hacker from North Eastern University in the USA. The essence of Napster was file sharing. It allowed users to access the files on the hard drives of fellow members and, as college students were early adapters of the service, the files they were most interested in were music files ripped from the CDs that their fellow members had bought and stored on their computer hard drives. By the time Metallica took their stand, the use of Napster was widespread, especially among those college students, and the genie was never going back in the bottle.

It's well documented that the Recording Industry Association of America (RIAA) had already commenced legal action against Napster and, despite suggestions to the contrary, the recorded music industry did try to negotiate common ground with the service.

But even while this was happening, the next generation of file sharing services called Grokster and Kazaa were already up and running. There was a war being fought, but the identity of the enemy kept changing – and there were many within the music business questioning whether the alleged enemy was, in reality, an enemy at all. Napster was at least capable of coming to the negotiating table; the later services, based in offshore tax havens, were largely unmanageable.

Napster wasn't the first time that digital music files had been shared – far from it. And Fanning certainly didn't invent MP3 files. They were

WELCOME TO THE JUNGLE

a German invention of Karlheinz Brandenburg, at the Fraunhofer Institute. And even before that in 1994, three Americans had established the International Underground Music Archive using uncompressed WAV files that needed several hours to download. Music, and its transfer, has always been at the forefront of the digital frontier.

What Fanning had achieved, though, was to write a program that indexed the files held on the hard drives of the computers of people who joined the network. Napster didn't store any files, so the alleged copyright infringement came from the individual users, not the service itself. Napster was essentially a service where you could window-shop for music you knew you liked and discover music you might like. It then became a user-based library, except the lenders didn't care if the borrowers never returned what they found on the shelves. Napster's valuable asset, then, wasn't the music but its network of users. Is it any wonder the owners of the copyright in the sound recordings wanted in – those people were the traditional customers of the record companies.

History now shows that Napster was willing to sell out to the major labels for a billion dollars, but this would have allowed consumers free access to the labels' music, making the deal unattractive to the labels. It was simply too great a shift from the long-standing paradigm to be acceptable. Had the labels accepted this deal, they may have been able to control access to digital music, but for how long? The debate over that question is probably beyond the scope of this book.

The key question for Napster was whether they could actually monetise their network. People were happy to be part of a free network that gave them access to music other network members had acquired, but what if they had to pay a subscription to be part of it? Remember, this was in 2000 when there was a real reluctance among consumers to use credit cards online and the logistics of collecting even a small fee from users were challenging.

ANDREW WATT

It's now arguable that the record companies weren't as backward as they have been portrayed. One company, Bertelsmann, the owner of music company BMG, even gave Napster a US$60 million loan in the hope they would develop a legitimate version of their service.

Music companies existed on a business model that returned high profits for low investment and consumers who were willing to play inflated prices for low cost merchandise (ie those cheaply manufactured pieces of plastic called CDs). Faced with the prospect of a service that brought the price of music down to a realistic level, and in so doing shrunk the labels' net revenue and margin, it wasn't illogical for them to delay the inevitable as long as possible.

But the future was already fast arriving.

After RIAA lost an initial court case against Grokster in 2003 in America, it changed its approach and filed suits against 261 users of the service, identified via their IP addresses. Not surprisingly these lawsuits, with the threat of huge payments of damages, were a public relations debacle for the industry organisation. In one ridiculous situation, the RIAA sued a grandmother who clearly had no concept of what a download even was. Some of these cases continued to drag on in the courts for many years.

2003 - iTunes Arrives

In April 2003, Apple launched the iTunes store. This was only after the major labels had tried their own legal download platforms, one called PressPlay and the other Music Net, and both had failed to catch on with the public.

Apple's iPod device wasn't the first portable MP3 player to be marketed, having been preceded by the Rio, among others. Incidentally the company behind the Rio device, Diamond Multimedia, had also

WELCOME TO THE JUNGLE

been on the receiving end of an RIAA lawsuit claiming that the device contravened the Audio Home Recording Act, a 1992 statute in the US. A court had ruled against RIAA, because the Rio was merely a player and not a recording device.

When the iPod was released it wasn't an immediate success due to the difficulty of accessing content, so Apple's plans for a legal paid download store were fast-tracked, firstly with the co-operation of Warner and soon after from Universal. The price of a track was set at 99 cents and of this the labels received almost 75% leaving relatively little for the retailer iTunes. However, the retailer was owned by the same company selling the devices that played the songs and that was were the real money was being made. It was a smart strategic move by Apple. The relationship between the purchased tracks and the player was unbreakable and it created a powerful nexus for the technology company. By 2004 the iTunes store had sold 200 million songs and consumers were now addicted to the idea of buying 99-cent songs rather than US$15 albums. Yet the labels were still faced with artist contracts that required them to invest in the recording of full albums, which some consumers no longer wanted to purchase.

Some artists, such as AC/DC, decided that they wouldn't sell music on iTunes to ensure that their audience – loyal fans who weren't inclined towards singles – would continue buying the band's physical albums.

Eventually, by 2005 the US Supreme Court finally handed down a decision in the Grokster case that limited the ability of file sharing technology to usurp copyright law, but by then the bird had flown. Music sales continued to fall and with that came the need to lay off record company staff and a drop in spending on the promotion of the recordings they offered for sale. It was a seemingly continuous downward spiral.

ANDREW WATT

The landscape had changed forever.

Todd Rundgren was ahead of his time in this regard. As an innovator he was talking music downloads long before they were the industry standard.

> **[TODD RUNDGREN]:** "I can't claim to be completely prophetic, but I have had some inside knowledge about the way this industry works. When it got to the mid '90's and Napster became a threat to the typical way that record labels were doing things, I had already been through it. I had been involved in a project that was supposed to deliver on-demand music into people's homes and not a single label would consider putting their music on a server. Indeed the whole idea of people downloading music scared them. They wanted to control their audience and the whole way they would get music delivered to them and as it turned out people want to be under that kind of control. They wanted to decide how they should have music delivered to them, so the collapse of the whole model was inevitable. You have to understand your own audience then how are you going to succeed?"

It's easy to be critical of the response of the recorded music industry to the advance of the digital world and much of that criticism is valid. However the music business was clearly the 'canary in the coalmine' as these changes stampeded forward on a wave of technological advancement.

A report in the Sydney Morning Herald by Bernard Zuel in 2012 suggested that illegal downloading was still rampant in Australia, saying, "Australians download music illegally more frequently, by head of population, than any other country. At the same time we also happily pay

WELCOME TO THE JUNGLE

for downloads and still buy physical albums at a rate which surprises the industry worldwide. According to a survey of downloads from bit torrent sites conducted by Musicmetric, a self-described data and analytics company, Australia, with just over 19 million downloads, placed sixth in the top 10 for music downloads in the past year. The top downloading nation was the US which, according to Musicmetric, downloaded music 96,681,133 times, more than double the next nearest nation, Britain, which had a little over 43 million downloads. However, by size, Australia with a population of 23 million for those 19 million downloads was comfortably the most frequent user of unofficial or illegal sites."

Brett Cottle is one of Australia's most knowledgeable music industry figures and as the head of APRA, he's had a front-row view of the reaction from the industry.

> **[BRETT COTTLE]:** "It's true that for a long time the music industry suffered from the reputation of being resistant to new business models and new technology, but in truth if you look at all the content industries now, you see that it was a case of the music industry having suffered the onslaught of new technology before the other industries did. The music industry went through this terrible period, having to deal with massive level of change. The value of the industry declined very significantly over a period of years but it's now on the way up and it's found a way to deal with the new technology. It's changed its mindset; the labels are no longer obsessed with controlling the whole distribution process. They realise that it is about running a business – money in, money out. The other content industries are at a much earlier stage in that process and are now having to come to terms with that massive change. Viewed historically, I think it's just that the music industry had to deal with that change first."

Australia was one of the keenest adopters of digital music sales. Artfacts made the following statement about digital music sales:

ANDREW WATT

"**In terms** of digital consumption, Australia was the first market in the world where our growth in digital outpaced our fall in physical sales, even prior to the uptake of music streaming subscription services Spotify, Deezer and Rdio. IFPI estimated the digital music market accounted for 38% of Australia's recorded music sales in 2011, placing it amongst the leading markets at that time in terms of digital uptake internationally, behind the USA and Canada. The IFPI notes a range of factors boosting the digital music sector internationally, including major players expanding their services into new markets, new players entering the market, the emergence of new partnerships, the continued advance of subscription services, positive developments in the legal environment in specific countries and the rapid growth in devices such as smartphones and tablets."

2017 marks the 14-year anniversary of the launch of iTunes and for a generation of music consumers, it's difficult to remember a time when that form of retail didn't exist. The iTunes store changed the way consumers made their music-buying decisions and in particular shifted their habits from buying albums to single songs. However, albums remain economically important.

The Artfacts website suggested, "The 'a la carte' model (where the consumer pays per track or per album) has contributed to a trend towards sales of single tracks, away from albums. Single digital tracks now make up the majority of units sold. However their smaller unit price means they only account for 15% of wholesale market value. CD album sales have fallen from over 50 million units in 2006 to 30 million units in 2011, yet they still make up 66% of market value, with higher average unit prices than digital music."

Digital music marketing has been a growth area and Jackie Krajl has been one of the leaders in the field in Australia. She was an early employee of iTunes in this country.

WELCOME TO THE JUNGLE

[JACKIE KRAJL]: "By the time I went to iTunes there was a buzz. iTunes had already launched in the US and Canada and in the UK, and Japan launched just after I started in Australia. People were excited. They had seen the success in other territories and were really looking forward to what would happen in Australia and how iTunes would impact. It was a new frontier because iTunes launching in Australia was like a big digital flag being put into the ground. There were services that happened prior to iTunes and they definitely paved the way in terms of the digital space and they had introduced both the industry and the market place to the digital space. But you can't dispute the impact iTunes had in any territory."

The Emergence of Streaming

The changes haven't stopped yet and in fact perhaps the biggest shift in music consumption is still emerging. The most recent evolution is the arrival of streaming services like Apple Music and Spotify, along with internet radio services such as Pandora. These services allow consumers to listen to huge libraries of music – either for free, if they are prepared to have their listening experience interrupted by advertising, or for a relatively small monthly fee they can listen uninterrupted. As at March 2012 there were an estimated 32 legitimate digital music services in Australia, and the number has increased considerably since.

This is really what the labels wanted to turn Napster into, but 10 years ago the internet environment probably wasn't ready for that, either in terms of the quality of the streaming experience or the ability to extract payments from wary consumers. Now there is the prospect that the paid download model as dominated by iTunes may only have been a transitional solution – that access to music is now about service and access, not ownership.

ANDREW WATT

It's interesting to compare the streaming model with the operation of You Tube. Nobody "buys" content from You Tube and the most popular content is inevitably preceded by paid advertising. Yet people seem comfortable with that situation. If you want to watch a viral clip of someone getting bitten on the bum by a pesky dog, you are content to sit through a 15-second advert first. However the streaming services are asking you to pay a subscription to avoid hearing advertising before hearing the song of your choice. How cheap do subscriptions have to be before enough people will buy them to sustain a business?

And for the owners of recordings – artists and labels – they key point to remember is, when someone subscribes to a streaming service they are agreeing to pay for music, not necessarily *your* music. You are yet to make a "sale" of your music until they select your track from the millions on offer.

Thomas Heymann was the managing director of Deezer's Australian and New Zealand operations for over a year in 2013-14 and is now at Pandora. Coming from an international background working at major labels and as an artist manager Heymann is well placed to comment on the future of streaming.

> **[THOMAS HEYMANN]**: "In a couple of years' time, everyone will be on streaming. I think music streaming will contribute to more jobs in other sectors because music will be more popular. Artists will sell more concert tickets, more merchandise. Music streaming is basically connecting the artists to the fans, which will result in more business and more jobs."

The jury is still out on the sustainability of the streaming models, especially in the face of the launch of Apple Music globally. How many free users will they convert to paid users and if they don't make those conversions, will the advertising support the free streaming model? There's already been heated debate about the share of the revenue

WELCOME TO THE JUNGLE

making it into the hands of the artists, with almost daily articles being posted bemoaning the meagre amounts being received.

Late in 2014 the hugely successful recording artist Taylor Swift made headlines when she withdrew her music from Spotify stating: "I'm not willing to contribute my life's work to an experiment that I don't feel fairly compensates the writers, producers, artists and creators of this music. And I just don't agree with perpetuating the perception that music has no value and should be free."

Scott Borchetta, of Swift's record label Big Machine, later claimed that other managers and artists are supporting the stance. "There's a big fist in the air about this. Spotify is a really good service, they just need to be a better partner", he was quoted as saying at the time.

In response Spotify boss Daniel Ek, has argued that with 50 million active users (now said to be double that number), 12.5 million paying subscribers and $2bn of royalties paid out to labels and music publishers since 2008, Spotify's policy of not restricting music from its free users is the most effective way to drive subscription sales.

This is really no different than the discussions about artist royalties from the days when most of the revenue was generated by CD sales in physical stores. The debate still centres around the concept of free music and what the owners of copyright in sound recordings are prepared to give away in order to develop a market that may or may not be there for paid content.

There is also a concern among artists that the Spotify model has a worrying sub-plot – the fact that the major record labels receive an equity benefit from the model.

As was reported by The Guardian in 2014, "It's fuelled by distrust of the fact that major labels own at least 18% of the company through equity stakes granted when it was negotiating its first licences in 2007 and 2008. Some artists suspect that those labels are holding out for big windfalls if and when Spotify either goes public or gets bought, and fear that the proceeds – as well as the large advance payments Spotify makes to labels whenever it renegotiates its licensing deals – will not be shared fairly with musicians.

Transparency

It seems to be a question of trust between labels and their artists that still fuels the debate. At a music business conference in 2014 U2 singer Bono commented, "The real enemy is not between digital downloads or streaming. The real enemy, the real fight, is between opacity and transparency. The music business has historically involved itself in quite considerable deceit."

Daniel Ek also points the finger at the intermediaries. "Lots of problems that have plagued the industry since its inception continue to exist. We've already paid more than $2bn in royalties to the music industry, and if that money is not flowing to the creative community in a timely and transparent way, that's a big problem."

In 2015 Rethink Music, a project of the Berklee Institute of Creative Entrepreneurship published a report entitled Fair Music Project that emphasized the need for greater transparency in the recorded music industry. The project was headed up by Allen Bargfrede, one of the world's leading authorities on the digital music world.

The Report found that there were 164 billion on-demand streams in 2014, up 60% from 2013. Streaming constituted 27% of the US recorded music market in 2014 and it was estimated that there would be 191 million paying streaming service subscribers by 2018. The report suggested that around 70% of the revenue generated by streaming services was paid out to rights holders but labels retained

WELCOME TO THE JUNGLE

around 73% of that money before the remainder was distributed to artists.

The Report made a number of recommendations regarding this industry relating to copyright reform and the disclosure of the path taken by funds generated by the industry suggesting that the technology now existed for instantaneous tracking of the use of recordings and songs.

There's no doubt that while the current debate is centred on the streaming model that the final chapter of the digital music revolution is a long way from being written.

> **[ALLEN BARGFREDE]:** "Streaming is growing exponentially and the up-take has been really, really fast over the past few years. I think we are still five years off from a critical mass in streaming and who knows what comes after that. Is streaming the end business model? I don't know. Everyone thought that iTunes and digital downloads was the way it was going to be but when you look at it that was dominant for maybe five or six years. Digital is a continuously evolving landscape."

> **[COLIN DANIELS]:** "Streaming is both an opportunity and a threat, but I think we are more clear on the opportunity than we are on the threat. Obviously the opportunity is that it's a new income stream and a discovery platform. That's what they are telling us and that's what it looks like at the moment to the naked eye. I think it's too early to tell. With any developing business sometimes the strangest things will surprise you. No one ever predicted Facebook, no one predicted You Tube. I don't think we can say, 'here is the future'. I don't think streaming is the future of the music business on its own, but it will play an important part. We don't know yet if we can make money from

it and I think it would be silly from the business viewpoint to put all the eggs in that basket and call that the future."

[JACKIE KRAJL]: "I think it's still a little too early to make a call on streaming. I know that streaming services are taking a bit of a bashing right now around the amount of money that is being paid back to artists. If streaming services see their numbers get good growth over the next few years, then the entire thing changes. I think it's important to note that in all the territories where streaming services have launched, downloads have also increased. So streaming services aren't necessarily taking a slice of the digital pie from download services, they are actually growing the entire pie which is really encouraging for the industry. At the end of the day, streaming services are offering a legal option for music fans and the industry should be really happy that consumers are getting more and more options in how to consume music legally, rather than only giving them a few options and pushing them to P2P and to illegal downloading."

The internet is by definition a worldwide platform and the businesses that exist as on-line solutions are global businesses. Even though streaming services rolled out progressively across various territories, that didn't prevent the industry having to think across borders. This is a discussion that extends well beyond the borders of Australia, and indeed beyond the Western world.

Ruuben van den Heuval is an Australian music executive who spent at least a decade working in the Asian market, largely in the emerging digital space. He is now Head of Music Partnerships – Asia Pacific for Google Play. His experience is different to many of his contemporaries.

[RUUBEN VAN DEN HEUVAL]: "Digital is the transfer from something being a product – something that is created and

WELCOME TO THE JUNGLE

then sold – to a service. If you are in Hong Kong or Taiwan and you are living in a 20 sqm flat with your mother and grandparents and aunt and uncle and a few siblings, the idea of having a CD collection is ridiculous. So the growth of digital in those places happened very quickly. Look at those places where the biggest aspirational item is a mobile phone. That is the statement to the world.

Digital has advanced very quickly in those markets. What I am seeing now is this massive shift towards the idea that the idea of ownership means nothing any more. It's all about the experience. I've got 20 million tracks in my pocket and I can listen whenever I want for a small monthly fee. That's about the experience, not the ownership. Whether it's ad supported or whether it is a subscription model, that's where it is going. Based on the Asian experience, I think the ownership model will one day be dead in Australia."

Charles Caldas, late in 2016, offered some very clear observations on the impact of streaming as it sits currently.

[CHARLES CALDAS]: In the last three years we have seen the initial growth spurt of streaming where no-one was quite sure what impact it was going to have and whether it was going to change the business positively or negatively. We've now seen streaming gather this extraordinary momentum and in some ways *become* the business and the future of the business. We have a lot more clarity about what its done to the eco-system and what its done to the overall business of labels.

One of the things we have really learned is the streaming model in itself is much more democratic than the physical model ever was. Even the biggest retail store in Australia probably carried 1000 titles and if you weren't part of that thousand you had no available market. The catchcry of independents was "if only they stocked my record, it would sell". We were stuck behind these tight channels to market and it was a model that suited the companies with the most financial power. The genius of the major labels was being able to control what was being marketed to people, at what time, through which key channels. So they were able to buy their way on to radio, into mass media advertising, they could control what artists appeared on television. You married all that with the fact that if a person walked into Sanity or Brashs the first thing they saw was what had been on television that weekend, which was the same as what they heard on the radio. As a consumer if you were into a niche type of music you had to walk past all the heavily marketed mainstream products to get to your niche.

That problem has disappeared. Now everything is in stock, all the time, everywhere. The dynamic of that is interesting. In a Spotify environment you can search for what you know you like and that will bring up a playlist that the music you like is on and then you will discover other things on that playlist that you like. From a music fan point of view, you don't have to walk past music you are not interested in to get to the music you do like. Instead you have all this curation and recommendation to help you find what you like. You combine that with the fact that when something is recommended to you it is available instantly – you don't have to order it in. The discovery process is no longer about the music that is stocked in your local record store, it's about all the music in the world."

Perhaps the final frontier is the concept of a Global Content Marketplace – not just for music but for all types of digital content. To achieve this though will require an enormous amount of legal discussion across borders. Experts suggest that this is still a long way off and until then challenges of differing copyright laws in different markets remain.

WELCOME TO THE JUNGLE

[ALLEN BARGFREDE]: "I think in an ideal world that's what we need to move to. Copyright has borders; content does not. At some point we have to recognize that and reform the law and start to be aware that the world is flat. It's frustrating to people to have this fragmented market for content but I think we are decades away from true globalization of it… and getting there is going to be a huge challenge and we are now just beginning that discussion. Getting past the initial discussion to getting people to agree to it and getting it passed is a very long process."

The Evolution of Streaming

Perhaps the most significant emerging question to arise out of the streaming industry is its impact on creative funding. If a streaming service really is just a 'celestial jukebox' then will the tendency be for people to use their services to play music they already know they like, or will discovery via playlists become the great legacy of the emergence of streaming? If streaming becomes the dominant delivery platform, then it will generate revenue for artists and music that are already known, but it may kill creative funding of recording from new artists who are not likely to be heard on a streaming service boasting millions of tracks that are better known.

In the first edition of this book in 2014 several pages were spent discussing the impending arrival of a streaming service called "Daisy" based around a company called Beats Electronics – best known for their Dr Dre line of headphones. Beats had announced Trent Reznor of Nine Inch Nails as its chief creative officer intending that he would help develop Daisy into a streaming service that will "bring an emotional connection back to the act of music discovery", according to a company statement. Leading music business executive and famed former record producer Jimmy Iovine was also involved.

ANDREW WATT

In early 2013 it was announced that new investors had provided $60m for Daisy to expand its operation. Those investors included Len Blavatnik's Access Industries and Australia's James Packer and Texan billionaire Lee M Bass. Blavatnik had already purchased the Warner Music Group and had invested in another streaming services, Deezer.

In May 2014 Apple had announced that it had purchased Beats for $3 billion – certainly a hefty acquisition, even for Apple. There had been a lot of speculation about what the Beats acquisition would bring to Apple, which already has an existing streaming radio business and very healthy third-party relationships in headphones, speakers and other peripherals.

In 2015 Apple's own streaming service Apple Music was launched with great fanfare.

It's probably too early to determine if Apple Music will become the dominant player in the streaming market but as the following comment from Apple observer Rene Ritchie suggests, the tech giant is in the music streaming market for the long haul:

"I believe everyone at Apple…went into Apple Music with the best of intentions. I believe they wanted to make a great service. Whether it's the right idea and the right implementation of the idea is something Apple still needs to prove. Apple needs to prove Music is something that's better than what came before, and better than the sum of its parts."

So what is the state of play? With a reported paid user base surpassing 40 million subscribers — and reportedly 55 million additional listeners on its free, ad-based service — Spotify currently holds the lead. Apple Music, as of September 2016, is reported to have at least 17 million subscribers. Although that is less than half the size of Spotify's paid user base, that is still impressive when you consider that Apple Music went

WELCOME TO THE JUNGLE

live in June of 2015, nine years after Spotify's founding. Apple Music offers a three-month free trial and a discounted family plan. Apple's service claims to have 40 million songs which is superior to Spotify which claims "more than 30 million". That's something that other competitors, like the new Amazon service or Jay Z's Tidal simply can't match.

Spotify tends to be the "go-to" service when it comes to playlists. For example, Spotify's *Discover Weekly* playlist lands in the subscriber's feed every week providing a two-hour playlist of personal music recommendations based on the subscribers listening habits, as well as those who listen to similar artists.

Amazon's on-demand music streaming service became available in October 2016. Amazon Music Unlimited, is a on-demand competitor to the likes of Spotify, Apple Music, and Google Play Music. Amazon has done a number of things to differentiate Music Unlimited from its competitors, but the most notable one is its price: the service will be available to Amazon Prime members for $7.99 per month or $79 per year (in the US), which is cheaper than the premium levels of Spotify or Apple Music.

It's obvious that the final view of the streaming landscape is far from clear and there are a good many cards still to be played yet. The future might be here but the real future is still in the future.

> **[CHARLES CALDAS]:** "The exciting thing at this particular juncture is that there is enough value in the streaming industry to make it interesting. That much money flowing into the industry attracts innovation and new ways of distributing, consuming and monetizing music."

Grass Roots Impact

There are now so many platforms available to promote an artist's music that it's almost an impossible task for an artist, or their support team, to be across all of them. The challenge is not finding a platform where you can be heard, it's being able to shout over the white noise. As veteran US industry expert Ted Cohen says of artists in this environment, "The most important thing now is that you have to take responsibility and you have to take action. And there's no one to blame any more. You don't have a manager any more to blame. You don't have an agent. You don't have a label. You don't have any of these people that you can blame. Even if you do have a manager, even if you have an agent, the days of saying 'it's your fault' are over. You need to take ownership of your career; you need to take responsibility for what happens."

For artists, this level of responsibility may be daunting. There is a distinct divide between those artists for whom marketing and career development come naturally, and those for whom it's the antithesis of everything they believe themselves to be. There is nothing inherently wrong with being an artist who does not want to participate in the marketing process, but it means they need to accept their reliance on support from people such as managers and agents, and those people need to be prepared to accept the challenges of working with artists of that ilk.

The evolution of the industry isn't lost on leading Australian managers like Bill Cullen. Cullen is one of Australia's most respected managers and he has witnessed first-hand the changes in his business as a result of changes in the recorded music industry.

> **[BILL CULLEN]**: "It feels like we are doing twice as much work as we were doing eight or 10 years ago and I think that's to do with the shrinking of the record business. The labels used to offer a lot more service and we've had to step in and fill those holes, or just let it collapse for the artist. As managers we are still trying to come to terms with the fact that we are still getting paid the same, but doing more work. You can't go and say to the artist that we now need 30% commission because we are doing more work.

WELCOME TO THE JUNGLE

It's easier to have an audience because the internet is global, but is not necessarily a big audience. There are a whole lot of much smaller niches but that doesn't mean you can have a career there. You can reach a kid in Norway but how do you monetise that?

The first person interviewed for this book was Bertis Downs, an American lawyer who for around 30 years has been the lawyer and business advisor to R.E.M., a band whose career paralleled and symbolised the evolution of "alternative rock" and its infiltration of the mainstream. Downs negotiated what was at the time the largest record deal ever signed by a band when R.E.M. signed a multi-million dollar, multi-album contract with Warner Music.

When asked whether someone entering the music business now is actually entering the entertainment, media or technology businesses, Downs provided a revealing comment that has stood the test of time.

[**BERTIS DOWNS**] "They are entering the ubiquity business. We have gotten to the point of the *celestial jukebox*, to use a few buzzwords. We've got to the point where music is like water. Music is everywhere. Paying for music is voluntary, so you've got to figure out a way to deal with the new math. The new math is very different to the old math. The old math was based on a premise that if somebody liked your music they would go out and buy your music. Now, the new math is that, at best, they are going to download a song, or maybe an album, and even that top line math is very different to another time. More likely they are going to get it for free, or something that is very close to free, like Spotify. It's not so much your song that people are paying for, it is *every* song. If they happen to consume your song you are going to get a slither of some pennies that might eventually add up to a dollar, which might eventually add up to something more. It's still early days to see how it's going to play out. Maybe it's all going to be fine and it's still going to be a significant income stream for a band, but I think now the way you go about making a career out of it has so many more variables, so many more opportunities and so many more pitfalls. We're in an age where people get music for free most of the time, that's just the reality of it. At best you're looking at a very different set of equations and how you are going to make that add up. Does it mean it can't be done? No? Does it make it harder? Yes. Has it ever been easy? No."

Downs makes several good points. Firstly – in some ways – nothing has changed. The business is still about what it always was: finding a way to connect those who make the music (the artists) with those who want to listen to it (the consumers). And wherever there is that aspiration there is a need for people to provide the services that make up the process that achieves that aim. The more important your service is and the more skilled you are in its provision, the more likely that you will be remunerated for providing it.

My Path into the Industry

MARIANNA ANNAS

"I started out as a music lawyer. I found myself going through law school, doing arts-law and increasingly realising that I was never going to be a conventional lawyer. I'd been a music fan for as long as I could remember and it made sense that if I was going to actually finish law school and do something with my law degree, then absolutely, categorically the only area I was going to work in would be music. I got a job with Shane Simpson and worked with him for three years and then increasingly realised that I was not built for a law firm environment. At the end of that time, an in-house legal and business affairs role became available at BMG and I took that. I ended up working at BMG for five years, but the last three were overseas. I spend a couple of years in Sydney, and I was transferred to the New York office and I spent three years there. I came back and went to EMI in the same role as director of business affairs. So I spent a lot of time in in-house roles and then I decided I wanted something a little bit more than a legal role. I've never underestimated what having the legal skills meant though. I think they are a phenomenal asset to anyone who works in a business that is so intellectual property and contracts-based. I'd always particularly liked music publishing and I'd always handled music publishing agreements in my business affairs role. ABC Publishing approached me about the role of head of music publishing and that's where I ended up."

CHAPTER 3

COPYRIGHT, CONTRACTS AND THE RECORDING INDUSTRY

While it's easy to imagine a new player coming into the music industry fuelled by an entrepreneurial spirit and a passion for music in any of its forms, it's more difficult to imagine someone inherently excited by the law of copyright. It would, however, be a huge mistake to underplay the importance of copyright in the new music industry. As much as the means of making reproductions of copyright works have evolved and become ridiculously simple, that hasn't changed that fact that the works are protected by the law of copyright and hence require the permission of the owner before they can be reproduced or publicly performed.

The Importance of Copyright

Anyone seeking to have a career in the music business – or at least in the business of the exploitation of recorded music - will still need to be well versed in the concepts and limitations imposed by copyright law. A working knowledge of the law of contract is also essential in any business and the music industry is no exception.

In his book, *When The Writ Hits The Fan*, legendary Australian music business lawyer Phil Dwyer opens the chapter on copyright with, "The business of music is about the creation, accumulation and commercial exploitation of copyrights individually or as part of a catalogue. Copyright is the bricks and mortar of the music industry."

WELCOME TO THE JUNGLE

Marianna Annas started her career as a lawyer in the music business. She worked in business affairs roles in major record companies both in Australia and internationally and she now heads a music publishing company, ABC Music. She is very well placed to comment on the importance of legal knowledge in the music business.

> **[MARIANNA ANNAS]:** "It's hugely valuable. The two main areas that consistently come up as relevant on a daily basis, are copyright and contracts. Invariably you will have to address an issue around copyright or contract every single day."

Copyright law is about creativity. It was first introduced as a matter of public policy because society recognised that innovators and creators should be entitled to protect the fruits of their labors and be encouraged to make new works, knowing that they would be entitled to the benefits that may flow when their work is used. The first copyright laws were enacted in Britain in 1710 and in the US, copyright law was introduced in 1790 to protect the creators of maps, books and charts. In 1909 the US laws were extended to protect musical works.

Copyright isn't a music industry concept, but it's the cornerstone around most businesses in the recorded music industry are built.

Copyright Basics

The basic principle of the law of copyright is that someone who creates an original work has ownership of it from the moment of its creation. Once ownership is established, that person has the right to restrict or allow other people to deal with what they own on the terms and conditions that they see fit. Important among these rights is the right to allow or restrict the right of another person to use what the first person owns to make new products or creations, and to make copies or duplications of the first person's copyright works.

ANDREW WATT

The rights belonging to the owner of copyright in a creative work can be described as the rights of "control", "permission" and "remuneration".

In the music business two main copyrights exist.

- Copyright in the song – This is owned by the songwriter and it exists from the moment the song is written and expressed in some form, either by recording it or notating it in some way. The mode of expression need not be sophisticated. Copyright protection does not extend to a mere idea in the head of the creator; the expression of that idea, however basic, is essential. A song consists of two copyrights: one in the lyrics and another in the music. These two copyrights can be created and controlled by the same person if that person writes both the words and the music. Two or more people can collaborate on a song, and when they do they will jointly own the copyright in whatever part they contributed to.

- Copyright in the sound recording – When a recording is made of a song, copyright in that sound recording is owned by the person making the recording. In effect this is the person who paid for the recording; the contract between the owner of the recording equipment and the person paying for the recording will normally state that the ownership of copyright in the sound recording will belong to the person who is paying for the recording – once they make the agreed payment. This is normally a very good incentive to ensure payment for services, something that studio operators are well aware of!

The key rights provided – by the law – to the owners of copyright in either songs (musical works) or sound recordings is the right to publicly perform the works (which includes the broadcast on television or radio and any other public performance) and the right to make

WELCOME TO THE JUNGLE

reproductions of the works (which includes making copies of recordings, which naturally involves making copies of the songs that have been recorded). It's probably no surprise then that these rights form the foundation of the recorded music industry and play a significant role in relation to live musical performance too.

Reproduction of Copyright Works

When a person or company wants to make a recording of a song they seek to exploit the rights held by the owner of the copyright in that song.

Let's go back to the making of a sound recording. When a song is going to be recorded the songwriter is giving permission for the recording artist to use their work (their song) in the creation of a new work (a sound recording). That sounds simple enough when the songwriter and the recording artist are the same person (you are giving permission to yourself!), but it's less straightforward when the two are different people and might not even know each other. Obviously it wasn't reasonable to expect each songwriter to negotiate and agree on a license fee with each potential artist who might want to record their song, especially for songs that become very popular. It became obvious that a system was needed that standardised this process of negotiation and value setting.

Mechanical Licenses and Royalties

This situation was dealt with by internationally recognised laws being passed that determined that a payment should be made by the owner of a sound recording to the owner of a song used in that sound recording, and the amount of that payment would be determined by the law. This payment was known as a "mechanical royalty" and the permission that was granted by the songwriter to the artist recording their song was known as a 'mechanical license'.

ANDREW WATT

This meant that, even if the songwriter and the recording artist were the same person, the songwriter was entitled to a payment when their song was recorded. This is fair because the songwriter may not necessarily benefit from the sale of the recording (as they may not even be involved in its creation) and yet the songwriter's creative work, the song, is being used as a part of that recording.

Think, for example, of the song *The Locomotion*, written by Gerry Goffin and Carole King. This song has been a hit several times, beginning with a 1962 recording by singer Little Eva, later by an American rock band called Grand Funk Railroad and finally by Kylie Minogue. Obviously King and Goffin were not involved in the sound recording by any of those three artists, so they would not directly benefit from the sales of the sound recordings. However, every time a recording of that song is made, the songwriters are entitled to a mechanical royalty from the owners of the sound recordings; in each case a different record company associated with each of those artists.

Record companies realised there was little they could do to avoid paying mechanical royalties to songwriters who were not connected to the artist – it was a legal requirement. However the companies argued that if the artist wrote the song, they should have some flexibility in the permission they gave. Hence in most recording contracts, artists were asked to accept a mechanical royalty below the standard statutory rate on songs they had written. These songs were referred to as 'controlled compositions.' This was one way that record contracts were stacked against artists who wrote their own songs.

Even with this standardised system in place there remained an administrative and logistical need for the owners of the copyright in songs to be represented with respect to the collection of their mechanical royalties. Accordingly AMCOS (Australian Mechanical Copyright Owners Society) was formed as an umbrella organisation for those copyright owners. The songwriters are able to grant their "reproduction" right to

WELCOME TO THE JUNGLE

AMCOS who in turn will collect mechanical payments on their behalf. AMCOS was established in 1979 to manage "mechanical royalties", that is the reproduction or copying and storage of music in different formats. This covers copying of songs and compositions by record labels or other parties to sell them on CD, DVD or online.

Public Performance of Copyright Works

When a song is publicly performed the copyright owner is entitled to be paid for this use of their work. Public performance can be done in two ways – either a musician or a singer performs the work in public (at a venue, either formal or informal) or the song is publicly 'performed' via the medium of a recording of that song (as happens on radio, television, in gyms, cafes, nightclubs and hundreds of other locations, thousands of times daily). If the song is performed via the medium of a recording there are actually two copyrights being used – the copyright in the song and the copyright in the sound recording. Both copyright owners are entitled to be paid.

A similar situation exists with respect to the collection of the performance income. The songwriters, and for that matter the owners of the sound recordings, have neither the time, resources or inclination to pursue every organisation that uses their copyright works for the payments they are entitled to. Again, in these situations, collective action was required and the two groups of copyright owners are represented by collection societies. Songwriters grant their "performance rights" to APRA (Australian Performing Rights Association), established in 1926, to manage the performance and communication rights of its members.

In the case of the copyright in the sound recordings, those copyright owners grant their performance rights to the PPCA. Established in 1969, the Phonographic Performance Company of Australia Limited (PPCA) is a national, non-government, non-profit organisation that represents the interest of record companies and Australian recording artists with respect to the performance rights in their work.

APRA and PPCA work in a similar way. Rather than make individual collections on behalf of individual copyright owners from those businesses using the copyright works, APRA and PPCA provide licenses to those businesses that enable them to use all those works covered by the societies for a fixed annual fee. A complex series of license fees have been calculated covering the various users of musical works and recordings and can be found on the societies respective websites. Of course the societies are able to enforce the payment of their fees because failure to have a license while performing works is an infringement of copyright.

APRA and PPCA operate and work independently as they represent different copyright owners but moves are being made to streamline this process.

On December 15, 2016, APRA/AMCOS and the PPCA announced they had signed a Memorandum of Understanding to develop a single public performance licensing system under the name OneMusic Australia. The new one-stop promises a much simpler process for businesses and public places to obtain, manage, report on and pay for the licenses they require to play music.

OneMusic Australia will covers both recording and musical work performance rights and will be introduced during the second half of 2018. In the interim the collecting societies announced they are committed to a period of "intense industry consultation" to help shape the project.

The joint venture follows the introduction of OneMusic NZ three years ago. However, until the launch of OneMusic Australia, it will be "business as usual" with both APRA/AMCOS and PPCA.

WELCOME TO THE JUNGLE

Performers Rights

In this section we look at the rights of Performers who participate in the making of recordings. This is different from the "performance rights" that are one of the bundle of rights owned by a copyright owner, and are administered by APRA and PPCA. The difference is subtle but significant. "Performance Rights" refer to the rights given to the copyright owner relating to the performance of their works (songs or sound recordngs). "Performers Rights" refers to rights provided to those individuals that perform on recordings – these people may be quite separate to those who either wrote the song or created the sound recordings.

There is no performers 'copyright' in Australia – quite simply because performers do not create a work as defined by the Copyright Act 1968. However the *Copyright Amendment Act 1989* (Cwth) gives performers the right to take action over unauthorised uses of their performances. The performer must be able to show that the offending party ought to have known the recording of their performance was unauthorised. It's a different power than that conferred by copyright and has been described as a 'neighbouring right'.

Susan Cotchin operates a Melbourne based business called International Royalties Rescue, that manages neighbouring rights on behalf of those people who contribute to the creation of sound recordings. She describes the term this way.

> **[SUSAN COTCHIN]:** "A song can earn money by being placed in a situation like a film or game. But you can't hear a song without a sound recording. So there are two separate rights. The sound recording is usually owned by a record label because they paid for it, but in order to make a sound recording we need performers and contributors like producers, sound engineers and musicians. So "neighbouring rights" refers to those

rights that "surround" the performer on the sound recording, whose involvement is not captured under copyright."

Value of Copyright

Ownership of copyright in a song entitles the owner to control how that song is used, including who can make the first recording of it. Keep in mind that the songwriter and the person recording a version of the song do not necessarily need to be the same person. In fact, the advent of the singer-songwriter was a relatively new phenomenon; for many years most successful recording artists did not write their own songs. As a result, the ownership of song copyright was very important.

Entire businesses were built around employing salaried songwriters to write songs that were then pitched at recording artists. These songwriters would 'clock in' and work a nine-to-five day, with the products of their labours being owned by their employers. The famous phrase "Tin Pan Alley" refers to a specific place: West 28th Street between Fifth and Sixth Avenue in Manhattan, where a number of these businesses flourished. Tin Pan Alley was where aspiring songwriters came to pitch their work. Songwriters who became established producers of successful songs were hired to be on the staff of the music houses, even though sometimes their work was attributed partially to a member of the company to maximise the return to the company. The very successful songwriters, such as Irving Berlin, were sometimes able to start their own publishing companies.

Assignment and Licensing

It's one thing to establish that the owners of copyright in a creative work have the right to control the use of that work and then allow (or deny) third parties the right to use it. The next step is to establish a framework that enables the copyright owner to systematically enforce those powers and be remunerated when that happens.

WELCOME TO THE JUNGLE

This is done through the laws relating to assignment and licensing.

An assignment of copyright results in the ownership of a work transferring from the creator (for these purposes called "the assigner") to another party ("the assignee"). The key point is that the ownership of the copyright work is transferred.

For example, when an artist makes a sound recording, our initial understanding of copyright suggests that the artist, as the 'creator' of that sound recording, would be the owner of the copyright. But if a record company had paid for the recording they would feel justified in requiring that the ownership pass to them. To ensure this happens, their recording contract with the artist would include clauses assigning the copyright of the recording to the company.

A licence of copyright act based around the giving of permission and thus can take different forms depending on what permission is being given. The word "licence" in legal terms means much is it does in everyday terms. If you have a licence to drive a car, you have been given permission to drive a car. By licensing the copyright in your work you are giving another party permission to use that work for the purpose of the licence. Let's use the same record company and recording artist example, except this time the artist has paid for their own recording. In this situation they are unlikely to want to assign the copyright to the company and the company is unlikely to expect to become the owner of the copyright, because the company did not pay for it to be made. However the record company may still want to manufacture and sell records embodying the sound recording and the artist may want the company to do that. The likely approach would be that the artist would license the recording to the company for the purpose of making and selling records, but they would not assign the copyright to the work.

ANDREW WATT

The distinction between an assignment and a licence is obviously very significant and these terms form the basis of most agreements in the recorded music industry.

When a third party wants to use a copyright work, they must obtain permission from the copyright owner. Thus, for example, when a film or television company wants to use a song in their production they must get the permission of both the songwriter and the owner of the sound recording, most likely the record company. When permission is granted it is facilitated by a licence agreement, called a Synchronisation Licence.

Ownership of Copyright in Sound Recordings

The basic principle of copyright is that the creator of a work is the owner of the copyright. At first glance you may think that the creator of the sound recording is the musician or group of musicians who recorded it. At a basic level, that is true. However the reality of the early methods of recording is that the technology (or machinery) involved in making those recordings was very expensive and as a result few musicians were able to make recordings themselves, as discussed in the previous chapter.

However business people soon realised that there was a demand for the recordings of certain musicians, and if they were willing to pay for the making of those recordings, they could benefit from the sale of those recordings to fans. This was the genesis of record companies. Essentially their business model was to pay for recordings that the musicians could not pay for themselves and sell those recordings to the public, at a profit. Their business challenge was to select recordings to make that the public would buy in sufficient numbers – much as the challenge remains today. The chapter on A&R looks more deeply into this 'talent selection' role.

WELCOME TO THE JUNGLE

The record companies had to entice the musicians to transfer, or assign, their copyright in the recordings they made to the company to allow the company to make copies of the recordings. In order to entice them to do that, they offered to pay the musician a royalty for every copy of their sound recording that was made.

For the artists the more copies sold, the greater the royalties they would receive, so the record companies would try to convince the artist that the company would be able to maximise the sales by showing they had marketing, promotion, distribution and sales expertise. They would consider it to be legitimate to take out some of those costs of doing business before calculating the royalty payable to the musician. Once these arrangements were put into the form of a contract, both the record company and the artist would have some degree of certainty about what was going to happen to the money generated by the sale of recordings made by that artist.

The standard arrangement whereby the artist would assign copyright in the sound recording to the record company had one further complication in the US. Under US copyright law, the assignor of rights is entitled to terminate the assignment any time within five years of the assignment's 35th anniversary. In other words, the transfer of ownership is really only a long-term license. This relates to assignments made after January 1, 1978. This means that as from January 1, 2013 these reversions of copyright came into effect.

It was expected that much litigation would arise from this, as the record companies attempt to argue that the essence of their agreements with the artists is not in fact an assignment, but that the work was originally a work-for-hire that did not require an assignment for the company to claim ownership, despite the word "assignment" being featured in the contracts.

A December 2012 article in *Billboard* magazine explained the situation well.

ANDREW WATT

While albums released in 1978 are the first batch eligible for possible reversion of ownership to pass from labels back to the artists, so far the only acts to file notice of termination for master right recordings with the U.S. Copyright Office include Pat Benatar, Journey, Devo and Billy Joel.

Although 2013 theoretically is the year that master sound recordings' copyright licenses begin to expire for albums and can revert from labels to the artists, no one is sure what exactly will happen.

But label executives insist their companies will be largely unaffected by the law becoming a reality and think it will continue to be business as usual. So for now, it's unclear if master recording copyright reversion will be a big issue for the industry, as artist advocates argue, or another overhyped potential disaster like the Y2K issue turned out to be at the turn of the millennium."

The practical outcome might come down to the value of the sound recordings that the artists may get back. Given the ease of digital distribution, there may now be real value in the artist getting control of these works and making them available for download and streaming, themselves and skipping the middle man.

So far the reversion law has only been considered by the courts in one US case. A copyright transfer termination (reversion) request was made by Victor Willis (member of the Village People and co-author of such hits as "Y.M.C.A.") in January 2011 to French music publisher Scorpio Music S.A and their US administrator, Can't Stop Productions, Inc. In return, Can't Stop Productions filed suit challenging the validity of Willis's terminations. Scorpio first argued that Willis's work should be classified as work-for-hire – the argument expected to be used by most labels and publishers. Willis successfully regained control of his copyright in this case.

WELCOME TO THE JUNGLE

In 2016, the Duran Duran case tested whether the reversion right meant that songwriters who assigned their copyrights to music publishers outside the US could still automatically reclaim control of their songs within America after 35 years. When Duran Duran members Simon Le Bon, Nick Rhodes, Roger Taylor and John Taylor, and former member Andy Taylor, sought to reclaim the American song rights in their first three albums and a James Bond theme *A View To A Kill*, their publisher –a Sony/ATV controlled company called Gloucester Place Music – insisted that their 1980's publishing contract, governed by English law, didn't allow such a reversion. Duran Duran said that if Gloucester Place Music won it would set a dangerous precedent, in that publishers could circumvent songwriter rights provided by US law through the UK courts.

The judge agreed with the publisher, ruling that the wording of Duran Duran's publishing agreement "would have conveyed to a reasonable person… that the parties' intention was that the 'entire copyrights' in the compositions should vest, and remain vested, in the claimant for the 'full term' of the copyrights", meaning that the US reversion right, which already existed at the time the publishing deal was done, would not apply when 35 years expired.

It will be interesting to see what follows, noting, of course, that this situation remains based in American copyright law and wont necessarily apply to rights outside of the USA.

Copyright and Downloads

Downloading occurs when the digital file you obtain is delivered via the internet and is stored on your own device, whether that be a computer, an MP3 player such as an iPod, a USB drive or a CD. You become the owner of that file, to the extent that it is stored on your device and you are in control of its use. The best-known site for obtaining legal downloads is iTunes.

ANDREW WATT

The retailer, for example, iTunes, is able to offer those tracks for sale because they have been given permission to do so by the copyright owners of the sound recordings.

Initially these copyright owners of recordings were the record companies, but in recent times services have emerged that allow artists without record companies to offer songs for sales by iTunes and other retailers. Tunecore is the most prominent of these services although there are now many of them. By using Tunecore, artists (and labels) can have their music placed on most of the significant download or streaming services for a fixed fee. Tunecore also offers a publishing royalties collection service that collects royalties for songwriters – mechanical royalties for reproduction of their songs, performance royalties when their songs are embodied in recordings that are performed, and even print and synchronisation royalties.

Initially iTunes set the price of a download at 99 cents per track, but in recent times there has been more scope for price differentiation.

The fee that is paid to the copyright owner by the retailer is usually paid to the owner of the sound recording, who in turn pays the artist and the publisher (or writer) the mechanical royalty that is due.

However, even this relatively straightforward arrangement has led to some controversy, particularly in the case of the relationships between artists and record companies.

This book used the word "license" to describe the legal relationship when a copyright owner gives someone permission to exploit the work. It is arguable that the record companies are giving iTunes a licence to provide those songs to the public for a fee. After all, they are not selling them a physical CD, as was the case with bricks-and-mortar retailers, and they don't have to invest any money in packaging and

WELCOME TO THE JUNGLE

distribution. However record companies are loath to describe that arrangement as a license for a significant financial reason.

In most recording contracts, the royalty paid to an artist on "sales" of their music is in the vicinity of 10% to 18% of the recommended retail price. However in the same contracts the split between the artist and the label on music "licensed" is normally 50/50. This is because the costs to the label of licensing a recording are minimal compared with those for a sale and thus the recording artist should receive a larger percentage of the resulting income. Of course, this was intended to refer to licences such as synchronisation licenses for use in film, television or games and most of these contracts were written prior to the advent of downloads. It's no surprise that labels like to avoid the use of the word 'license' when dealing with iTunes – they would obviously prefer to pay the artist 10-15% of the revenue received, rather than 50%.

This conflict was actually tested in the courts by Eminem and the US courts found that a digital download should be treated as a sale rather than a license of music, despite it having no physical product exchanging hands. This wasn't a great result for artists who clearly would have preferred that a download be characterised as a license than a sale.

Copyright and Streaming

Streaming occurs when you are able to listen to a song on your device, but only by being connected to the internet. The file is never downloaded to your device, but remains on the server of the streaming provider. You have permission to do this as often as you want, provided you maintain your subscription to the service. Such a subscription generally costs between $10 and $15 per month. Some streaming models allow you the same access for free, but the listening experience is periodically interrupted by advertising. It is expected that new variations of this model will continue to emerge as we saw in the previous chapter.

The owners of the copyrights provide access to the music by way of a licence given to the service provider in return for a payment calculated using a formula based on percentages of subscription revenue. This revenue is collected by the labels - for the sound recordings and the collection societies such as AMCOS - for the mechanical royalties. In Australia the APRA/AMCOS website states "APRA/AMCOS has available a license for subscription services (including subscription services that provide streaming and cloud-based options) at 9.0% of the relevant revenue, subject to certain minima."

According to Kobalt Blue's Simon Moor, the publishing industry has adapted well to the new paradigms

> **[SIMON MOOR]:** "Yes, I think we have worked that out. The publishing business has always been adept at recognizing that there are multiple income streams and has never fallen in love with one income stream. Where the major labels were making so much money from the CD format, they didn't develop those other income streams sufficiently. The publishers always worked in synchronization, licensing, performance, print, as well as mechanicals and for that reason we were always aware of the potential and how to maximize these income for songwriters. We knew what the collection societies did and there are some really forward thinking collection societies out there working on behalf of publishers and songwriters and achieving a lot. When Kobalt put a deal in place with YouTube to pick up third party revenue directly we were one of the first independents to do that."

Another publisher, the vastly experienced Ian James of Mushroom Music, agrees that the publishing industry is well across the new developments, although it has required some quick thinking.

WELCOME TO THE JUNGLE

[IAN JAMES]: "The interesting thing at the moment as we enter into this digital world is that, in a lot of licensing, there are no established parameters and there are no real signposts. You are making it up as you go along. APRA has a guy whose job is to work out licensing schemes for the new users of music. So he's been in negotiations with Spotify and with Pandora and he was the guy that did the original negotiations with iTunes. You've got to be across this stuff and you have to know what to charge for it. The trouble with precedent is that after you operate in a particular way for a period of time everyone says, "OK, that's the landscape, that's what we can expect to pay". The landscape you start off with quite often becomes the one you are stuck with. It's one of those dilemmas – you want to provide access to new players, but you don't want to set rules that are going to murder you."

Although James believes that the industry has dealt well with extracting payments from the streaming services, he still questions whether artists remain vulnerable to sharp accounting and definitional practices.

[IAN JAMES]: "We are right across it. Because the publishing business can do this collectively behind APRA, we can come to some consensus about what is a better way of doing it on an industry-wide basis. With the record labels, when they start taking equity in the new start-ups, it creates a dilemma.
It means that some of the money that could have been called revenue could be diverted and called something else so that it doesn't flow through to the artist. If everyone actually tells the truth about their numbers and doesn't try to rip everybody off, there will probably be room in the boat for everyone. If there is going to be dodgy behaviour, there probably wont be room for everyone."

James point is that when a label gives permission for its recordings to be used on a service – and gets paid for giving that permission – that money is revenue for the label. In theory that money should be shared with the artists, but given that the money is a payment for access to the label's catalogue, rather than 'sales" of any particular artists recordings it's difficult to attribute that payment to a particular recording or recording artist. It becomes 'consolidated revenue' rather than revenue on which royalties should be paid. This again raises the question of transparency as discussed in Chapter 2.

> **[CHARLES CALDAS]:** "In this environment the transparency issue is important and will continue to be a big point of debate. The biggest impediment to it is around contracts between the artists and the rights holders – are those contracts out of date and do they reflect the way the industry looks now or are they reflecting an industry that doesn't exist any more?"

Copyright and Technology

As was also considered in Chapter 2, one of the big changes in today's industry is that the technology involved in making recordings has evolved markedly and, as a result, is now much cheaper and more accessible to musicians. Consider, for example, the cost of digital storage. It's almost embarrassing to think how much it cost to buy memory capacity only a few short years ago.

Remembering that one of the main reasons record companies came into existence was that the cost of making recordings was beyond the means of most musicians, this changes the balance of power between the musician wanting to reach their audience and the record company wanting to profit by facilitating that connection.

Let's look at it from the record companies' viewpoint. When people buy a copy of a sound recording, they are paying not only for a physical product (e.g. the vinyl album, the cassette or the CD) but also – and

WELCOME TO THE JUNGLE

in fact even more – for the recording contained within it. Thus the record companies have always been concerned with unauthorised reproductions of the recordings they owned, seen by in their initial reactions to file sharing services.

When blank tapes were introduced, allowing people to make copies of their records, the record companies' concerns were expressed in terms of breach of copyright, it was a legal response to a commercial threat. Their investment in making the recordings would be undermined if people were able to get copies of them without paying for them.

When sound recordings were turned into digital files that could be shared quickly and easily over the internet, the record companies were alarmed for exactly the same reason, only this time the means of reproducing sound recordings were instantaneous and literally millions of copies of a digital file could be made very easily. This was "home-taping" on steroids!

This issue continues to centre around copyright. One of the main benefits of owning copyright in something is the power to control, restrict or permit reproduction of the work. In the digital age, not only do people have the ability to reproduce sound recordings, without permission, in an almost undetectable way, but this ability is shared by millions of people at a very low cost. The technology has outpaced the ability of copyright owners to enforce their rights. For a business based around the ownership of copyright and the investment required to create a body of copyright work, the undermining of the protection provided by copyright is a massive blow.

While it would be an obvious statement that copyright law simply needs to be changed to keep pace with changes in technology that is a lot easier said than done. As Allen Bargfrede explains there are many obstacles in the way of that, particularly in the USA.

ANDREW WATT

[ALLEN BARGFREDE]: I don't think that copyright is catching up at all. I think the EU is about ten years ahead of the US – the US is so hamstrung by lobbying interests that the ability to make any updates to copyright is almost impossible. The US Register of Copyrights is really pushing the need to make copyright reform now but the EU – because they are trying to coalesce 27 countries into a single digital market is ahead of the US. The US law was written 40 or 50 years ago and there has only been two major updates to US law dealing with on-line content and the last one happened in 1998. There's a lot of different interest to look at – it's not just the content producers, it's the content distributors. It's a complicated world and every time you try to change something it's probably going to have a negative impact on someone and they are going to fight against it.

Charles Caldas looks at the issue from both the perspective of commercial gain and the need to expose art to a prospective audience.

[CHARLES CALDAS]: The good thing about the way the web is evolving is that you can maintain control of your creations and you can choose to give them away. A healthy copyright system is one that allows the people who actually made something to make the decisions about how and where it is distributed. The thing that we are always talking to people about is that we are not trying to wind the clock back here; we are looking at what the new market looks like and what it might look like in five years time. As a rights holder – an artist or as somebody who is trying to make a living out of being in the creative industries – what do you need to do to be successful? You need to be able to give things away to get people to listen to your music, but you also want to be able to pay the bills and get to the point where you will be able to have a long term or even short-term career doing what you want to do by virtue of what you create.

WELCOME TO THE JUNGLE

> If you make something that you eventually want to make some money out of you need people to see it. With music you have to, at some point, make the decision that you are going to give everything away and make money from playing live, or I'm going to get people to seed fund my recordings by giving them music for free. These days the opportunities are limitless."

Putting to one side the impact "free" distribution of music has on the business of the record companies, it also changes the relationship between the labels and the artists. If one of the main roles of the record company is to invest in the creation of sound recordings and maintain control over their distribution, then a great deal of their relevance is seemingly removed if they are not needed for the purpose of funding recordings and they have lost the ability to control – and get paid for – the distribution of those recordings.

Record companies will still argue that they add something to the value chain in this process, due to their ability to promote, market and distribute recordings to the widest possible audience. It's an argument that is hard to dispute. The question is - does that still entitle them to own copyright in the recordings?

Although the nature of the business is changing greatly, the central element remains the same – it is a business where the musicians are trying to connect to the audience that wants to hear their music. Copyright is the agent that allows them to do this with some certainty that their labours have the potential to be remunerated.

Re-Sale of Digital Files

Consider the differences between an MP3 file and a CD in terms of the owner's ability to sell what they own. If you buy a CD from a store and decide to sell that CD to your friend, there is no legal impediment to that transaction. You own an asset – a piece of plastic – and you sell it. Clearly there has been no reproduction of that asset in that transaction. This relies on a legal doctrine called "first sale doctrine", that suggests those who make the first purchase of a recording are able to re-sell the physical goods without the authority of the copyright owner.

However, if you buy an MP3 file from iTunes and decide to sell it to you friend, the only way you can do that is to sell them the entire device on which that file is stored **or** make a copy of the file. Given that few people want to actually sell their device to their friend, their only choice is to make a copy of the file and transfer that. It's the act of reproduction that creates the copyright infringement.

Yet many people would feel they have every right to on-sell something to their friend if they have legally purchased it. It was only the technology that was stopping them. How was it possible to sell a digital file without re-producing it?

This question may now be closer to being answered. In March 2013 it was reported that Amazon had been granted a patent on technology that allowed it to re-sell 'used' digital files, described as a "secondary market for digital objects".

Amazon first applied for this patent in May 2009. It defines digital objects not only to include e-books, but also "audio, video, computer applications, etc." bought from an original vendor.

The patent states, "When the user no longer desires to retain the right to access the now-used digital content, the user may move the used digital content to another user's personalised data store when permissible and the used digital content is deleted from the originating user's personalised data store."

This is similar to a process offered by a digital start-up called ReDigi, and the subject of yet another lawsuit by the Recording Industry

WELCOME TO THE JUNGLE

Association of America (RIAA). Responding to the Amazon announcement ReDigi issued its own statement; "the Amazon patent is further proof that the secondary market is the future of the digital space and that there is no turning back."

CNet journalist Lance Whitney explains it like this;

> "You'd start off by housing your purchased music, videos, apps, and e-books in your own online storage space, just as many of us do today. When you get tired of listening to the same songs or reading the same books, you can move those items to someone else's storage space. The moved items are then deleted from your own space. Amazon's patent would impose a limit on the number of times a digital item could be transferred to another person. When that threshold is reached, the ability to move that specific item would be suspended or cut off permanently. The seller would receive some type of credit in return for moving the item, while the buyer would be debited a certain amount. Amazon itself would charge a fee for the transaction, which could be collected from the buyer, the seller, or both."

If Amazon's patented technology can allow people to make a sale of a digital file in a way that does not constitute it being a reproduction, but an actual simultaneous transfer and deletion, they may have unlocked a legal second-hand digital music market. The situation exemplifies why copyright law needs to try and keep pace with technological innovation.

Copyright Education

There is an educational element to this discussion also. The recognition of copyright and the right to compensation underlies the establishment of Music Matters in the UK in 2010. The Music Matters campaign revolves around an educational website featuring advice on legitimate ways to buy music. The site provides content including a series of animated short films telling the stories behind artists such as Kate Bush, Nick Cave and The Jam.

When it was launched, the aims of Music Matters were explained by analogy with the gradual changes brought about by anti-drink driving campaigns, where consumers' behavior is gradually changed by education. The Music Matters campaign now has individual websites for the US and ANZ as well as the original UK site. In Australia Music Matters is being project managed by an Australian/ NZ steering committee comprising members from ARIA, AIR, APRA/AMCOS, AMPAL, AAM (Managers), AMRA, labels and music publishers.

Another Australian initiative emerged in 2014. Australian music, TV and movie companies launched an on-line program to encourage content users to seek legal sources of online content.

Funded by ARIA, Foxtel, News Corp Australian and APRA AMCOS, Australian Screen Association, Copyright Agency Ltd and Village Roadshow amongst others, the Digital Content Guide is an online portal to industry-approved, movie, game and sport streaming and download services.

ARIA CEO Dan Rosen commented at the launch of the Digital Content Guide, "Often we haven't communicated to the Australian public as well as we should have....Widespread copyright infringement on the internet is an ongoing problem for the creative industries and we have been told that at times consumers have been confused about what is or isn't a licensed service. The Digital Content Guide can help consumers find the content they want from the many licensed sources available in Australia today. These licensed services support the creative industries

WELCOME TO THE JUNGLE

by ensuring money goes back into those industries and those who invest in them."

Productivity Commission Report

In late 2016 the Australian Government released the Productivity Commission's report into Australia's Intellectual Property Arrangements. The report has been praised for the way it tries to balance the needs of innovators who invest in the creation of new works and expect to be protected in the exploitation of the rights they have invested in, with laws that prevent people from making new inventions and creating new works, because access to existing works becomes fraught with danger of infringement.

The Productivity Commission's view is that copyright law is not balanced, and that our laws are "skewed too far in favour of copyright owners to the detriment of consumers and intermediate users". The most notable and controversial recommendation in the report is that Australia should introduce a "fair use" exception for copyright infringement, which allows people to use copyright material in ways that are "fair", without asking for permission first as has been extremely significant in the US.

APRA/AMCOS, as well as agencies in other content industries have all stated emphatic criticisms of the report. APRA/AMCOS stated, "The report is a blunt attack on Australia's creative industries, unashamedly promoting the interests of those who exploit Australian content over those who create it. APRA/AMCOS is dismayed that the Commission has ignored the submissions and evidence provided by the Australian music community during the consultation process. The factual inaccuracies, disparaging language and alarmist assertions from the draft report not only remain but have been re-stated with renewed fervour and single-mindedness. The rights of Australian songwriters and composers to earn a living have been overlooked by economists in Canberra in favour of the profit making interests of the multi-billion dollar technology and educational sectors".

Brett Cottle further said, "At a time when artists and the wider music industry are finally starting to see a return from streaming services, the Productivity Commission report proposes a raft of changes that will distort the commercial environment in which music licences are negotiated. These changes will allow global technology firms to reduce their bottom line - to the detriment of Australian music creators. The question must be asked, what problem is the Productivity Commission actually trying to solve? Are online services floundering in Australia? Are they finding it difficult to launch in this territory without the protection of an expanded safe harbour scheme? Of course not. Australia is consistently one of the first international markets in which any new digital music service decides to launch. Why? Because Australia already has one of the world's most stable, fair and efficient copyright systems."

This was clearly an emphatic statement by APRA/AMCOS and it is clear that the law relating to intellectual property and copyright in particular is likely to be a very hot issue over the next period of time. No music industry participant can afford to the ignorant of these discussions.

My Path into the Industry

JESS DUCROU

"I was pretty wayward as a youth! From a very young age I was staying at my schoolmates' houses and we'd pretend we were going to the movies and we'd go to nightclubs and take drugs! By the time I was 14 or 15 I'd moved on from the club scene and I'd religiously read the gig guides and I'd collect flyers for shows and paper my bedroom with flyers. I was just so keen on live music. When I was around 14 my mum took me along to the Trade Union Club, and I saw Nico and Died Pretty. It was probably around that mark, as a 14 or 15 year-old that I knew I wanted to work in the music industry in some form, and probably in the live side. I thought I wanted to be a band manager, but I don't think I really understood what that was at that age. I started at Red Eye Records, a retail store, and I worked there for about four years, which I loved and met a lot of people that I've gone on to form business partnerships with.. I went to from Red Eye to *Rolling Stone* and in that transition I started doing an Associate Diploma of Accounting at TAFE. I wasn't doing it because I wanted to be an accountant, but I wanted to know how to run my own business and know how the finances would work. There was a music agency called Music Staff and there was a job advertised as a booker at the Lansdowne Hotel. It was like my dream job. So I begged and pleaded and did everything I could to get the gig. Ultimately my job was to get bums on seats in the venue because the publican wanted to sell beer. I was able to really cut my teeth in that job, and I met a lot of people. I think having that venue perspective has been incredibly valuable for me as a festival promoter."

Chapter 4
The Live Music Industry

While the past 20 years have seen enormous changes in the recorded music business, one constant has been the desire for audiences to connect with musicians in a live environment.

Music is an integral part of people's lives and has been for thousands of years. However the prominence of live music is people's lives is constantly under challenge. Even in the past 100 years, the interest in and demand for music has managed to survive the introduction of film, television and video games, not to mention the evolution of hundreds of sporting, recreational, cultural and social pastimes that do not inherently rely on music for their existence.

Yet it would be folly for the music industry to think it is immune from the impact of leisure alternatives.

Michael Coppel has been one of Australia's leading concert promoters for several decades, after starting his music industry life as a retailer with Melbourne's iconic record store, Gaslight. In 2011 Coppel sold his business, Michael Coppel Presents to international live entertainment giant Live Nation and is now the head of that company for Australia and New Zealand. He's also one of the smartest people in the Australian music business and has views on what live music is really competing with in this day and age.

WELCOME TO THE JUNGLE

[MICHAEL COPPEL]: "We have a much more competitive market. If you go back 15 or 20 years, people's entertainment budgets weren't so committed. Now if you look at a middle-class family they have a Foxtel subscription, they have broadband, they have four or five mobile phones on contract – so there are hundreds of dollars each month that they have spent before buying a concert ticket. We are competing with those committed expenditures and we are very much an impulse buy.

We are competing with the movie industry, which has been extremely successful in marketing itself and it has obliterated the music industry in most of the major media. Ticket pricing has [become] so high through greed and high guarantees, that people who used to think they would go and see eight or 10 shows a year are now seeing two or three shows a year. There was a survey that Live Performance Australia did on ticketing trends in Australia and the one thing that came out of that was that if you wanted to double the size of the entertainment industry, just persuade people to go to shows twice a year rather than once a year. It shouldn't be that hard to do."

However what is also evident in virtually all of those alternative activities is that music can be part of the product mix and actually enhances most of those innovations, whether it be sports, movies or the mobile phone. When Bertis Downs and leading digital thinker Jim Griffin speak of music being the "ubiquity industry" as discussed in Chapter 2, they are referring to music's role everywhere from our shopping experience to our travels and commutes, to our sporting and recreational environments and in every room of our home if we wish. That might help copyright owners with finding revenue streams for recorded music, but it may present more of a threat to the live performance market. Unlike a CD or a DVD, when the concert is over there is no chance of selling any more tickets.

ANDREW WATT

[**MICHAEL COPPEL**]: "You are selling a perishable commodity; once the tour ends, every seat that is unsold remains unsold. It's like the airline industry; once the plane takes off, every empty seat is worth nothing."

Even in this scenario though, live performances of music remains a major industry that isn't going away. It's also worth noting that the Australian live scene is recognised on the world stage. Included in the nominations for the awards promoted by live industry bible Pollstar for 2013 – 2015 are a number of Australian figures, events and venues, including Michael Gudinski, Michael Chugg, Michael Harrison and Michael Coppel (in fact anyone named Michael!) as International Promoter of the Year, Bluesfest as International Festival of the Year, Rod Laver Arena as International Venue of the Year.

There has been a strong suggestion that the live music scene was immune from the challenges faced by the recorded music industry. That's partially true, but the live industry has had its own set of challenges resulting in its own upheavals. The changes have been more evolutionary than revolutionary, but that doesn't mean they haven't been significant. On both local and international levels, the business is virtually unrecognisable now from how it looked 20 years ago.

There's no doubt that the live music scene is the subject of a great deal of study and consideration and it seems in recent years there has been a recognition that it is deserving of close monitoring and attention.

The establishment in 2013 of the National Live Music Office headed by John Wardle was a part of this recognition. The National Live Music Office is funded by APRA/AMCOS and the Australia Council and is responsible for many of the behind-the-scenes pushes for policy overhaul that will benefit live music and live music venues.

WELCOME TO THE JUNGLE

In 2014 Wardle was joined by at the National Live Music Office by festival and tour management veteran Damian Cunningham who will work with the music and government sectors to boost the live music scene. Cunningham, who has worked on the Peats Ridge, Big Day Out, Splendour In The Grass and various community festivals, came on board as the new Director Of Audience & Sector Development.

This initiative is one in a long line of attempts of bring live music on to the agenda.

What follows is a greatly abbreviated review of the evolution of the contemporary live music scene. For readers interested in taking a far more interesting and interpretive look at the local live music scene Clinton Walker's *History Is Made At Night – Live Music in Australia* (Platform Papers, Currency House Inc.) is essential reading. There are also a number of great anecdotal books by the likes of Michael Chugg and Michael Browning that give eye witness (and often hilarious) insights into the live scene.

The Local Scenes

The thriving live scenes in Melbourne and Brisbane weren't always the way they are today. Brisbane, in particular, was previously regarded as a challenging environment for original live music. While Melbourne always had a history of live venues in areas such as the CBD, St Kilda, South Yarra and Richmond, there had also been a strong suburban circuit of pubs in suburbs like Sandringham (the Commodore), Mt Waverley (the Village Green), Frankston (the Pier) Kew (the Prospect Hill) and Preston (the Croxton Park). Several of these venues still operate. It wasn't unusual to find touring bands like INXS or Divinyls playing that string of venues in a five-night Melbourne tour.

In the "80s, Sydney boasted a strong underground scene based around Surry Hills, and some large gigs on the northern beaches, along with

ANDREW WATT

a major venue called Selinas at the Coogee Bay Hotel, just down the road from Bondi.

Brisbane had traditionally been a relatively quiet music city although every now and then bands such as the Saints, the Go-Betweens and later Regurgitator and Powderfinger emerged from the northern capital, and in the two earliest cases became internationally regarded bands – quite possibly more prominent in Europe and to a lesser extent America than they were at home.

The emergence of these bands has been attributed as a response to the relatively oppressive political regime in Queensland through the "70s and "80s. This view was provided by writer, Andrew Stafford in his excellent book *Pig City: From the Saints to Savage Garden*. Stafford, however, argued that the bands in question arose despite the live music scene, and not because of it. A second edition of Stafford's book was published in 2014.

In other cities, the emergence of nightclub culture and late liquor licenses in those venues had a major impact in Melbourne and in Sydney, and later in Melbourne, poker machines became the preferred option for many publicans for attracting crowds. Although there was a lot of so-called "alternative" music being recorded and played on radio, many venues, particularly in the suburbs, were finding covers bands – and that annoying new invention, "tribute" bands – were safer options for attracting crowds. In later years, changes to liquor licensing laws in Victoria led to the emergence of numerous small bars that often had neither the capacity nor inclination to host original live music.

Studies and Activism

In their 2008 paper *The Death and Life of Great Australian Music: planning for live music venues in Australian Cities*, written for Griffith University's

WELCOME TO THE JUNGLE

Urban Research Program, Dr. Matthew Burke and Amy Schmidt considered the Melbourne position.

> "Despite the abundance of small venues, there remain perceptions that the Melbourne live music scene has been under threat from incompatible development. In 2002/03 the *Fair Go for Live Music* campaign was initiated by Vic Music, a not-for-profit organisation that acts as an advocate voice for musicians and others in the music industry in Victoria. The campaign was in response to concerns over the loss of venues within Melbourne, including the need for first-occupancy rights of existing venues, the effect of new residential development and complaints, and the resultant loss of venues or loss of live music operations... Those involved in the campaign said there was exceptional support and interest for the initiative from venue owners, lobbyists and members of the public and this was supported by other informants, though by no means was public support universal, with residents' groups critical of venue operators in key suburbs."

In Sydney, the small pubs of Surry Hills fell by the wayside one by one, becoming victims of urban gentrification. Many of the landmark venues are now high-priced apartment blocks.

In June 2013 the City of Sydney held an event to discuss the state of live music in that city. Hoodoo Gurus leader Dave Faulkner, one of the most engaged artists of recent decades, gave the keynote address. The following excerpts from his speech provide a good summary of some issues – firstly the issue of poker machines.

> **[DAVE FAULKNER]:** "Why has live music been dying in Sydney?
> Firstly, there's no denying the relaxing of laws governing poker machines and other gambling devices in pubs has had a huge

impact on live music across the state. Although actual poker machines weren't introduced until a bit later, beginning in 1984 the Wran Government allowed hotels to install up to five gambling machines, euphemistically called "Approved Amusement Devices" The argument is often put forward that poker machines subsidise other less-profitable parts of a hotel's business, such as the bistro and perhaps even live entertainment, but anyone who has spent much time around serious pokie players will know: they want to be left to indulge their mindless addiction in near-absolute silence. Well, apart from all those annoying jingles, chimes, bells and whistles. Many establishments simply don't have the room to separate entertainment and gambling areas, so often it's the entertainment that has to go.

Faulkner also considered the impact of urban gentrification and the 1980's POPE laws in his articulate way.

[DAVE FAULKNER]: That brings me to another huge problem for live venues: neighbours! Rapid and profound gentrification has resulted in many traditional live venues finding themselves cheek-by-jowl with belligerent, litigation-happy residents – otherwise known as NIMBYs. A thriving, buzzy neighbourhood attracts well-heeled homebuyers who come for all of the excitement and amenities – then immediately take steps to shut them all down. In the late "80s, the NSW government brought in the ridiculous POPE laws – POPE stands for Place Of Public Entertainment. Every pub, club and tavern, no matter how small, would no longer be permitted to put on live entertainment, no matter how limited, unless they first applied to be rezoned as a Place Of Public Entertainment. Neighbours were suddenly able to lodge objections to venues that had been operating without controversy for decades. When – or if – that

WELCOME TO THE JUNGLE

was ever approved, the venues then had to apply to bring their facilities up to the new code, which included providing extra fire exits with disability access, disabled toilet facilities, total soundproofing, power isolation switches – this last item alone cost $80,000 to install – with annual inspections. After all this, there was still no certainty that the licence would continue from one year to the next as a few aggressive neighbours could always get the POPE licence revoked afterwards. Though on the face of it many of these things sound desirable, disabled access and so on, for most of the venues affected, the expense of compliance meant they had to spend hundreds of thousands of dollars with no certainty that they would be allowed to operate afterwards. Many of them just threw up their hands and gave up."

Finally Faulkner was able to provide more recent and better news.

[DAVE FAULKNER]: "It only took 25 years to happen, but I'm glad to say that those POPE laws are now ancient history. Three years ago the NSW Government introduced a simpler and fairer approval system for live entertainment, mainly thanks to the efforts of concerned activist and music-lover John Wardle. John waged a campaign almost single-handedly over many years to get those laws revoked. Not long before that happy event, our crazy, anti-competitive liquor laws also became a thing of the past and there has already been a big upswing in the number of small, funky venues offering niche entertainment around this city as a result.

Of course, these wrong-headed laws have caused incredible damage to our live music scene over a very long time – 30 years in fact – and there are still many challenges ahead. One of the biggest challenges facing us is what we can do about the lack of medium-sized licensed venues, those fabled beer barns of long ago. Many of them have simply vanished, extinct like the dinosaurs, now overgrown by forests of pokies or re-purposed as super-screen sports betting lounges, partitioned off with coffee shops for 'gamers' so that they can get a quick, cheap snack and hurry back to their 'gaming'. Are those showrooms lost to music forever?"

Two of the most famous venues in Sydney were the Annandale and the Hopetoun Hotels. The booker of those venues through much of their glory days was Millie Millgate, one of the most popular people in the Australian music scene – and now the head of Sounds Australia. She suggests that Sydney simply has a more difficult real estate environment for live venues, but this isn't always the decisive factor.

[MILLIE MILLGATE]: "It's all relative, and the Sydney-Melbourne conversation will always go on. There's a different expectation of what a good night is and what a successful night is. When you look at the costs of establishments and renting the properties in Sydney, the costs are so high that what those venues need to bring in through the door every day has a big impact on their capacity to trade. But even with that aside, you've got so much regulation as well. And sometimes it's just unfortunate and you can't put it down to any one thing."

Meanwhile in Brisbane, conditions were changing and by 2007 the emergence of Brisbane as a music power was complete. Dr Matthew Burke and Amy Schmidt had this comment to make in their paper about the reasons for Brisbane's rise.

"**In early** 2007 international music magazine *Billboard* listed Brisbane as one of the international 'hotspots' for music, with a particular focus on the Fortitude Valley area as the breeding ground for successful bands such as Powderfinger, the Saints and the Go-Betweens. Yet historically Brisbane has been criticised as unsupportive of live music and having a 'dearth' of

WELCOME TO THE JUNGLE

live performance spaces. A set of threatened venue closures and the furore over the complaints closing down live music at the Press Club in Fortitude Valley in 1999 led to the *Save the Music Campaign* being initiated by industry representatives, venues, lobbyists and some patrons to successfully pressure local and state government to intervene. That intervention took the form of the *Valley Music Harmony Plan* (2004) which significantly altered planning and liquor laws within a designated 'Entertainment Precinct'. This place-based approach was distinct and unique in the Australian experience. The Entertainment Precinct is legislated and enforced through Brisbane City Council's Planning Scheme – *City Plan 2000* and respective Local Plans and the *Brisbane City Council Amplified Music Venues Local Law 2006* (Brisbane City Council 2006) as legislated by the *Local Government Act 1993* s956G. It has changed the balance of power in dealing with noise problems in clear favour of the venue operators"

While the authors of this paper question whether one dominant entertainment precinct is a sustainable solution for a city the size of Brisbane (when compared to Melbourne, where several entertainment hubs exist), there can be little doubt that Brisbane's "Valley" scene has had a very positive impact on the music emerging from there.

Melbourne's live scene has made a strong recovery though, firstly in Brunswick and more recently in suburbs such as Northcote and Thornbury. Another interesting development has been the re-purposing of suburban RSLs as live venues. The Oakleigh, Elsternwick and StKilda RSLs now also serve as the Caravan Music Club, the Flying Saucer Club and Memo Music Hall respectively, targeting slightly older audiences who remember the earlier eras of music south of the Yarra River. While there are ongoing discussions about many issues in Melbourne's venues, it does seem that the city's live music culture has always been very resilient.

ANDREW WATT

Victoria also seems to be the state most able to activate grass-roots support for live music. Faced with the closure of the much-loved live venue, the Tote, due to the costs of regulatory compliance, in 2010 the Melbourne music community was drawn to action. SLAM (Save Live Australia's Music) was born.

SLAM is a collective of non-politically aligned, independent, music-loving citizens. To date SLAM has had no funding and is run by volunteers, although in 2013 it ran a Pledge Music campaign to generate sustainability funding.

In early 2010, the SLAM Rally drew about 20,000 people to protest against Victorian Liquor Licensing policies that unfairly linked live music to high-risk activity such as alcohol-fuelled violence.

The Live Music Accord was signed on the eve of the rally and SLAM spent a further seven months negotiating the Live Music Agreement, where it was officially announced that *live music does not cause violence*. A new Law was introduced in Victoria in December 2011, where Live Music was recognised in the Objects of the Liquor Licensing Act.

Since then, SLAM has lobbied and contributed to the Premier's Round Table for Live Music in Victoria, with outcomes including more laws changed to cut red tape, reformed planning policy and licensing laws – including calling for a review of EPA measures – building codes, all-ages gigs, a code of conduct for venues when dealing with musicians and educating government on issues facing musicians and the sector.

Now SLAM is an Australia-wide organisation undertaking initiatives in most states. It's worth noting, too, that while many issues considered by SLAM relate to licensed venues, their support for live music extends to any place that music can be played.

WELCOME TO THE JUNGLE

After furious lobbying on December 12, 2013, Victoria's then Minister For Planning Matthew Guy told parliament the then state Liberal Government will ensure the agent-of-change principle is implemented into negotiations with venues to protect them from noise and planning issues. The Agent of Change principle was gazetted as part of new regulations in September 2014 that were intended to "...address key challenges faced by the industry such as noise management, building standards, over-regulation and compliance which threaten the viability and growth of live music venues and the industry as a whole."

Of course the issues relating to live music remain on-going and by the time these words are read there will be a further series of issues being fought and won between live music advocates and government. Probably the best advice for industry participants is to recognize that vigilance is constantly required.

The stakes are high though. A survey conducted by NMIT in 2012 found there are around 120 clubs, bars and hotels offering live music in Melbourne's CBD as well as 17 larger theatres and concert venues. Every Friday and Saturday night around 97,000 people attend popular music performances in the city, generating an average turnover of around $5.4 million per weekend in ticket sales, door entry, food, drink and merchandising.

As it stands, it is probably fair to say that the live scenes in Melbourne and Brisbane are still relatively strong while Sydney remains somewhat disappointing for a city of its size and international standing. The controversial and broadly despised 'Lock-Out' laws in Sydney have clearly not helped music venues or Sydney nightlife generally. As of January 2017, Sydney's lockout will be pushed forward to 2am, while the last drinks curfew will be pushed forward to 3:30am for "live entertainment venues" only — which seems to be defined as "venues that offer genuine live entertainment, live performances or art and cultural events" — inside the lockout zone of Sydney's CBD and Kings Cross. There's plenty left to play out in this issue.

International Significance of the Local Live Scene

In her current role as head of Sounds Australia, Millie Millgate also realises that a strong domestic live scene is essential if the aim of Sounds Australia – to develop export markets for Australian music – is to be fulfilled.

> **[MILLIE MILLGATE]:** "We can create these opportunities and get as many eyeballs [as possible] on the Australian artists and really make sure their time in the overseas markets benefits them – but if we don't have the amount of acts coming through, what we are doing overseas is going to have no impact. In order to set Australia up as an exporting nation, which is our goal, we need a strong and healthy and robust base of that pyramid. The infrastructure in Australia needs to be strong.

Live Music Under Review

In several states, 2013 was a significant year for the live music industry. In New South Wales and South Australia, comprehensive reports were presented to each state government on ways to both nurture and develop their live music industries.

In December 2012 the City of Sydney established the Live Music and Performance Taskforce, with a brief to advise Sydney City Council on how to best support its live music industry:

In late 2013 the taskforce handed down their report, an impressive 70-plus-page document, titled *Live Music Matters: Live Music and Performance Action Plan*.

WELCOME TO THE JUNGLE

The report made 57 recommendations designed to provide more live music and performance in Sydney in four areas: Development Controls and Noise, Building Code of Australia, Liquor Licensing and Audience and Sector Development. The key recommendations of the Plan included reviewing the Sydney Development Control Plan 2012 to recognise and reinforce existing areas of live music and performance activity, as well as supporting the growth of new centres in appropriate locations – again seeing the impediments to live music as being within a regulatory framework.

Other recommendations included the creation of a mediation plan to resolve noise complaints, providing information and temporary and permanent venue creation, holding further talks (in the form of a symposium) relating to live music sustainability, undertaking research into noise issues and local government interactions and looking into the relationships between international and local live acts – all worthwhile objectives.

The Live Music and Performance Taskforce had an interesting make-up. Alongside long-time live music activists such as John Wardle were several academics who have participated in similar activities in the past, along with representatives of the APRA/AMCOS, the Australian Hotels Association and community radio. Notable by their absence were anyone who actually works at the coalface of the contemporary music industry – no agents, managers, labels, promoters or music venues. However, despite this, the Task Force appears to have identified some significant regulatory issues and offered some worthy approaches to dealing with those issues. Their report is certainly worthwhile reading.

Similarly in South Australia a report entitled *The Future of Live Music In South Australia* was delivered by Martin Elbourne, the quaintly titled "thinker in residence". Elbourne founded the Womad festival

ANDREW WATT

in Britain with Peter Gabriel and has had a long involvement in the Glastonbury Festival. He is also creative director and co-founder of the Great Escape in Brighton (Europe's leading music showcase), co-founder of M for Montreal (one of the main Canadian showcase festivals) and co-founder and promoter of NH7 festivals held in Pune, Delhi, Bangalore and Kolkata (the leading contemporary music festivals in India).

This report provided 49 recommendations in a range of areas that were not dissimilar to those considered by the NSW taskforce, including audience development, trade and economic development, and regulation. A key recommendation was the establishment of the South Australian Contemporary Music Advisory Council by the state government, which would report directly to the Premier and have the specific aim of increasing the size and value of the state's music industry.

Elbourne's report is an outstanding piece of work. Due to his extensive experience at the industry coalface, he brings a very practical context to his work. In particular his insights and recommendations regarding music education are vital and forward thinking. This paper should be essential reading for anyone participating in the music business, not just in South Australia.

In Victoria, the City of Melbourne appointed a group called the Music Advisory Committee to assist in the development of a Music Strategy for 2014-17. The result was a document with a number of suggested initiatives under six themes. In 2015 and 2016 that Committee hosted the Melbourne Music Symposium attended by local and international academics and industry people.

Late in 2014 the University Of Tasmania called for responses to a survey it conducted in order to understand the intrinsic value of live music. The project, titled *Cultural And Economic Contributions Of Live Music*

WELCOME TO THE JUNGLE

Making In Australia, and was designed to compile data through which policy makers and regulators will be able to make better-informed decisions when it comes to Australia's live-music landscape, sought to construct the most comprehensive picture they could of Australian live music consumption. The study was a joint initiative of primary backers the Live Music Office in conjunction with the City Of Sydney, the City Of Melbourne and the South Australian state government, as well as personnel from the University of Technology, Sydney, and RMIT.

The survey results were published in 2015 as a 41 page report and are important reading for anyone involved in live music operations and policy-making.

Changing Times For Live Music

All of the changes to the live music scenes have been gradual and marginal, but what's important to note is that the scene is in a constant state of evolution. For many key players, it's a case of balancing the tried and true methods of generating live music business and embracing new opportunities.

Frank Stivala of Premier Artists is a doyen of Australian artist agents. He's been in the business over 30 years and has clients who have been with him for most of their and his career – household names like Ross Wilson, Joe Camilleri, Daryl Braithwaite, James Reyne and Mark Seymour. The Australian live music scene would look a lot different if it weren't for Stivala.

> [FRANK STIVALA]: "When I started, it was the pioneering days of agents and we invented a lot of the situations we have now, like the door deal and pub rock. After doing the job for the first 12 months, I figured there was a career to be had in

the music business. Up until then my folks had been saying, "Go and get a real job". After that things evolved and bands got bigger and the whole pub rock thing exploded and there was serious money in the music business. I wasn't motivated by cash, but it helped. I had a passion to be involved in the music business and I was a frustrated musician – so that led me into being a behind-the-scenes man."

Richard Moffat has been the most prominent live music booker in Melbourne, and perhaps Australia. His activities have cut across festivals such as Falls, Groovin' The Moo and the St Kilda Festival, as well as his previous history booking the Corner Hotel, the Northcote Social Club, the Workers Club and Sydney's Newtown Social Club. He's very optimistic about the state of the live scene, in Melbourne particularly.

[RICHARD MOFFAT]: "Things are changing really quickly and all for the best as far as I'm concerned. It's an amazing time for music. New bands can get really big really quickly, so that whole 'pay your dues forever and a day' thing has gone. I really like that. There used to be a problem that there would be a whole lot of bands that I liked, but it would be really hard to support them. These days if a band is organised and has good songs and if they get their social networking set up early, they can be selling out rooms within three months. It's happening so much with so many different bands. The actual gatekeeper people are totally out of the way now – the radio programmers and labels and people that used to manufacture bands getting big are completely irrelevant now."

The Agency Landscape

Through the '80s and '90s, the Australian band-booking agency landscape was dominated by two related agencies, Melbourne's Premier

WELCOME TO THE JUNGLE

Artists, and Sydney's Harbour Agency. The common link between them was an ownership stake held by Michael Gudinski. Every few years a new agency would emerge and try and challenge that two-state power base, but the challengers rarely lasted. This changed though in the past decade with new agencies finally getting a foothold. Now there are more agents and more artists on agents' rosters than ever before and businesses like Select, Village Sounds, New World Artists, 123 Agency (a now thriving agency formed in 2013 by former Premier agent Damian Costin), Wildfire Agency (formed in 2013 by Mark Lackey – ex Village Sounds) and others are succeeding, while Harbour and Premier continue to hold a big slice of the pie.

> **[FRANK STIVALA]:** "A lot of younger people came up through the ranks and figured there [was] a career in the music business and a career in being an agent. As the industry grew and the whole business expanded, it left a lot more room for new people to come into the picture and there are always people looking for change. We are very loyal to our roster and they are very loyal to us and we have a strong adult contemporary top-end of the roster with people we have been involved with for 30 years. We were pretty busy keeping the legends as legends – the easy thing is to make someone famous, the hard thing is to keep them famous! With us working hard on those artists, it did leave room for other people to get involved in the business."

One of the most significant of those relatively new players is Artist Voice, a company formed around 2010 by Matt Gudinski (son of Michael) and former Harbour agent Brett Murrihy. This move has been extremely successful with Artist Voice being absorbed in 2015 into the global William Morris Agency. Murrihy has become WME's Head of Asia Pacific for Music, reporting to WME Music Head Marc Geiger.

ANDREW WATT

"We have admired what Brett has built at Artist Voice, and are incredibly excited to welcome him and his team to WME | IMG," said Marc Geiger at the time of the acquisition. "We share the same passion for our artists and entrepreneurial approach to business that made this partnership a natural fit. This addition will help us continue to elevate the level of service we are committed to providing our clients around the world."

The increasing number of agents has been beneficial to managers, who now have a lot of choice about where they place their artist's live booking business.

> **[BILL CULLEN]:** "When I set up this business it was actually a conscious thing to not have all the artists with the same agent. Having lived and worked in England for five years I realised that there was no reason why you should be with the same agent all the time. You pick the right agent for the right act. It has changed. Agents have become more important. Back 10 years ago, the agent's job was to go out to the promoters and get as much money as they could. Now it's flipped around. It's not about pulling as much money out of an individual promoter as you can, it's about being strategic, picking the right venues and you need an agent who does a lot more than telephone sales. There's a lot more strategy involved now. We talk all the time and we have a shared vision about what we want."

Live Venues

Despite a number of well-documented issues facing live venues the live scene remains strong.

As recently as 15 years ago it would have been inconceivable to have a live venue operating seven nights a week with viable shows. In the

WELCOME TO THE JUNGLE

past couple of years, it is almost impossible to find a night where the Corner Hotel or the Northcote Social Club is empty.

For Tim Northeast, a partner in these venues, it's been a combination of well-operated venues and a buoyant market for good live, original music.

> **[TIM NORTHEAST]:** "It's something that we have worked hard to achieve and it's taken a long time. Secondly, the live music scene is particularly strong at the moment. That's a reflection of the fact that as album sales fall, bands have to tour. I think the festival market has stretched the touring calendar across the full calendar year, whereas it used to be more cyclical. It used to be very much that all the bands toured in summer and autumn, whereas winter was very quiet. There's a certain section of the market that doesn't like festivals and prefers to see the band in a more intimate space. That's where it's worked very well for our venues, so we can get those sideshows and cater for that market."

Brian Lizotte, who has operated three Lizotte's restaurants in NSW, offering dinner-and-show options, has a less positive view of the impact of festivals. While he provides the kind of intimate venues that Tim Northeast talks about, Lizotte believes the festivals often suck the available talent out of the market.

> **[BRIAN LIZOTTE]:** "I think the festival industry and perception of the cultural festival in the mind of the general public is still alive and well and the amount of festivals has had a huge impact on us. The festivals are lucrative for the acts and so we miss out on many occasions [on artists] that would have normally played our room, but who now do the festival circuit. People are getting their fix of that style of music in that environment, especially for the younger generations. It's a constant

struggle to get some of these acts into our rooms so we can have some success as well. Some of them start off in our rooms and then the festival circuit will lift them to the next great height and the managers and agents know that. Sometimes we have to take the crumbs on occasions, which I'm not happy about, but I understand why it happens. But my biggest hurdle is that I can't get the acts when I want them."

For Pixie Weyand the dynamic young owner of Brisbane's iconic live venue The Zoo, (and the 2016 Telstra Young Business Woman of the Year for Queensland), the challenge is more about understanding what a live venue can offer.

[PIXIE WEYAND]: "We cant compete with the corporate backed venues in terms of paying guarantees so I have to think outside the box a little bit and try and be innovative. For me it's about the experience. I want to create an experience for the bands and have them walk away from The Zoo thinking it was so much fun to be here."

The Touring Market

If you look through the international touring listings in the street press in any city at any given time, you're likely to see more than 100 contemporary music acts listed. It wasn't always this way.

Australia has always had some of the best and most resilient concert promoters in the world. Michael Gudinski (Frontier Touring Company), Michael Coppel (Michael Coppel Presents), Paul Dainty (DCE Group) and Michael Chugg (Chugg Entertainment) are among global leaders in their field. But even with the standards being set by these promoters, it was uncommon to see them with more than two or three shows on sale at any one time.

WELCOME TO THE JUNGLE

Several factors conspired to make Australia one of the world's most active touring markets. As it has with so many other businesses, the rise of the internet has made it possible to build international audiences online, so that there are now many acts with audiences keen to see them in Australia, sometimes without having a particularly visible profile.

Emily York, whose company Penny Drop tours many smaller, more niche international artists, is able to do so without the support of traditional media.

> **[EMILY YORK]:** "We definitely don't operate in that world. We don't rely on commercial play in order to get something going. Having so many different avenues to get music out there has changed a lot. I might discover an act, but there was a time when if I didn't have even Triple J airplay, I might not be able to make something work. The experience I've had is that, if the act is good, I can make it work – on varying levels – with or without the support of some of those traditional outlets that I would have needed a few years ago."

It may be a good thing that promoters are less reliant on mainstream media to help build awareness of a tour – because as Michael Coppel observes, there is greater competition for that traditional media space. He has some strong thoughts on how the music business has dropped the ball in this area.

> **[MICHAEL COPPEL]:** "If you look at any major newspaper, the coverage that music gets compared with the coverage that film gets, it's about 1 to 10. That's because the studios have made sure that their headliners are available and accessible for journalists to do pieces on and they provide good material that can be used to create strong stories. By contrast you have

to pull teeth to get most musicians to do interviews to promote themselves. You wouldn't expect Bob Dylan to speak to any journalist that wanted to talk to him, but in the pop market where the artist clearly needs to get as much exposure as possible, I've had artists that I've had to beg for months to get one phone interview. The material, the artwork, the photos, the videos that they give you are often second rate and cheaply done. You look at that and realise that we, as an industry, don't promote ourselves well."

Australian Currency v US Dollar

Another important factor in recent years has been the strength of the Australian dollar. Most international acts traditionally get paid in US dollars; this allows them to budget their tours accurately and not be exposed to movements in the currencies of the countries they tour in. Having established their fees in $US the act's agents are happy to shift the currency risk to the local promoters. With the Australian dollar constantly rising in the past decade (though at the time of writing it is significantly below parity with the $US at around 0.72 cents) it has meant that often our promoters have actually ended up paying less for the artist than they had originally budgeted, making tours more successful. The cost of buying $US shows has almost halved in terms of Australian dollars in the past decade. Obviously international agents are aware of this advantage and inevitably will adjust their prices accordingly, but it's clear our promoters are not behind the eight ball from the beginning as they once were, although the last two years has seen a reversal of that advantage.

Leading Australian music writer (and label owner and sometime promoter) Stuart Coupe published an excellent book in 2003 called *The Promoters*. It's a thoroughly entertaining ride through the rollicking adventures of Gudinski, Chugg and co. In that book Coupe makes the

WELCOME TO THE JUNGLE

following observation about currency issues. "Another major factor that has hurt Australian promoters over recent years is the weakness of the local dollar compared to the American dollar and the English pound. Overseas artists, not unreasonably, expect to be paid in the currency of the country they live in – that's the currency they pay their fellow musicians, personal bills and booking agent and management commissions in. Why would they possibly come to a country and accept being paid in Australian dollars? They can earn real money in the northern hemisphere and it's not as far to travel. Australian promoters have had to get used to artists who say it's simply not worth their while to come to Australia – and if they do, the promoter is paying the majority of his expenses in American dollars or English pounds – but only selling tickets for Australian dollars. Doesn't make it easy."

How times have changed. In 2003 there was a positive outlook posted that suggested that with a bit of luck the Australian dollar may break through the $US.70 barrier. At the time it was hovering in the mid-.60s. It's little wonder there have been so many more international tours in the late 2010's with the Australian dollar at parity with the US dollar. The challenge will be for our market to remain this buoyant should there be a downward shift in the Australian dollar and possibly return to the 2013 levels.

New Promoters

The combination of the (now relatively) strong Australian currency, alternative means of promoting and building an audience for non-mainstream artists and increasing expertise in the art of touring international artists now means that concert promotion is no longer the exclusive province of a select group. Gudinski, Chugg, Dainty and Coppel (the latter now under the banner of Live Nation) are still prominent and other experienced players such as Andrew McManus and Gary Van Egmond still regularly tour artists – but they have now been joined by a host of other promoters while Peter Noble's Bluesfest and Bluesfest Touring appear to grow bigger and more remarkable every year.

Meanwhile Jess Ducrou and Paul Pittico's Secret Sounds – responsible for both major festivals and stand alone tours announced a joint venture with Singapore-based Now/Live. The JV, dubbed Secret Sounds Asia will see tours making their way through Asian territories on the way to and from Australia.

Late in 2016 it was announced that Secret Sounds had joined with Live Nation with the global company taking a majority shareholding in the Australian business, encompassing Splendour in the Grass and the Falls Festivals. The deal also involves Secret Sounds' touring, sponsorship, PR, artist management and domestic agency businesses. The acquisition was international news in December 2016, with Live Nation president and CEO Michael Rapino stating, "Splendour in the Grass and Falls are the two most iconic festivals in Australia. Jess [Ducrou] and Paul [Piticco] have created events that attract the biggest artists in the world but still feel uniquely Australian. We look forward to partnering with them to find new ways to grow our live event footprint across Australia."

All the Australian promoters are solid players and all seem to have found either a significant niche or built sustainable business models and relationships with agents, managers and artists that allow them to create a strong backbone for their companies. But Chugg explains that the credibility and equilibrium of the industry can easily be upset by promoters who don't have the experience or knowledge of the market entering the game, and aim for too much, too soon.

WELCOME TO THE JUNGLE

[MICHAEL CHUGG]: "There's too many promoters in Australia, far too many, and the bigger problem is when idiots get into the business who don't know anything. There was one concert/festival that lost about $20 million. They paid international acts three to five times what they are worth. That impacts on everything. The punters lose confidence and international agents think they can get as much money as they want in this market. They don't give a fuck about the punters or the ticket prices or the other promoters. The punters know the difference between idiots and legitimate promoters – they pick the vibe up. But it doesn't help when the media actually prints bullshit that they are fed by these people."

Michael Coppel doesn't deny the right of new promoters to enter the market; he just wishes they would bring a dose of realism to their ambitions.

[MICHAEL COPPEL]: "If you walk in the door waving a cheque for 2 or 3 million dollars that some idiot has given you the ability to write, some agents will just take the money and run and think that Australia is far enough away that nobody will find out where the bodies are buried. Look at Stone Fest (a two-day festival held at Sydney's Homebush Stadium in 2013 that only ever ran once). There is no way the agents for the acts that headlined would have accepted those offers from a major promoter. But if some newbie walks in and offers $5 million for an act to headline a 68,000-capacity show, the agent will think they just won the lottery. So long as the client is prepared for the potential embarrassment of playing to 10,000 people in that huge space, the agent will take the money and run."

Not every new promoter will draw the ire of the establishment. There is a whole set of promoters doing successful and well-promoted tours who didn't exist a decade ago who are welcomed by the industry.

ANDREW WATT

In many ways smaller promoters who are forced to work within restricted budgets and as such learn the value of a promotion dollar, are better for the future of the business than new inexperienced players entering at the high end of the market.

The newer players are coming from some interesting segments of the industry.

Merchandising company Love Police started a touring operation with a small tour by swamp artist Tony Joe White, which has now expanded into a series of regular tours for artists like Gomez and key Americana acts. Love Police is now the Australian tour promoter of choice for the Black Keys and in 2014 launched the Out On The Weekend festival as a vehicle for Americana style acts, along with the Boogie festival at Easter.

Several music distributors have entered the fray and taken on the role of tour promoters, forming separate divisions to do so. Shock started Ragged Company Touring, while Inertia have a successful division called Handsome Tours, which has been responsible for tours from artists such as the War on Drugs, Grizzly Bear, the XX, Metric, the Mountains Goats, Lou Barlow, Foster the People, Explosions In the Sky and Bon Iver, as well as the Fairgrounds Festival.

> **[COLIN DANIELS]:** "That's Inertia being a service company. It came about because there were artists that wanted to come to Australia and we wanted them to come to Australia and no other promoter wanted to tour them. It came about out of necessity."

On a smaller scale, Melbourne-based indie label Mistletone began releasing cool music and then almost by necessity started touring some of the artists they released. Their touring division is now very well established with dozens of tours completed from the likes of Kurt

WELCOME TO THE JUNGLE

Vile, Sharon Van Etten, Beach House and Ariel Pink amongst many others.

David Williams was managing director of Shock at the time they got into the touring business. He has opened a new touring business where he partners in some tours with Metropolis Touring, another relatively new promoter.

> **[DAVID WILLIAMS]:** "Shock initially got into touring in a small way as a result of a particular artist that we were promoting for CD sales. We wanted to get the artist into the market to perform because we felt that if people would see this artist they would fall in love and buy the album. The touring companies were looking for a contribution and we realised that if we were to tour that artist, the worst that could happen is that we could lose the amount of money that the touring companies were asking us for as a contribution. We realised that we may as well do the tour ourselves. We did start to develop the live touring side of the business. Shock started to move away from that and as I moved away from Shock I moved into the touring side."

There are many others specialising in particular genres and eras of music. Blue Murder specialise in punk and hardcore, often working with Destroy All Lines. Metropolis Touring focuses on alternative genre artists like Peter Murphy, Stan Ridgway, They Might Be Giants, Kitty Daisy and Lewis, Epica, and Bob Mould and have previously toured acts as diverse as Ace Frehley, Barry Adamson, Motorhead, Pendulum, the English Beat, Gary Numan, Ice Cube and Imogen Heap – all artists that have identifiable audiences that are accessible from outside mainstream traditional media. Tim Pittman's Feel Presents goes for quality artists such as Henry Rollins, Dirty Three, the Sonics, Redd Kross and Urge Overkill, all of whom appeal to fans of past generations of music. Feel also combined with iconic Australian band Hoodoo Gurus to curate the Dig It Up! Invitational, a concert series that bought together a host of relatively obscure international bands as a tribute to garage rock. And the powerful Unified Group operates the fast emerging heavy music festival Unify – Heavy Music Gathering.

None of these promoters were active in the 1990s, but there seems to be room for all of them now. All of these promoters appear to have made it over the hump that separates sustainable businesses from entry-level gamblers, but as Stuart Coupe again points out in his book, it can be a treacherous road at the beginning; "A promoter operating on these levels can have a series of good tours and make a couple of hundred thousand dollars, begin to think it's an easy business – and then be financially destroyed with just a couple of tours that fail badly…This level of promoters simply can't compete with the established promoters, so spend their time looking around for artists that they hope no one else has thought of touring, but have a cult audience in Australia. And ideally they are artists who want to come to Australia for reasons other than money. These tours often happen because the artist really wants to come to Australia and can't imagine they'll have the opportunity otherwise, so they are prepared to make big compromises in the fees they request … These are promoters living on the very margins of the business, both financially and in terms of the artists they work with. Frequently they are just learning about deals and structuring tours, so they are at their most vulnerable – as are the artists they tour, as the chances of one of these promoters not having the resources to pay their bills at the end of a tour is extremely high".

> **[MICHAEL CHUGG]:** "A lot of people you see come along, see the business and think they would like to be in it. They get involved and they go out of business just as quickly as they got into it in most cases. One of the areas that's been really bad has been the hip-hop area, where there have been a lot of people get involved thinking they can get it happening and then the acts end up not coming and people end up not getting paid,

and the kids lose confidence in that whole scene. That's not good for anyone."

There may be a negative side to the apparent ease with which artists now tour Australia.

[LUKE O'SULLIVAN]: "I think the demise of the record companies has had an impact on the venue scene because artists have to tour more because that is their livelihood. Previously they might not have toured as much, so that has helped the live scene. But with the amount of festivals that are on now, we found that there is more supply of acts coming into Australia than ever before, but they are also coming out more regularly. And because they are coming out more regularly it diluted tickets sales a bit. Some bands came out three times in 18 months. It used to be that people would go and see a band because it was a special event and they might not see them for another five years, but people might think twice about seeing a band, because they are getting a bit spoilt."

For venues like the Hi-Fi/Max Watts and the Corner, the risk falls largely on the promoters. Obviously the venues want shows booked into their rooms that sell more tickets rather than less, because a full venue normally leads to higher bar sales and greater box-office commissions. For these venues, it's not so much about how much the booker likes the artist, it's about how well their room will work for the promoter.

[RICHARD MOFFAT]: "There's a bit more maths to it now than there used to be. All the statistics are online. You can see a band's level of Facebook likes and You Tube plays or whatever and that's a mathematical thing. We know when a band is going to sell out, and we know that because we spent five minutes on the internet looking at their statistics. When My Space first came in there were little bands that had massive numbers of My Space friends who never pulled a crowd, so clearly there was a way to manipulate the figures but for Facebook and You Tube it seems relatively reliable. So these days it sometimes feels like it's more about maths than art or science or anything curatorial. It's not like I've always booked the best bands – and I would love it if we could always do that – but we book bands that we think other people want to see. A band being good is not really the impetus for us to book what we book."

Targeted Events

It's not just at a pub and venue level where the influx of international tours has had an impact. Twenty years ago no one had thought of staging concerts in wineries. Now, the A Day On the Green concert series provides a reliable and thoroughly enjoyable alternative for audiences who perhaps have tired of seeing music late at night in sticky-carpeted venues, but who are still active and well-funded music fans. Heritage acts such as Rod Stewart, Elton John and the Eagles had always been huge concert draws in stadiums and arenas but A Day On the Green showed that older artists, one level below those superstar acts, could be successful draws if promoted as part of an "experience" beyond that of a mere concert.

Michael Newton, who with his wife Anthea formed Roundhouse Entertainment to stage the A Day On the Green concerts, looks back on his decision with a great deal of pride.

[MICHAEL NEWTON]: We were promoting a club at the same time, which gave us some sort of security, which was fortunate. But

WELCOME TO THE JUNGLE

it was a really big call. We sold our house to have enough money to pay our way, which was crazy and looking back on it, I don't know how we did it. It was a lot of outgoing calls! Us calling wineries, us calling media, us calling bands, us calling potential sponsors, just trying to sell the concept. It probably took three or four years of travelling, finding the wineries and setting up the circuit, getting media partners, some of whom we still work with today."

Festival Boom...and Bust?

It's almost hard to believe that the Big Day Out started in 1992. Bluesfest began as an outdoor event, the Byron Bay Music Festival, around 25 years ago. For a long time it felt like these two events were the only two contemporary music festivals on the landscape. This wasn't true of course – genre-specific festivals had existed prior to this, but it took the Big Day Out in particular to establish Australia's festival culture. The idea of a travelling event taking in at least five and up to seven cities was something that had never been attempted so after its first year as a Sydney-only event in 1992, from 1993 it was established as a major national event on the musical calendar.

Few would have predicted the boom that was to follow. Newcomers to the industry won't recall the momentary challenger to Big Day Out, 1995's Alternative Nation touring festival that failed as a result of terrible weather and some curious booking decisions, while others like V2 and Summersault also came and went, despite having strong vision behind them.

Michael Coppel has an interesting perspective on the festivals that didn't survive. He has participated in several and believes that sometimes promoters are too quick to give up on a festival project, or are simply unwilling to sustain the early losses that will eventually turn around once a strong festival brand has been established.

ANDREW WATT

[MICHAEL COPPEL]: "Frontier and I co-promoted Alternative Nation in the '90s. It didn't work. It ran for one year and had fairly massive losses and we gave it away, but in retrospect with the growth of the festival market, we should have persisted. We should have made a three to five-year investment and I think it could have turned into something that would have been as competitive as any other festival in the marketplace. When I worked with Richie McNeil the first time, we did a thing called Apollo 99, a dance festival at the Melbourne Docklands, with a number of acts that became very prominent subsequently. Again it didn't work and lost money and so we lost the appetite to do it again. Often life is too short to keep working what seems to be a pointless avenue. We had the Narara Festival in the "80s. The first one was very successful and the second one was a debacle, despite having what now would be a bill that would fill a 100,000 capacity. We gave it away; we lost the site. Because we were concert promoters, we were too busy on the day-to-day stuff to stick with it."

Even with the premature demise of some festivals, there has been a remarkable success rate for a market this size, and those entering the music business now won't know a world that didn't include Bluesfest, Splendour in the Grass, Laneway or Falls. There are also numerous smaller events dotted across the landscape that have stood the test of time – Meredith and Golden Plains continue to flourish. None of these events have been around forever, although it can be difficult to remember a time they weren't.

While these events have provided a rite of passage for a couple of generations of festival goers, they've also been the breeding ground for numerous new industry participants who were bitten by the live music bug while attending one or more of these events.

WELCOME TO THE JUNGLE

For several years now doomsayers have been flagging the notion that Australia has too many festivals for the size of the market and that there will inevitably be a rationalisation of the market with some events falling by the way. In 2013 that began to happen with Harvest and Pyramid Rock cancelling, and Homebake also going on hiatus after trying to change its format.

Of course the biggest upheaval has been the demise of Big Day Out – the former heavyweight of the festival scene sliding into the sunset, with a revival highly unlikely.

In late 2015 there was another major casualty with AJ Maddah's Soundwave and it's associated Soundwave Touring collapsing in a torrent of acrimony and bad press coverage.

Festivals have another benefit. Established promoters use festival appearances as launching pads to break new artists in Australia, then bring those acts back for their own headlining tours later on.

> **[MICHAEL CHUGG]:** "A lot of people understand that they can go to festivals and they can see their favourite acts and they can also discover acts they've never heard of. That's one of the things about Bluesfest, and Laneway is similar. Every year Danny Rogers puts on acts that no one has ever heard of and they will blow up just before they get here or they will blow up during the festival. That's exciting. That fits into our plan and direction because we tour more young acts than anybody else because we believe that's how you build your business."

For artists and managers though, the festival boom can be a double-edged sword. It's easy to become too reliant on the festival circuit and lose sight of the need to build an independent fanbase beyond that market.

ANDREW WATT

[MICHAEL GUDINSKI]: "Festivals are great gatherings, but they are really social events. It's great for new acts to get in front of people on small stages and spread the word. Acts need to know when they are in a position to move on from that and do their own shows. A lot of acts get themselves well overexposed by doing too many festivals. In England when the festival season is on, you'll have seven festivals with the same five headliners."

Electronic Dance Music Festivals

The other twist in the touring market has been the emergence of EDM (electronic dance music) as one of the huge growth areas in live music in the past decade, and somewhat belatedly some of the world's biggest music promoters such as Live Nation and SFX are infiltrating that scene in a major way internationally.

In recent years the EDM scene was dominated by three promoters – Future Entertainment, Totem One Love and Fuzzy – though many micro-businesses have flourished in the scene. Big developments occurred in 2013 though, with SFX buying Totem One Love, while Future was effectively taken over by Michael Gudinski's Mushroom Group and later shut down. Fuzzy continues to operate strongly with a string of events such as Parklife, Field Day, Shore Thing and Harbourlife, and in 2013 added the travelling event Listen Out.

In 2014 the Mushroom Group took an equity interest of the Sugar Mountain festival in Melbourne that blends an eclectic musical line-up with fringe and experimental art exponents.

Frank Cotela and Dror Erez are two of the partners of Totem One Love, and were the promoters behind the Stereosonic and Creamfields events.

WELCOME TO THE JUNGLE

[DROR EREZ]: "Dance music changed the day people started dancing in front of each other and all turned around and faced the stage as if it were a rock band. That only happened in the [past] 10 years, at least in clubs."

[FRANK COTELA]: "I laugh at some of the traditional music industry people who talk about the arrival of [EDM]. It's been big business in Australia and England for the [past] 25 years. We've been selling records, we've had clubs that were full, there have been festivals. The big change that I noticed was in 1988 and 1989 when the English scene came to Australia. That was the definitive change in dance music in this country."

Of the established promoters Michael Coppel was the first to recognise the emerging importance of EDM, and promoted tours from artists related to the scene like Portishead, Massive Attack and Faithless. He even partnered with Richie McNeil, who later became a director of Totem One Love, in a dance festival as far back as the late '90s. Both Coppel and McNeil know the EDM scene requires special knowledge.

[MICHAEL COPPEL]: "I don't think any of the established promoters do EDM successfully, except episodically, and it's become a huge market. Things like Stereosonic and Future Music Festival have been what a group of younger promoters have picked up on and made themselves successful. They understand the music and the audience and they know the artists and they can compete with anyone because they have that feel for the field they are working in."

[RICHIE MCNEIL]: "There's always been a spirit and a vibe with EDM that has been anti-establishment to an extent, and anti-brands. It's more prevalent in the underground dance scene than say punk or metal. When you actually meet them and you have a trance guy and a techno kid and someone who is into house music, at the end of the day, even though they are all into different kinds of music there is still a common spirit where everyone is thinking in a similar way."

Millie Millgate, from Sounds Australia, is another from a pub background who has observed the growth of the EDM market and its successful industry players.

[MILLIE MILLGATE]: "I went along to an Electronic Dance Music conference and I was fascinated by how much of an eco-system there is there, and how many people are involved and operating and they are people I haven't come across in almost 20 years in the industry. They are out there bringing in money and running sustainable businesses and the dance world has really led the way when it comes to just getting up and doing it."

International Waves

The past decade has seen enormous changes in the international landscape and the repercussions are being felt in Australia.

The biggest upheaval came in 2005 with the birth of Live Nation, an American concert powerhouse formed as a division of Clear Channel Communications, the country's largest radio station operator. In 2010 Live Nation merged with US ticketing provider Ticketmaster to form Live Nation Entertainment.

Live Nation states that it annually promotes over 22,000 events, including music concerts, with total attendance exceeding 50 million people.

WELCOME TO THE JUNGLE

Within months of its formation Live Nation owned or operated 117 venues, consisting of 75 US and 42 international venues, including 39 ampitheatres, 58 theatres, 14 clubs, four arenas and two festival sites. In addition, Live Nation had contractual booking rights at a further 33 venues. In 2006 Live Nation acquired the House of Blues chain, comprising 13 venues across America.

An early Live Nation strategy involved signing major artists such as Madonna and U2 to deals that embraced their entire careers; not just live performances, but recording and merchandise. A similar deal with Jay Z followed.

Internationally, Live Nation made acquisitions in the concert promotions business in numerous European and South American countries and a number of venues and festivals in the UK, including Glastonbury, Reading and Leeds and Latitude Festival.

There continues to be big movement around the Live Nation business. In February, 2011 Irving Azoff, the world's most prominent artist manager, sold his Front Line Management business to Live Nation for $US 116.2 million, in the process becoming the executive chairman of Live Nation.

In December 31, 2012 Azoff resigned from that role, and has since founded a new company with Madison Square Garden Co. that includes rights management, live music and sports management elements. Front Line remains a Live Nation business as part of its Artist Nation unit, employing 90 managers representing about 250 artists, according to regulatory filings. In the nine months ended September 30, 2012 Artist Nation had revenue of $298.6 million, or about 6.8% of Live Nation's $4.38 billion in revenue. The changes continued into 2013 when Live Nation effectively bought out the management companies behind both U2 and Madonna.

ANDREW WATT

The impact of Live Nation has been felt in Australia. They opened an office here in April 2010, and in April 2012, announced they had bought the Australian touring company Michael Coppel Presents for an undisclosed amount, with Coppel heading the new Australian operation. At the time Michael Rapino, president and chief executive officer of Live Nation said, "We have worked with Michael Coppel on a number of tours over the years and are now extremely pleased to be welcoming such a well respected and successful promoter into our international network. Australia is the sixth-largest music market in the world and an increasingly important touring market for international artists. It represents a significant part of our opportunity for international growth."

Coppel himself expects the interest in our market by international players is likely to continue.

> **[MICHAEL COPPEL]:** "I think it is increasingly internationalised. I think the business has gone from a series of smaller and mid-sized regional promoters in all markets to an internationalized business where you have Live Nation, AEG, Virgin Touring and C3 all eyeing this market. Australia ranks in the top five or seven touring markets in the world. America is pretty much spoken for and so Australia, S.E Asia, India and Japan are the emerging markets and the last frontiers. It's not surprising that the international operators are looking at Australia increasingly and it becomes a clustering effect. Once Live Nation move in, then AEG have to move in, and then C3 have to move in. It's the sort of thing you see on the high street, when one retailer opens up, then all its competitors are opening up, up and down the street."

The internationalisation of our touring market didn't stop with Live Nation. In early 2012, another major announcement came when Big

WELCOME TO THE JUNGLE

Day Out and American concert promotion giant C3 Presents (the company behind two of the US's top music festivals: Austin City Limits and Lollapalooza) revealed that they would collaborate in the continued growth and expansion of the Big Day Out Festival with C3 Presents purchasing half the Big Day Out business. With the demise of Big Day Out only time will tell whether C3 Presents, a Texas-based company headed by Charlie Walker, Charles Attal and Charlie Jones will have any continuing involvement in the Australian market.

My Path Into The Industry

ANDY KELLY

"Like a lot of managers, I started out playing music. I played in high school bands. I had older brothers with really good record collections and they had guitars and I thought that was a really cool thing. We started forming bands when I was 14 in high school. I was fascinated with all the stuff that happened behind the scenes. I was fascinated with the idea of backstage and what happened in a dressing room and what being on tour was like. I'd see the occasional footage of a band on tour and it seemed like the greatest life – to play every night and to stay in a hotel! It seemed to be like this incredible alternative way of living, in the same way that some people ditched everything and went surfing in those early days.

Now is actually very much part of the establishment, like most other industries, but back then it seemed so mysterious. It's still mysterious, but at that time it was harder to find out how it all worked. I never thought about it as a career path and I never, for a second, thought I would end up working in it. When I got a job in a record store it was a dream. In the "90s I became more interested in why things didn't work. I had friends in bands and we would help each other out and two of those friends ended up as my business partners. But there was no real plan that that would happen.

I was friends with Andy Cassell from high school. We used to go and see bands together and talk about music and then we became friends with Pete, our other partner, who played in a band. He was doing a law degree, so he had that background, which was really good. We weren't really looking for certain things in each other – it just sort of happened."

Chapter 5

The Relationship Between the Live and the Recorded Music Businesses

It's easy to assume that the two main parts of the music business – live and recorded – are two halves of a whole. In reality it is more complex than that.

While there are clear connections between the live music business and the recorded music business, there are also deep distinctions. It often seems the two sides of the industry attract different personalities.

People such as Mushroom Group founder Michael Gudinski are rare – having substantial and vital interests in both the recording and live performance side of the business. By comparison Michael Coppel never found himself charmed by the idea of having a record label, despite his initial foray into the business as a record store owner. Powderfinger manager Paul Piticco operates record labels and is heavily involved in festivals and concert promotion heavyweight Michael Chugg, has had great success with Chugg Music artists Sheppard.

In the reverse, it wasn't until very recently (which shall be explained later) that record companies, major or independent, began to delve into the live side of the music business.

There remain some very powerful people whose interests stay on one or the other side of the industry.

WELCOME TO THE JUNGLE

[JESSICA DUCROU]: I've always wanted to work in live music and to a degree I always have. It's not like I started off working in labels and moved across to the other side of the fence. And I do think there is a little bit of a fence, between the two areas – the recording industry and the live industry. Maybe it's the mathematician in me, but I like the instant result of planning a show and watching how people purchase tickets and seeing what the result ends up being. I just have a very strange fascination with that process. There's nothing vague about it. You put a show on, you set a ticket price and do the best you can to present it and people are going to come or not. I haven't moved over to the recording side because it hasn't interested me. I think the divide has become greater because the way people buy music has changed and there is a lot more focus on the live side of the industry and maybe I was lucky that I started on the right side of it."

Of course, Ducrou doesn't turn a blind eye to what's happening with bands' releases and what media and radio coverage they might be getting. It's obviously one of the factors she considers in determining the viability of a tour, the size of venues a band might be able to fill and even how a tour might be routed.

There may be signs for the future though that some emerging players could be tightening the link between live and record music. Misteltone Enterprises is an independent label and touring company, established in 2006 by husband & wife team, Ash & Sophie Miles. The touring side came first and it was almost by accident, or necessity, that a label element evolved. Now both sides of their business are prolific and marked by very good taste.

[SOPHIE MILES]: "It was kind of by design; we were touring Ariel Pink (our first ever tour) and we realised he did not have a label in Australia. A good friend of ours was working for a distributor and encouraged us to start a label, so we took him up on the offer so that Ariel could have his amazing album House Arrest released in Australia, in time for the tour. Once we started a label, incredible music kept coming our way. We've never had to seek it out."

In the EDM market Future Classic operates a highly successful label, featuring the likes of Flume and Chet Faker, but the company is also involved in events and touring as founder Nathan McLay explains.

[NATHAN McLAY]: "I am fascinated by most areas of the business so it has been fun getting our hands dirty with all of these areas. We enjoy working with others. Laneway Festival, The Museum of Contemporary Art, Sydney Festival, Vivid, etc are all relationships that have been very rewarding. We learn a lot from working with others and have been very lucky to have some great partners over the years."

On the distribution side, the importance of record sales is seen as a less definitive measure of a band's popularity than it once was.

[COLIN DANIELS]: "The biggest change to me is that record sales are no longer the biggest indicator of an artist's popularity. In the past it was the single indicator of how popular an artist was and now it's not. You have situations where we might have sold 3000 records and I'm seeing 12,000 people buy concert tickets for that artist."

For Michael Coppel, the use of record sales is now only one indicator of the potential for a tour, even at the level of acts that Live Nation tours.

[MICHAEL COPPEL]: "It's still a factor, although it's not so much about records sold and the downloads are important.

WELCOME TO THE JUNGLE

They might not have sold a lot of albums, but if there are a million downloads of four or five singles then you are damn sure there is a market there for that artist. We still talk to the record companies, not just to see what they have achieved in terms of album sales and downloads, but you also see what their promotional plan is – if they have an investment in that artist's career, if they plan to bring them out to do a TV show, or if they have given up on a release. The rationalisation of staff levels at all major labels means that you have a very short window with any new release and if it doesn't work they move on to the next one. They just don't have the time to stick around and work albums six, eight or 10 months into the lifespan of its release. That's always an inquiry you make and you also look at the online information; the Facebook likes, the Twitter followers, the level of activity you can discern. You look at what the media says, although that's sometimes a product of what the labels do to get coverage for new releases and it's not necessarily reflected in public interest. It all feeds in and if you are [of] a generation that is actively interested in music, then what you hear in clubs and socially would influence it as well."

Michael Chugg agrees that the level of support from record companies has changed over the years.

[MICHAEL CHUGG]: "Years ago the record companies would do combined marketing deals and they would put money in, but that's not happening any more. We still get supported at a PR level, and with record releases. But our business is very much stand-alone these days."

Tim Janes is one of the most well-liked music company people in Australia. In a career that has spanned several record labels he has seen the landscape change dramatically.

ANDREW WATT

> **[TIM JANES]:** "Agents and managers don't rely on the labels any more and they don't put their hands out as much as they used to. On the first Black Keys album, we gave the promoter 10 grand tour support to help get them out here. That would just never happen now! You couldn't give tour support when you are licensing a band for one territory. That seems a lifetime ago."

Promoters such as Penny Drop's Emily York have lower expectations of record company support for tours. She's come into the business in an era where she did not rely on that marketing support, let alone financial contributions to her costs.

> **[EMILY YORK]:** "You have to understand it from the label's perspective. I imagine it's hard to justify if they are not seeing any album sales off the back of it. Maybe they got to a point where they thought, 'Hey this just isn't working, the reward we are getting for the time we put into this just doesn't add up'. I definitely don't feel any sourness towards labels dropping the ball, but I know that I will do whatever I need to do, by any means necessary, to get the artist to connect here. If that means supplementing the work of a label then that's just what we have to do."

The Real Relationship Between Recorded and Live Music

There has always been an imbalance where record companies would invest recording and marketing funds in an artist, resulting in that artist gaining a significant profile and being able to tour successfully, and yet sometimes the label fails to recover that money from sales of recordings.

Equally though, the artist felt like touring was their only refuge and means to make a living, when faced with a large unrecouped recording

WELCOME TO THE JUNGLE

and marketing advances that meant they were unlikely to ever see any money from recording royalties. It's easy to see why, for some artists, the label that starts off as their new best friends quickly becomes perceived as the enemy when they realise that they are unlikely to ever receive a royalty cheque. Conversely, their agent, who seems to be their only source of immediate income, becomes their preferred and happier relationship.

This often lead to an antagonistic relationship between the artist and the label, with the artist manager caught in the middle; and they too would have a conflict of interest, because their commission on the live work was sometimes the only thing keeping the doors of their management business open – especially if they had agreed not to take commission on recording advances, which was the norm. The manager would want, or need, the artist to play live, whereas the record company would want the artist working towards their next recording, in the hope of seeing some return on their investment. There are obviously conflicting financial agendas.

It's not always that way though – a good label will recognise that all the members of the artists team can work towards a common goal. There are many label people totally committed to the broader career of their artists; former major label head, Mark Poston, was one of them.

> **[MARK POSTON]:** "There is nothing more pleasing about our job than working with Australian artists. We want to break Australian artists and we want them to have success and we want them to have careers and make money. There is nothing wrong with artists making money out of their art. Where the music industry got it wrong was that we were so slow to react to piracy and it's really heartbreaking that only a small number of Australian acts get to break through and live the dream. They do it because they have no other choice. They have the music

bug and they were born to make music and be artists and they have to follow that."

Nevertheless there was a period where major labels realised that they needed to tap other revenue streams, beyond sales of recorded music, if they were to remain capable of investing heavily in artist's careers.

The 360 Deal

The result was what became known as the 360 Deal. Under these contracts that began to gain some currency in the 2000's, the record company would receive a percentage of the artist's income from touring, merchandise and any other income stream in return for their investment in the artist's recording career. They – sometimes quite rightly – felt that the investment in the recording and the marketing dollars put behind promoting that recording were the catalyst for other income, even though the recording itself may not recoup those costs.

The arguments for and against these types of deals were very simple. The record companies argued that the changing nature of the industry meant they deserved to recoup their investment from any income that investment generated, and the companies started characterising themselves as "entertainment" or "music" companies rather than "record" companies.

The artists took the view that it wasn't their fault that the bottom had fallen out of the record companies' business model of selling recorded music, and there was no reason why they should have to compromise their other income streams to pay for the record companies' problem. Further, the artists pointed out that record companies, with a diminishing workforce, were actually offering less service, so the labels should actually receive less, rather than the greater cut they were seeking! They also argued that the labels didn't have any expertise

WELCOME TO THE JUNGLE

in touring or merchandising, so should not be entitled to earnings in that area. In response, many record labels made some none-too-convincing attempts to create touring and merchandising divisions.

Ultimately, the situation came down to what it always does – the balance of power between each artist and the label. An artist who didn't need the label's support to make their records and tour would be less willing to accept those demands, whereas a less self-sufficient artist would be prepared to sacrifice more to get that support.

> **[DENIS HANDLIN]:** "The business of a record label has diversified and the relationship between the record label and artist is more of a business partnership. The common goal is to create a successful long-term artist career. The broader rights deals have come about through this development as much as the changing market place. Major record labels have significant expertise across marketing, digital, promotional, finance, legal and media management to value-add in a significant way to the artist's career. Through this partnership, the artist can concentrate on creative and performance aspects when all these business aspects are properly provided in this way."

The jury is out on whether the 360 Deal was a success. Manager and label boss Michael Parisi, who sees things from both sides believes the model was flawed.

> **[MICHAEL PARISI]:** "I think the labels failed dramatically because they didn't have the infrastructure to support the 360 Model. Had they been serious about it and really built a management structure or a merchandising arm within their companies, it might have worked. As a manager, I don't mind the idea of giving away a cut of the artist's income streams, but the labels have to earn it. I understand that they can't sustain their

model on music sales alone and I'm happy to help them earn revenue, but they have to give me something back. And that never really happened. Now with a lot of the deals overseas, the majors have stopped offering 360 services. Now it's just straight recording. They will sign you for recording and are happy to discuss the ancillary stuff down the track. It's gone the full circle again."

Adam Jankie, CEO of the Illusive Group of Companies, believes that independents are well placed to operate in this 360 manner due to their inherent ability to find new revenue streams.

[ADAM JANKIE]: "It's because the traditional business model of a record company no longer applies to the modern music industry. The income derived directly from music itself has decreased, but it's also starting to pale into insignificance against the other revenue streams. Therefore those companies that have a single business model where all they are trying to do is sign rights for music, and then exploit that music, are having a hard time deriving enough income. Modern music companies have to change their business model to apply it to the current market place, and in order to do that they have to start generating revenue through other areas, whether that is doing cross deals or taking on specific roles internally or creating companies to do it. The knowledge of someone who understands the recording side of the business can also be applied to any other area, because the skills that that person may have in publicity and marketing and on-line strategy now also applies to touring, merchandising and everything else."

It is an interesting analysis to make. One of the world's greatest record companies is Beggars Group headed by Martin Mills, a revered and hugely influential figure. Beggars Group consists of five labels – XL,

WELCOME TO THE JUNGLE

Rough Trade, 4AD, Matador and Young Turks. Mills took an interesting approach to the 360 concept a few years ago – effectively setting out to prove they weren't suited to it! Beggars executive Ruth Barlow explains.

> **[RUTH BARLOW]:** "Martin always knew it wasn't for us but I think he wanted to demonstrate that. We got involved with promoters. We experimented with festivals, we got involved with merchandising and it all failed. It failed because we knew that our expertise was finding great artists, having great A&R and putting out great records. I was sent out there to fail! But it has evolved over the past few years and now the recorded music community and product managers and labels work so much closer with the live music community. So part of my job is still to be an ambassador for that."

These days the line between "live" and "recorded" is being blurred. Whereas once when an artist used to play live it would hopefully encourage audiences to go and buy their album, now a live recording viewed on You Tube was more likely to be seen as an alternative to listening to that same artist's recorded music streamed on Spotify. Effectively the streamed live performance was music consumption that cannibalises the type of consumption that a record company actually gets paid for.

> **[RUTH BARLOW]:** "A couple of years ago we noticed that a lot of festivals were wanting to record our artists. Not just Glastonbury and Coachella but a lot of other festivals as well. I think it was triggered somewhat by You Tube saying to festival promoters that they should set up their own channels and become content providers. We started to get a lot more requests through for permissions and we were being told it was part of the performance fee – the artist has got to be recorded

and live streamed. And we got to thinking – "Well, that's not right." - because the artists were our exclusive recording artists and what the festivals wanted was a recording license. After a lot of thought we decided that we would embrace that but be smart about it. We were being told "Hey, its great promotion", but this was a time when streaming was really starting to become the way people consumed music and so we asked what exactly was it promotion for? If the consumer was listening to a live concert on You Tube that consumer wasn't then going to go "Now I'm going to listen to their album". There are only 24 hours in a day. So now my job is caretaking that area, setting some boundaries, educating people that if streaming is the future of our business, we want our business to be protected in that environment."

The "360 Empire"

The Australian industry has become notable for the emergence of business structures that unite recording, publishing, agency, live events and touring and other businesses such as merchandising and marketing under one umbrella.

The multi-business model isn't unique to Australia; in fact, the idea of having multiple business units that form part of a larger group is quite common internationally. When *Billboard* magazine names its Power 100 for the Music Business, one of the top spots inevitably goes to manager Coran Capshaw, whose empire included the huge Red Light Management Group (which employs around 60 managers, servicing over 200 artist clients), promotions company Starr Hill Presents and record labels ATO Records and TBD Records, branding and sponsorship businesses (Greenlight and New Era) along with many property investments in theatres and venues and an equity stake in festivals such as Lollapolooza, Austin City Limits and Bonnaroo. Capshaw

WELCOME TO THE JUNGLE

came from a background that exposed him to the marketing savvy of the Grateful Dead. He's an intriguing character who doesn't often speak publicly about his business, but he told *Billboard* that "our artists benefit from our collective overall experience and knowledge in the marketplace, in every area."

Roc Nation is another international example of this approach. A joint venture between Jay Z, Jay Brown and Live Nation, Roc Nation is a multi-faceted business offering a range of services to artists. However, in an interview with *Billboard*, Jay Brown didn't want to call Roc Nation a "360."

"I just want to say that our company can provide services from every stream," he said. "From the merch side to the touring side, publishing, producer management, artist management or a label – basically every venture that an artist is a part of or not a part of, we can offer that. We can be in business with an artist and not manage, but we can publish. We don't have to have everything."

The Mushroom Group was an early Australian example of this approach. The model has now been restructured to be probably more powerful than it ever was, incorporating Mushroom-branded businesses (publishing, events, film and sponsorship, creative & marketing), the Illusive companies, agency operations Premier and Harbour Agencies, interests in merchandising (Love Police ATM), A Day On The Green (Roundhouse), several labels including I Oh You, Ivy League, Liberation, Liberator and Wunderkind and, of course, the powerful touring company Frontier.

> **[MICHAEL GUDINSKI]**: "A lot of people have looked at what I have done and modelled themselves on Mushroom. We were ahead of our time; we had the 360 deal, but we had the companies to support it. We were never greedy enough or smart enough, depending on how you look at it, to try and cross-recoup."

ANDREW WATT

Manager Gregg Donovan (who now has interests in recording and publishing) can see why artist management enterprises are well placed to expand into multi-service businesses.

> **[GREGG DONOVAN]:** "We are starting to see a centralisation of the business. There are not many industries in the world that split up their income streams like we do. It's quite a unique business. To have record companies, publishing companies, management companies, agencies etc. is quite strange. It does make sense to centralise. Managers are in a great position to deal with that centralisation because they are the ones who have been in the best position to see how all those income streams work – as [Eleven Management's] John Watson would say, we are in the centre of all the spokes in the wheel. We see how all those things connect."

A great example of this is former Powderfinger manager Paul Piticco who has collected a series of enterprises alongside his management business including record labels Create/Control, Nook Nook and Dew Process (which has released albums by Sarah Blasko, the Living End, the Panics and Mumford & Sons). He and Jess Ducrou launched a touring company Secret Sounds, which owns Splendour in the Grass and Falls Festivals (now in partnership with Live Nation). It's a model not dissimilar in approach to that of Coran Capshaw.

> **[PAUL PITICCO]:** "I realised very early on that so many areas of the music business are reliant on the success of another facet of the music business. For example, tickets don't sell if records are poorly promoted. Radio/media need tours and festivals to promote and align [themselves] with and in turn the events need the media support for awareness to sell tickets …. and so on. I guess I most liked the idea of when I really loved a band of being able to bring something to them they needed and wanted and in turn I could then have a relationship with them

WELCOME TO THE JUNGLE

of some kind. Ultimately it's about being adaptable and always being able to have something to offer. Here's a rarely-shared home truth. I started the Dew Process label and Splendour at virtually the same time and I really didn't expect to get both off the ground …I thought surely I will completely screw one of these ideas up…. I was hedging my bets basically with my first ventures outside of management … but I got lucky!"

In Melbourne, Jaddan Comerford and Ben Turnbull turned the Staple Group into a multi-faceted business powerhouse, including the UNFD brand (recording, management, publishing and merchandise), event and tour promoter Destroy All Lines, agency Archery Club, street teaming business Small World, indie community Purple Sneakers, clothing label Mistake, mobile app developer Zapp and creative agency One Meaning Communicated Differently. Businesses were added organically as new opportunities became apparent. They subsequently split the businesses and both continue to be successful with their respective enterprises.

[JADDAN COMERFORD]: "Initially it was more just organic growth, just plugging gaps that we saw there. From where we were sitting we didn't see that those services were being offered, at least to our sector of the industry. We took the approach that if no one else was doing it, we may as well do it ourselves.

The thing that tied them together was management. We started managing acts that were in the clubs, but also on the label, and that's what created the first major growth and the creation of multiple entities. The way we did it has been very hands-on and even with artists that have just signed to our label or just signed to our management or publishing, we were very hands-on and we were very involved in many ways."

What is important these models and business groupings is that the artist isn't forced to use all the services on offer within the group. Unlike a major label trying to leverage artists into a so-called 360 deal, the idea of a interrelated group of companies means that each company stands alone and the services it provides must stack up against another service provider in that area.

> **[JADDAN COMERFORD]**: "We are an a la carte business. As soon as we become a shotgun-to-the-head business we won't be what we set out to achieve. Our accountants and business advisors might argue with us on those points from time to time, but I just believe that if you abuse the trust that you have with your clients, then you are not going to have much left."

Adam Jankie explains the approach in a similar way.

> **[ADAM JANKIE]**: "Some acts we represent as a label and do their merchandise, but we are not their booking agent and we are not their manager. Others we do their bookings and their merchandise but we are not their label. There are a lot of artists that we do not have directly signed on our roster, but we represent them in some other way. We thought the smart thing to do would be to vertically integrate rather than outsourcing things. That's when we started to expand and start doing those things. It became a natural progression to start business after business and start feeding them all into each other and in the process signing more and more acts to the various businesses to keep them sustainable."

My Path Into the Industry

BRETT MURRIHY

"I came from a different background. I wasn't an ex-musician or a manager or anything of that ilk. I'd completed a sports psychology degree in Brisbane and moved to Sydney when I was 21. Music had become an obsession. I'd see live gigs all the time and I was always buying records. Even though I'd finished my degree, I knew I wanted a career in music.

I fortuitously answered an ad in Drum Media for the Harbour Agency. To even attain an interview, Tony Grace made me yell "show me the money!" down the phone at the top of my lungs! To be honest, I had very little understanding of how any agency operated. At that time agents were the pariahs of the music industry. Touring representation was not the main focus for the artists and the record labels controlled the power and the money. A&R was the key job at the label. The Harbour Agency gave me great training, from my start in the mailroom to my time as senior agent. They taught me from the ground up. I realised, however, the role of the agent needed to become more professional and modernised in this territory and for me to attempt this, l needed to start my own agency at Artist Voice."

CHAPTER 6

NEW MODELS AND CHANGING TIMES

In the ever-changing environment of the music business, there is always going to be a new angle, opportunity or business model to emerge that challenges the balance between the players. In many ways, the music business is the perfect industry to be the breeding ground for this. While there are real motivations for some incumbent players to maintain the status quo – examples of this abound in the worlds of record companies, music retail, venue operation and festival promotion – there are equally motivations for outsiders to gain access to the carefully guarded ground.

Artists want to play and record and have their music heard by an audience. If there are gatekeepers denying them these opportunities, then it is likely they will try any angle to get around those gatekeepers. There is no government quota restricting the number of musicians making music and you don't need a qualification or license to get involved! Opportunities to service the needs of artists will inevitably bring about new business models being developed and tested.

When smart people see things being done in a way that could be challenged or improved, change will usually follow.

Changes in the Landscape

The music industries are fertile ground for fresh thinkers. They may be the likes of technology entrepreneurs such as Daniel Ek (Spotify)

WELCOME TO THE JUNGLE

or Tim Westergren (Pandora), or innovative artist managers such as Coran Capshaw, Scooter Braun (Justin Bieber) or Troy Carter (former manager of Lady GaGa), or executives pushing the envelope at companies like iTunes, Live Nation, Clear Channel or even companies such as Coca-Cola or Red Bull.

Perhaps the best statement of the new pressures coming to bear is the slogan for Troy Carter's management company Atom Factory – "Discover. Develop. Disrupt". His company's self-description via their website is revealing:

"Atom Factory is a multi-dimensional entertainment and artist management company based in Los Angeles, CA. Founder and CEO Troy Carter has been a pioneer in the music industry, seamlessly bridging entertainment and technology. Constantly employing innovative methods to create authentic experiences for fans, Atom Factory has caused a paradigm shift in the entertainment industry. Atom Factory is uniquely positioned to meet the needs of its clients due to its partnerships with A\IDEA, a creative think-tank and branding agency, and AF Square, an angel fund and technology consultancy. Led by executive teams with far-reaching and diverse professional experience, Atom Factory provides unparalleled service to their diverse roster of clients."

Carter's description of his enterprise is a very different way of looking at the music business. Carter, Scooter Braun and Madonna's manager Guy Oseary are all very active in technology investment, both in music-related fields and broader social media applications. In May 2013, the *Billboard* profile of Oseary stated:

> **"The music** business that Oseary came of age in from the late '80s to the early 2000s could rely on album sales and touring as principal revenue streams. No more. Being a manager in the age of disruption means staying abreast of every ripple and

current in not just pop music, but social media, technology and even consumer products. Promotional opportunities and brand partners are constantly surfacing. Some demand attention and evaluation; others need to be sought out and understood before they cannibalise your business.

In part, that puts managers such as Oseary, Carter and Braun at the forefront of emerging technologies, able to spot investment opportunities as early – if not earlier – than seasoned venture capitalists. This trio invested early in Turntable.fm, SoundCloud and Spotify. Together, they're helping redefine not just the profile of a music manager in 2013, but also how Hollywood's gradual merger with Silicon Valley (or 'Silicon Beach', as some have dubbed it) unfolds."

That is a revealing statement and one that could equally apply to participants in the Australian music industry. It's big business at the exciting and disruptive end of town, yet the essence of the approach of people like Carter and co. remains about developing and exposing artists through whatever means are available. It's not surprising that Carter now has another role - "Global Head of Creator Services," at Spotify which means he will work with musicians, songwriters and labels on behalf of the streaming company.

The Australian Experience

While operators like those just mentioned have the benefit of working in the epicentre of the entertainment and media universe, there is no reason why Australian entrepreneurs can't emulate their thinking towards the new music business. The CEO of ARIA, Dan Rosen, believes this generation is privy to a time of great opportunity.

[**DAN ROSEN**]: "I think it's an optimistic time for the business. It had been a very difficult decade with the transition

WELCOME TO THE JUNGLE

to digital, and the music industry was the first industry to be really transformed by the internet because a music file is only a small amount of data and you can trade that on a narrowband connection, whereas now we are moving to broadband movies and TV and retail and everybody is being severely affected by it. The music industry went through it first and it didn't have the opportunity to look at another industry to see what was going to happen, so it was a difficult time. I think we were the first industry to start working out the first business models and we've worked quite innovatively to present music fans with legal ways to get music so they can make money start flowing through to the industry. I think it's a very exciting time; it's probably never been a better time to be a music fan because you can get music anywhere, anytime and on any device."

Adam Jankie exemplifies the sense of opportunity pervading the Australian business. He instinctively understands the new era drivers that power the business.

[ADAM JANKIE]: "Things are moving at such a fast pace now that it's all about innovation, and coming up with creative ways to expose content – music, pictures, imagery, anything that's associated with the artist. It's about exploitation of content, not just exploitation of music directly anymore. It's all about, 'what's the next thing?'."

Jankie uses an observation of the changes within the famous Mushroom building in Albert Park, Melbourne, to explain the recent evolution of the local music business, in all its different forms.

[ADAM JANKIE]: "This building paints a picture of the broader industry as well. When Matt Gudinski and I started out there wasn't anyone within 15 years of our age. There [weren't] 30-year olds working here then. In the [past] 10 years everything has changed. This building has got more people under the age of 35 than it has people over the age of 35. It's an interesting sign. The older people are still in very high executive roles, but all the marketing and promotion areas have been taken over by a new generation of people, because the age of technology is changing things quicker than anyone can catch on to. There is new shit popping up every day, new revenue streams, new ways to exploit music and content. We have to keep up to date with what's going on in terms of technology and exploitation, but the other core part of the business is finding the actual artists, both on a label side and the touring side; finding what's popular and what's next."

For Nathan McLoy, of Future Classic, being of the digital generation is a huge benefit.

[NATHAN McLAY]: "I grew up with digital. My first serious music job was setting up the digital department for Inertia and it was really exciting being part of one of the growth areas of the business. Digital music and social media has made the business more egalitarian that has been an exciting development and continues to bring a lot of new opportunities."

Despite the huge number of new ways to monetise people's passion for music, the business still doesn't exist without music. Leading manager Andy Kelly exemplifies why some people find themselves on the business side of the industry. It's really no different to what drives Troy Carter's diversified business.

[ANDY KELLY]: "We were driven by thinking … our friends' bands were good and we couldn't work out why they weren't getting shows or why no one would put their records out. Why

WELCOME TO THE JUNGLE

people like things that you might be involved with is completely intangible, to be honest. You don't know why people like things. You know what music you like, but you don't know whether other people are going to like it, so all you can do is build this thing and have a plan and stay on top of it as much as possible."

For Vanessa Picken, one of the leaders in the area of digital marketing of music, the changes in the industry are clearly technology-driven, but even from that perspective she sees that the music itself remains the key driver.

[VANESSA PICKEN]: "Definitely. It's just identifying where the opportunities are. The way in which we consume music, the way in which we research, the way in which we gather information and even the way in which we write content is all coming to us in multiple forms. The way in which social networking allows people to communicate in real-time has opened up opportunities even further. I think it has broken down a lot of the barriers that we would have seen traditionally in how you would have marketed or found music. It's just so much more accessible and that's an exciting time for everyone and the doors of that potential are just starting to open. Every single component of music and the industry itself is becoming stronger for that fact. People talked about the death of the music industry because no one was buying music, but in actual fact it just became more fragmented. Traditionally it would have been just the sales coming through from physical retail and being on tour, but now there are so many more channels to market in which you can monetise if you want to, or you can give it away for free to get a fan. It's all about making your own opportunities and cutting through the clutter and that's why marketing is really important. And at the end of the day, if you want to sell music you still have to have really good music."

ANDREW WATT

Clearly there are opportunities there for creative thinkers and those who are not satisfied with the status quo, and that can only be a good thing. However there's a cautionary note to this theme. Anyone thinking that the "new music business" is some wild frontier where there are no rules is kidding themselves. Part 1 of this book has deliberately sketched out a history of the business, as well as highlighting several of the most recent pivotal moments. The smart operators know there is much to be learned from the past. Many of the structures that have always governed the business remain in place today.

Artist manager Joel Connolly illustrates this point.

> **[JOEL CONNOLLY]**: "It is simplifying it to say there is an entirely new way and that there are no more rules. That's not true, because there are rules and you still abide by some of those rules. We try and do different things, but you do need to have a really good understanding of how things work and what does work. A lot of those things do come from the '90s and the '80s. But now there is less guarantee that those ways are going to work. You have to figure out that there are risks involved in those ways and what you can do to give your artist more of a chance."

During his 20 years at Shock, company co-founder David Williams oversaw thousands of releases and employed hundreds of people. Williams sees that the core business of the music industry remains the same, even if the business models, by necessity, evolve.

> **[DAVID WILLIAMS]**: "Ultimately artists are artists; they are not business people. Art and commerce need each other. Artists need someone to put their art into a form that is saleable and to make it available in the market and that's what a music sales/marketing/distribution company can provide. What we are all doing is taking music to the market and trying

WELCOME TO THE JUNGLE

to get people to invest their emotions in that music and be a part of it."

With that important perspective in mind lets look at some of the key developments.

Monetising Video

When You Tube first emerged as a dominant platform for user-generated content, few people considered its implications for the music business. It was seen as a threat to the visual content industries – film and television – as it paved the way for the public to post copyright material for general viewing, and even to create content their peers found more compelling and personal than that created by corporate media.

The music industry's initial concern came from artists and managers who were concerned that rough footage from live performances was appearing at a fast rate and that footage often wasn't well shot or edited. There were some concerns raised on the basis that such actions were infringements of performers' rights.

However, the ground has shifted again and now the owners of copyright material are embarking on a new strategy – monetising You Tube content. This is done in a number of different ways including the most simple - via the You Tube advertising partnerships program, where posters of content get paid a royalty when their content is viewed.

The Guardian newspaper reported in January 2013: "Some indie labels say about 30% of YouTube ad revenue goes to You Tube and owner Google and 40% goes to the owner of the recording (usually the record label). The label gets another 20% of the ad revenue if it can claim ownership of the video; that is, it's an "official video" and not a video of someone dancing to the track. And last – and least – the songwriters/publishers get to share the remaining 10% between them."

The Cooking Vinyl label was quoted extensively in the report, suggesting that You Tube revenues are growing rapidly and labels are becoming more sophisticated in their approach to the platform, with different approaches to advertising being more effective in different countries. The label concluded that You Tube is likely to become their most important revenue stream in the future.

Vevo

In 2009, Sony Music and Universal Music, in conjunction with an Abu Dhabi media company, launched Vevo, a music video platform aimed at monetising video content under their control. EMI also contributed content to the site, although they were not equity participants.

Vevo launched in Australia in April 2012, as a joint venture between its international owners and MCM Media, later re-named Authentic Entertainment. Australia was the fourth country behind the US, Canada and the UK to have a stand-alone Vevo site. It was touted as being especially curated for the Australian market, with localised content and advertising sales.

In late 2016 radio network Southern Cross Austereo (SCA) purchased Authentic Entertainment inclusive of its Vevo business. After five years of Authentic Entertainment developing the Vevo brand and service in Australia, SCA now takes over Vevo at a time when Vevo is the largest premium video advertiser funded offering in the country, delivering over 170 million streams a month. Vevo is also set to grow with the announcement that Warner Music, the last major label that was not part of Vevo, are now contributing their content to the Vevo offering.

WELCOME TO THE JUNGLE

Impact of Video

The implications of the emergence of music video platforms are many, most notably the idea that artists will again have to consider the merit of an investment in music video, which for most of the first decade of the 21st century were seen as a low return exercise. Could this see a re-emergence of music video as a vital marketing tool (and possible revenue stream in their own right) and could this again shift the power balance between the artists and the labels that may have the capacity to fund videos where artists do not? Then again, the technology exists for artists to create low-cost compelling video content, so maybe this empowers artists even further?

Adam Jankie believes the future of video content exploitation has arrived, and in his role as manager of Bliss n' Eso has taken some innovative measures to be at the forefront of it.

> **[ADAM JANKIE]:** "Monetisation of video at the moment is coming from ad share and revenue programs with You Tube. You, as the rights holder, whether you are the artist or the label, allow You Tube to place advertising on your video and whenever someone clicks on the video you get a percentage of what You Tube gets from the advertiser. The more hits you get, the more money you make, depending on the demographic of who is watching it and who the advertiser is. It's starting to monetise. But it still doesn't justify spending huge amounts of money on video.
> Bliss n Eso, as part of the strategy that 'content comes first', have made a conscious effort that whenever the band had significant activity, they would hire guys to film it. The band invested in equipment back then and they have created all sorts of content. They have recorded every single performance they have done since 1999. It's all archived, we have boxloads

of tapes, hard drives, mini DVs and it's all catalogued. This got bigger and bigger over the years to the point we decided that the future of content in video was by giving it away for free and generating income via a third party, whether it was people sponsoring the video or advertising on it - the same way You Tube and Vimeo work. In order for us to get ahead of the game, we realised that we actually needed to hire someone to work for us full time to be the creative director and producer of content for the band. We poached a guy out of the action sports industry who was working for Red Bull and clothing companies. He had 10 years' experience shooting skaters, BMX, motocross, all of this stuff. We saved a fortune on film clips because this guys directing all the clips himself and the band owns all the equipment in-house. So if the trend of people streaming music off You Tube and Vimeo continues to go up, that works well for us, because we'll keep generating income for our bands through that. If we can't monetise it now, we can monetise it in the future."

Another new revenue stream has emerged from the You Tube platform. Many songs are used by video posters as soundtracks to their visual content, and in many cases amateur 'artists' perform cover versions of songs. Initially these uses were something of a black hole for the copyright owners, with their only approach being to try and prevent those uses rather than profit from them.

However, in 2013 AMCOS developed a deal seen as a landmark in the use of music on the platform. The deal is with Australian and New Zealand YouTube partner network Boom Video, which will grant Boom's content creators access to the catalogue of songs represented by AMCOS' members, which includes both local and international publishers. Boom Video's network of creators includes video bloggers across content such as music, comedy, fashion, film, food and drink,

WELCOME TO THE JUNGLE

how-to and parenting. This agreement grants these creators legal access to the massive collection of songs, for which a license will be paid back to the artists and copyright holders, while the creators will now also be eligible to take a cut of the advertising surrounding their channel.

You Tube Evolution

There's a cautionary note to be struck with You Tube though. You Tube has something like a billion users, compared with Spotify's 100 million. Yet the music industry revenue generated by You Tube is less than 10% of the revenue generated by Spotify. Clearly there is some work still to be done in that space. In fairness to You Tube music only makes up a small part of its content and it's parent Google claims to have paid out $3 billion to copyright holders. The platform continues to make goodwill gestures to the music business including opening up its YouTube Spaces with their high-tech production facilities to artists and the industry, presenting artist showcases at SXSW, Coachella and elsewhere, offering YouTube Music Insights tools to help artists with optimization and being having an investment in Vevo.

In 2016 YouTube launched an initiative to develop music talent under the name *YouTube Music Foundry*, which gives artists new tools and guidance on how to successfully grow their presence on the video platform. All Foundry content is available for free on the main site as well as on the YouTube Music app. Among the tools artists are learning to use now via The Foundry include live streaming video production, a rapidly growing technology that over the last several years has grown exponentially, especially since the advent of Facebook Live.

Extending Revenues

Beggars Group is clearly one of the smartest music companies on the planet – having global success with Adele, but also having a roster of the most important and innovative artists releasing music this century.

ANDREW WATT

They have come to realise that there is a blurring of the line between marketing, promotion and sales now where the "transaction" of buying and consuming music has shifted from an exchange of money for a piece of plastic. Beggars executive Ruth Barlow explains the thinking.

> **[RUTH BARLOW]:** "What we have to acknowledge now is that marketing, promotion and sales have merged. They are all the same thing. There is no such thing as promotion because promotion used to be directed towards getting a sale, but now consumption of music is a sale. So we have to try and direct audiences to official streams and official videos. Everybody wants to record the artist but we have to pick and choose who we allow to do that. We have to protect certain relationships – those that have supported the artists for a long time. Our artists still think of their album as their art. They see their live shows as a very different experience and someone wants to capture that for whatever reasons they see that as an add-on to their art, not a replacement for their art. Our artists are still most interested in that moment in time, that moment in the evolution of their art that is their album."

Another English based company Music Glue is also taking a new approach to generating artist revenues. Their on-line platform allows independent artists to create a shopfront that sells everything from downloads of music, to merchandise to concert tickets in a single place – effectively cutting out middlemen at every point.

Mark Meharry is CEO of Music Glue and sees his platform as part of a new set of economics.

> **[MARK MEHARRY]:** "There's a shift in the access that artist's have to their fanbase. The origin of that was social media but in the last five years artists have access to a global fanbase. How does that change the entire industry? We've had an industry based on long supply chains and the economics of scarcity.

WELCOME TO THE JUNGLE

Now we are in the economics of abundance where artists have direct access to their fanbase and those long supply chain models are irrelevant now. There are no gatekeepers; there is no-one that can actually sprinkle dust on an artist and make them famous. All that is bullshit. It's about building a fanbase, building a relationship with that fanbase and then commercializing that relationship. So what does that commercialization part of it look like? We don't think it looks like Spotify and iTunes and dealing with Ticketmaster and Live Nation. If you've got a tool where you can reach out to those fans globally and become a global retailer then you can chuck out all the middlemen."

Music Glue started as a direct-to-fan ticker seller and had great success with the likes of Mumford & Sons, but quickly realised that this was only part of the potential of their platform. Meharry now evangelises the notion that artists and fans can serve each other better by speaking directly in a transactional way.

[MARK MEHARRY]: "Managers are realizing that you don't create hype around your band so you can broker deals with a whole bunch of companies in the hope that might make your band successful. That doesn't work anymore. For artists and managers that's a difficult cultural shift to make from the old supply chain model of manufacturing goods and distributing goods to retail to get access to consumers. Bands have direct access to consumers and can sell directly to them. It's not about DIY – its about providing a very professional service as good as iTunes or Bravado. And the fan wants to pay money to an artist. One in three transactions that we process involve a second item – because they are buying from the band – it's not Ticketmaster and its not Apple that they are buying from.
We are getting bands that upload their music on to the platform, give it away for free, build up a database, upload a few

> different pictures for shirts, without manufacturing any stock, so you still haven't spent any money, do some shows, with free ticketing to build up an audience. So you have ticketing, merchandise and digital content and on the page you can allow streaming so people can listen while they are having a look around the page. Zero expense, zero risk."

The notion of there being no gatekeepers can be disputed however. For many artists the prospect of doing everything for themselves, direct-to-fan is daunting or in other ways unattractive. And not every potential corporate partner is sitting down waiting for that artist to call like a cab on a rank. This is where Sat Bisla's model of providing access and opportunity comes in.

> [SAT BISLA]: "There are still gatekeepers. You can stand outside the White House but without an invitation from the President you are not going to get in. That's not changed. It is still a relationship business and sometimes you need someone to create that relationship."

Patronage and Crowdfunding

As Music Glue would suggest the biggest impact the internet and social media has had on the music industry is in closing the gulf between an artist and their fans and potential fans. It's a cliché that the best thing about the internet for artists is that any artist can now reach an audience. The worst thing about the internet for artists is that any artist can now reach an audience. The barriers are down, but they are down for everybody.

The challenge for any artist and those working with them as managers, agents and consultants is how to exploit this access. But because everyone has the same opportunity, competition is fierce.

WELCOME TO THE JUNGLE

One of the most frequently discussed models that has been embraced by the music industry has been *crowdfunding*. This has seen fans or supporters invest in many aspects of the creative process, most commonly the recording, marketing or distribution of albums.

Websites such as Kickstarter, Pozible, IndieGoGo and Pledge Music have all seen numerous creative projects funded by fans, either pre-purchasing albums, before they were recorded or contributing to some other aspect of the process usually in return for a "reward" offered by the artist.

While the concept of crowdfunding is not limited to the creation of music – and in fact has been used for any number of ventures across technology, creative arts and business – it is particularly suited to music because of the immediacy of the fan response mechanisms and the ability to strike an emotional chord with supporters.

While crowdfunding has become a buzzword in recent times, the concept is actually almost ancient; again, we can learn from history.

Artistic patronage has been around for a very long time. As far back as the Middle Ages and the Renaissance, artistic works were commissioned and paid for by patrons. This arrangement would be a contract between the artist and the patron that specified the payment, some of the details of the work, a time frame for completion, and what theme the work might reflect. This level of control sometimes reflected the attitude of the times, where the artist was not considered to be a great creative or cultural innovator, but rather a tradesmen whose skills could be used and paid for.

The comparisons between both the record company model and the crowdfunding model are obvious. It's also worth reflecting that when artists cite "creative control" as one of their reasons for not wanting to sign with a corporate record company, in the distant past the level of control required by the funding partner – i.e. the patron – was often extreme.

Patronage also plays a large part in the history of music. Through the Baroque and Classical periods, composers not on payroll of the church would need to find a patron to support their work. Those composers with a history of impressive work would usually be successful in finding patrons – but not always. Vivaldi had what could best be described as 'bad PR" that resulted in potential patrons shunning him, while some composers who effectively worked the patronage circuit were paid to create work that has not necessarily stood the test of time.

In many ways it's no different to a mediocre band getting a record deal because they had a good manager. The history of labels is littered with bands whose work is best forgotten, just as there are numerous artists who have the potential to make great music, but who cannot cope with the business machinations required to get that music heard.

In the traditional patronage model, for the patrons there was added reward beyond having access to the art they supported. The social standing of the patron also benefitted from their dealings. Supporting a number of artists indicated wealth and a philanthropic spirit that was respected in the community.

The modern concept of crowdfunding replaces the idea of one patron with a larger number of smaller patrons who share the load of supporting the creation of an artist's output. However, there are still examples of individual patronage. Iconic Australian band, the Church, openly credit their continuation to the patronage of a wealthy American fan funding recordings on a speculative basis.

WELCOME TO THE JUNGLE

[**STEVE KILBEY**]: "He's a professor from America, he's rather wealthy and 12 or 13 years ago he popped up at a gig at a time when we were struggling a bit and he offered to help us finance projects and tours and underwrite costs. He was as good as his word and, really, the Church would not exist without this guy at all. We wouldn't have gotten through the hard times.

If I was a zillionaire and I met an artist I really admired, I'd be happy to say "Here's 10 grand, go and make another record". What else do you do with your money once you've bought the Ferrari and the yacht –you can look around and realise you can help a favorite singer or a favorite band. It's a great thing and it's an age-old tradition. I would be completely happy if some geezer turned up and said, 'Hey Steve I'm going to put you on a hundred grand a year and you are going to write songs and paint and write poetry for me' And usually the bolder and more original and strange you are, the more you need a patron. Thank God they are out there."

Crowdfunding Models

Most crowdfunding models are relatively similar. The artist or their manager devises a series of rewards based on different levels of support from fans. The basic level of support is usually a pre-purchase of the album – if that is what is being funded – either in digital or physical form. Higher levels of support result in increasingly more exciting rewards, often of the "money can't buy" type (although money is exactly what is buying those rewards!). Well-structured reward hierarchies are able to bring the fan increasingly closer to the artist, or the creative process, giving the fan not only a reward, but a reason to become an evangelist for the project.

Most crowdfunding models won't allow rewards that make the fan a commercial partner in the process, or make them a profit participant, as this would likely require registration under corporate laws governing commercial syndication or investment schemes.

From a legal point of view, the fan does not obtain any ownership in the copyright of the resulting work. This allows the artists to retain copyright, something that crowdfunding models proudly trumpet when trying to entice artists to use their platform.

Each of the major crowdfunding platforms operate slightly differently. Pledge Music is exclusively used for music-related projects, whereas Pozible, Indie GoGo and GoFundMe are broader, the latter being used for everything from charity campaigns to personal projects. Where Pledge Music reviews project submissions and only allows those that they think will attain their funding goal, at Indie GoGo there is no filtering of project proposals. Kickstarter's music projects only comprise around 20% of projects, with video games, design and technology featuring heavily.

Kickstarter's headline maker was prominent independent American artist Amanda Palmer, whose campaign targeted to raise $100,000 raised over US$1.2m. While the campaign was clearly a monumental success, it did create a further problem for Palmer – having to then justify how she would spend the additional funds she received beyond the minimum she required. Even in a world where the artist was providing an agreed reward for people who signed up willingly, there was still some resistance to the idea of them making a profit! The supporting public may still require a degree of transparency.

While there have been numerous examples of artists successfully funding projects through crowdfunding platforms, there are also some warning bells. There is a risk that crowdfunded recording will simply result in a series of vanity projects – albums being recorded that are only ever heard by the 100 or so people who financed its creation.

WELCOME TO THE JUNGLE

Eventually, when those people see no escalation of an artist's success, they may drop off the bandwagon.

The message is that the artist needs to have a plan for their crowdfunded work beyond playing it for friends and family.

> **[NICK O'BYRNE]:** "I'm worried that we are going to see a whole lot of bands that think that crowdfunding is the answer to all their problems. But the principles remain the same. If you are not a good band with a good fan base, it's not going to change anything for you. If you are a good band that would have sold 10,000 albums in Australia anyway, then of course it will work for you."

Benji Rogers is the founder of Pledge Music, one of the most innovative music crowd-funding platforms. English based, Pledge has a strong American presence and in 2013 hired their first Australian employee, Scot Crawford, formerly of Shock Records. Crawford has overseen some great Australian projects for Pledge Music since his appointment.

Rogers sees crowdfunding as a game changer, but has taken the model and the thinking behind it further. He views it as part of the music business's broader model, not an alternative to it.

His logic – and it is accurate – is based around shifts in the power relationship and the risk profile of investing in an artist's recording.

It works like this: when a record company pays for a band to record an album, the record company assumes all the risk of that recording. Sure, the band faces a prospect of making a record that doesn't sell – and hence they will receive no income from it, and they will be left owing an unrecouped balance to the record company – but they won't be directly out of pocket. And as an advance against royalties, the recording fund paid by the company is not refundable by the artist, it is only recoupable out of future royalties. The financial risk is clearly with the record company, so to compensate them for taking that risk, they ask for a higher return in the event that the album sells and makes money. It's hard to begrudge them that, even though it usually leaves the artist feeling under-compensated.

Let's change just one factor. If the record company does not put up the funding for the recording, the risk profile for the company changes immediately. Instead of having to recover the recording funds before they can start seeing a profit, they are able to see profits from the first sales. Not surprisingly, this situation allows them to strike far more balanced and fair deals with artists, as the pressure to recover outlays before seeing a return on investment is nowhere near as intense. It's not a case of being more generous, it's simply a case of reduced risk profile.

This thinking is hardly revolutionary. Successful artists who have been able to fund their own recordings have always been able to strike better deals with their record companies because the balance of power has shifted. The problem is that not many artists, in the greater scheme of things, have been in a position to fund their own recordings. Even if they did, it simply meant that the risk of the recording shifted entirely from the record company to the artist, who was left to face an unacceptably high level of risk. Only superstars were in a position to risk funding an album that may not sell, because for a superstar artist with a huge fanbase, the risk of a complete flop is comparatively small. Even with advances in recording technology, for many artists the level of funding required needed third-party investment.

This is where crowdfunding comes in. If you replace the risk for either the record company or the artist with risk undertaken by

WELCOME TO THE JUNGLE

another group of people, the position changes for everyone. If the recording budget is funded by a number of fans, the risk is spread, reducing the exposure for each of them. Their risk is in fact limited to the cost of the reward they have signed up for. If you buy a pre-release copy of the album, the worst thing that can happen is that you don't like the album. If you sign up at a higher level then presumably you saw a reward or inducement on offer that excited you sufficiently. The only risk you take is if the artist fails to deliver on the reward – and there are protections against this – but even then the outcome is not likely to be financially devastating. Effectively the risk of making that recording has shifted to the fans – who don't see it as risk to begin with!

The Pledge Music model takes this a step further. Rather than simply target artists who don't have record companies, but who do have fans (they hope) Pledge is now taking on projects from signed artists. By harnessing fans via the Pledge platform, the artists are able to strike a better deal with their label – they can use the label's marketing and distribution services, but don't have to endure draconian deals to do so – because the risk for the label has been eliminated.

> **[BENJI ROGERS]:** "It comes down to risk. It's very hard for someone who is going to buy the rights to some music to take a risk, because the reward is shockingly low now. If you can adjust that risk in some way and change the way the risk is received, all of a sudden you can spend differently and smarter and you can start to build a business.
> **I went** to the bank once and said I wanted to borrow some money. The banker said to me 'how do I know I'm going to get it back?' Fair point. I had no job, I had long hair and I was a musician. So I understood why he wouldn't lend me anything and if he did, I [understood] he would want to get 300% interest!

ANDREW WATT

When a musician signs to a record label, there's two types of risk they can take if they think it's the greatest thing they have ever heard: they can bet the farm on it and they can give an egregious deal or a fair deal. All the risk at that point lies with the label. If a label is going to spend $100,000 on your band, it wants to make $100,000 back with $100,000 profit. If it goes wrong it's going to cost the label $100,000 and its time. What does it cost the artist? Some hopes and dreams. Ultimately the artist will be able to move on and play live which the label won't be a part of.

What we designed at Pledge was the platform for the artist to say to the fans 'I want you to be a part of making the album, and as it's being made I'll take you along on the journey'. Part of the pledge goes to the charity of the artist's choice and the fan can get involved to the extent of a CD, a signed CD, a lyric sheet, poster, house concert, all the way up. When a label runs the campaign, they know within the first few hours whether something is going to fly..

We had a band raise something like $120,000 after being dropped from a label and then the same label came back and said, 'let's do a deal'. The terms were unbelievably fair because the label doesn't have to risk that $120k. Therefore the label becomes a partner in the process not the sole risk taker."

Helping artists move away from entirely self-funded recordings has flow-on effects for the rest of the recording industry. Artists who self-fund and self-record often end up with records that sound like no money is spent on the recording. They often sell accordingly and leave the artist remaining as a hobbyist. If fans are able to fund the project to a level that the artist feels is necessary to make a great recording, suddenly a whole new set of players get involved. For example, record producers who previously were out of work because no one could afford to work with a producer are back in the game.

WELCOME TO THE JUNGLE

[BENJI ROGERS]: "The producer will take a discounted rate and something on the back end, because they know the back end will be worth more because you will have a better product in the marketplace. The producer wins because they can charge the fees that they want. The engineers win because they can work with the producer and become the producers of tomorrow. The fans get better sounding albums."

Whenever there is a new platform, there is a need for experts knowing how to best work with that platform. It's no different for crowdfunding, or its more advanced offspring like the Pledge Music model. Crowdfunding sites are littered with projects that are pitched badly, have unenticing reward models or unrealistic expectations of their fans or own potential. Assistance is clearly needed.

[BENJI ROGERS]: "One of the reasons why we are more expensive than a crowdfunding platform is that we have that expertise built in. You get someone who is trained to do it. Sometimes it will take a few days to get these things launched because you will go back and forth with our team to make sure what you are offering will work for you, and how you will go fulfilling what you offer."

The essence of the Pledge Music model is that the fans are not end consumers who may or may not be willing or able to buy an album on the record company's designated release date; rather, they are participants in the process. This effectively extends the 'release window' from a couple of weeks to the length of time it takes to fund, record and release the album. Instead of word-of-mouth starting when the album's release is imminent, fans begin talking about it when the funding opportunity is announced. And they can 'buy' the album any time from when the funding window opens to when it is actually released, all before the album even hits iTunes or bricks-and-mortar retail.

ANDREW WATT

Crowdfunding changes not just the relationship between the fan and the artist, but between the artist and the record company, and the record company and the fan. All three participants can be winners if the process is managed correctly and cleverly. But again it isn't a magic formula. For the model to work it needs artists who make good music that fulfil fans' expectations, labels that understand their role as a service provider and managers who are able to coordinate and orchestrate a successful meeting of the minds and support the recording and release processes with the rest of a band's strategy.

> **[BENJI ROGERS]:** "My whole thing is this: there's a very black-and-white decision. A band can try and get everything from a label and in that case they are at the label's mercy. Or they can get everything from the fans and then go to the label and say, "This is what I've got, do you want to help me sell to everybody else?" And in that black-and-white moment you need a manager to do that work for you. If you are not willing to invest that amount in helping your fans be part of the process, why should a label invest in trying to force you to do that?"

New Live Opportunities

Alternative music funding models, revenue and new methods of music consumption are not the only areas of change in the music business. The live side of the business is also evolving rapidly as audiences and live music enthusiasts seek new experiences and new forums to experience their music.

Australian pub rock culture is alive and well, particularly in Melbourne and Brisbane. While the live industry faces challenges in the form of urban gentrification and the on-going evolution of licensing laws, OH&S standards and public liability insurance, these challenges shouldn't mislead anyone into thinking the live scene is an endangered species.

WELCOME TO THE JUNGLE

[EMILY YORK]: "I think there was a lot of doom and gloom and you read about it in the paper every week, but I think it's actually a great time for live music. There is a myth surrounding certain venues, and although it's really sad when those venues come to an end, sometimes there is this doom and gloom that I just don't think is real. I understand that people are very passionate about some venues and they get upset when it comes to an end, but overall the scene is healthy and it's really vibrant. Again, if the act is good, you are going to sell tickets and the venue will do well. If a festival is well programmed, the festival will sell tickets and everyone will go and have a good time, because the acts are great and they will buy a ticket next year. I think it's a lot healthier than we were led to believe."

York's thoughts are echoed by Richard Moffat, who believes you need to experience the live music scene in other countries to realise how good we have it here.

[RICHARD MOFFAT]: "I've spent a lot of time in London and New York and other places and I honestly believe that Melbourne's music scene is better than any in the world – by a considerable distance. Quite often you go to gigs in London and New York, and there is no vibe. The band will be playing to 50 people and the same band could tour Australia and sell 800 tickets at the Corner. I've proved that to myself a hundred times over. In those overseas venues often the PA is awful, the staff are rude, the room is tiny and pokey and there is no air-conditioning. In Melbourne there is a much higher volume of people that go and see live music and the quality of production and the rooms are considerably ahead of any other city in the world."

But the relative strength of the scene doesn't mean that changes are not happening. There is a constant cycle of venues opening and closing, in any city, at any time.

ANDREW WATT

What's more interesting is the trend towards presenting music in non-traditional venues or producing events that capture the imagination of the music-seeking audience.

These days, gigs take place on trains, trams, in people's backyards, at markets and in pop up venues. Live music has been woven into everything from cricket matches to cruise ships, to zoos and this has meant that music industry professionals were called upon to program, book and produce the music components of these events.

The opportunities presented by live music are acutely obvious to the marketing side of the music business, which in turn can pitch those opportunities to brands and their marketers.

> **[CARL GARDINER]:** "As we all know there has been a number of changes in the commercial model of the music industry, and revenue from live performances or revenue stream related to live performances is becoming increasingly important. Australia's been blessed to have a really good live music scene and that's where some of the best opportunities lie. Agents like Brett Murrihy get that. What a sponsor can do for a fan within a live music environment is pretty obvious, whether it's making the ticket price lower or making the level of production better or whether it's a genuine on-site experiential opportunity. Quite often when I'm talking to clients and looking at the sort of briefs I get from them I look at live music-related opportunities as a cornerstone of fulfilling the brief."

My Path into the Industry

MICK NEWTON

From an early age I wanted to work in entertainment but I didn't know where or how. I ended up doing a PR degree at RMIT with thoughts of getting in behind the scenes in promotional PR or something like that. I ended up working in a consultancy that was pretty corporate, straight, 'suit and tie' sort of thing. I really didn't like it. At the same time I was managing a couple of little bands – friend's bands – and I got to know a couple of the guys at Premier. I'd see them at gigs and I got to know them. I hassled them for a job, even though I was probably around 26 and completely over-qualified to be the poster boy. I remember having an interview with Frank Stivala, and he told me he thought I was over-qualified. I took a fair drop in salary but I really wanted to give it a go. I could wear board shorts to work and go to gigs and it was really good fun. While I was the poster boy, I began booking a couple of small bands for gigs and got to know a few people by doing that and after about a year I became a full time agent.

CHAPTER 7

INTERNATIONAL AMBITIONS

A crucial area to undergo enormous change is the prospects of Australian artists entering international markets. The global market is becoming increasingly closer due to technological innovation, cheaper international travel and communications, and the prospect of doing business without having to completely rely on the patronage of the traditional gatekeepers if the artist chooses not to.

> **[BRETT COTTLE]**: "I think that is definitely true. When it comes to talented successful writers and artists negotiating deals, I think that it is very much true that the power is with the artists and their advisors these days. I don't have a lot to do with those negotiations, but I think everybody now knows that you can now negotiate with a publisher or label internationally. You are not only dealing with the Australian market when you are looking for a deal; it is truly a global market. That wasn't the case in the past. The pathway to international success was always doing a deal here and getting the label to support you internationally through their connections. That's no longer the case, so I think the power has shifted substantially along with the fact that it is a do-it-yourself world for the great majority of artists".

Danny Rogers is one of the most successful Australian music entrepreneurs on the international stage. As the co-founder of Laneway Festival (with Jerome Barazio) he has done what many thought was

WELCOME TO THE JUNGLE

impossible – export a festival. Laneway has now been held in New Zealand, Singapore and Detroit. As co-manager of Gotye (with John Watson) and manager of Temper Trap, Roger's thoughts on breaking international markets from Australia are both enlightening and enlightened.

[DANNY ROGERS]: "From the start of working in management I asked myself, 'is this an artist/group that I'd be proud to showcase at SXSW? Would they make an impact at Glasto or Coachella? Can I genuinely imagine this act sitting alongside the world's most exceptionally gifted artists in a few years' time?' If the answer is yes, and that's very, very rare for me, then it's a very exciting proposition. From the start of managing, I always had the goal to try and make the artists I worked with an international reality. Knowing how competitive it is from trial and error, I quickly learnt that the artists needed to share that same vision.

To manage acts just for Australia is completely fine and you only have to look and truly admire someone like Bill Cullen and the unbelievable job he does for Paul Kelly or the incredible work that Paul Piticco did with Powderfinger to see that working Australia is more then enough to build lasting and fruitful careers. I also know that both acts would have loved and deserved bigger international careers, but because of the timing of these acts, it didn't quite happen for them. That gives me a heightened appreciation for what we've been able to achieve. Personally, I'm excited by rolling out campaigns that have multiple countries in the mix. It's culturally stimulating, you always learn so much and when it works, it's a very satisfying feeling. With the festivals, I guess from all the travels and releasing albums overseas, I came to the realisation that [Laneway] could also go global."

ANDREW WATT

In her role as head of Sounds Australia, Millie Millgate has championed Australian artists and managers seeking a foothold in international markets. She has seen the dawning of a whole new era.

> **[MILLIE MILLGATE]:** "As recently as five years ago, it was like you had to build an Australian story – you had to have sold X amount of units, you had to have toured the country so many times, you had to have certain chart positions – before you could get anyone's attention, and it was ultimately because you were trying to target the major labels which were your access to international markets. That has changed so much. You've got these acts that can put some tunes up and find some fans through analytics and other ways to monitor where their audience might be. Now the thing that people are going for in the first instance is definitely not the label. It's about getting their team in order, whether that is working with a radio plugger in North America, or getting an agent on board and then maybe thinking about what your distribution might look like. A lot of acts are just looking at digital releases just to get a look at the market. The whole methodology has changed and if you look at examples of acts that have had breakaway success like DZ Deathrays or the Jezabels or Flume, it's been before debut albums have been released here. It is a different process now and the idea of releasing territory by territory is obsolete. Everything has made it easier to get overseas and our dollar to be worth more once you get over there, but you have to have done your research and be prepared and be able to put on a great live show."

But as a word a caution, Australian artists or labels need to be realistic in their ambitions and what is required to fulfil them. Rev. Moose (not his real name!) operates a radio promotions company called Marauder servicing the US market.

WELCOME TO THE JUNGLE

[REV. MOOSE]: "The best way that people can start whether it is a company or a band is to identify what they want in the market and do a self-analysis as to whether that is reasonable to pursue. Do they have the talent that is appropriate for the market? They have to be critical about that. It's going to require a budget of some kind – time and money – and often people overlook one or the other of those. People under-estimate how much time its going to take to break into a new market and the US being the biggest music market it takes more time and money and focus and effort. You need it to be a strong focus of yours and not just a dream."

The access point could come in any number of different ways depending on the artist and their material. There is no single formula for knocking down the door – if there was every one would use it!

[SAT BISLA]: "It starts with the songs and then a vision for the artist to reach their vision. We look at different platforms and relationships and access areas that will be the path of least resistance to build a foundation for the artist and their songs. That could be any place, anywhere, any platform. It might make sense for a song to be launched with a brand, it might be at radio, it might be a synch. It might be live."

For Jaddan Comerford, the international market hasn't so much been an ambition as a natural extension. He sees his business as being a small global music business that happens to be based in Australia rather than an Australian business hoping to expand overseas. In 2013 he signed Melbourne artist Vance Joy to a long-term recording contract with Atlantic Records, before the artist had even released an album in Australia, a contract that bore plenty of fruit in 2014 and 2015.

[JADDAN COMERFORD]: "A lot of the relationships that I now have have got to do with the success of Vance and they weren't available to me before. That being said I did have a network that I could tap into that allowed me to move things in the directions that I wanted to much quicker than if I didn't have those relationships. The initial Vance Joy relationship with Atlantic actually came about because of our relationship with Roadrunner Records and The Amity Affliction, because Roadrunner's parent company is Atlantic Records. So you make the most of any networking opportunity but it will only go so far if you've got something to talk to somebody about."

[**PAUL PITICCO**]: "I think inevitably the recorded music market will globalise in such a way that you can control the release and promotion of music from wherever you are. We aren't there yet, but that's where it will end up. Touring obviously will stay market-specific while there are national boundaries, and holograms remain lame!"

As a small and definitely indie Australian label Julia's Wilson's Rice Is Nice also has its eyes on overseas markets and has invested time and effort into making those inroads.

[**JULIA WILSON**]: "I've been going there for a long time, slowly, slowly meeting people and building bridges and avenues. It's been such a long process but it feels like now seven years later there is a little bit of recognition and acknowledgement. It's been a long time coming but it's an exciting thing and a necessary thing for Australian artists to have that avenue to release in the States."

For label Remote Control the majority of their success has been achieved by licensing international albums for release in Australia from international labels like Beggars and 4AD. That resulted in Remote Control releasing Adele's albums in Australia among a host

WELCOME TO THE JUNGLE

of others. But increasingly they too are looking at taking Australian music to international markets.

> **[HARVEY SAWARD]:** "We are a bit more focussed now on our local roster because I feel quite strongly that there needs to be some strong Australian labels to support some Australian bands whereas I don't necessarily feel that the rest of the Australian industry goes along with that. Bands and management have an aim to sign with a US label or a UK label where in reality 90% of what those labels sign is going to be from their own backyard. Our passion over the next couple of years is to sign Australian bands that we can work successfully overseas. We've spent a lot of time recently hiring US publicists and talking to people about partnering up on things. We are a sought after home for Australian bands in Australia but we want them to trust us with the rest of the world as well."

Matt Gudinski sees the internationalisation of the market for Australian labels as inevitable and essential.

> **[MATT GUDINSKI]:** "It's still a frustration of mine that although we work with a number of artists on a global level there will still be a number of artists that we don't work with globally. In this current era that makes it hard. Australia is still our focus but for the artists where we do have global rights we've been able to find various pockets in the world that do pick up on those artists. So we look at the world as one big territory and while we break down and target certain regions, based on the culture in those regions, we do look at most of our set-up on a global approach. There was a perception out there which has almost been eliminated now, that to have success internationally you had to sign with an international label. I think that's changed a lot over the past five years and the

majority of artists that we have developed in recent years we do have worldwide rights to."

Manager Andy Kelly has had international success with artists such as the Vines and Jet. For Kelly and his partners in Winterman Goldstein, the appeal of international markets is both necessary and exciting.

[ANDY KELLY]: "If you live in Australia you have to think that way. It's very hard to sustain a life just operating in Australia with Australian acts. I actually take it as a given that people would think that way. Part of it is the adventure and the unknown. You get to go and learn all these new things in different countries and meet new people and see different ways of doing things. That's a massive and exciting part of it too; those things that you get to do that you can't put a price on. It's about all the people you meet and the experiences you have as much as anything. Maybe you will make some money and maybe you won't, but you might have this incredible enriching life. It can be incredibly hard, but I know it's no harder than working in a restaurant. Playing to 10 people in Grand Rapids, Michigan can be a bit of a bummer, but at least you are in Grand Rapids, Michigan and you are going to be somewhere else the next night. And you are never going to know unless you try."

[JOHN WATSON]: "We would only sign a new artist if we felt they had serious international potential. There are a number of reasons for that, but to be totally frank the main one is that I enjoy the challenge of working overseas – particularly in America. There's something compelling about working in the biggest market in the world and once you've got a taste of it, it's highly addictive. I've been blessed to have four artists get a serious shot in the US over the last 17 years – Silverchair, Missy Higgins, Wolfmother and Gotye. We've had gold records (or

WELCOME TO THE JUNGLE

bigger) with each of them, so that's really the benchmark we'd set for any new project."

Manager Bonnie Dalton spent several months based in the UK, and for her it was an essential move to make, both for her artists and herself. The only real question was one of timing for the artists she works with.

[**BONNIE DALTON**]: "When they're ready – simple as that. Only it's not simple because there's no one-size-fits-all answer, ever. I'd only been managing [Melbourne band] Husky for nine months by the time we'd done a worldwide record deal and sent them off on tours across Germany, the USA and Canada, but I certainly wouldn't recommend that for every band. It's a matter of weighing up how ready the music is, but also how good the live show is and what set-up you have already internationally – there needs to be a lot of interest before the band gets on a plane or it's a wasted trip. Very importantly, however, you also need to consider cash flow and make sure that you have a plan for the band in terms of getting overseas again and again and again once you make the first trip. If that first one goes well, it will just be the start, so you need to take a long-term view. For Australian bands I think that the tyranny of distance can be a blessing as much as it is a curse because you can hide away in relative isolation from the rest of the world until you're ready to launch them as a 'brand new discovery' elsewhere, but it does take a lot to get them back into those other territories time and time again."

[**SAT BISLA**]: "Social media stats are secondary. More important is personality, the attitude, the passion and the work ethic of the artists and the manager. Social media is a tool and tools can change. You can pick your tools as needed. Some A&R

people are very data driven and I think that is a big mistake. For the most successful A&R people their No. 1 data research tool is their gut. As a fan, as a consumer I couldn't give a shit if an artist has a million views on You Tube. It's about my connection to the music and so it's not important to hit a certain point of social media engagement before aiming ovcrseas."

For some artists the first step of their international path to engage an agent that will assist in opening up live opportunities for touring and festivals in the international territory.

Rob Ziferelli is a leading agent at the United Talent Agency and he thinks that an international agent will only work for an Australian artist when they form part of a well-orchestrated plan.

[ROB ZIFERELLI]: "For me it's all about the plan. I need to understand the music first and foremost because it's a different pitch depending on where you are heading. The singer-songwriter scene is a lot different to the rock scene for example. It's really important to me to see that the artists and their team have it together and they have a plan. Sometimes artists need development and after a couple of decades in the business I'd like to think that I can see the potential. But the main thing is to see a plan and a team around the artist because that romantic idea of "discovery" is like winning the lottery."

Highly respected LA-based manager Peter Leak has always been willing to push outside his home market when attempting to break an artist. Some US-based managers and labels had been accused of not recognising territories beyond America, but times have changed. Smart managers like Scooter Braun and Troy Carter are huge proponents of developing "difficult" markets and Leak is another who has an "all-of-world" view.

WELCOME TO THE JUNGLE

[PETER LEAK]: "I think it's really important to try and understand as many markets as you can. The markets are changing all the time; new markets are being developed. The traditional markets that have been there a long time are always important – North America and Europe – but now the Asian markets are opening up more and more and they are really important. As a manager, the more information you have and the more ability you have to have an influence in those markets yourself is invaluable, because the major labels are cutting back on their staffing more and more and you are finding yourself dealing with international departments who want to do their best, but are stretched incredibly thin. A lot of times their job is just scheduling and I'm not sure how easy it is for major labels to get a lot going for a new artist, unless it is made a global priority. If you don't have that you are not going to get a lot of work done by your own label, so you have to constantly be looking for opportunities around the world yourself. The global market becomes more and more important and with the on-line opportunities giving you the ability to get to people, it's more doable, but it's quite daunting to find the time to do it all."

Working Overseas

Having international ambitions isn't limited to artists and those working with them. For people working behind the scenes having international experience can have enormous career benefits. Colin Daniels agrees that international experience is a huge positive to a career in music, or in any business for that matter.

[COLIN DANIELS]: "I was fortunate at a young age to experience the worldwide industry and not just the Australian industry. For me that's really important. You've got to understand how the industry works globally. That will benefit your career and it will help shape your thinking. I remember the first time I worked in Europe, I got the understanding that there were acts in continental Europe that were selling five million records, but only selling them in Eastern Europe and Italy and Spain and they were never going to work in England, North America or Australia. That didn't mean they weren't great acts; it just meant that they weren't right for that market. That helped me shape my thinking. In every country in the world there are different twists and different ways of doing business, not just in music but in any business."

Mark Poston agrees with this position.

[**MARK POSTON**]: "I definitely recommend working in another market and getting that experience if there is that opportunity. It might be overrated sometimes, but it does seem to be helpful if you have worked overseas. It holds you in good stead when you come back home. But more importantly than that, you just learn a lot, especially if it is a bigger or a more sophisticated market. You learn things that you don't even realise at the time and it will help you in your career. I always say to people that they should grab that opportunity."

Charles Caldas views his Australian industry background as a reason for his success on the international stage.

[**CHARLES CALDAS**]: "Australians as a rule have a great can-do attitude to work, and in setting up a business in a different country I was amazed at how different work ethics and work cultures can be. Australian's have a 'get on with it' attitude and there is not a lot of negativity in the Australian spirit. When there is political stuff going on – as there inevitably is in a global

WELCOME TO THE JUNGLE

organisation – I'm removed enough from it that I can just see it for what it is. It's like all of your clichés about the national characteristics come into play before your eyes, but I'm not aligned to any of that. The distance [away] that Australia is can be a real positive but it can also create an insular and inward-looking attitude. To be fair, that is phasing out and as the music industry is a more global beast, you evolve that stuff out of existence anyway. Australians do break through, and to do it you have to have a boundless ambition and a boundless confidence that says 'just because you are from here doesn't mean that the American market is not going to appreciate what you do'. It's about having this belief that what you can offer is going to be of value to people. That can-do attitude gets you a long way in a culture like the UK where there is a much more limit-bound mentality, rather than a limit-less mentality."

The eyes of the Australian music business are not confined to the traditional international destinations of America, the UK and parts of Europe. Increasingly, the Asian market is of real interest to many of our key players, from Danny Rogers whose Laneway Festival operates in Asia, to agent Brett Murrihy who opened an Asian office very early in the evolution of his Artist Voice business. Village Sounds have now followed suit in having a permanent Asian presence. An Australian executive who has worked for many years in Asia, Ruuben Van Den Heuval explains that there's more to breaking in to the Asian market than simply catching a plane.

[**RUUBEN VAN DEN HEUVAL**]: "The difference in Asia is that you are extremely foreign. You have to get very used to the idea that you are a foreigner. You have to assimilate into their ways and that's a long road. The road to China is many singular steps taken over a period of time. If you want to do business in China, you have to build relationships. You have to being willing to go back and have the same conversations over and over again and make it seem interesting. You have to realise that you are nothing, but the difference you can make is bringing an international perspective to what is a very parochial position you get in these different countries. My success has been the ability to bring people [together] from different parts of the world, different religions, different cultures and ideologies and make them understand that they are the same human beings. By doing that I've made money and been able to survive. The big opportunity in Australia right now is to go overseas and try and do something different. You keep going back and sooner or later it will work. People will remember you and introduce you to someone else and you'll become interesting to them."

PART 2
ROLES IN THE MUSIC INDUSTRIES

My Path into the Industry

JESS BESTON

"From a very young age I was obsessed with anything and everything to do with music, and was certainly known as one of the most 'musicy' people at my school. When I graduated high school, I went straight to Sydney Uni where I completed a Bachelor of Arts degree majoring in Music, whilst also having singing lessons with Opera Australia.

At some point during that time I fell madly, obsessively (scarily?) in love with Radiohead, Tool, the Smashing Pumpkins, Nine Inch Nails, and Blur among others and decided I had to give up this classical music malarkey and get myself to London.

I moved there when I was 21, and had the opportunity to work as assistant to the directors for the National Youth Music Theatre, so I grabbed it! We performed at the Edinburgh Festival and a Royal Gala Performance at Glyndebourne Opera House, which I also ended up performing in.

I then started work at HMV in Piccadilly Circus. I worked and travelled over those years, but I also met three awesome guys, and we formed a band called Motel 6. We didn't have a bass player so I bought one, and away we went. I taught myself bass guitar in the four weeks leading up to our first gig. I then also taught myself to play guitar (badly), and when I flew home to Sydney in 2001.

In 2001 I also got my first job at a record company, starting in licensing at EMI Music Australia, and then later moved into promotions. In early 2007, I was asked by Universal Music Australia to join them as A&R manager, and I said yes!"

ANDREW WATT

Roles in The Industry

Having established the length and breadth of the new music industry, and many of its fast evolving areas of development, it is obvious that career opportunities in the business are many and varied – and now far more diverse than ever. While the size of operations of some sectors has contracted, there are new sectors and service providers taking up the challenge of connecting music makers and consumers.

Part 2 looks at many of the areas of the business and examines the career opportunities that exist in each of these areas.

What is most striking about Part 2 is how different jobs within the music business can be from each other, and what the differences in the skill sets, the hours, the risk profile and the opportunities for advancement might be. Some jobs might be ends in themselves; desirable career destinations, whereas some jobs are stepping stones to other roles.

Some roles require little or no experience; others require detailed knowledge and a level of formal education. There are very few roles that are inaccessible to anyone based on gender or background, which is one of the great things about the business.

It could be argued that the key to having a long and financially sustainable career in the music business is identifying what part of that business interests you the most, intersecting that with what you are good at and finding customers who will pay you for that service.

People often find themselves starting in one area and moving deliberately…or accidentally…into a different area. Now there is scope to move between industries while still exercising the love of working with music, not only because there are a number of areas where skills and experience can be transferred between different roles, but because

WELCOME TO THE JUNGLE

the industry itself changes to make some skills redundant and other skills more in demand.

> **[DENIS HANDLIN]**: "In this business the moment you think you know it all, you know nothing. The ways to take music to the market have changed. We now have 24/7 access to consumers through on-line channels, forums, as well as smart phones, emails, databases and social media. The marketing skills have been augmented to understand the most effective way to position our promotion and marketing through these new channels to best connect with the target audience as well potential new fans. The industry uses more research information and is constantly gaining consumer sentiment through social media and online trends and staff with education and experience in these areas have entered the industry. Record companies also have a range of other roles including various content creation, digital delivery, computer programming and graphics based roles that play a key part in presenting artists information and communicating those materials to the fan base."

The music business is currently one of the fastest-changing industries because music is particularly adaptable to technological change and evolution of delivery mechanisms. Music is an end product delivering certain experiences in its own right, but is also an ingredient in other forms of entertainment or media. For this reason the music business, by necessity and for its own benefit, interfaces with many other areas of business and for that reason specialist roles tend to be created and adapted as those interfaces evolve. Examples of this include the roles of music supervisors in film and television and music sponsorship brokers, both of which are considered later in this book in greater detail.

It might be tempting to turn to the chapter on the job that you already *think* you want and read what those people already doing it have to say about it. The book is designed so you can do that. A better approach, though, is to read through all the roles and the expert descriptions and anecdotes accompanying them. If you are planning on working in the industry it's important to know where your niche fits into the big picture and how the different roles relate and interact. You might also discover your dream job is something you didn't even know existed!

Many people featured in this book started their career in the music business started in a predictable place – on the stage. The likes of Scot Crawford, Andy Kelly, Jess Beston, Gregg Donovan, Simon Smith, Keith Ridgway and Patrick Donovan all played in bands with varying degrees of success. Many well known musicians like You Am I's Andy Kent have combined successful careers on stage with responsible off-stage roles. Paul Gildea for example, has been touring lead guitarist for Icehouse for around 25 years while managing artists such as Motor Ace (which featured now powerful agent Damian Costin on drums), Michael Paynter and Stonefield. He sees some benefits in coming from that background.

> **[PAUL GILDEA]:** "I think it's been a double edged sword – on the one hand I may have greater empathy than some in terms of understanding the pressures and demands on the contemporary pop artist/band having been through the process. On the other hand the band/artist sometimes need a firm and even stern directive and I've been guilty of being too understanding in the past. I like to think it's a balance I've addressed with more experience."

So the message is – whether you are a musician or if you cant play a note – there are opportunities in the many roles detailed in the following pages.

Chapter 8

Major Record Companies

As suggested in Part 1, it's been a tumultuous couple of decades for major record companies. Challenges to their business model, erosion of traditional revenue streams and a perception that they had alienated their customers during the post-Napster years meant that cracks appeared in businesses that only a few years earlier had been bouyant and had cashflow that must have seemed like it was going to last forever.

Being signed by a major label was the holy grail for most artists (even those exhibiting an independent aesthetic) and while everyone knew there was plenty wrong with the major label system, it was also the game that most participants – artists and industry workers alike – wanted to play. Many idealistic industry players undoubtedly thought they could change the so-called evil empires from within; that they would miraculously be the rare artist or the executive that didn't walk away a few years later with a horror story to tell.

There are hundreds of stories of major label excess, corporate thuggery, dubious accounting, improper practices and outrageous indulgence and just about every major label has been the subject of several books documenting these lascivious stories. These books make for entertaining and sometimes jaw-dropping reading. There isn't an artist or manager or label executive who has had a lengthy career that doesn't have a story to tell, and only some of those stories are exaggerated.

WELCOME TO THE JUNGLE

The woes of the major labels were discussed earlier in this book and Michael Gudinski summarises them well.

> **[MICHAEL GUDINSKI]**: "The majors liked the way the business was running and as much as the independents were strong and could do things, the majors still ran the bulk of the business. They got greedy and they got fat and they fought new technology, not just in Australia, but around the world. That was the beginning of the change, where the record companies started to lose their position. The re-issuing of catalogues over the years in many formats, be it cassettes, 8-tracks, CDs etc. meant people would buy the same music again. It resulted in record companies shooting themselves in the foot. It resulted in a lot of over expenditure and indulgence. There were Australian albums being made that cost nearly a million dollars and videos around the world costing a million dollars."

Even so, it's no accident, even in 2016 and beyond, Gudinski's current labels enjoy a important working relationship with the largest major, Universal.

Majors In Perspective

A sense of perspective is needed. Probably half the people interviewed for this book have either worked for major labels at some point in their career, or at the very least had their career boosted, directly or indirectly, by having an association with a major record company. Most of these people are smart enough to admit that they wouldn't be where they are today without that experience.

John Watson provides that perspective.

ANDREW WATT

[**JOHN WATSON**]: "One general comment I'd make on this topic is that there's a really common, lazy habit that people have of thinking that all major label people wear black hats and all indie people wear white hats. It's a stupid and blinkered way to view the world. There are most definitely some evil people in major labels, but I can absolutely assure you that there are some evil people in indies too. Equally there are some sincere, decent hard working people in both types of companies. People shouldn't make the mistake of judging individuals based on the name on their front door. It's a case-by-case thing. I've seen majors do some heinous things to artists over the years but I've seen some indie labels do even worse. Young people coming into the business shouldn't wear blinkers when it comes to majors versus indies. Keep an open mind and call each situation as you see it."

Watson's sentiments are echoed by Colin Daniels.

[**COLIN DANIELS**]: "There are great artists and great people at indies and majors. I think it's really important to understand that. I'm not one of those people who are major label bashers. There is a time and a place and a right business model for every artist. For some, they choose the indie route and others need the guidance and the funds of a major. I've enjoyed my experiences working in both environments."

Also worth remembering is that the vast majority of recorded music sold, licensed, downloaded or streamed under any model, belongs to major labels. Whether you like this situation or not, it does mean that anyone wanting to work in the music business should consider the major label option. The three major music companies are where most music is controlled, and that's not likely to change in a hurry.

WELCOME TO THE JUNGLE

[ALLEN BERGFREDE]: "The major record label is not dead – it's the contrary. In fact I think that they are stronger than they have ever been before because they now have the ability to flex their muscle when it comes to licensing catalogue to streaming services and they still hold the key to artist development. It's impossible to find an artist that is a superstar without a major label involved somewhere."

Major labels are suited to marketing and distributing globally successful artists on a grand scale.

If the idea of participating in that activity sounds like an attractive career option, then a role at a major label is still highly seductive. It may be that the emphasis at major labels will change – one prediction is that they will become less artist development-oriented and evolve into marketing-driven companies with a significantly smaller roster of bigger global artists.

Breaking in via the Majors

These days there are far fewer jobs available at record companies, and the nature of these jobs has changed. For example, there is far less music retail to service, and so the team of sales representatives that each label has is far smaller. Historically, many people started their career as a sales rep for a record company and worked their way up.

Ruuben van den Heuval's story is typical of the time, as he relates his experience when working in a record shop on the NSW Central Coast.

[RUUBEN VAN DEN HEUVAL]: "During that time the reps from the record companies would come in and they had great mullets and I couldn't think of anything in the world that would be better than having a great mullet and driving around in a company car and visiting record shops. I wrote letters to everybody, but I couldn't get into the industry. Eventually I was able to get into a party for Demis Roussos and at that party I met people and I ended up with a job at Polygram. I did sales desk stuff and I filled in for reps. From Polygram I moved over to CBS. The head of HR asked me how old I was and I told him I was 18, and he said that he couldn't employ me. But I'd already signed my contract so it was too late! I was a sales rep there for a number of years and then Phonogram asked me to become a label manager. That was an interesting entry point into marketing at a very young age and I did a whole series of tours around Australia with a whole series of bands like the Black Crowes, John Mellencamp, Metallica and Dire Straits."

Label marketing and promotions teams have been trimmed and there are fewer mainstream media outlets that require attention. On the other hand, there are new forms of distribution and promotion in the digital realm and major labels have re-deployed forces into these areas. To be fair, major labels were well ahead of the game in some of these areas, even when the nature of the game was hazy. As discussed in the chapter on digital music marketing, some of the leading lights in that field began their careers at major labels.

The A&R departments of major labels have been known to have fairly high staff turnovers, but this area has also been a breeding ground for a number of people who have gone on to significant careers in the broader industry.

Leading artist manager Cath Haridy is one person who benefited from her time both at major label Warner and at Mushroom, which was a 'virtual major' at the time.

WELCOME TO THE JUNGLE

[CATH HARIDY]: "I had a short label experience, which was bookended with Warner. I had six months at Warner at the beginning of my label career and then six months at the end. In between I spent seven years at Festival Mushroom, which had the backing of a major label in that it was owned by News Ltd, but it worked autonomously like an independent. I think I was lucky, in that the experience I had in that company for seven years was very special. We had a smaller staff than any of those multi-nationals may have, so we all got to multi-skill in a sense. I wasn't just doing A&R, I was doing marketing as well and I was learning skills across several different disciplines. That was really helpful to me and has been ever since because management needs such a broad base of skills. I got to work very closely with people in sales and very closely with people in publicity and in marketing and also in the international department. We were all working pretty much on top of each other in an office space and you learn a lot when you are working so closely in such a confined space, with other people doing different things. We had people who were very willing to share their experiences as well and were willing to pass on information."

Haridy's experience highlights the major benefit of working with a substantial company. If a person is prepared to keep their eyes and ears open across departments, they can get exposure to everything from A&R to publicity, from marketing to sales, under the one roof. That can also be done at an indie label, but in that situation those roles are filled by one or two people.

For publicist Nicole Hart, the years she spent at major labels served her well later in her career.

ANDREW WATT

> **[NICOLE HART]**: "There were times at BMG when we were getting great A&R from overseas and getting incredible global acts and they were coming to the market and touring. That helped me foster really good relations with the media and realise the importance of attention to detail and care for your artists. It's so much about being honest and having integrity, and I think they are really important things to take into running your own company. There was a lot of pressure at major labels and I still have those same expectations now when I am trying to deliver a project, even though I'm my own boss. You are so well trained by the machines in what you have to deliver and that's just experience you can't get until you are under the microscope doing it."

With the major label there is room for career progression, if someone is willing to propel themselves forward.

Denis Handlin, head of Sony Music for Australia and the Asia Pacific region, maintains a strong belief in the ability of major labels to develop executive talent.

> **[DENIS HANDLIN]**: "The reality is, entrants to the industry have always been interested in starting at a major and we have a long and proud history of developing people that have worked here going on to extend their careers in other companies or parts of the industry. As we have diversified our business activities into online, digital, touring, films and artist management, the scope of roles available have also increased, providing staff opportunities to work in various areas to build experience levels. Overall we are seeing more applications from communications and music business graduates, but generally the profile of the aspirants still centres on passionate music people that

WELCOME TO THE JUNGLE

want to get into the industry and learn – whether that be in sales, marketing, promo or digital, finance or other areas. The fundamentals remain the same. The business is built on having passionate music people who are always increasing their skill set."

[DAN ROSEN]: "I think working at a record company is a very exciting option, whether it be at an indie or a major. It's a great time to work for a record company because they are innovating and they are coming up with new business models and charting new courses for their artists. We are getting to a point where record company sales are 50% digital, so if you are interested in the digital world and with how consumers interact with content online, then it's a fascinating time to work at a label."

New Talent Models

For some major labels, one of the game changers has been the emergence of television talent shows as sources of commercially important new artists. These artists arrive at the label with an audience already aware of them and the challenge is to keep and grow that audience. While there is a perception that these shows stifle A&R activity by creating overnight success stories, Michael Parisi sees it differently.

[MICHAEL PARISI]: "Those shows have made a big impact. I heard Michael Gudinski say that you will never get a Bob Dylan or a Neil Young from any of these shows, but what you will get is kids wanting to do something about their music career. It stimulates the industry. It gets people back to buying music. Talent shows have always been there, but they are more prevalent now. But there have been more failures than success stories coming out of those shows. And not everyone wants to play that game.

But I don't think they are bad things provided the artist knows what they are getting themselves into."

Denis Handlin is quick to dispel the suggestion that television talent shows have replaced the A&R function at record companies.

[**DENIS HANDLIN**]: "The perception is clearly wrong and ill informed. In Sony Music's case, we have a leading local artists roster of acts we discovered from the live scene and even the internet. We also have acts signed via the TV formats. Also it should be understood that many of the acts coming through the TV shows have been active in the live scene or honing their recording and singing skills for a number of years. But the fact is, most of our local acts are discovered by our A&R team through our network of contacts in the market and from our artists' recommendations."

Mark Poston viewed the image of major labels as being unnecessarily negative and emphasised the "team" approach to breaking an artist as one of the most rewarding aspects of that environment when he was working in the major label environment.

[**MARK POSTON**]: "There is always going to be a place for major labels and when we had interns or when we employed people, they all think it's a great place and they learn a lot and they find that people really care about music. They find that it can be a really great career path and that there are a lot of good opportunities. The great and beautiful thing about major labels is that you get a whole team of people that are working towards developing an artist's career or having a successful record. It was great and really pleasing when we had artists in the building and when we got together with the artists and

WELCOME TO THE JUNGLE

> their managers and they felt that. As cheesy as that sounds, it is really powerful. It's got a bit cool to be dismissive of that and I understand why some people prefer to be "indie", but there is something really powerful and attractive about a whole company that is working together to try and break an act."

John Watson is able to see through the emotion and bear down on the rational argument.

> **[JOHN WATSON]:** "Labels can still play an important role for artists, but they're often less central these days than they once were. The traditional label model probably works best these days for pure pop music which is still driven largely by mass-media exposure and brand associations, so if you're keen to work with those sorts of artists and in that sort of model, then a major label is a good place to learn the ropes. It's very hard work though as, typically, they have smaller staffs due to declining sales of recorded music. As such, most of the people there work incredibly long hours under quite trying conditions.
> Personally, the four years I spent working at a major label in the early 1990s were incredibly formative. I learned a lot and am incredibly grateful for the experience. These days I'm not sure it would be as much fun as it was back then though."

Major labels are, by definition, big corporations. And big corporations are driven by great leadership, whether that leadership takes the form of inspirational and charismatic individuals, or processes fine-tuned to produce results. For Denis Handlin, major labels provide great opportunities for people with leadership qualities to emerge and build rewarding careers.

> **[DENIS HANDLIN]:** "There are no prerequisites —the key attributes will always be a mix of instinct, passion, experience

and constant learning. The best leaders will make it their business to learn the business and create business. They will invariably know what they don't know and create teams with the required mix of skills that work in a united way to achieve the best results for our artists. Leaders will always know that the biggest room in the world is the room for improvement and create an environment where constant reinvention, learning and creativity is in place."

My Path into the Industry

SCOT CRAWFORD

"As a youngster I took an interest in both music and film and I pretty much made a decision at that stage of my life that it was a career path that I would like to follow. From there I went on to form a band at the age of 15 or 16 years of age and then I got an independent record deal at the age of 17. So I got experience as an artist in dealing with a record label, and as a songwriter dealing with publishing, as well as performance. When I got to the age of 19 I decided that the next thing for me to do was retail. I worked for HMV in retail for three or four years in product roles and later in store management roles. The next progressive step was usually into record companies. I was approached by BMG to become a road rep for them and I was known as the guy who was slanted more towards independent music. I got a call from Shock back then to be a product manager. From there I went across to MDS in an A&R role, which is what everybody wanted to do. I got swallowed into the larger Festival Mushroom family and looked after label management and A&R with Michael Parisi. I realised that my forte was more marketing and strategy and I became a strategic marketing manager for Festival/Mushroom. I went off and did a bit of time in sports media which wasn't at all my passion, but it got me involved in the technology side because the company I worked for did a lot of mobile technology development and ran the AFL websites. It was brilliant for me because it was a real escape from what I had done for a while and I had always been interested in the technology side of things. Shock wanted me to come back in a marketing role and so I came back to the music industry."

CHAPTER 9

INDEPENDENT RECORD COMPANIES AND DISTRIBUTORS

Although this chapter includes examinations of the roles of independent record labels and independent distributors, the two types of businesses are very different in their functions and objectives. They are considered together though, because the services they provide to recording artists are closely linked.

An independent record label or company provides services to recording artists pursuant to a wide variety of types of contracts that enable them to release the artist's music for sale to the public. The deals that they use range from providing funding to make recordings and all the services necessary in bringing those recordings to the market, through to deals that do not involve significant financial investment, but offer services that effectively partner with the artist for the release of that music. Depending on what investment or services they provide, independent labels may acquire ownership or part ownership in the copyright in the sound recording and their rights may be for a limited period of time or a restricted territory. Independent labels rarely, if ever, have the means to distribute the recordings themselves, especially physical products such as CDs. In the digital age, an indie label may well be able to place an artist's music on iTunes or on streaming services, but the ability to distribute physical product into music retailers is something they have neither the facilities nor the systems to do.

This role is played by a specialist business called a distributor. The biggest and most powerful distributors in the music business are, of course, the major record companies – Sony, Universal and Warner.

WELCOME TO THE JUNGLE

These companies have the size and the amount of recordings in their catalogue to maintain the infrastructure necessary to provide distribution services; a sales team, warehousing and freight and the administrative services to support these roles. In the era prior to digital distribution, any artist or label that wanted to get their CDs (or cassettes or vinyl) into the hands of the public via music retailers needed to strike up a relationship with a music distributor, either major or independent, and rely on them to do that job effectively.

The distribution deal is very simple. The distributor provides the sales, warehousing and freight services and keeps a fee for what they sell. It's a business model far from unique to the music industry and it's common across just about any business where physical products need to be delivered to retailers. Music distribution is really just a wholesale business.

The distribution facilities of major labels are not infinite and they are not willing or able to distribute everyone's releases. It's no surprise that the releases that take priority are those that are owned by the company itself and those it has invested in. Titles owned by other companies are inevitably lower in the pecking order for major label distributors.

This situation led to the formation of companies providing distribution services alone, to customers who may not have been able to achieve a distribution deal with a major label, or actively chose not to seek one – these customers were primarily independent labels and independent artists.

Internationally there are numerous independent distributors, while in Australia, only a small number of companies exist in that area, but those companies are well established.

[NICK O'BYRNE]: "Just like the majors, independent labels and distributors are not making as much money as they used to from selling recorded music. Most of them that are surviving are diversifying their business. On a lower level you've got a proliferation of very strong businesses entering the market. It's almost become two-tiered. You have strong small businesses with great ideas, really great labels that otherwise wouldn't have access to market are starting to peak up."

In this Chapter you will hear from an array of independents including the phenomenally successful Remote Control (Harvey Saward), a couple with major label funding or ties Dew Process (Paul Piticco) and Wunderkind (Michael Parisi), Australia's chart-topping EDM indie Future Classic (Nathan McLay), three truly independent operators Misteltone (Sophie Miles), Rice Is Nice (Julia Wilson) and Bedroom Suck (Joe Alexander) and three independent labels operating as part of larger music businesses UNFD (Jaddan Comerford), Illusive (Adam Jankie) and Midnight Feature (Mark Dodds). And we will get the global indie perspective from Merlin's Charles Caldas. That shows how diverse the term "indie label" really is.

Independent Record Labels

Australia has a long history of creative, resilient and influential independent record companies. From labels like Fable in the 1960s and '70s through to Mushroom, Regular and rooArt in the '80s and '90s and more recent labels like Eleven, Modular and Dew Process, Australian independents have been a highly attractive alternative for artists and their managers. Newer labels like UNFD, Future Classic, Golden Era, Mistletone, Rice Is Nice and I Oh You look set to continue that tradition

Working in independent labels has also been a vital career step for many successful people in the industry. For many, it's also the end game. Owning and operating a label is one of the most exciting prospects for anyone who loves music and while it's among the toughest challenges in the music business, it's also possibly the most rewarding.

WELCOME TO THE JUNGLE

Julia Wilson started her indie label Rice Is Nice with a graphic designer partner after she left the safer confines of Mushroom Records in 2008.

> **[JULIA WILSON]:** "I love all the people I worked with and I really respect them but I just saw a way of doing things differently and on a smaller scale. I don't have to have so many cooks involved and if I want to do something I just do it. It's DIY and I think that's the exciting thing about it. Working for a boss or a business means you don't have that freedom and that's what I like about Rice Is Nice, It would be great if one of the artists blew up but there is never any pressure for any of them to do that."

Joe Alexander's label Bedroom Suck was started out of a desire to get his friends records heard, or at least in a position to be heard. Those artists have included Totally Mild, Boomgates, Blank Realm, Bitch Prefect, Terrible Truths and others.

> **[JOE ALEXANDER]:** "I had a visual arts and music background. I did a Bachelor of Fine Arts at QUT in Brisbane and that was my thing for a while. I worry constantly that I don't have the marketing know-how or the business know-how, so I'm trying to learn by observing and speaking to people. But I feel like I'm getting a grasp on how the world works. I thought about rewinding and going back to school and getting a marketing qualification or something, but I haven't yet. There's a lot happening now with the label and I don't want to put in on hold. So I'm learning by doing."

Starting a label, and signing all your favourite bands, and imposing your immaculate musical taste on the masses is a romantic notion, but it pays to remember that the reality of it is that you are starting and operating a small business, with responsibilities that go with it. The responsibilities are not just to yourself (and your backers or investors if you happen to have any), but also to the artists who are signed to your label.

Michael Parisi operated a successful imprint in the '90's called Sputnik that signed artists such as 28 Days, Machine Gun Fellatio and Motor Ace, and now has another label, Wunderkind, that has been home to artists like Owl Eyes and Stonefield

> **[MICHAEL PARISI]:** "You absolutely have a responsibility to the artists you sign, but realistically you are going to make mistakes. But the better labels are the ones who make less mistakes. We second guess the market; we second guess the media. When I was the general manager of Imago Records I was doing A&R, accounting, everything. It was quite daunting, but I'm glad I was thrown in the deep end at that label."

Former Head of AIR Nick O'Byrne recommends starting a label as a fast track to getting your feet wet in the industry.

> **[NICK O'BYRNE]:** "If you go out there and you have some nous and you have some taste and you have some conviction you can build something that starts to get people's attention. A great example is I Oh You, or what happened with Jaddan Comerford's label Boomtown. He had a really good idea and stuck with it. I've seen lots of people do that now because they had the time and dedication to do that. It does take some knowledge, but the best way to learn is just to go out and release some music. What we found with a lot of AIR members is that they have learned their business through instinct and by doing it and the technicalities come a bit later on. That's not a bad way of going about it, but at the same time you don't want to be naive and be caught with a whole bunch of costs that you are not ready for."

WELCOME TO THE JUNGLE

[JULIA WILSON]: "I always wanted it to continue and I always wanted to have the label, but I'm not sure exactly how or why it has continued! So I expected it to exist but I didn't expect it to be this thing that it seems to be morphing into which is more of a supportive network for the artists than a typical record company. The artists all do things for each other or help with each other's records or videos, because that's the way you need to be. Maybe it is a money thing, because they can't all afford to be out-sourcing, session musicians or video directors. It's definitely a community thing and I think that's important for Australian music. I don't think about charts or record sales, so I don't make much money. I make some money through synch and those sorts of things but not from record sales. All of our artists are independent and they are all a little bit 'left' – that's the appeal to me. They are all quite varied but they all seem to make sense together even if genre-wise they are all different."

For Michael Parisi, one of the important considerations in operating an independent label is managing the expectations of artists and their representatives. It's not a case of the indies being better or worse than a major – but the services they are offer are different.

[MICHAEL PARISI]: "The biggest challenge – if you are a real indie label – is money and finance. There is a big misconception among artists that indies are going to do more for you, but they don't really have the muscle to do that. Even though indies do fight the good fight, they are still up against it. But the good thing about indies is that they can be flexible because they are masters of their own destiny. They can move quicker with the times and with social media channels. That's something that most majors don't have."

Paul Piticco has a similar perspective.

ANDREW WATT

[**PAUL PITICCO**]: "The internet and streaming services particularly have started to break certain media's stranglehold on developing artists. The playing field has not been completely levelled between the indies and the majors, but it is flatter than it probably has ever been. I think indie labels are evolving and adapting very quickly and I am excited by the next five to 10 years. Baby labels can have global reach easily these days and that is what [record label] Create/Control is all about – helping those labels and creating that infrastructure."

The positivity that Piticco provides is echoed on a global level by Charles Caldas in his guise as the head of Merlin, the umbrella organisation for independent labels.

[**CHARLES CALDAS**]: "In the last three years we have really cemented what we do for independent labels globally. We have had more labels joining from the main markets but we have also broadened our label base. We have 730 members from 49 territories whereas initially we only had ten or fifteen territories represented. We now have members from Nepal and Columbia and Indonesia which I think is an indication of the music market. In the last two years two thirds of the companies that responded to our survey said that their business was growing year on year and 82% of them said they were highly optimistic about the future."

As discussed in Chapter 6, Mistletone is an interesting example of the formation of an independent label. Originally started to release an album from an artist they wanted to tour who had no distribution in Australia, the label has blossomed. Now the challenge is to keep the roster manageable.

[**SOPHIE MILES**]: "We say no to so many good releases these days, just because it's so hard to sell records, so we need to be cautious. With overseas releases, it's usually a symbiotic

WELCOME TO THE JUNGLE

relationship as we look after both the label and touring side of things, this cuts out some middle men and makes budgets leaner for everyone. Our local artists are the heart of our label and we are very proud to work with outstanding Australian artists such as HTRK, Luluc, Montero, The Orbweavers, Ross McLennan and Wintercoats."

Despite the passion driven nature of independents there is a global recognition that independents need to band together on a number of levels.

In 2014 Australian independent labels and distributors including Future Classic, We Are Unified, the Mushroom Group, Inertia, Rice Is Nice, Elefant Traks and MGM signed up to a global declaration demanding a 'fair go' for indies regarding digital deals.

Global independent trade organisation, the Worldwide Independent Network's Fair Digital Deals Declaration was set up in response the YouTube's highly controversial 'take-it-or-leave-it' negotiations regarding their new streaming service. Over 900 companies from around the world have now signed up to ensure that digital download and streaming revenues are clear and proper for indie labels and artists.

"This declaration is about independent labels stating loud and clear that it is important that Artists are paid fairly and transparently under these complicated deals," Mushroom Group's Warren Costello said at the time. "One clear benefit for artists is that the label signatories need to ensure that their artists receive a share of any income paid on an entire catalogue basis, which in the past some labels may have kept to themselves,"

AIR Chairman David Vodicka also commented, "Increasingly, the majors seek to bury their obligations to repatriate funds to their artists, without whom they would have no business," This isn't a path that the independents seek to endorse and in fact see it as a great opportunity in promoting this attitude as a key selling point to working with independent record labels."

Independent Label Perspectives

Remote Control is one of the great success stories of Australian music. Formed by Harvey Saward and Steve Cross "with the intention to support under-represented music". Both came from A&R backgrounds at Shock and Festival Mushroom. In its first 15 years, Remote Control released records from artists such as The White Stripes, Adele, The National, Dirty Three, Sally Seltmann, Radiohead, The XX, Vampire Weekend, Wolf & Cub, Dizzee Rascal, M.I.A. Kurt Vile, The Mountain Goats Belle & Sebastian, Alabama Shakes and Interpol through a series of deals with international labels, in particular Beggars Group. In that relationship it's simply a case of the minds meeting.

> **[HARVEY SAWARD]:** "Very much so. We've worked with them for a long time and we admire what Martin Mills (Beggars charismatic owner) has done and he is very supportive of what we do down here. He's a great partner in terms of the advice that he can give us as business people. At times we might feel a bit disconnected from the people at the coalface signing the bands. Australia is still a long way away from the US and the UK and so sometimes we need to wait for a while and be patient and see what might work for us. There haven't been too many examples of things that have worked here that haven't worked there first. Sometimes we have artists that might have fallen outside the label where we originally worked with them and we'll continue to work with them directly."

Jaddan Comerford saw his label Boomtown eventually evolve and grow into what became UNFD, which remains a label, but under the same banner also offers artist management, label services (including

WELCOME TO THE JUNGLE

distribution and marketing), merchandise, publishing and business management. But the Boomtown label was what gave Comerford the calling card to commence his evolution through the industry, which led to the multi-business structure over which he presides.

> [JADDAN COMERFORD]: "I remember my first trip to Sydney about ten years ago when our lawyer introduced me to a whole lot of people. I went around and met these A&R people and publishers and I really didn't know what I was doing. We had an office launch party in Sydney a few years ago and I was talking to one of those people and now he is chasing me for business. I think we've networked quite well. We exist in our own space, but we do see the value of the wider industry, on a political level as well. We are not here to make enemies, we want to exist in the wider industry."

The Illusive label, operated by Adam Jankie and Matt Gudinski, shares some similarities with the UNFD operation. Illusive started as a touring company, but became a label when they realised some of the local acts they had opening for international acts were in need of label services. They originally started as a hip-hop label whereas UNFD has operated more in a punk genre, although in recent years has successfully broadened into other genres.

> [ADAM JANKIE]: "At that point hip-hop was so minimal in Australia that it would be the same three or four acts that would be the support act for any international hip-hop show. One of those acts was Bliss n Eso. After a few tours with these local acts, we started to realise that there was no proper outlet in Australia for their music or for urban music in general. We made an active decision to start a record label and sign a couple of acts and try and develop them. We'd worked with Bliss n Eso on a couple of tours and when their deal with

Obese expired we told them that we'd be keen to get them on our label and they were keen as well. At that time they'd sold six or seven thousand records, which was big for hip-hop in Australia, where just getting a record deal was unheard of, let alone getting a song on radio. An act that got a record deal was regarded as top of the food chain in Australia. The first record we released with them sold 12,000-13,000 units which in a physical market that was already starting to decline overall was pretty good. I started representing them on their tours and we got very involved on every level. All of a sudden we were their label, management, booking agent and helping out with their merchandising. It became a team, them and us."

Paul Piticco's Dew Process however is notably genre "un-specific", something that has been a deliberate approach from the label's inception, something made possible by Piticco's inclusive approach to his team.

[PAUL PITICCO]: "It's driven by the people in the building and their taste….no one persona specifically and I love it that way. It makes for a very broad array of artists. The important thing is that no matter what the music sounds like, we are trying to build careers and music that will stand the test of time in its genre. I think the diversity has also been part of the reason for its longevity. It transcends trends; it can move with them, but isn't beholden to them."

While the Mistletone label reflects the taste of its founders what seems to have defined the label is that the artists it works with are tremendously loyal. The label has grown but some of its artists have grown relatively faster and yet they seem content to maintain the relationships that nurtured them. It's almost the blueprint for the nature of a great independent label.

WELCOME TO THE JUNGLE

[SOPHIE MILES]: "We are very grateful that our artists have taken us with them as they have grown. For example, we have been with Beach House from the very start, and it has been a great joy to work with them as they have grown into a "big" band. They are the same people and so are we, so the way we work together is the same. It's more complex now, and our team has grown, but that's all good; we have all learned together as the band has increased its audience year after year. It has been a gradual process of growing from labour of love to serious business, so it's been relatively painless as we have grown organically and adjusted as we go along."

For Future Classic, a label that has established an incredible footprint in the electronic genre spearheaded by Flume and Chet Faker, the aesthetic of the label is important but it's never allowed to become more important than its artists.

[NATHAN McLAY]: "Our artists are what matters. Our own aesthetic and brand sits behind our artists and obviously we have a quality control that creates an aesthetic more broadly speaking. Jay Ryves our art director does a brilliant job of maintaining a standard and process to each project visually while from a music perspective we hope there's no one defining sound but rather again a unifying intangible element that connects everything."

Even for a label as successful as Remote Control developing that sense of community around the label is important.

[HARVEY SAWARD]: "That's something we have worked on the last couple of years as we have become more focussed on trying to build up a local roster. We've got great people out and about seeing bands and wanting to sign bands and we've tried to create an environment where they can do that. That's coming to fruition now."

In 2014 noted music company and distributor Inertia established a new imprint label under the supervision of A&R expert Mark Dodds. The label, Midnight Feature, promised to be an exciting artist destination. For Dodds, the creation of a new label needs to handled with equal parts care and passion.

> **[MARK DODDS]**: "In a marketing sense, I think early signings establish as label's personality. Broadly speaking, I don't think audiences care about labels. Audiences care about artists. If they care about enough artists coming from one place, they start to trust and care about a label. In that sense, a label's signings are integral to establishing a brand identity - the signings are the prism through which listeners will come to understand the imprint. That said, in truer cultural sense, I think a label's personality determines early signings. It mightn't be on the public radar, but a good label has personalities behind it from Day 1. These personalities drive the discovery of repertoire and how it's executed. If early signings are driven by passion, you shouldn't need to think too hard about signing "the right things" early to establish an identity. The personality already exists - and will come to make sense to more people over time."

Business Operations

Like any small business, an independent label needs to understand where to position itself in the market. It's all very well for a label owner to love every band that is signed to their label, but it's just as important to know how to market both those artists and the label itself as a business. Some business skills can be learned on the job, while others are common to the operation of other small business and thus can be acquired in a more formal environment.

WELCOME TO THE JUNGLE

[MICHAEL PARISI]: "If you want to start a label from scratch and you want to be the head of that label, then you need to understand everything about the business. You need to understand A&R, but you also need to understand accounting. You need to have people skills and know how to form relationships and you need to have a social presence. You need to have tenacity above everything else because it can be a long, slow, lonely road at times. It's not for the faint-hearted. You need to be passionate not just about the artists you are signing, but also about the business side of it. Business is very important. That's where it's worth doing a music course – to understand the fundamentals of how royalty accounting works and how publishing works and things like that. If you want to start a label I'd say, do a music business course."

[JOE ALEXANDER]: "For me the business side of things is more of a challenge. I feel like I've got a good handle on the creative side. But as you get into running your own small business the day-to-day stuff is a bit of a burden. But I worry more about the marketing side and how to get the music out there and get people to pay attention. At a label of our size you do become label, manager, booking agent, producer – you do everything which is great but it can be detrimental if you cant get it all done the way it should be done. I'm trying to learn how to bring people on board. We have a great team of young interns that have the same enthusiasm that we do about it."

Nick O'Byrne has observed that tertiary qualifications are not essential when operating a label and opportunities exist for people looking to contribute at a label level if they show the right attitude.

[NICK O'BYRNE]: "Marketing is a very important aspect of running an independent label. Some people have a natural flair for it that can be developed as they are running their business. I don't think a small indie would look at a person's uni degree if they were hiring their third or fourth staff member. That might get you an internship and if it goes really well for six months that would lead potentially into a job. But for me it's about self-motivation and your ability to find and make your own work within that business. A bigger business might be looking for someone with a more specific skill to fill a particular job, in which case you probably would need a degree, but I don't think that exists in indie world."

Perhaps the biggest challenge for an independent label comes with success. For Future Classic the success of artists like Chet Faker and Flume has taken them to a new level.

[NATHAN McLAY]: "For nearly the first 5 years of Future Classic I was working at Inertia for a day job while DJing a couple of times a week. In close to ten years there's been a lot of hard work combined with a DIY mentality about asking questions and trying things to learn how they work, getting inside projects be they A&R or running a tour or event. It's not easy to plan for that level of success but we're getting better at pivoting to what is required based on what's happening in a campaign and being adaptive."

For Julia Wilson at Rice Is Nice the label supplements its sales of music by bundling music with other products such as merchandise. It gives the label a character as well as more diverse product offering. She also supplements the label's operation by other related work.

[JULIA WILSON]: "I believe that people still want something tangible so perhaps that's me being an advocate for people purchasing something from bands other than just something digital. When everything is digitized you are losing that element of getting something from the band that is personal. Once they

WELCOME TO THE JUNGLE

have a tote bag or a cassette it gives their relationship with that band a bit more of a life or a talking point, rather than them just being in your computer. Sometimes we'll do a run of totes, rather than say vinyl as a cost thing if we cant be sure we are going to sell vinyl which is expensive.

I'm trying to talk to brands for income, I do music supervision as well and try and gets synchs for our music. It is hard to try and get paid running a label. I don't do it full time and I've had times when I think I don't want to do this anymore. But then something will happen and….off I go again!"

Deal Structures

One of the interesting aspects of the new labels is that they are not locked into deals and contract structures that were invented 30 or 40 years ago, in a completely different climate. Major label contracts emerged in a time when the four key elements – recording, manufacture, marketing and distribution – were vastly different than they are today. Independent labels naturally borrowed some of the key parameters from these contracts and it led to a proliferation of recording contracts that bore little relation to reality.

[JADDAN COMERFORD]: "Any old-world things that we picked up, we evaluated. We got old contracts from lawyers and things and we looked at them and went "Are you serious? That's not how you sign a band". We still make money signing bands the way we sign them, but it's totally different to the old way. Somebody said recently that there has never been a better time to start a record company than right now because the opportunities are there to correct the new way of doing deals. I wanted to try and make the deals shorter. One of my favorite things to do every six months is to actually pay royalties, rather than send out statements telling artists how unrecouped they are! I guess we just try to gear it in a way that everyone can make some money and everyone feels that they are getting something out of it rather than just a good vibe and a couple of free beers at the pub."

Paul Piticco operates three labels; Dew Process, Create/Control and Nook Nook, the latter being a singles-only imprint of Create/Control, but which also includes sponsorship, synching and touring/festival opportunities for the artists it works with. The two main labels operate differently. Dew Process has funding from Universal and offers different deals to the artists on the label compared with the more "license oriented" Create/Control model. In late 2013 Create Control announced label relationships with three influential American indie labels: Arts & Crafts, Vagrant and Innovative Leisure, indicating that its model had evolved from simply direct artist relationships into a role of representing like-minded labels from around the world.

> **[PAUL PITICCO]:** "I think Create/Control is a hybrid of a few things; it's a 50/50 license model; it's a services company. It's still a label in the sense we select what is released. I hope it captures the zeitgeist with regards to how bands and managers are starting to think. Do I want someone else to own my work? Some say 'Yes, it's OK if they pay for it' and some say 'No'. I guess we have a label in Dew Process for one group and a label in Create/Control for another."

With even indie labels now the ability to reach out and release records internationally has changed the way they look at signing bands.

> **[JULIA WILSON]:** "Originally when I started licensing bands I thought I'd just do Australia and New Zealand to keep the pressure off me and then I wasn't across the digital landscape as much. Now when I sign a band I kinda have to have

worldwide rights. I might generate a lot of PR here and that's going to get them something in the States. There is that potential. But if a band on my label get an offer from a huge label or whatever I'm not going to stand in the way because that ultimately going to be beneficial for me and their previous records. But the reality is that it is so hard to get any presence and if we are building it here the label and the band can do this whole thing together."

[JOE ALEXANDER]: " For the label to grow we have to be able to take the music overseas so we do sign our bands for the world. Originally it was all handshake agreements, but we recently started to get something done on paper – which is a really good idea! Generally the bands will own the master having paid for the recording themselves and we will license it from them for a term and hopefully for the world. Most of the bands self-manage and pay for the recording themselves through shows or merchandise sales or crowd funding. They are really independent."

Internationally for all the changes in the positioning of majors and indies, much remains the same. Peter Leak has been doing deals with international major labels for almost a quarter of a century and he's seen many things change. However the key determinant of the deal an artist receives from a record company remains what it has always been – the relative bargaining position of the artist.

[PETER LEAK]: "There is some more flexibility, but it depends what level an artist is at and where they are in their career when they approach the label. I think that a new artist approaching a major label is still not going to get a very good deal if they don't have very much going on, on their own, and it might not be the best situation for them actually. A major label often doesn't know how to start an artist off on a developing process, so I think it's up to the manager and often indie labels to start something off before it's even ready for a major label. If you go to a major when they really want you and ideally when there is competition, then I would think certain labels are open to cutting different kinds of deals, or even not signing things for the world which would not have happened a few years ago. But I would say that it's not vastly better for an artist now doing a deal with a major than it used to be unless there are labels fighting over the artist. And the money is a lot less actually – the amount of money that labels are prepared to spend on most things, but that's not necessarily a bad thing either."

Manager-Driven Labels

A number of independent labels begin life as vehicles for artists or managers who want to self-release recordings, and in this respect the idea of starting a label is something that managers should consider. Traditionally, managers are important sources of A&R and this often leads them to form independent labels, either by themselves or with the support of majors.

> **[NICK O'BYRNE]:** "It normally starts with a manager saying, 'No one is giving us a deal we want or we are not ready to sign a deal yet, so we are going to self release this album.' That leads to the artist and the manager acting like a label. A lot of AIR member labels are self-released artists. Paul Kelly is a member of AIR because he pays for all his own recordings, but it's Bill Cullen (Kelly's manager) that does all the administration of it. At some stage the manager has to say, 'OK, we can now get a better label deal for you than we can do by being the label ourselves'.

WELCOME TO THE JUNGLE

The End Game

Traditionally the business purpose of operating an independent label was twofold. Certainly label operators are hoping to sign artists and own or control recordings that generate income; at least enough to keep the doors of the label open. And as has been the case with many international indies, one very big artist can sustain a label for a long time. Then there is the second objective – to build a label that attracts the attention of a bigger company, usually a major label, who will come along and buy the label and its valuable copyrights – rewarding the label owner for the years of hard slog.

> **[MICHAEL PARISI]:** "My intention was always to do something with a major because they have the muscle. Working with a major allows a small operation like mine to utilise a team of 65 people in Australia alone. The end game for an independent is to either have a massive hit that keeps you in business for the next 10 years or you get to the point of finding a partner who might potentially buy you out in the end. The other thing that will happen – and its only a matter of time – is that three or four indies will partner up and start their own virtual major."

For Remote Control, an indie that continues to invest in staff and infrastructure, it's essential that there be the occasional hit come through the pipeline. It's a long time between Adele albums!

> **[HARVEY SAWARD]:** "It's pretty important in terms of being able to employ people and grow our levels of staff. Primarily our role is the promotion and marketing of the music and that's become a much bigger job than when we started in 2001. The traditional media is still around but now there is all this new media as well. We started off as Steve and myself, one

publicist and someone going to Triple J for us in Sydney. Now it's Steve and I and about six publicists! You wouldn't want to have two or three years without a couple of really big selling records!"

Michael Gudinski enjoyed the experience of selling his record company Mushroom to News Ltd in the '90s. It was a once-in-a-lifetime deal and now he has the luxury of having a broader perspective on the rewards of operating a record company.

[MICHAEL GUDINSKI]: "There are independents and there are independents. There are people who are independent, but they are relying on money from a major, and then there are those who are truly independent using their own money. Then there are people who are scraping together money and it's week-to-week to feed yourself. When you are independent you've got the liberty of being a lot more of a leader. The end game to me is to enjoy what you are doing, break new artists, work with artists that appreciate you, be honest with them and do your best for the artists, whatever part of the business you are in. I never had an end game. It might look like it was much more planned than it was."

In late 2013, Australian Music Industry Network (AMIN) announced a great initiative called Release, a five-stage program designed to help independent label owners from Australia and New Zealand grow their businesses. It's an educational and mentoring program (including residential labs and workshops) that aims to help independent label owners operate in a more professional way and benefit from the advice of experienced industry operators. In a similar way that the Control program assists emerging managers, the Release program is a positive step in the evolution of the Australian indie label landscape.

WELCOME TO THE JUNGLE

[MATT GUDINSKI]: "There's always going to be room for alternatives and there's always going to be room for independents."

Independent Distribution

The role of independent distribution has tended to reflect the retail landscape. The more retailers there are, the greater the need for businesses that service those retailers and provide them with the product range that they want to sell. Australia has had many distribution companies operate over the years and not surprisingly many of these emerged at a time when the retail market was buoyant and consumers were buying recorded music in physical formats and in large numbers. Back in the '70's and '80's, major retailers such as Brashs and Allans had numerous stores and music was a big part of their business, and just about every suburban shopping centre had an independent record store, usually operated by knowledgeable and enthusiastic staff. Through the '90's, Australian retail was dominated by the Sanity chain, which took a modern approach to retail – high energy, young staff, active promotion and tough bargaining with distributors. International retailers such as HMV and Virgin opened big retail outlets in capital cities, but a number of strong independent retailers still managed to hold their place in the market due to having specialist knowledge or 'alternative credibility'.

In this strong retail environment, it was understandable that new distributors would arrive on the scene to service both the large-volume retailers and the numerous labels and artists that were releasing music that couldn't get into the catalogues of major labels' distribution arms.

A number of small distributors such as Musicland were set up, but the business of independent distribution really kicked up a notch with the formation of an offshoot of the Mushroom Group, called MDS

ANDREW WATT

(Mushroom Distribution Service). In subsequent years this company was joined by Hot, Shock, Rocket, MGM and Inertia, among others. There were also distributors that specialised in genres such as jazz, classical, country or folk that did big business.

These distributors were fantastic launch pads for many careers. There are numerous people interviewed in this book that got their start at MDS or Shock, including some, like Charles Caldas, that have gone on to take prominent places on the world stage.

However, the business of a music distributor has changed. While they are still a vital link between the labels (and artists) and retail, there is a lot less physical retail to deal with. Sanity is a very much smaller operation now than it was, with a very limited range and there are now very few independent retailers – although those that survive are much-loved destinations for music buyers. JB Hi-Fi is clearly the biggest customer for music distributors, but their recorded music sections are shrinking, as higher-margin product ranges like electronics and computers take up more floorspace. Interestingly the space allocated to higher priced vinyl is increasing. Big department stores such as Myer maintain only a token selection of music.

It's a pattern that has been seen globally.

David Williams is one of the most experienced people in the independent distribution business in the country. He sold out of the business he founded, Shock, in 2012 and now operates his own touring and consultancy business. He is well placed to consider the role of independent distributors in the current climate.

> **[DAVID WILLIAMS]:** "There's always going to be room for independent sales and marketing. The actual physical distribution of it can be given to someone who is just involved in

WELCOME TO THE JUNGLE

warehousing and, in fact, that is potentially the more sensible way to do it. You can spend a lot of time having to deal with the operational side of making sure that there are discs getting put in the boxes and going out and getting into the stores. I do believe, though, that there is scope for independent sales, marketing and publicity companies. Maybe there are too many of them in the market now. When Shock started out there wasn't too many others doing this, and then for a while there was MDS. There was enough for both of us, but in the end MDS was merged into the whole Mushroom Festival deal and there wasn't anyone again. Now you have MGM predominantly working Australian artists and you've got Inertia and you've got Fuse doing a fair amount of imported product. Against that you've got JB Hi-Fi taking less and less new releases."

Inertia is one of the most proactive companies in the distribution business, largely because managing director Colin Daniels doesn't see it as being in the distribution business. Daniels views Inertia as a business providing services to artists and labels, one of which is distribution. His comment below has already featured in this book, because it applies to most businesses in the industry but it bears repeating in relation to how he sees Inertia.

[COLIN DANIELS]: "We used to be a distribution company, now we are a service company. We help [artists] with making music, with touring, with merchandise. We'll do their accounts for them if that's what they need. It's about what the artists need. It's our job to do what they need us to do and that will constantly change. There will always be content creators and there will always be a content business and in reality that is about the artist. You have people that create content and then you have a servicing industry built around that. I'm not in a circle of creating content, I'm in a circle of servicing content."

ANDREW WATT

David Williams sees the role of the distributor in a similar way now, and the smart operators have embraced the new world rather than bemoaning the reduction in physical outlets.

> **[DAVID WILLIAMS]:** "The positive element about what independents have to offer to artists and labels is that they do try to provide the best service they can for who they take on. You do end up with product people who are trying to do the utmost for every release and it's almost like they are trying too hard, because they can't provide the service any more, simply because the retailers can't take all those releases. Artists expect them to do wonders and get their CD into every JB Hi-Fi and every independent shop and when that doesn't happen, they think that the distributor is not doing their job, when the problem actually is that there just isn't enough interest from the retailer to carry that title.
> Distributors are quite dynamic in the digital market and that's where more of the focus will go. I think that long term there will still be a physical market but maybe there will be another specialist player that can deal in that market. If you look at vinyl and the growth in vinyl sales, that's a specialist market and potentially CDs will go the same way. There will be some demand, but it will be specialist and there will be scope for more successful independent retailers again as physical product becomes more niche."

The international landscape for distributors is under threat. It's a simple mathematical exercise. Distributors are still essential for labels that rely on sales of physical product. Until recently, that meant just about every label. The distributors have been able to use that to leverage the labels into granting them the right to digitally distribute product as well – even though digital distribution is something the labels could probably handle themselves. But as physical sales decline, some labels are beginning to question the wisdom of giving distributors a slice of digital revenue.

My Path into the Industry

IAN JAMES

"My first job was at APRA in 1976. It was an advertisement in the *Sydney Morning Herald* for a licensing representative to go and talk to the people who ran the venues, the jeans shops and the pubs. It wasn't a senior position by any means. I would have completely missed it except for the fact that my wife knew someone who used to work at APRA and had pointed me in the direction of applying for the job. I didn't get it because I had no qualifications or experience whatsoever in the music business, but what I did have was a degree in economics. That told them something about the fact I could think and talk and add up. I was fortunate in that the person they chose for the job was a booking agent who spent the rest of the week continuing to book his own bands and was fired at the end of the week. That was pretty much the pattern at the time – you had to get into the business by accident or at least by some fortuitous series of circumstances. That was mine. The interesting twist in the plot was that about three months later the licensing manager told me that he was resigning and that I'd be running licensing in Australia for APRA. When I was 25 that was a rather large task to take on board. I'd still had no training whatsoever in any aspect of the music business."

Chapter 10

Publishing, Synchronisation and Music Supervision

The business of music publishing evolved from a very basic principle of copyright law and a very basic premise about songwriters. The legal principle is that songwriters are the creators and owners of copyright in the work that they do – songs – and they are entitled to benefit from any situation where their work is used; reproduction in any form, public broadcast, or performance or adaptation for any purpose. In reality, most songwriters don't have the time, the resources or the inclination to identify or collect what is rightfully theirs.

The core functions of a music publisher are to carry that burden on behalf of their songwriters to maximise the value of those entitlements and ensure that the assets – the copyright in the songs – are protected from infringement or other damage. The business model of a music publisher is to provide those services in return for a fee that will normally include a slice of the revenue they collect on behalf of the songwriter, and often a share in the copyright in those songs, at least for a period of time.

If that paragraph makes sense, you are a long way towards understanding what is traditionally one of the most creatively important, economically viable and financially significant parts of the music business.

The prominence of the music publishing business as a part of the overall music industry landscape has varied over the years – but the reality is, music publishers have never been anything less than absolutely vital to the business structure of the industry and the business models on

WELCOME TO THE JUNGLE

which just about every segment is based. No record company can exist without knowing that mechanical royalties are payable to the songwriters whose songs are being recorded and released. No venue or music festival will operate for more than a very short time without being confronted by the fact that payments are due to the songwriters whose works are being performed at that location or event. No television or radio station can exist or no motion picture can be made that features any music at all, without a music publisher being involved.

The role of the music publisher is one of the most pervasive across the industry and yet for new people entering the business, it's sometimes an area they overlook or as Native Tongue publisher Jaime Gough says, "the fundamentals of what a publisher does are often one of the most misunderstood areas of the music industry."

Scope of Publishing and Key Concepts

There is a perception that publishing is one of the less adventurous and exciting areas of the business – it doesn't have the perceived glamour of working for a record company where you think you are going to be rubbing shoulders with deliriously talented artists on a daily basis, or the immediacy of concert promotion that brings the intoxicating adrenalin rush of seeing and hearing a crowd react to a band on stage. After all, one of the most-used phrases in the music publishing business is "copyright administration". How exciting could that possibly be?

The answer is – <u>very</u> exciting!

> [MARIANNA ANNAS]: "I believe that music publishing is the heartland, because I think great songwriting is the heartland of the whole music business. There is nothing more fantastic than working with great songwriters and great songs. It probably is a stable area, because when you work as a music publisher you manage rights in songs. There are various rights attached

ANDREW WATT

to songs and each of those rights has a corresponding income stream. You are working very multi-dimensionally as a music publisher. At a record label level it can get a bit linear – you are literally working with a recorded piece of music, which is only one of the formats that a song can be embodied in.

One minute I'm organising a co-writing session with one of my writers and someone else for someone's album. The next minute I'm getting them on to a songwriting camp for *The Voice*. The next minute I'm pitching one of their songs to someone in Nashville who is looking for songs. The next minute I am negotiating a synchronisation license for *Underbelly*, because they have gone nuts over one of my writer's CDs. Then I've got *Home & Away* wanting instrumental versions of someone's CD because they want versions of songs without vocals. Then I might be getting approached by someone elsewhere within the ABC, to suggest a writer to score sixty minutes of a documentary. That's all pretty diverse. And that's not counting the people that I am looking to sign and do publishing agreements with!"

A copyright work is created by songwriters when they write a song and the decision that a songwriter needs to make at some point in their career is whether they have a catalogue of copyright works that is large enough or in sufficient demand that they need help to administer it.

In the traditional publishing model when a publisher agrees to help a songwriter in administering and maximising the returns on their copyrights, they take ownership of those copyrights. The business of publishing has therefore been about consolidating a large collection of copyrights, and enhancing the value of that collection.

This business model was exemplified back in 1985 when Michael Jackson bought the publishing rights to 251 Beatles songs – ironically outbidding Paul McCartney himself. The purchase price was £47 million. The Beatles catalogue had been owned by a company named ATV

WELCOME TO THE JUNGLE

that had acquired a business called Northern Songs, which in turn had been the vehicle for the ownership of the Lennon-McCartney songs. It wasn't until 2008 that Jackson sold the catalogue to Sony. That catalogue has now been valued at somewhere between $400 million and a billion dollars, depending who you ask. Any valuation of a catalogue of songs though is able to be quantified – simply by estimating the revenue that flows from the exploitation of the songs to determine what that revenue is likely to be projected into the future. It's a calculation that doesn't require any subjective appreciation of the quality of the songs at all – in these circumstances, accountants rather than music critics are the arbiters of value

New Models

That model is under some challenge. An example of the new thinking is Kobalt Blue, the publishing company discussed briefly in Part 1. This company takes the view that publishers are service providers and their model should be more about being paid for the services they provide and less about what copyrights they can own.

> **[SIMON MOOR]:** "In the past companies have offered their services, but in return a songwriter would have to assign their copyright for at least 10 to 15 years and face giving up a fairly large slice of their income. That ultimately leads to a conflict of interest between the songwriter and the label or the publisher. In the services model there is no conflict of interest. There are often no or smaller risk advances which reduces any cause of conflict. Under the services model the interests are much closer aligned – and if they drift too far from being aligned the writer or artist can leave and take their copyright with them. Our model is based on a services model. We wrap our deals up into an administration type framework, and at the same time provide a suite of services – collection, creative services, and synchronsiation etc.

ANDREW WATT

The challenging conditions for the recorded music industry in the past couple of decades have laid the foundations for the Kobalt model. With record sales diminishing, the revenue coming to songwriters, via their publishers, from mechanical royalties, was also diminishing. This had the effect of reducing the publishing advances that publishers could pay songwriters, and then in turn these reduced advances caused songwriters to question the merit of giving away their copyrights to the publishers.

> **[JAIME GOUGH]:** "For almost twenty years now digital has been talked about as the thing that is going to change the industry but the overall industry revenue is increasing. Publishing used to be a very safe industry and in many ways it's still a safe industry. It used to be reliant heavily on mechanical income but when sales slowed down dramatically that chunk of mechanical revenue disappeared off the bottom line for music publishers. Some publishers took a while to adapt but eventually they all did and went more into the synchronization world as a way to make money from musical copyrights."

While traditional publishers do offer administration deals where they do not take ownership of the copyright, Simon Moor says this won't necessarily advantage the writer when they find their songs competing for attention with those of writers whose songs are owned by the publisher.

> **[SIMON MOOR]:** "The end result for a writer or artist who has done an admin deal under a traditional publishing model is that they may get their income collected and paid back to them, but any creative work or any sync work will be minimal because that publishing model favors writers where the publisher is getting paid three times as much as they are getting on an admin deal. If they have two songs, they will always go for the one they are getting 30% of, over the one they are getting

WELCOME TO THE JUNGLE

10% of. In our services model, all of our songs attract the same fee if they are placed in a film, so it comes down to the best song for the placement. That system works for everyone."

Marianna Annas believes the model of a publisher as a service provider is certainly upon us and this has implications for the importance of acquiring the copyright in the work – in the case of the publisher, in the song.

> **[MARIANNA ANNAS]:** "I think a lot of people have recognised that the demand is for services and possibly services that traditionally artists have felt they haven't adequately gained from record companies or publishers. If that's what artists want, then artists, record companies and publishers need to become less hung up on copyright ownership. You don't need to have worked with artists and creators for a very long to know that copyright ownership is quite coveted for that community. I think copyright ownership is totally overrated, but it's the Copyright Act that we have at the moment. It's structured around licenses and assignments and it's easy to get hung up on copyright ownership. If a deal is structured so that services are being provided and the remuneration for the creator's work is being adequately covered, then I think there is cause to argue that we need to be a bit more relaxed about copyright ownership."

The evolution continues though. Earlier in the book the business of Tunecore was introduced. With the advent of multiple platforms for digital music delivery, Tunecore emerged as a service that, for a small flat fee, could make artists' sound recordings available across those platforms. Tunecore also offers a publishing administration service. For a flat joining fee of US$75 plus 10% of the royalties they collect, Tunecore offers to collect publishing royalties from up to 13 different royalty streams in over 60 countries. Their marketing line is "you didn't become a musician to become an expert in copyright and foreign exchange". Like the closely related recording industry, the publishing industry is becoming increasingly about the provision of service and less about copyright ownership.

The Business of Publishing

While publishing can be an immensely satisfying area of the business, the business of publishing isn't easy. Legal knowledge needs to be combined with creative instincts. Because there is a perception that there is money to be made in publishing in a low-risk scenario there is often a temptation for record companies, management businesses or even tour promoters to establish a publishing division or subsidiary. It is usually a more difficult proposition than they expect. Mushroom Music's Ian James has seen a number of start-up publishing 'bolt-on' attempts come and go.

> **[IAN JAMES]:** "People have always known that publishing is where the money is! The mechanics of it are quite complex, but the basic principles are quite simple. When you are licensing a song for film or television you really do need to understand how to construct a proper license and what rights you should include and not include and how much you should charge for all that. There is a well-known series of train wrecks of people who tried to bolt on a publishing company to another business and didn't know what to do with it. It's not that easy to be a publisher."

And it's not necessarily becoming any easier. In fact, with a reduction of services being offered by record companies faced with challenges to their business model, that burden has fallen increasingly to publishers to pick up some of those services.

> **[MARAIANNA ANNAS]:** "What I have observed is that there seems to be a trend at the moment where there is a perception

that you don't need a record label, but you do need a good manager and a good publisher. On one hand I understand that, but on the other hand that has had the effect of creating a void where some of the services and some of the roles that the label would normally undertake are not being undertaken, particularly where the manager is inexperienced. It's creating a lot of pressure on publishers to do stuff. I'm finding myself trying to get journalists to review CDs and those sorts of things —which I am happy to do, but I do find I am spilling over into the management role more than a publisher has had to do before. There are a lot of inexperienced managers at the moment, so I feel like I have to step in, but at the same time it is not really a publisher's role to do so."

Publishers are also likely to be at the forefront of the battle over digital dollars as the disparity between what the owners of sound recordings receive as compared with the owners of songs under the new models. It's expected that publishers will be active in the fight for greater returns for their writers.

[ALLAN BARGFREDE]: "I do think the publishers are starting to flex their muscle and as a result the musical composition holders are going to get paid more. Do they need to get paid equal to the owners of the sound recordings? There is an argument that a song can be covered and there be a future income stream whereas a sound recording cannot. I don't know if its going to hit parity but I do think that publishers are having some success with the argument that they are not getting a sufficient amount from streaming as compared with the owners of sound recordings. Publishers pay more to their writers than record labels pay to their artists and our research suggests that labels are not necessarily playing fair when it comes to streaming services."

ANDREW WATT

Publisher – Songwriter Relationships

The relationship between a songwriter and their publisher is often the most enduring of that writer's career, frequently outlasting those they have with their record companies, agents, managers and even members of their own band. And a songwriter's career can regularly outlast their time as a recording artist or performer – if that's what they also do. It flows from this that the publishing business is based around the control of assets that provide recurring and reliable income rather than the constant search for the next big thing or the need to fill another room with paying customers. Maybe it's the relative security or reliability of the business model that makes publishing one of the areas where people tend to stay employed for a long time.

So while publishing is considered a relatively conservative part of the business, that certainly shouldn't suggest it lacks creativity. The earliest role of publishers was developing a catalogue of songs that could be pitched at the recording artists of the day and this era, centred around what became known as Tin Pan Alley, represents one of the most important eras in the music business. Today, publishers range from those who are relatively passive – being collectors of royalties due to their writers – to very creative, where they are constantly seeking new ways to enhance the value and earning potential of the catalogue while developing the artistic visions and outputs of their writers (such as by facilitating collaborations with other writers and creative participants from other industries and artistic fields).

The A&R roles in publishing companies are significant and in Australia some of the best 'ears' in the business work in the publishing area; people like Peter Karpin, Craig Hawker and Linda Bosidis. The talent discovery function in publishing companies has become even more important as major labels are signing fewer new artists and an increasing percentage of artists who are not necessarily writers.

WELCOME TO THE JUNGLE

[IAN JAMES]: "Over time we have noticed that the publishing A&R has been as cutting edge as the record labels and quite often we are signing acts before or at the same time as they are signing to record labels. The resources in the big labels are depleting."

[JAIME GOUGH]: "There are a lot of publishers and a lot of songwriters and it's really competitive when you come across a great songwriter that you want to work with because chances are you are not the only publisher that has figured that out!"

Craig Hawker is the A&R director of Sony ATV, the publishing arm of the Sony music businesses. He's worked with numerous artists and songwriters in both record company and music publishing A&R roles, and he finds the ongoing relationship he has with the songwriter's catalogue one of the great upsides in the publishing world.

[CRAIG HAWKER]: "I think there's lots of crossover to the basics of the roles, but if anything, I think A&R within a publishing capacity offers an almost limitless ability to be creative. Of course, we still work to cycles of record releases for artists, but when an album or song has had its moment in the sun from a chart perspective, we can continue to find ways to keep generating revenue for a song through sync and licensing, or by finding other artists to record that song and extend its life in ways that are perhaps not the priority at a major label. We also represent songwriters and producers who are not artists and don't rely on an ability to tour and it's up to a publisher to find them opportunities with other artists to co-write or place their songs with other artists to record. On the publishing side we also have the freedom to sign and work with artists who might be signed to any of the major labels or an independent one, or those kind of writers who specialise in composing music for film or TV, so we work closely with screenwriters, music supervisors, producers and directors which is a big difference to most major label A&R."

Breaking into the music publishing business is a challenge. For many participants, a place in publishing is a natural progression from a role in a record company. For others it's the first port of call in the music business.

Ian James sees some experience outside the music industry as being advantageous in some jobs within publishing.

> **[IAN JAMES]:** "We decided to create a position marketing the catalogue of the publishing company. We needed someone who had an understanding of social networking, someone who understood the digital world and where these copyrights were being used quite often without our approval. We needed to understand that landscape if we were going to work in it. The job also was about pushing our catalogue out to areas other than the traditional film and television deals that we had for a long time and our ongoing relationships with ad agencies.
> We got about 275 applications. They came from a variety of backgrounds, but I realised that a lot of people that came from the music and allied industries were there because they were in the right place at the right time. We ended up with someone who had a marketing degree from Adelaide University and who was working in a book publishing business – more trade books than fiction. I felt like I was fishing in a pond that not too many other people in the music business had fished in as far as I could tell."

Music Supervisors and Sync Agents

If Bertis Downs is correct and music is in fact now the "ubiquity" industry, there is nothing so ubiquitous as the use of music in various forms

WELCOME TO THE JUNGLE

of visual media. There's obviously nothing new about film and television using music to create an emotional impact in a scene (or to help conceal some of the shortcomings in the visual storytelling!), but the industry of music synchronisation has grown enormously in the past couple of decades.

A music supervisor makes the connection between the visual content creators (producers, broadcasters and agencies) and the music providers (record companies, publishers, artists and songwriters). They are usually employed by the content producers or networks and so, effectively and contractually, they are working for those businesses rather than the music businesses, but inevitably they work closely with the music businesses as both a customer and a service intermediary. When licensing music for use in film, television series or advertisement, a music supervisor needs to get agreement from both the owner of the copyright in the sound recording (usually a record company) and the owner of the copyright in the song (usually a publisher). For this reason, music supervisors are often former employees of music publishing companies and, to a lesser extent, record companies because they have a background and understanding of the licensing requirements of those sorts of companies.

Kim Green runs freelance music supervision and licensing company, Music Licensing Pty Ltd, and she began her business after a long career at publishing companies such as BMG, Polygram and MCA.

> **[KIM GREEN]:** "I'm biased, but I do think working in publishing is the best way into this role. I spent almost my entire working life in publishing companies. I actually started at a record company, but quickly got into the publishing side. I think the publishing side of the industry is more complicated than the record company side. When you work in publishing companies, you really get to understand what intellectual property is all about. At a record company you know you are selling a tangible

thing, whereas in a publishing company you have to understand that you are not selling anything you can hold; you are selling rights that are embodied in that intellectual property. That can take a long time to click with people, but once you get it, you understand all the applications for that. There are lots of businesses that do licensing and they would be a good place to start – record companies and, for that matter, merchandise companies or computer companies – it's all licensing product and intellectual property to a degree."

Music supervisors don't automatically come from a publishing background though. Bernard Galbally has been a highly effective and respected music supervisor at Mana Music and his music industry background was in venue operations, tour promotion and artist management.

Galbally describes his role as a mix of creative and administrative functions.

> **[BERNARD GALBALLY]:** "It's about 20% creative and 80% admin and negotiation. It's finding musical solutions for people that want to use music in their own creative endeavours. We concentrate on film producers, television producers and advertising agencies. They are people that want to use music in their work and we help facilitate that and take all the headaches out of that for them."

Kim Green echoes this thought, emphasising that there is some misinformation about the job description for a music supervisor.

> **[KIM GREEN]:** "I get emails from students who think they are cut out to be music supervisors because they love music and know a lot about a certain type of music. People think we sit around and watch movies and listen to music and think about

WELCOME TO THE JUNGLE

how certain songs would be in certain scenes, but in fact what it is about is having the contacts to find the songs that clients already know they want and understanding the rights that you need to secure for those clients. It's then about exchanging contracts that cover them for what they need. There is a lot of research, a lot of administration and a lot of negotiation involved. You have to have really good contacts before you even start thinking about pitching song ideas to film projects, and you really need to be very organised from an administrative point of view. The majority of my days are spent in front of the computer doing spreadsheets and contracts and requests and negotiations and budgets."

To illustrate her point, Green says that one major project she worked on in early 2013 required 84 different contracts for pieces of music. It doesn't leave a lot of time for casual listening to music.

While they are acting on behalf of the producers, the music supervisor often has to manage the expectations of their clients. For some producers of television, film or advertising, music can be somewhat of an afterthought and, as a result, they don't want to spend that much money on it. It's not always a big part of their overall budget. It often falls to the music supervisor to educate their clients on the reality that music owners expect to be paid for their content too.

[BERNARD GALBALLY]: "You get the odd person who is surprised at the value of music, but then when you explain that they are wanting to utilise someone's piece of work to enhance theirs, they usually understand it. But I do think Australia does get charged a lot for music compared with other territories around the world for sync fees. As a music supervisor you are trying to get the best deal for your client and get those fees lower, but I obviously understand that a fee has to be paid if you want to exploit someone's work in your own work."

ANDREW WATT

> **[KIM GREEN]:** "That's a hard question. Some producers absolutely do understand the value of music, but because budgets for film and television in Australia are so small anyway, and the projects themselves are expensive to make, there is never enough money in the music budget. But the majority of them will try and be reasonable in their music budgets. Some of them will talk to me about what songs they would like before they do the budgets, so they can try and create a reasonable budget and that's a great situation. Filmmakers know that they need to set aside a realistic budget, but they are forever surprised at what 'realistic' is!"

Producers tend to approach and use their music supervisor in one of two ways. They will either already have a clear idea of what song they want and it becomes the music supervisor's job to go out and get that song for the best price they can. Other times the music supervisor will get a brief from the producer regarding what type of music they might want, or what the music is supposed to convey, and the music supervisor will then source a range of available songs that might fit the brief and budget.

> **[BERNARD GALBALLY]:** "If it's a feature film we will often work with the producer and director in pre-production about the musical palate they will be looking for, and from there we will start pitching song ideas and putting together mix tapes for them and getting their feedback. It involves reading through the script and seeing where sourced music might be used and talking to them about score music as well."

While the value of sync opportunities, both as an income earner and a promotional opportunity is great, the reality is that there are far more songs that sync places and artists and managers need to lower their expectations in this regard. The success of sync needs to be a two-way street and the rights holders need to be able to respond to opportunities quickly.

WELCOME TO THE JUNGLE

[BERNARD GALBALLY]: "It's just one of many areas that you have to be aware of and respond [to] accordingly. The big thing with sync that many managers and record companies are not aware of is that when we are seeking approval for a film or TV series or advertisement, time is critical. You need responses back within 24 to 48 hours. Publishing companies understand this and they are structured accordingly and often you will get the publishing approval back very quickly, whereas record companies are still a bit in the stone age. A request will go to a licensing person who will send it off to the label people and then it will go to business affairs, before it even goes to the manager and the artist. You can be waiting three weeks or longer for a record company to get back to you, but in that time the producer will want to re-record the song and not use the label's recording."

While both Green and Galbally are contract-based service providers to producers of visual content, there are also roles for music supervision within production companies, networks and advertising agencies.

[KIM GREEN]: "Some of the big TV companies like Fremantle that do some of the big music-driven shows have in-house music supervisors and clearance experts. Most production companies don't have those people though, and I do deal with most production companies. Some of the networks require that their in-house producers clear things themselves for promos, and sometimes promo departments clear their own songs. And for some shows the music is covered by a blanket license from APRA, so they don't need a music supervisor."

For Green, operating as a freelance music supervisor gives her freedom in selecting the projects she works on. She developed an expertise in licensing music for theatre with a important project being the stage production of *King Kong*.

[KIM GREEN]: "I've got the luxury of working the way I do because I don't run a big company with lots of staff and overheads. That's good and bad of course because it means I'll never get really rich from it! But I get to choose what I work on. I concentrate on film and TV and theatre and I don't do advertising. There are a lot of people who do that and do it well, but it's just not me."

The skills developed as a music supervisor are international in their application, however to be successful in international markets, it also takes a contact base to complement those skills.

[KIM GREEN]: "I do have quite a lot of relationships because of the international projects I've worked on. You are of value to a client because of your relationships with the music licensors and if you live in Australia, you get friendly with the people you are dealing with on a day-to-day basis. Licensing is done pretty much the same way wherever you go, but you have to have the contacts and the knowledge of what fees are normal and reasonable in those territories. But you can do jobs for overseas clients and still live in Australia too. You have to be willing to take the odd late-night or early morning phone call though!"

My Path into the Industry

JOHANN PONNIAH

"The reason we started was to pay the gas bill and basically we are doing what we have always done, which is work with our friends and music that we love, whether it is putting a party on as a basis for showcasing the music, or whether it is releasing music and making film clips. The reason we put our first record out was because I was managing a band called Howl at the time (later called Hunting Ground) and we couldn't find anyone to put their EP out. So we thought we'd do it ourselves. Then through friends of friends I met Bleeding Knees Club and we put that record out and that went really well. Around the same time, I was talking to our friends DZ Deathrays who I met because I was tour managing Howl. Howl were too young to hire vans or tour manage themselves, so I went with them – even though I was only one year older than them! So it's very much just been a natural progression and I know a lot of people do say that, but that's just how it is. If I had to put a date on when it became a legitimate business I would say it was the day when we did a joint venture with Mushroom, but nothing has really changed since then. Obviously we get to work with some great people and things, but in the way we think about it, nothing has changed at all."

Chapter 11

A&R

A&R, or Artist & Repertoire, is an area of the music business that causes excitement among new people considering entering the industry – especially if they are serious music fans that have a belief in their own ability to pick great artists in the early stages of their career.

Talent identification is a sexy part of most businesses though. Whether you are trying to select a yearling that will grow up to win the Melbourne Cup, or an AFL draft pick who will become a Brownlow Medallist, the ability to see a future star is always highly valued.

But A&R is also a misunderstood function in the music business. Originally – as the words suggest – it was about finding a recording "artist" and putting that artist together with material that they would record – the "repertoire". It arose from the era when recording artists rarely wrote their own material and hence the role of identifying and obtaining suitable songs for recording artists to record was vital. In the past 40 years the role of A&R has changed significantly, although the title A&R – somewhat quaintly – remains.

Another big misconception about A&R is that it involves hanging around with rock stars in recording studios, doing whatever rock stars do when they are in search of "creative inspiration". Well, yes, that may be what happens – about 1% of the time! The rest of the time is spent working within your organisation – whether it be a record label, publishing company, agency or management business, justifying your

WELCOME TO THE JUNGLE

decisions and working the angles to try and make the talent signed under your watch successful. The A&R role can be the most celebrated in the industry when everything goes well, but it's also the direction where fingers are pointed when the hit records dry up.

So what exactly does an A&R person do? Jess Beston provides a major label perspective from her time at Universal prior to creating her own A&R consultancy.

> [JESS BESTON]: "As an A&R person at Universal, I scouted bands I liked and when my bosses agreed, and the band was into it, we negotiated a contract with them and their manager and we signed them to the label. I was then given a budget to work with the band on their album. The band, myself and the manager would pick a producer, we would get the songs to a stage everyone was happy with and make sure we had a really great track listing for an album, discuss the final track listing with the producer, and off to the studio they would go! I would usually join them for a week or two of the recording process to make sure everyone was happy, productive, getting on, and we were getting some great tunes down. We would then mix and master the record, and I would then project manage the creation and production of the artwork, videos and photos for the project. So A&R within a label basically also means you are the band's creative manager within the record company, and a bridge between band / management and the label. I worked on all the bands' albums, videos, artwork and photo shoots, and I was responsible for delivering those things to all other departments and getting them super pumped about my bands!"

These days, A&R has a much broader meaning than the old function of matching songs with recording artists. Now it encompasses the whole process of talent identification, bringing that talent into your particular corporate (or less-than-corporate) system and developing that talent into a revenue earning "unit" within your business structure. Hence the A&R function isn't confined to record companies – publishers are looking to identify songwriters whose work will generate revenue across diverse income streams, while agents are looking to find touring artists that will generate commissions on their live work. Managers are looking for artists that will break through on many levels. The A&R function can take place at any stage of this process and there are now no set patterns as to which arm of the business is likely to get on board first.

> **[CATH HARIDY]:** "A&R is interesting because the definition of A&R has changed so dramatically over the [past] 50 years. Like management, there is no one single way of doing that job. I speak to A&R people all the time who do their job in completely different ways. Some just work on the basics of recording and get really into song structure and sonics, and then drop it all when the recording is finished and pass the project on to marketing. Others are really hands-on through every step of the process and really champion and guide the project, like an internal manager. That's the way I was as an A&R person at Festival Mushroom and I think that's where I got a lot a lot of skills and grounding in many aspects of management. So when I moved into management, I found there were so many skills and actions of the job I had been doing that translated perfectly."

Leading manager Gregg Donovan confirms this.

> **[GREGG DONOVAN]:** "In this day and age, A&R is being done by managers and agents. I'm hearing about bands for the first time through agents more than anyone else these

days. It used to be A&R guys. They were out all the time, they were constantly on top of it and they knew about bands months before anyone else. Now I'm hearing from the guys at agencies who are telling us about stuff early and it's because live music is so strong. A band like Paper Kites in Melbourne was a good example of this. Steve Wade at Select was already booking them because Richard Moffat at the Corner told him about them. They had sold out the Corner. He checks them out online and he contacts the band, gets them on the roster. He talks to me about them for the Josh Pyke tour. We put them on as an opener; they had already sold out the Corner, so it was a no-brainer. We loved them on that tour and so we signed them to management. All that came from the band creating their own live world, their own success online, building their own community and that was what attracted us to them."

One of the most intriguing aspects of the A&R function is the fact that there are no formal qualifications for the job. Great A&R people can come from just about any area of the business. Music media has supplied some very good A&R people in Australia (and a couple of very bad ones). There's been a couple of music lawyers perform well in the A&R role (and a couple perform very badly). There's been A&R people emerge from the sales departments of record companies and others from booking bands in live venues. Various managers have taken on A&R roles for record companies with varying degrees of success. And of course record producers and musicians themselves have transitioned into the A&R role. The challenge and the opportunity is that anyone who loves music and wants to work in the industry probably feels qualified to be an A&R person. Nobody actually believes they have dodgy taste in music!

[**MICHAEL PARISI**]: "The A&R role has changed and it hasn't changed. The way we listen to music has changed dramatically and the way we discover music has changed dramatically. When I started in A&R it was about relationships and it still is to a large extent. You befriend the agent or the young lawyer or the venue owner and you get tips from being on the street. And that still happens, but more so now, online is so crucial. There are labels in America that have people scouring the internet to find new artists. Ultimately though, it still is a flesh-and-blood process. You actually need to see the band and meet them as people before you would decide to sign them. Having 100,000 Facebook fans doesn't mean that you are a better band; it may mean that that they are good at digital marketing. I've seen bands that have heaps of followers, but they are still crap bands!"

Mark Dodds is one of the newer breed of A&R people in Australia. As A&R and Australian Music Manager at Inertia he has worked with the likes of Big Scary, Glass Towers, Seth Sentry, The Delta Riggs, Zeahorse, Money For Rope and Mantra, as well as labels including Elefant Traks, Rice Is Nice and Stop Start. He sees the A&R process through new eyes. It's no longer as one-dimensional as discovering a band in a pub in an obscure support spot.

[MARK DODDS]: Seeing a band live is still a hugely important facet of identifying talent. But it's rarely my primary point of contact. The speed with which music is disseminated and adopted nowadays means you can't always wait for an act to have a full "set" of songs before engaging with them, let alone a live set-up. The most talented acts can be on and off the market before they've ever set foot on the stage. Soundcloud, blogs and even radio (especially with the advent of Unearthed) deal in the currency of good songwriting. If you hear a song which truly captures you, it's a thread worth pursuing. If they can perform live, great. If they can't, perhaps that can come later.

WELCOME TO THE JUNGLE

> More often than not, seeing a band live isn't about identifying talent - it's about identifying how far along that talent is. Are they ready to burst out the gate immediately, or do they need more time to develop their persona and confidence? Are they ready for more spotlight, or are they okay where they are for now?"

Nathan McLay of Future Classic works a similar way.

> **[NATHAN McLAY]:** "My background is as DJ and Chad (who does A&R with me) and I are immersed in a pretty deep community of artists around the world connected to that scene. But we still listen to demo's and go to shows; performing is just as crucial as recorded materials so we do still have that traditional process in some ways."

For Sony ATV's Craig Hawker, the A&R role has become increasingly democratic. Where once, particularly internationally, A&R directors were able to build a reputation in one genre of music – such as the legendary American A&R John Kalodner did in hard rock – these days an A&R person needs to be able to "shape-shift" seamlessly.

> **[CRAIG HAWKER]:** "I think one of the most important requisites for A&R (at least in major label or publisher terms) is having a genuinely broad interest and understanding of all kinds of music. There are plenty of specialists in certain genres of music who do one thing and that can work for them, but I think diversity is really important in building a successful roster of writers/artists. If you can't sit down with a country artist one minute and a left-field electronic artist the next and figure out what really makes them tick, you potentially limit your ability to attract the best new talent. Every artist has different needs creatively and it's vital you can figure out the

best way to meet that need and deliver your artist and label success."

The question, however, is not whether you can find music that you like – it's whether you can play a part in bringing that music to life and into a form that will find favour in the marketplace. Then you have to hope that the rest of the world shares your opinion. A&R is an inexact science.

[**MICHAEL PARISI**]: "A&R is probably the most subjective concept in the music industry, because one man's treasure is another man's trash. As Ahmet Ertegun said in his book, *The Last Sultan*, he had two ears – his outer ear and his inner ear. The inner ear was his commercial ear and his outer ear was the one that loved jazz and punk and all the things that you wouldn't think he would like. He had a sensibility that drove him to sign acts. It allowed him to sign Led Zeppelin before they became Led Zeppelin. It's a fine line and it's really tough to maintain the balance sometimes, because you are always second-guessing the market. It's a tough role and it can be a thankless task, because you are hoping the market likes the same thing you do. Sometimes you get it wrong; in fact most times you get it wrong! I've had a lot of success, but I've had failures, and anyone who tells you they've had a 100% success rate is kidding themselves."

[**CRAIG HAWKER**]: "We have access to more music than ever before and people's attention spans are shorter and as a result, music has become more disposable in some ways and more desirable in other ways. The internet is the infinite jukebox and it's hard to keep up, but it also means more opportunities to succeed and if you look hard enough through all the clutter, the good stuff rises to the surface much faster."

WELCOME TO THE JUNGLE

At Universal Australia Jess Beston was involved in signing a number of artists including Children Collide, Dukes of Windsor and Gyroscope, before forming her own independent A&R consultancy Tiny Monster. She summarises the A&R process, as she sees it.

> **[JESS BESTON]:** "A&R does not necessarily take place within the confines of a record company. To me, A&R is the process of being able to spot talent, then give the advice and support needed to nurture and grow that talent, whether you are working within a record company structure or not. My favourite part of what I do is working with amazing bands who I have totally fallen in love with, helping them really hone their songs, their sound and their live show in order to achieve the things they want to achieve, and pairing them up with the right people to create an effective and passionate team around them. I also really enjoy helping artists find the right photographer to work with, the right video director, the right behind-the-scenes EPK guy … all that stuff is super fun and exciting and all part of the overall A&R role in my opinion. As an A&R person you need to have an absolute understanding of your artist's music and future, what the artist wants and needs, and the creative vision you and the band and management share, in order to then translate that to others effectively, inspiring whomever you are working with and getting them motivated about your artists. It is also about helping your artists overcome any possible creative hurdles to deliver the best possible songs and release they can at that moment in time."

Mark Dodds sees the role as being more service oriented now – in keeping with the overall Inertia philosophy. He accurately points out that the days of a band being pretty much helpless until an A&R person with a cheque book comes along are well and truly over. As artists are able to be more self-sufficient the need for A&R to get involved is a much more selective process.

> [**MARK DODDS**]: "The most distinctive element of A&R in the current environment is that, most of the time, you're identifying and discovering talent at the same time as thousands of others. Even the most proactive scout is often encountering an artist after several thousand Soundcloud spins (which could have been racked up within hours) or blog posts. This change is important because it means artist development, which used to happen behind closed doors, now takes place in public. There's so much artists can do themselves nowadays in terms of releasing music, engaging with their fans and generating buzz - and things take off fast. As A&R, if you're granted the privilege of stepping into their world, it comes with the expectation that you can help them develop - give them guidance, introduce structure and ideas - without necessarily halting their momentum or driving a wedge between them and their fanbase. It's a delicate balance."

For Michael Parisi, deciding whether to sign an artist is determined by very subjective grounds, beyond his assessment of their commercial potential. Though he is speaking in a recording A&R context, his words apply equally to management, agency or publishing.

> [**MICHAEL PARISI**]: "The first question I ask myself is 'can I see myself working with this act? Do I actually like them?' Because if I don't like them, I probably wont work well with them. Do I like what they stand for? Secondly, can I see this artist go beyond the following they might already have? There are so many boxes to tick. Do they have the drive? Do they have a management team around them?"

WELCOME TO THE JUNGLE

From a management perspective Andy Kelly sings from a similar hymn book.

> **[ANDY KELLY]:** "I definitely don't want to work with anyone we don't like. That would make no sense at all. Now that we are older we really feel like you have to have a Sydney Swans, "No Dickheads" policy. By the same token there is a payoff between unbelievable talent and the ability to function like a normal human being. I think that was most pronounced in the case of the Vines. We had a very good relationship with Craig [Nicholls, the band's volatile singer-songwriter], over a long, long time but I would never say that we were friends in the normal sense. It was crucial to have that relationship because had we not had it, it would have imploded a lot quicker than it did."

A&R in the Digital Age

Technology has impacted on the A&R role. There was once a time when the only chance that an artist would have to make a decent recording was if someone else was willing to pay for it. In that world, A&R people were the gateway to the holy grail of making a recording, and the A&R person had to be able to assess an artist's recording potential based purely on their live performances or perhaps a basic demo tape. As Craig Hawker puts it, "the gatekeeper mentality is dead". The availability of cheaper recording facilities now means that artists can often make release-quality recordings at home (depending on the nature of the artist and the genre in which they work). This has had a huge impact on the A&R role as it no longer necessarily involves working with the artist on raw, undeveloped material and shaping in into a great release.

That's not to say that every great record will be made in the lounge room, like Gotye, Flume and Chet Faker have done recently. It's horses for courses.

ANDREW WATT

[CRAIG HAWKER]: "My feeling is that there will always be a need for traditional studios. I'm all for both traditional studios and home studios, but there's something to be said about what happens to music in the hands of a skilled producer, mixer or engineer who has learnt their craft in a traditional studio. Could a record like the Beatles' White Album ever be recorded at home? I doubt it."

The nature of releasing and promoting music has also affected the A&R role. Ever since the advent of iTunes, artists and labels have been thinking more in terms of singles rather than albums, as consumers sought to buy their music one track at a time.

[MICHAEL PARISI]: "We have learned to accept that releasing a bunch of singles ahead of an album is not a bad thing. But we used to do that back in the day. It gives you a chance to know who your market is and to maybe learn from your mistakes. It doesn't change the way you view your signings or potential signings though. What iTunes taught the market was how to buy music again. Now the single business is massive. There were acts that sold 700,000 digital singles."

Another impact on the A&R role is the increasing globalisation of fans' access to music. Very rarely now will an artist be signed purely on the likelihood that they will be successful in a domestic market. Most A&R people have international aspirations for their signings from the earliest stages of their careers and the world market is increasingly accessible.

[MICHAEL PARISI]: "It's easier said than done. We always aspire for our artists to do something overseas. In most cases the tyranny of distance won't allow for it because it's still an expensive proposition to re-locate or try and break an act by remote control, but as an A&R person – particularly for a major label – you have to think that way. There is a ceiling that you can reach here and you have to look for fresh markets all the time and you have to have that mentality if you are going to succeed in A&R."

For Jaddan Comerford, operator of the UNFD business and manager of Vance Joy, the international aspects of A&R show just how far the international talent identification process has evolved.

[JADDAN COMERFORD]: "Perhaps it's got something to do with people being interested in Australian music or maybe it's just that a good song can instantly be heard on a worldwide level. But if you've got a song like *Riptide* by Vance Joy, there's no hiding that song. We got on the front foot with Atlantic who signed the act eventually, but between that initiation and the signing we would have been approached by at least 60 record companies worldwide. We were still getting approached by record companies months after that because they didn't realise that the deal has been done. That is because they are hearing it on Soundcloud or You Tube. The reality is that music can now create its own momentum, whether it's Flume or Flight Facilities or Gotye; if you've got a good song, people will find it. The record companies in the US have research analysts in the A&R department who just sit there studying the iTunes charts for all the different countries, scouring Soundcloud, Hype Machine, all of that stuff. A lot of people that contacted us weren't even A&R people; they were research analysts."

My Path into the Industry

JAKE GOLD

"I was actually a singer in Top 40 bands when I was in high school, just for fun. In a lot of ways we didn't have a lot of other distractions, there wasn't video games, there wasn't the internet, so basically it was music. That was 100% of the youth culture and I was really into it. I started hanging out with my friend's bands and became a lighting guy. I lived in LA and then a friend's band got a record deal in Toronto, so I went back to become their road manager and lighting guy. The band split up a month after their record came out and then they reformed and I became their manager. That was in March of 1981 and here we are 31 years later.... I was about 23 years old. I didn't think about how hard it could be, I just thought I'd try that. Interestingly enough, there is this bunch of guys that I play cards with from high school. We get together every couple of months and we were sitting around one night and one guy said, "Jake, you are the only guy out of all of us who actually got to do what you wanted to do." I asked him what he meant by that, and he said, "I don't know if you remember, when we were in Grade 6, there was a talent contest, and there was three girls who wanted to enter the talent contest, and you said, you would be their manager". Apparently I rehearsed them for two weeks and they won the talent contest. I was 11. Maybe I was always destined to be a manager."

CHAPTER 12

MANAGEMENT

The role of the manager has always been one of the most vital in the career of the artist. It's often the first role that anyone wanting to enter the music business will think about, and for many it's the first step they will take when crossing the line from being a fan to being an industry participant. There is something very pure and basic about the relationship between the artist and manager. The artist believes (or hopes) they have the creative genius, and yet rarely are they able to translate that genius into business processes. The manager believes he or she is the conduit between the creative work and its appreciation by an audience.

Management probably is the only role where the perception is that the artist's interests and those of the service provider are truly aligned.

It's also an all-consuming role exemplified by Andy Kelly, one of the three partners in management company Winterman Goldstein.

> [ANDY KELLY]: "You have to be aware that it's not going to be a job; it's going to be your life. If you think of it as a job, then it's a shit job. You probably work for ten years before you see any money if you are lucky. If you go into it thinking that it's a massive gamble and you don't know what is going to happen, then you will be alright. It's just so unusual to be able to make it a career and there are so many things that affect it. You will get calls at midnight about the mastering of a track or someone

WELCOME TO THE JUNGLE

can't get their baggage checked in. It's an enormous amount of diplomacy and keeping a cool head while the fire is raging. It's your life and it's not just a job and it defines everything that you do.

It's got to be collaborative. It can't be the manager saying you should do this or you should do that. And equally it can't be the artist telling the manager to do this or that, or else you may as well be a personal assistant. It's got to be a continual conversation where you are working together."

There are times when managers' and artists' interests can conflict. Most notably this occurs around the need to perform live. For many managers their only cashflow occurs when the artist is performing live, so there is a temptation to have the artist performing when strategically their time might be spent better on other creative activity. This is often one of the first dilemmas a new manager has to resolve.

How a manager determines this dilemma will often come down to the business model they adopt and what they are hoping to achieve – are they looking to work exclusively with one artist in the hope of a stellar career or do they seek to build a roster of acts all contributing to a revenue stream for a management business? Does the manager simply hope to create a wage for themselves while providing services to the artist? In some cases, management might be seen as an adjunct to another line of business.

> **[MICHAEL GUDINSKI]:** "Now you are managing a group of rights. There are a few forms of managers. There's very few of the great old school Colonel Tom, Terry Blamey, Paul McGuiness, Elliot Roberts, Jon Landau-type managers. They would be at 85-90% of their artists' gigs and that would be the only thing they would be doing. That's great if the artist is that big and they can afford to do that. Now you can be a very

boutique type of manager or you can be owned by a corporation, or you have to manage a lot of acts. These days acts don't play 50 weeks of the year like they used to, so for a lot of time the manager doesn't see any income, but the acts still expect a lot from their manager."

Australian Management Tradition

Australia has a long history of remarkable management relationships. Gary Morris and Midnight Oil, Chris Murphy and INXS, Terry Blamey and Kylie Minogue and before that, Glen Wheatley and the Little River Band were all internationally successful pairings, while later teams such as Paul Piticco and Powderfinger, Wheatley and John Farnham and Rae Harvey and the Living End were all teams that stood the test of time in the domestic market. There's other managers such as John Woodruff, Michael Roberts, Michael McMartin and Rod Willis who established the level of professionalism that distinguishes the Australian business.

For Terry Blamey, the manager who guided Kylie Minogue's career for about a quarter of a century, one of the great challenges in management is maintaining a long relationship with a client, something he achieved better than almost anyone. He puts it down to one word.

> **[TERRY BLAMEY]:** "If I were to answer this with a single word, it would be "honesty". Many may be surprised to hear that even slightly dodgy practices guarantee a short run in this industry. There are times when it may seem easier to answer a tricky question with a white lie – but believe me, it's not worth it. For example, if you've been too busy to do something which your artist has asked you to do, you may be tempted to lie when asked if it's been done; however, *'sorry I've been so busy I haven't done it yet'*, will be a much better answer in the long run. You can then get straight onto it!"

WELCOME TO THE JUNGLE

Paul Piticco was able to maintain a long and extremely fruitful relationship with Powderfinger for the entirety of their career. He linked up with the band very early on in his career and, essentially, grew alongside them. He agrees with Blamey that most artists will recognise and acknowledge hard work from their manager.

> **[PAUL PITICCO]:** "I think I was extremely lucky that the band I fell in with had a democratic/team-based philosophy. My advice though for younger managers is that, like a marriage, you need to be very sure you work at the relationship and never take it for granted and never let them take you for granted. Artists are generally strange fish in the sense that they're both very confident and very insecure all at once and you need to know how to read those moods and to adapt accordingly. And, above all, work hard for them day and night. If you're truly busting your hump for them they will look past your foibles - of which I had many - as I really was self trained and learned as I went."

> **[BILL CULLEN]:** "There are some managers who manage their mates from school and end up becoming the biggest managers in the country, like Paul Piticco. There was an element of luck there, but he has proven that he was the right guy for the job. I feel like I chipped away for 10 years or so before I had any success. There are different ways of doing it. I had time to work out what my style was and what sort of acts I wanted to work with. I worked with another manager for five years and I learnt a lot; what to do and things I wanted to do differently. I tour managed a lot as well. There are all these different entry points."

The Scope of Management in the New Music Business

Management is equally the hardest and the most rewarding role in the business. When a management relationship is successful it can be the most exhilarating sphere of the business, but few relationships can be as deflating when they go sour as that between an artist and manager.

The role of the manager has become even more important in the past decade. With record companies downsizing and signing fewer artists, the manager has had to take on further tasks or even assist the artist in operating their own label. The traditional business arrangement between the artist and manager hasn't really changed though. In most cases the manager takes a commission on the artist's earnings of between 15% and 20%, a figure based more on tradition than any real objective valuation of the worth of the manager's contribution to the artist's career.

> **[CATH HARIDY]:** "In the [past] 10 years it has changed totally. When I started in management in around 2006, it was at the end of the management heyday. Labels and publishers and everybody else were starting to cotton on to the fact that management was actually quite a free deal. Managers took their percentage of artist income and their job was really to be a conduit between all the different parties involved in releasing an album, and continuing to build an artist's career. There wasn't really a need for the manager to go in and get hands-on with the marketing plan, or to physically go out to media with the album or try to source deals or employ teams and coordinate a complete strategy. Now that's what a manager has to do. A manager is everything to an artist and more, and the broader skill base that person has, and the more life experience that the person has, the better they will be. The 15 or 20 percent that you earn from an artist is probably no longer accurately reflective of the work that a manager will put into an artist over a three or five-year period."

While the decline in recording royalties is often considered to lead to a loss of income for the manager, this is somewhat of a myth. An artist

WELCOME TO THE JUNGLE

in a traditional record contract only receives recording royalties when they have recouped the cost of their recording (and its promotion) and in reality this didn't happen very often.

> **[JOHN WATSON]:** "The declining sales of recorded music are typically (and wrongly) viewed by most in the media as a *revenue* problem. In fact, most artists never got royalty cheques in the first place, so it makes much less difference to their bank accounts than is commonly thought. The declining sales of recorded music are actually creating a *muscle* problem. Labels have shrunk and so have their marketing/promo budgets. At the same time, media has fragmented so the 'to do' list has doubled at the same time as the people who traditionally did the marketing and promo work have halved. The challenge for everyone in the business is how do you bring sufficient marketing and promotional efforts to bear in a world where labels are much less equipped to perform the task? The solution requires everybody else – manager, artist, agent etc – to roll up their sleeves and help spread the word too."

Bill Cullen concurs and points out that some of the costs that record companies no longer incur actually makes it easier for an artist to recoup, as there are less expenses that need to be repaid before an artist gets their share.

> **[BILL CULLEN]:** "The fact was that it was really rare for artists on major labels to ever recoup, so you actually weren't getting any recording income. But what we relied on were these big machines that spent a lot of money on marketing and we would be able to ride off that marketing to sell tours and convert into publishing income. Now it feels like we don't have that, but for the first time ever all of our acts are actually recouped because the record companies are not spending half a million dollars

on making a record and $150k on videos. So now there is actually a stream of income from recorded music which there never was, unless you were a multi-platinum artist. In the past even I've had triple platinum artists who were not recouped because the records were expensive and film clips were expensive and overseas tour support was expensive. Now you don't get any of that and so you don't have to recoup it."

So it seems the economics of artist management are not as extreme as some would like to make out. However, the workload is clearly heavier and the degree of responsibility is immense.

Paul Piticco has also seen the role of the manager evolve relative to that of the label. He sees this as a great time for managers to step forward and be the driving force (with their artist) in determining how that artist is positioned and marketed.

> **[PAUL PITICCO]:** "I think labels have certainly lost ground to some degree, in the sense that they were the conduit for the media to get to the artist in years gone by, but now managers and bands are making the decisions about how the artist is seen by the world. The first point of direct contact is online through social media. Most labels, or at least the 'smart labels', are now promoting and marketing 'what is', rather than 'what they want it to be' like they did 10 years ago. That power and responsibility should have always been where it is now … with the artist and manager. It is a great time to be a manager, as long as you understand your requirement to promote and market the band and you can articulate their vision."

Bill Cullen also sees the marketing aspect of management as the biggest growth area.

WELCOME TO THE JUNGLE

[BILL CULLEN]: "In the past 10 years, the changes have been constant. In a lot of ways it makes what we do really interesting because one project is never the same as the last one or the next one. It used to be that it felt like there was the same approach to take with every artist, but I feel now that every artist – and every project by every artist – you have to look at it differently and think about the potential market in different ways and how you get to those people. It used to be a case of getting on commercial radio and the record company would do TV advertising and some billboards if it went really well. It was a total mass-marketing approach. Now it's become a lot more about marketing to an artist's fan base and developing fan bases bit by bit. The way of getting these people is changing. Things pop up and then vanish just as quickly. The essence is the same though – it's about getting to audiences in a more incremental way, rather than a mass blast that everyone will take notice of at the same time."

International manager Peter Leak has also seen artist's expectations change. The time when a manager regarded getting their artist signed to a label as the endgame has long gone.

[PETER LEAK]: "I suppose in the so-called 'old days' an artist would think that if you got them a record deal, you had done your job. The manager then had to be there to get the record company to do what they were supposed to do, but the manager wasn't expected to do it all themselves. Artists are more aware now that a manager has a lot of different hats to wear and has to have a lot of different areas of knowledge. But having said that, the artist hopefully knows that artists have to be doing a lot more too. There is a lot expected of an artist in this day and age. It's probably not enough just to be talented; they have to have drive and they have to work really hard on social media skills and things like that."

Responsibilities of Management

There are numerous jobs in the business where mistakes can be corrected and there's a system of checks and balances built in to ensure that any errors don't have catastrophic effects – concert production is one such industry for obvious reasons. When staging a concert, a promoter isn't likely to leave building the stage to someone who is learning on the job. However, artists frequently leave the management of their careers to managers who are doing exactly that.

There is a legal issue involved in this discussion. There are duties built into the law of agency, upon which the management relationship is based. For example, a legal agent has a duty to act in good faith and to follow the instructions of the principal in the legal relationship – that being the artist in the artist-management relationship. But beyond the legal duty also lies a moral duty that the manager must remain acutely aware of.

Even highly accomplished managers such as Rae Harvey admit that plays on their mind.

> **[RAE HARVEY]:** "Don't be afraid to admit you don't know the answer and ask the question. You have responsibilities to other people. That was my mantra when I was starting out, that I was never going to fuck up because I'm too proud to ask a question. If you fuck up your own business, that's fine, it's yours. If you fuck up your artist's career, that's a big problem to be responsible for."

For Terry Blamey, it's important to understand where the line between creative and business management blurs.

WELCOME TO THE JUNGLE

[TERRY BLAMEY]: "Some managers get more involved in the creative side than others; however, interfering too much in A&R or styling, for example, can lead to conflicts. Nevertheless it is absolutely essential for the manager to help the artist to source required creative collaborators and, more importantly, to manage the relationship with such personnel, including the logistics and all financial, legal and other business aspects."

John Watson has an analogy that he uses to describe the role of the manager. He's used it several times at conferences and it remains a very accurate description of the manager's role.

[JOHN WATSON]: "When explaining the manager's role to people, I typically begin by asking them to imagine the artist and manager as the hub of a wheel on a bike. Ideally the manager and artist should have complementary skills sets – one is strong in the areas where the other is weak, so that together they cover all the bases. Together they form the hub. Then out from that artist/manager hub you have a series of spokes. Each of those spokes is a different member of your team – agent, publisher, publicist, accountant, lawyer, crew, producer, marketing people, promotion people, sales people etc. Once all the spokes are in place you've hopefully got a wheel that can take the artist's career where they want it to go. The job of the hub – both artist *and* manager – is to *strategise* a career plan and to then *coordinate* and *persuade* each spoke to work in service of that plan. To torture the metaphor, the manager and artist need to get that wheel rolling in the right direction. The interface between the manager and each spoke will be much better if there's at least some level of understanding of that person's job. In truth, if you've got the right team, then the manager will probably be worse at the task of every spoke than the specialist who's been employed to do it. S/he will be worse at law than the lawyer, know less about booking a show than the agent, have fewer radio relationships than the promotions person and so forth. However, in order to keep those people working in the right direction, the manager typically needs to have some *understanding* of the spoke's job."

It's important to remember that the hub in the wheel consists of both the artist and the manager – and in today's music business both are required to be active participants. As a touring musician turned manager Paul Gildea has an interesting viewpoint on the role of the artist in the relationship.

> **[PAUL GILDEA]:** "I work for the artists, the more they can challenge the process in both presenting me with changing priorities and developing options for the business model, that is their band/ act, the better for all. I think everybody needs two jobs in this business. It's always been the classic singer/ songwriter but it should now be the guitarist/photographer, keyboard player/graphics aficionado the bass player/social media biographer. Music and musicians have to relate on so many different levels now and with such determined gusto that if you aren't all pulling together to cover the levels that represent your 'compelling' story then the story can become less compelling. It's rigorous and hard work to be successful – it requires a dedicated effort from all."

There's another analogy that is often used to look at the role of the manager. Think of the manager as the ringmaster of a circus. The ringmaster's role is to keep the show moving along, introducing each act, who in turn comes on and dazzles the audience with their skills. The ringmaster throws from the lion tamer to the trapeze artist, to the clowns, to the jugglers, calling on each to step up and do their thing when their moment arrives.

WELCOME TO THE JUNGLE

The manager's role is similar. The manager has to know when to call on the agent to activate touring opportunities, the artist's lawyer to deal with emerging legal situations, the publisher to create a synchronisation opportunity, the publicist to let the media know what is happening and the digital marketing person to engage the artist's fan community with the operation. And then to co-ordinate all of those actions to create a smooth and compelling show that is the artist's career.

Both the 'hub-in-the-wheel' analogy or the 'ringmaster' analogy are accurate, but the one thing it doesn't take into account is that the spokes keep changing. While some artists and mangers have team members that are constant throughout their careers –perhaps publishers or agents – the challenge is that no two albums, no two tours and no two situations are exactly the same. That's also part of the fun.

Band manager Bonnie Dalton (Little Red, Husky) subscribes to this view.

> **[BONNIE DALTON]**: "I really enjoy the diversity of the role, the constant challenges and being part of the ongoing development of artists' careers. There's really no repetition and it encompasses so many different experiences and forces you to develop so many new skills because you're constantly 'in the deep end'. Experience can better prepare you for what to do, but there's always something brand new that you've never faced before because your artists, their directions, ambitions and paths are always going to be different from one another, but also from record cycle to record cycle. Beyond that, the music industry itself grows and changes so rapidly that you need to adapt quickly. It can feel at times like the possibilities are endless and every time you feel you've achieved something

great, you realise that it was actually just a stepping stone to the next bigger, more exciting thing – from local touring to international releases or wherever it is your artists want their career to go."

[**MICHAEL PARISI**]: "Unless the manager and the artist are driving the team, it's not going to work. If you left it to your label or your agent or your publisher, it won't happen. The manager's job is to get them all together. Managers have to drive all the conversations and get them to the point where they met. That's what the manager strives for every day. Even majors are just becoming another service provider, albeit different services to those that an indie might provide."

Twists in the Management Tale

The world of crowdfunding gives an interesting insight into the role of the manager. Benji Rogers of Pledge Music is well placed to see how important the manager is in that process.

[**BENJI ROGERS**]: "I think that managers are the key, understanding that the job of the manager is to organise the team around the band. You can de-risk your investment significantly as a manager because you are a party to all streams of income. The manager's power is fairly weighty right now and what I think a lot of managers are going to ask in the future is, why do I need a record label, what can't I do in house? But that said, the smart manager can take the story that they have built and then they leverage it against a fair record deal. There are some brilliant managers doing these unique joint venture hybrid deals with labels now. In management you will become part-label, part-publisher, part-sync guy, part-agent."

WELCOME TO THE JUNGLE

The speed of decision-making has also increased. As is the case with jobs in many industries, managers are now on the clock 24/7 and are forced to make decisions on the fly. And as someone who is that 'hub in the wheel', the manager has to be up to date with every aspect of the ever-changing business – whether it's in the live environment, the recording industry or any of the other industries that artists now expect their manager to master.

> **[BONNIE DALTON]:** "I guess the biggest shift has probably been in terms of technology because you just have to be onto the 'next thing' so quickly and be able to figure out immediately how to get the most out of it. Finding the time/resources for research and development in that area can be a challenge, particularly because delegating to a third party isn't always something artists are happy to do. They're right too, because ultimately social networks should be their direct access to fans and the nature of it means it should be unmediated. There's also the creativity required in this 'new music business' where you don't necessarily have to take 'no' for an answer if you can find a way around what could previously have been a road block. If a major label doesn't sign your band or a radio station isn't playing it, there are more options than ever before to find an audience anyway. In fact, the options for releasing music have become almost endless, so navigating your way through all of those decisions becomes harder, because for every decision there are multiple combinations of outcomes – that's fantastic because it gives you so much more scope to tailor your artist's career to suit their specific needs, but it also makes the decision-making process a lot more complex. Oh, and let's not forget the crunching of budgets, where the kind of advances and tour support that used to be standard investments in artist development from labels are largely a thing of the past."

ANDREW WATT

Co-Management

One of the greatest challenges in management in Australia is that it's often a lonely business. One solution to this is to manage in partnership with another manager. Obviously the downside to that is that commission revenue needs to be split, and in most cases there is barely enough revenue to support one manager, let alone two or three. But management partnerships can work. Australia's Winterman Goldstein is a three-way partnership between Andy Kelly, Pete Lusty and Andy Cassell, a structure that has allowed them to not only manage artists successfully, but also build a successful label and publishing company under the Ivy League brand.

> **[ANDY KELLY]:** "There's no way I was the kind of person that could have done it by myself. I completely credit Pete and Andy with being able to do it. When we started they were quite fearless and I don't think I was like that. They had an incredible amount of belief that they could do things and I was dragged along with that. There was camaraderie and it was like we were a band. We all started at the same level and everyone had different ideas and ways of doing things and we complemented each other."

LA-based manager Peter Leak has also managed artists in partnership and it has worked for him.

> **[PETER LEAK]:** "It can be a great thing having two people managing an artist together, but equally the communication has to be really great. I have seen situations where partnerships have been created on an artist and each person thinks the other one is doing more than they are and so things don't get done or not done right."

WELCOME TO THE JUNGLE

Management Groups

The other development in recent times is the creation of large management groups – collections of managers operating under a banner, sharing resources, back-office support and intelligence. International management conglomerates like these are often the size of record companies, with many staff and departments. In recent years much of the power in the business has shifted to these mega-management corporations, where large numbers of salaried and incentive-driven managers work under one banner. Examples include **Q Prime** which has offices in New York, Nashville and London and represents Metallica, Red Hot Chili Peppers, Josh Groban, Muse, the Black Keys, Snow Patrol, Eric Church, the Mars Volta, Cage the Elephant, Gillian Welch and Silversun Pickups, among others, and **Red Light Management** that represents almost 200 acts across eight cities.

Peter Leak is an extremely successful international manager. His early successes came with artists such as 10,000 Maniacs, Cowboy Junkies and Grant Lee Buffalo, who he managed under his own company. He later joined forces with Terry McBride at **Nettwerk Management** where he managed or co-managed Dido and Avril Lavigne to worldwide multi-platinum success. Leak now works under the banner of Coran Capshaw's Red Light Management where he is able to merge his own sizeable reputation, experience and contact base with the resources available to Red Light managers as a group. It's an undeniably powerful combination.

> **[PETER LEAK]:** "Different people enjoy different environments. I had my own company for a long time and at the point when I did join up with Nettwerk I felt that it was just time to align myself with a bigger set of resources. The business of management has become so sophisticated and there are so many things that you want to be on top of, it's great to have a

team of people around you to help you with that. The idea of being in a bigger management company is that those services exist to benefit the managers and the artists that they manage too. I think that is something that worked at Nettwerk and it's certainly working for me at Red Light. It's an environment that I enjoy. Red Light, for example, has a radio promotion team, a marketing team, they have film and TV sync people – they have people to provide all those services. They are all things that as a day-to-day manager you don't get to do yourself; there are just not enough hours in the day."

There's nothing even approaching that size in Australia where managers tend to be solo operators. Publisher Ian James of Mushroom Music makes a good observation.

[IAN JAMES]: "What is not happening here yet, but it is happening in America, is that the big management companies are behaving like full service labels. They have people on staff that do licensing, they have people who do marketing, they have people who do PR. So the really big companies are taking over the role of the labels in a lot of ways and reducing the role of the label accordingly. We haven't got to that critical mass yet, but in America there is enough volume to be able to afford the staff, to be able to become a replacement for the record labels."

An emerging Australian company like UNFD does have a staff of people in the management side of the business but, on the whole, that approach is undeveloped in this territory. UNFD are certainly modelled in that way.

[JADDAN COMERFORD]: "There is strength in numbers. Management is a very fickle game. You can have a hot act and go set up your office and hire an assistant and do a couple of trips around the world and all of a sudden that act might stop playing, or release an inferior product or they could void your contract and go to another management company and all of a sudden your business does not exist any more. Whereas if you partner up with a company that has multiple acts and multiple revenue streams you have some security on a financial level, but you also have relationships that you can leverage and I think there is a lot to be said for managers working together to create a bigger picture and a better place for the artists they work with. We set up our business in such a way that we can minimise our risk so there is always a revenue stream there to fill the gap if one revenue stream was to leave."

Leveraging relationships is the strongest reason for working under the banner of a management group like Red Light. There is plenty of give and take between the managers, although they all remain fiercely committed to their own artists.

[PETER LEAK]: "Red Light has a pretty high degree of communication between the managers and between the services people and the managers. There are a lot of resources available and a lot of emails going out saying, "Does anyone know how I can get in touch with...." And within five minutes a couple of people will come back with an answer. So it's a good environment for sharing information but at the same time, every manager is still very much doing their own thing. Managers do team up to work together on certain artists, particularly if there is a geographic reason for doing that. Red Light has offices in London, LA, Nashville, New York, Charlotte, Vancouver. So for example if I was interested in managing an artist who was based in London, I could partner up with someone in the London office."

ANDREW WATT

Managers working independently often find themselves with decisions to be made and only a few places they can turn to for advice. As Rae Harvey suggested earlier, getting that advice may save you from destroying a client's career. Gregg Donovan agrees.

> **[GREGG DONOVAN]:** "Absolutely. Good advice directly relates to success and money. As well as people like John Watson and Michael McMartin, there are a lot of guys in America I talk to all the time. I think it's invaluable and you are nuts if you don't do it. In an industry like this when everything changes every day, you need to talk to other people. You need to have a support network like that. It gives you confidence to work harder and better."

> **[BONNIE DALTON]:** "There's a lot of 'who you know' as well as 'what you know', so having those people looking out for you and putting in a good word at the right time is very important. More importantly than that, however, is the fact that there's no rule book for management, so having a mentor to watch and learn from is a really crucial part of professional development. It can be a really isolated role in a lot of ways and knowing that there's an experienced person you can call and seek advice from, discuss things with, or even just chat (or occasionally vent) to is just so helpful. Hearing 'back yourself Bonnie' from someone I really respect has made a huge difference to my confidence on many occasions too."

While Dalton is correct in saying there is no management rulebook, there are places young managers can go to get assistance and career development opportunities.

Cath Haridy is a huge believer in the process of continuing education and mentorship for music industry professionals. She's clearly smart

WELCOME TO THE JUNGLE

enough to know that there are always things you don't know and listening to those more experienced than yourself is invaluable.

> **[CATH HARIDY]:** There are great programs out there. One I was involved in is called Control, which is funded in part by AMIN, along with AAM [Association of Artist Managers]. They sponsor a three to four-day course for managers who are at mid level who want to learn more about the intricacies of being a manager both psychologically and from a business perspective. The course is so valuable. I learnt a lot about creating a business plan through that course and I learnt a lot about the psychology of management as well. It changed my life and everyone else who is involved in it says the same thing. It was good to know that there were things that I was encountering that other people felt exactly the same way about and that there were ways of being able to deal with challenging situations.
> The other one that is really good for entry-level managers has been the JB Seed. That starts from a different place and both are very valuable. The more short courses and really thoughtfully put-together courses that exist on that level, the better. I believe that you really need to be skilled up in this job and if you don't have the skills when you get involved you need to go out there and get those skills."

She also advocates industry involvement as an important element of both giving back and gaining insights into the way the business operates. As well as running her own business, Haridy has been the chairperson of AAM.

> **[CATH HARIDY]:** "I think if you are going to get involved in an industry that you are getting something out of, then you need to give something back. I believe that being involved in something like AAM, which has a very strong advocacy line in

it, is very important. I think that is the responsibility of anyone who gets involved in the industry and benefits from it in some way. We are all working in what is a relatively small pool and there is not a lot of access to funds other than what we commercially make for ourselves. You are also strengthening your network of peers and not only are you benefiting by having your ear to the ground, you are also developing close relationships with people who are in a similar position to you who may be able to be there for you when you need advice or help. And there isn't a point in a management career when you don't need advice or help. Management is such a living, breathing thing that I don't think you can ever know everything and you've got to have that support. Plus you get a lot of direct benefits from being involved in something like that, whether it be discounted flights or discounted delegate passes to conferences. I really enjoy it because you feel like you are helping to build something that will be important to people well after you are gone from the scene."

Leading Canadian manager Jake Gold (the Tragically Hip, Adam Cohen and many others) is even more clear about his involvement in various Canadian music industry organisations.

> **[JAKE GOLD]:** "I was one of the initial founders of the MMF (Music Managers Forum), but I went away from it for a while when I was living in New York. What I realised over time was that some of the information that I wasn't necessarily getting was only going to the people that were a part of those groups. So I decided that with my expertise and my years behind me and all the experience and credibility I had, that it was time to enter these organisations. I could enter as a board member and really be participatory and really contribute. At the same time I could strengthen relationships and really have a much

WELCOME TO THE JUNGLE

bigger field to play in as a result. I soon discovered that it was better to be in the room where the decisions were being made, rather than standing outside waiting to hear what the decision was. That's a part of it. You give up your time for free, but in return you get information before everyone else does and be part of shaping potential regulatory things that are going to affect you and your clients. It is self-serving and everyone in the room admits it, but also you are in there for the good of the industry. That's the give and take."

Structuring a Management Business

Some managers consider themselves to be equal members of the band, with the only difference being they play the calculator, laptop and mobile phone, rather than guitar, bass or drums. They structure their business based on this principle. In this scenario the manager and the band members are all equal and share the profits from the enterprise in equal shares. This has the obvious advantage that the manager and the band members are all equal partners in the business that they all contribute to.

Other managers like to operate a business entirely separate from that of their clients and be a service provider to those clients. This allows them to take on multiple clients and offer services to each of them without having their fortunes tied to the success of one. Legally the structure is a more secure one for the manager because their relationship with the artist will always be seen as that of an independent contractor and it not likely to be perceived as a partnership.

As an independent business, a manager needs to consider their own 'brand' and not sublimate it to that of the artists they manage. It's generally a brand based on the way the business conducts itself in the business.

ANDREW WATT

[**BONNIE DALTON**]: "I think you do that regardless of your intention because your brand is really your reputation and between bands, within the teams you work as part of, and in the industry beyond them, you make an impression through the work you do, the career paths/decisions of your bands and just what you're like in person. It's not an industry that follows processes in regards to qualifications, resumes or interviews; networks are close and people rely on the reports from trusted sources. There is a consistency across everything Minnow & Co. does and anyone who works with us shares the same approach to management, but it's not so much a 'customer facing' brand that needs to mean something on its own."

Whatever approach a manager takes, as important as it is for a manager to take great care of the business of their clients, they should always remember that they are themselves running a small business. It's easy to get so caught up in the daily challenges facing your clients and forget that you are no use to those clients if your business ceases to function properly itself.

Risk and Return in Management

The other consideration is the prospect of multiple income streams for management businesses. Sometimes commissions are slow to generate and managers need to have a back-up form of income to assist in keeping the doors open while their artists proceed through the creative cycle.

As Gregg Donovan points out, the manager's income stream is entirely dependent on the success of the artist and the relationship with that artist being maintained. That can sometimes be a risky business.

WELCOME TO THE JUNGLE

[GREGG DONOVAN]: "For the first few years as a management company, I was doing tour management and band management. It took me a while before the success that Grinspoon were having was able to keep me in a living and allow me to have a full-time assistant. I kept my toe in the tour management camp for years. Everybody I know in this business did part-time bar work or whatever it took to survive. For us it's been really important to grow this company, and it's even more important now to start diversifying because managing artists is such an unknown factor. It's so hard to ever feel like you've got anything stable. As a manager you don't own anything, you've got no business assets. You might have a great roster of acts and you might believe in all of them, but none of that is 'owned'. I can't sell those contracts and morally I wouldn't because it has to be a personal relationship. You do start thinking, 'what will I do when I retire?'. If I was running a newsagency or a butchers shop, you sell the business."

[RAE HARVEY]: "Even with the first Living End record I wasn't making any money from them, yet I helped fund their album because we didn't want to sign a deal straight away. I was only in a position to do that because I was a tour promoter as well, and the tour promoting was what I lived on. None of the bands that you take on make you money in the first couple of years unless they have a overnight smash and that doesn't happen too often."

The question of money at the beginning of a management relationship is problematic. It's often early in an artist's career when they need most hands-on attention, but that is also the time when they are generating the least income to allow the manager to give them that attention. Bertis Downs, who went from being R.E.M.'s lawyer to their virtual manager, believes the prospects of investing your time and energy into developing an emerging artist now faces some serious competition from more immediate opportunities.

> **[BERTIS DOWNS]:** "People generally don't get into this because of money. They get into this because it's what they want to do, because they love it. I read an article that said that we have come to a point where if someone wants to invest… where are they going to invest their money? Are you going to invest your money and your time, your resources and your energy in building up a band or are you going to invest it in writing a new app. Sadly the answer is the second! It's a much better bet. So where is the investment in bands going to come from? Is it going to be completely a DIY world? Managers serve a useful function, to keep bands from having to return every phone call and to meet all the people that don't have anything to do with the art. Plenty of bands don't have managers, plenty of bands just do it on their own, and maybe more and more are going to do it on their own because it's going to get harder and harder for people to get involved because of the new math."

While the manager often invests time and/or money in the early days of the relationship hoping to recoup it later, the other exposure they have comes at the end of the relationship.

For the manager – and for live agents as well – the risk in their business is once the relationship with the artist either expires or breaks down, the entitlement to commission ceases. In some cases the manager may be entitled to receive a reducing commission on revenue derived from contracts that were entered into during the term of their management agreement, but this isn't always the case and it doesn't always result in significant ongoing income. Anyone entering into a career in management needs to know they are not building up a bank

WELCOME TO THE JUNGLE

of tangible, realisable assets that will sustain them long after the management relationship ends.

On the other hand management does provide a fantastic basis of knowledge about the industry that can then be used in other areas. There are numerous examples of managers going to take other roles in the business, using their contacts and knowledge.

Paul Piticco was able to build a group of businesses around his role as manager of Powderfinger. It's a model that has been utilized very successfully internationally by some of the most powerful players in the business. A prime example is Coran Capshaw, a manager who started his management career with the Dave Matthews Band. Capshaw segued the success of that act into one of the biggest empires in the music business including a multi-city artist management conglomerate (Red Light), music venues, a record label and equity positions in major music festivals.

For Piticco, the factor that allowed him to build a business that included record and publishing companies, management and festivals without compromising his relationship with his flagship client was to include them in the evolution of his business.

> **[PAUL PITICCO]:** "I always make sure I look after my partners and artists and I made sure that if there was something that had a chance of being seen as a distraction from the band's business I would give them an interest and at the same time use their draw and notoriety to aid that new business. I thrive on new ideas and new ventures. It's part of who I am and I love building teams and the camaraderie and to do that everyone needs to feel they're needed in some way in that process – big part or small."

ANDREW WATT

Smart agents like Brett Murrihy recognise that management is great training for potential players in every part of the industry.

> **[BRETT MURRIHY]:** "Doing an internship at a management company is probably the best training you can get. They are the lifeblood of the business and without the managers our business doesn't work. That would be my advice – to do an internship at a good management company. That way you are dealing with agents, dealing with labels, dealing with publishers and dealing with artists and you are seeing every part of the business and from that you will get an idea of what area of the business excites you most. So if you see an artist that you think has been handled well look it up and see who is responsible."

My Path into the Industry

PETER FOLEY

"We started doing gigs in the lounge room because we couldn't go out. We had a disabled child, Jack, who had muscular dystrophy. It was a way of us bringing the world to us because we were so limited in what we could do because he had a lot of needs. I ran into Mark Ferrie at a festival in Mt Beauty, which was my home town and he offered to come down and do a lounge room gig and it started from there. One day we had 70 people for a Dave Graney gig in our lounge room. My son died about two years after we started doing those. I'd started doing a couple of gigs at the Oakleigh Bowling Club by then, and he died a couple of days before a gig. We decided to go ahead and do the gig and Stephen Cummings was the act we had on. It was a fantastic gig and so I think my son really inspired us to continue it. I When he died I couldn't really contemplate doing another house gig, because he was such a big part of that and it was going to be difficult for me to ever do a normal job again. I wanted to do something meaningful. I know it's a fun business, but it has a great community vibe. I couldn't do it if it was just another gig, and that's why we do a lot of meaningful shows. So he's the inspiration for us doing this and I think there is this emotional content in there and I think that's what people connect to and it's the key to our success. People know that we are serious and committed and we care about what we are doing and they keep coming in big numbers."

Chapter 13

Venue Operation and Band Booking

The overwhelming message coming from venue operators is that it's a very rewarding area of the music business, but also one of the toughest in which to survive. There's nothing more immediate than the thrill of watching a crowd respond to live music in a space that you have created for that purpose; there's nothing more frustrating than having to deal with many of the regulatory issues involved in operating licensed premises.

Australia has a proud history of live venues for contemporary music and many of our leading industry figures cut their teeth operating or working in live venues. Taking a position at a venue, whether it is in administration or on the hospitality side (bar or bussing) puts you in immediate contact with the frontline of players in the business – the bands, their crews and their management. And there are far less enjoyable jobs to do while you are making your way through university. The challenge is how to segue those entry-level positions into an ongoing career.

There are numerous issues involved in operating a music venue and only a few of them are music related! Once the venue has a talent booker the major operational issues are much the same as any of those relating to operating any licensed hospitality venue – staff, stock, patron management and regulatory compliance. There are numerous examples of venues opening and closing because the proprietor was too enthusiastic about the music side and not diligent in administration.

WELCOME TO THE JUNGLE

The Corner Hotel and Northcote Social Club are two of Melbourne's most successful music venues and have now been joined by a Sydney "sister" venue, the Newtown Social Club. The venues are owned by Matt Everett and Tim Northeast. Part of the success of the operation is that the owners have never lost sight of the fact that they are running a hospitality venue, just as much as a music venue. They are doing something very right. Prestigious US magazine *Pollstar* named the Corner in the Top 10 venues in the world based on ticket sales and venue capacity.

> **[TIM NORTHEAST]:** "We run traditional pubs that have music, which is different to a theatre-type operation, where people come in and watch the show and then leave. You've got to look at it as hospitality or you won't survive. People come and pay to see the show, but they are still expecting to enjoy a certain level of hospitality, whether that's the ambiance of the venue or the quality of the food and drinks. We've talked about that philosophy as a group. We've always looked for a pub that can do music rather than just a room."

Brian Lizotte's three venues in NSW have been among the most loved in the country. Lizottes has established a brilliant reputation amongst artists as being places where hospitality extends to the back of house.

> **[BRIAN LIZOTTE]:** "My history in the industry goes back to those days of being the first to arrive and the last to leave and the welfare of the artist was everything. My philosophy is that if you look after the artist, the rest will look after itself. A lot of other venues don't have that philosophy, but I think it's a very important thing. If musicians are happy they will go on and do a great show and we always get testimonials from the artists on stage about our food, or how well we look after them and if they are re-enforcing that to the audience, that's gold for me because the customers respond to that."

Peter Foley, operator of the Caravan Club and the Memo Music Hall in suburban Melbourne, has similar thoughts.

> **[PETER FOLEY]:** "There seems to be a thing in Australia that a lot of musicians complain about the way they are treated. They get treated well here, but I don't think what we do is anything incredible, so they must get treated pretty badly elsewhere. In Europe they get treated as guests and feted."

Pixie Weyand took over the loved Brisbane venue The Zoo in her mid-twenties in 2016. It was a huge leap of faith for her and she's bought both energy and innovation to the space.

> **[PIXIE WEYAND]:** "One of the challenges is getting people's trust. You can almost see people thinking, "She is new to the industry, how is she going to do it? Does she understand how it works?". There is so much love for The Zoo and that adds to the pressure. I've got staff that are older than me and have been here longer and I understand that I have to gain their respect. As an independent music venue it can be financially daunting. We are absolutely a small business and that can be a little bit scary. But waking up every day and having a job that I love makes it worthwhile."

Venue Operations

Venues such as the Corner operate on a "room-for-hire" basis, meaning that promoters book the room and stage an event in the way they want to stage it. The venue provides the staff and infrastructure (which includes bars, PA, stage and ticketing) that enables the promoter to operate an event and sell tickets to an audience. That raises the question: exactly who are the "customers" of a music venue – the promoters who hire the room and stage the show, or the fans or patrons that pay their money, frequent the venue and provide the bar takings?

WELCOME TO THE JUNGLE

[TIM NORTHEAST]: "We really go out of our way to make sure the bands, promoters, tour managers and production crew are all welcome and looked after, so again it's extending hospitality to those people as soon as they walk in the room and identifying that those guys are going to be repeat customers in a venue like this. A promoter might do up to 12 shows at the Corner in a year and they often use the same tour managers and road crew, so every time those guys walk in the door we want them to have a good experience and a warm welcome. On the punter side of it, there are a lot of people in Melbourne who love their music and they will come to the Corner a few times, to many times a year and you have to keep a consistent product for them, because Melbourne's a competitive place and if you are not up to scratch you'll soon find out."

Sometimes venue operation might involve supporting a new promoter who may flop and never be seen again or may become a key hirer of the venue for the next decade,

[TIM NORTHEAST]: "If someone pitches a show that we think is going to work, we will obviously try and take the show on. We have shows from every promoter in the country – there's no one that we won't do shows with. Over the years we've seen new promoters come into the market and we really go out of our way to help those guys along and offer them some guidance on how to set the show up well and market it the right way. We have a really strong publicity team at the venues that helps promoters in promoting their show well. We were early adopters of social media strategies which worked well."

Former Managing Director of the Hi-Fi Group Luke O'Sullivan explains the organisational structure he had in his business.

ANDREW WATT

[**LUKE O'SULLIVAN**]: "People often think that I held up one end of the bar four nights a week and I'm loading in beer and cleaning the floors. It's not really like that. We set the business up into commercial and operations divisions and each division had a general manager. Under Operations General Manager oversaw the Sydney, Brisbane and Melbourne venues and he had an operations manager that sat underneath him. He dealt with the key suppliers because obviously there's millions of dollars of stock that gets delivered into the three venues, and that stock had to be managed. The operations manager attends all the liquor licensing forums in the three cities and they are usually with other people in the industry and the police, liquor licensing and government. So we have open dialogue with those three key stakeholders. Then each venue has a venue manager and those venue managers are responsible for staffing, rosters and bar management, as well as cleaners, repairs and maintenance. The venue managers do two days and three nights and the two days are all task-orientated, getting ready for the operation for the nights. Then the nights are another whole thing in itself, when they are looking after up to a dozen security and up to a dozen bar staff and bussies, plus tour managers and promoters, to say nothing of 1000 to 1400 punters coming in."

The business of venue operation can be divided into two sets of challenges – internal and external. The internal challenges include booking and presenting the bands, including the production issues, marketing and promoting those performances and operating the hospitality side of the business – which includes everything from staff, to stock, refrigeration and kitchen, and repairs and maintenance. The external challenges involve dealing with licensing and council issues and liaising with police and other authorities. None of these activities

WELCOME TO THE JUNGLE

will directly help a venue operator sell another drink or attract another customer to the venue, but they are very important.

> **[TIM NORTHEAST]:** "To be sustainable people have to realise that they need to keep re-investing in the business and the building they are running the business from. Venues have a very high level of wear and tear; there's constantly stuff that needs upgrading and repairing. That is an issue in terms of cashflow and you need to manage that as well."

Jon Perring, along with two partners has operated a number of small Melbourne venues. He's acutely aware of the range of issues confronting a venue owner.

> **[JON PERRING]:** "A major part of it is dealing with the regulators and all the business crap that goes with that. You've got to be on top of all that stuff, otherwise you don't survive. You can't be naïve about it. Most people in some form of creative industry feel like they don't really want to deal with that stuff. But you do have to deal with it, and the better you deal with it, the more time you can devote to what you want to do. You've got to be on top of that stuff yourself or resource it up accordingly, which means you have to employ book-keepers and managers and all that sort of thing. There are lots of people around that work in hospitality and it's probably more fun working in a music venue than a straight café or whatever. But its hard work – it shouldn't be glorified in any way. Working in a bar is tough."

> **[TIM NORTHEAST]:** "These days there's probably five regulatory bodies we have to report to, not to mention the on-going issues with planning in inner-city Melbourne. The cost of dealing with them is substantial. I do spend a lot of time dealing

with them and the level of compliance with OH&S and essential building services really has become a serious part of our job and we have to set aside enough resources to manage that."

Another perspective on venue operation is provided by James Young, co-owner and booker of Melbourne's famous Cherry Bar and more recently Yah Yah's. As much as band bookings are obviously important at Cherry, Young also puts a lot of time and effort into working on the brand of his venue. It's an area that many venues overlook – expecting the talent to fill the room, rather than giving the room its own personality.

> **[JAMES YOUNG]:** "It doesn't matter what you stand for, just make sure you stand for something. Cherry's brand is that we believe in local music and late night rock n roll, and I think it's important to bring a personality into your bar/brand. So the Cherry Facebook, for example, isn't just about boring gig listings, it is a pop-culture commentary supposed to amuse and connect to like-minded people. If you enjoy the humour, the observations, the personality then the bar is made for you."

Pixie Weyand strikes a well-considered balance between the administrative functions and the branding of the venue.

> **[PIXIE WEYAND]:** "I think as I've moved through my business journey I've learned to take things more slowly. A lot of people think I'm a hundred miles an hour now, but I'm actually mellow now compared to two years ago! I've learned that if I have an idea to sit on it for a while and see if I think its still a good idea when I wake up in the morning. There are days when I do all the standard stuff like rostering and ordering but a lot of my time is put into developing the brand of The Zoo. There's so much more potential to grow the brand than just being a venue."

WELCOME TO THE JUNGLE

Employment In Venues

The live industry is responsible for a lot of jobs. Luke O'Sullivan estimates that at any one time the Hi-Fi Group had around 100 people on the books. Of these, there are around 15 that work in full-time capacities, either in central administration or in managerial positions. The rest of the staff are people taking initial steps in the industry or supporting either studies or a creative career. There is a lot involved in operating a venue that doesn't come with a manual. The ability to adapt and learn new skills will see you rise through the organisation.

> [LUKE O'SULLIVAN]: "There's no doubt that the more skill sets you've got and the more competent you are in a range of areas the more employable you are. But having said that, people acquired skills as they went along in our group, because a lot of people who worked in key roles in our business came from venues. That's what we tried to promote. On the commercial side of the business we moved towards getting more skilled professional people in that space because it became more important, but we still wanted them to have the right cultural fit. But on the operations side we had people who are now in management roles who started off working in security or working on the bar or working on the door and then found themselves working in the office."

> [TIM NORTHEAST]: "We generally get two kinds of people working here. There's those who love music and think it's a foot in the door to the music industry. Just loving music is usually not enough to convince me that they are going to be a great long-term prospect. Sometimes those people like working in the bandroom and listening to the music, but they are not focused on developing themselves. There are also students that come through as a good fun uni gig, while they are on

the road to somewhere else. Those people are great, because they are often studying and they are focused and they have a reason to be doing a job. But for the long-term staff you really need to have a passion and a love for live music, but also an understanding that it is a business and if you are going to make a career out of it you need to work hard to make a success of it."

Many of the venue operators in this chapter operate multiple venues. Basic economics suggests that there are economies of scale in the business and a central administration system can the spread over several venues that do essentially the same thing.

[TIM NORTHEAST]: "Each venue stands on its own two feet from a financial point of view, but we perceive there are advantages in being able to book multiple venues. From the perspective of the booking team and the marketing team, rather than employing people just to market one venue, we think we can spread their work across a couple of venues. It also increases your buying power from a media point of view. A promoter will also look at you as a bigger, more viable option for booking shows when you have multiple venues of different sizes. The model we are trying to put forward is that we are able to provide that consistency of operations across different size venues. The Corner and the Northcote are obviously different brands, but people in the industry know that they are linked and we are trying to push the same standards across both venues."

Future of Live Venues

There's no doubt that the Australian music industry has been shaped by the strength of the live scene. Most of our leading industry figures cut their teeth either operating venues or booking bands into venues, or managing those bands or even playing in those bands. Thousands

WELCOME TO THE JUNGLE

of lives have been changed by something they saw, heard or felt in a live venue and hundreds of deals have been done by industry players while leaning on the bar at a live gig.

Yet fears are constantly held for the live scene, mainly because there is concern for the viability of live music venues as businesses in the face of increasing competition, challenging regulations and harsh realities of the real estate market.

The importance of keeping the live scene strong cannot be overstated and, according to Frank Stivala, one of the people who played a part in creating pub-rock as we know it, the responsibility starts with the artists themselves, and those advising them.

> **[FRANK STIVALA]:** "Traditional venues are always going to be the backbone of the music business. At the moment there are not enough acts to feed those venues where they can have continuity. Back in the '80's you'd have good pubs all over the country doing two and three nights a week and getting decent crowds every night. We've got the acts, but they are not working as often and they have a different mentality about working. In some cases that might be right and in other cases it's definitely not right and it's overly precious. So the bands need to support those venues and let's hope the venue owners don't get tired of it and turn their venue into a food joint or put an extra 20 pokies in where the band room was. The new generation of acts need to support them and develop that pub culture to keep those venues alive."
>
> **[MICHAEL CHUGG]:** "Local venues are very buoyant at the moment. There seems to be a lot of action out there. There are a lot of young people doing shows and a lot of young bands that we haven't heard of working well. I think it's pretty good to be

honest. Bands doing festivals only and not touring became a major concern though. That's what happened in England and Europe too – a lot of acts no longer did tours; they just did festivals. I think there is a time to do festivals and a time to do your own tours."

Band Booking

What sets a music venue apart from a regular bar is, of course, the music. And there the idea of being the person responsible for booking the talent in a band venue is one of the most immediate jobs that people eye off when looking at breaking into the business.

However, if you are more inclined towards the music, the starting point in the live context is simply booking the talent and leaving the operation of the bar – the selling of drinks and the maintaining of a license – to the owners. That's obviously a simplification; no venue owner is going to persist with a venue booker who books bands that don't make any money for the venue, and the booker needs to understand and contribute to the overall business objectives of the owner.

One booker who has had an incredibly enduring career is Richard Moffat. As the booker for the Corner and the Northcote Social Club, he booked two rooms that rarely spent a night closed. He has some interesting views on what the job actually involves.

> **[RICHARD MOFFAT]:** "I love it when a crowd is out having a great time watching a band – whether that art transforms their lives beyond that night, I don't know or care. We are not selling anything people take away as a souvenir other than the experience of the night. It's very much about entertainment. We love it if people come early and eat and chat to their friends and watch the band and stay and have a drink at the end. The

WELCOME TO THE JUNGLE

venues make money from the beer and food sales, they don't make money from the tickets. Everyone that I have ever worked for has needed the connect of money over the bar for it to make financial sense and to keep running the venue running and all I care about is keeping the spaces sustainable so I can continue to book bands. I've often wondered what I would do if I was given the magic venue that had a house crowd every night and there was always people there and I could just book great bands, but that's like a myth and a fantasy. There is literally no venue anywhere in the world that has the mythical house crowd that is there every night."

While venue owners usually take a great deal of time, effort and money in building a venue that reflects their tastes or personalities, there's a question about whether the venue can attract an audience or whether it's the bands that draw the fans. While promoters, booking agents and managers are obviously interested in the quality of the PA and the size of the stage, do they actually care about the aesthetic of the venue and whether the front bar does good counter meals?

[RICHARD MOFFAT]: "I actually do the opposite to what most people do – I try to erase the personality of the venue completely. I really like neutral spaces. I like to book a space that can have an acoustic folk act one night and a black metal act the next night, and a blues act the next night. I try to make the spaces neutral and then try to have as wide as possible advertising and marketing reach. People might only go to the venue once a month or once every three months, but when they go they love it and we do not max out any one crowd. That's the model we built at the Corner."

Mary Mihelakos who has booked many Melbourne venues including the Evelyn, The Prince of Wales and Yah Yah's sees there being both an over-supply of bands and venues.

ANDREW WATT

[MARY MIHELAKOS]: "I used to know every band until about 2005 and now there is just so many of them and you can't keep track. Sometimes you find yourself getting tricked into putting on bands that tell you they are really good, where in the days when I was first booking venues I knew who every band was and exactly how many people they would pull. There are so many venues in Melbourne these days that people don't have the same loyalty to live music rooms that they did 10 or 15 years ago. When I first started going to gigs there was five or six music venues that everyone would go to on a regular basis. Now there's actually too many. You hear people getting upset when a venue shuts, but sometimes it's almost a good thing, because we have too many venues and some of them are empty half the time. I'd rather have 50 great venues than 100 average venues."

Richard Moffat also looks to bands and their managers to ensure that a show becomes an event, taking the view that people won't show up just because they have an inherent desire to support live music.

[RICHARD MOFFAT]: "The reasons why bands do or don't play in a space are really intangible and they are a lot to do with the connects of the people who are running it. We try to keep really diverse and keep it focused on 'event shows' as much as possible. I've never really been a big believer in the idea 'hey its Friday night, people want to go out and see original music'. I don't know of anyone who sits on the couch thinking that. That didn't feel real when I started and it doesn't feel any more real now. People generally go out to see stuff that their friends want to see and to hang out with their friends. It's the 'connector friend' that knows of the band that will be the one that gets the enthusiasm going."

There is no training that will guarantee you a job, let alone success, as a band booker for a venue.

WELCOME TO THE JUNGLE

[JON PERRING]: "Venue bookers come from all sorts of places – community radio, musicians who have been around for a while. In order to book a venue, the prime thing that you need is that you know a lot of people. You've got to know how to hook into the network. It's not really something you can be trained for. You just need to know who are the people doing things and get some kind of idea about who is attracting an audience. There's a commercial side to it. It's not just beer and skittles and listening to CDs. That's the big myth. Remember how everyone had to have a demo and send it out to everyone? They never got listened to. I don't know any bookers that ever listened to those things. It's sad because people put a lot of effort into producing those and it wasn't relevant."

In 2016, the Venue Collective, a company booking Melbourne venues (the Corner, Northcote Social Club, 170 Russell and Shebeen), the Newtown Social Club in Sydney the Woolly Mammoth in Brisbane and the Max Watts chain, stepped back from its multi-venue operation. Most of those venues now have in-house bookers working for that single venue. The Venue Collective was headed by Ben Thompson and had unprecedented influence across Australia's live landscape. It will be interesting to see whether that model arises again.

[BEN THOMPSON]: "The benefits of a multi-venue booking operation are lower costs to venues (booking, publicity and advertising overheads) and the ability to work with acts, agents and promoters to route several dates in the one phone call or email. At the same time as we were booking shows into multiple venues nationally we were also building communities of music lovers throughout the country and a marketing database to promote the shows that we booked."

ANDREW WATT

A career in venue booking can be a launching pad into other areas of the industry. Frank Varrasso, who features in the chapter on promotion and publicity, is one of Australia's most highly regarded radio promotions people, but he cut his teeth booking bands and doing promotion for Melbourne pubs. Richard Moffat has parlayed his venue booking into festival booking. In Sydney, Millie Millgate made a name for herself as the booker at the Annandale and Hopetoun Hotels and became known as one of the most helpful and approachable people in the Australian live scene. She's taken that experience and reputation with her into her current role as the head of Sounds Australia, an organisation that supports the export of Australian music. Her background at the coalface in live venues serves her very well.

> **[MILLIE MILLGATE]:** "It helped me understand what it takes from the early stages of a band's career. I think the basic principles apply every time you tackle the next stage of the lifecycle of an artist. It really is the same formula over and over again. The things that I tried to instil in acts when they were getting their first shows at the Hopetoun were things like promoting the show and picking the right supports and getting a good engineer. All of those sorts of things that go with a show at that local level are absolutely the same principles they should apply when they are in Austin for SXSW or New York for CMJ, or Britain for the Great Escape. It's the same when you move from your local venue, to your interstate touring, to your international touring. If you get it right from the beginning and get the basics right and if you are not afraid to ask those questions, it will put you in good stead to have the capacity to go all the way through. If you get those building blocks right, it's absolutely going to help."

My Path into the Industry

FRAZER BOURKE

"I started by doing mobile DJing. I got sick of doing 21st and 40th birthdays and having to buy all these records that I had no interest in whatsoever. So I started off running a goth-industrial club on a site in Kings Cross in Sydney on a Wednesday night, basically because I had all these records that I wanted to play and I couldn't play them as a mobile DJ. I started running more alternative clubs, and then an "80s club called Retro. Within doing that I would sometimes put on bands. That then led to buying a club, which sucked the life out of me. I did nightclubs – either running club nights or running a club for probably 10 or 12 years. I couldn't make a living doing that and so I had to find a full time job. I then started booking the Big Top in Sydney in the Luna Park complex. It had been open for about a year and hadn't had any shows, so I got that up and running as a venue, which I did for two or three years. I started the Come Together festival there and also the New Year's Eve event there. I was watching how Chugg and Frontier and Coppel were doing things and seeing why they had been in business for so long and why they were so good at it. Then I started doing Civil Society, which was the touring arm of Inertia, the first record label to do a touring company here in Australia. You try different things and it's a case of finding a balance between doing what you love and being able to put petrol in the car!"

Chapter 14

The Agent

The business of artist agent has a history almost as old as entertainment itself. Based in the idea that the skills and experience required to be a great entertainer or artist are inherently different to those required to obtain work for such talented individuals, the role of the agent came into existence. The business of an agent is founded upon the broader law of agency which, in simple terms, permits one individual to represent, negotiate, make agreements and enforce those agreements on behalf of another individual, provided that the second individual has given permission to the first individual to do so.

The agent, in the entertainment world, is simply the artist's authorised representative, and as such the relationship between the two is based on both legal principles and trust, where the artist believes the agent will represent them in a way that reflects well on them and fulfils their expectations of the relationship. The agent essentially stands in the shoes of the artist, so that those people dealing with the agent can rely on the fact that what is agreed by the agent will be fulfilled by the artist.

Despite some obvious similarities, the agent plays a different role to the manager. Traditionally, in Australia, the agent represents the artist in relation to live work – concerts, appearances and tours – and is generally not involved in the artist's recording or songwriting. The manager however, as seen in a previous chapter, is involved across the board, and helps the artist prioritise the various aspects of their career

WELCOME TO THE JUNGLE

and co-ordinating third parties that become stakeholders in it. An agent rarely, if ever, has any interest in the copyright created by an artist's work and will not receive a payment in relation to the exploitation of that work. An agent's compensation is derived entirely by commission on the revenue earned from the work they sourced for the artist. Thus, by definition, the agent is unlikely to be earning commissions from artists who are at home writing songs, in the studio recording or doing promotional work supporting an album release that does not include paid live shows.

> **[FRANK STIVALA]**: "All an agent owns is a relationship. Most times it's a handshake relationship where you can get screwed any time if you don't deliver. Very few agents do written agency agreements – it's basically relationships and handshakes. There is no real tangible asset there except the credibility that you build up over the years. It's like a marriage – if the artists want to be there they will be there, if they don't want to be there, they will leave. The only thing that a contract does is to complicate the relationship with legal razzamatazz, and it might stop someone from jumping hastily. But the bottom line is, if someone doesn't want to be there, you let them go because otherwise it becomes a bigger aggravation. You've go to have enough faith in your own ability to keep them.
>
> A manager will get a slice of the publishing, a slice of the recording, a slice of live and a slice of merchandising. Unfortunately in an agent's world, you only get a slice of the live income and if the act doesn't work because they got a big record advance or a publishing advance, then the agent doesn't make any money. So you need a lot of acts to support your business."

The role of the agent has always been perceived as cashflow or income oriented. The relationship they have with the acts they represent has never been seen as a tradeable asset, and in fact, as Frank Stivala points out, most agents have not even had contracts with their artists, which would set a fixed length of time to the arrangement. Unlike record companies or publishers who own copyright, or even managers who sometimes are entitled to post-termination commissions, the agency relationship has always been regarded as being in the "good while it lasted" department. That might be changing in some booking agent relationships.

> **[ADAM JANKIE]:** "Traditionally, the way a booking agent works is that they would do a deal with someone, selling a band to someone, and let's say they generate revenue of $100,000 and so the booking agent takes 10% straight off the top. Traditionally people would just turn over booking agents whenever they wanted to. An agent-client relationship wasn't a commodity. Now the rights of booking are actual rights that people sign away for a period of time to a booking agency. There is a value on those rights now, in the same way there was a value to traditional rights management in music or copyright. Things have become more complicated in terms of rights management."

Logically, if an artist has a successful album then the demand for them as a live performer will also increase and the fees they can command for those performances will also increase. More performances at higher fees naturally leads to higher commissions being earned by an agent booking those performances. So naturally, agents were happy to see artists doing the work necessary to release and record new albums and make those albums a success.

From the record company perspective, an artist touring to large audiences in strategically important markets can certainly help to make a record more successful, or even turn around a faltering release into a break-even project. Labels would generally work with agents, via the

WELCOME TO THE JUNGLE

artist's manager, to try and ensure that the touring schedules around a release were a positive contribution to their overall marketing plan for that release.

These days, high-quality agents tend to be more pro-active and they will be involved in the planning for an album release right from the beginning of that cycle. Rather than just waiting to be asked to 'book some dates' almost as an afterthought, the agent is now an integral part of the team, even taking up some of the slack where labels, managers or publishers might be under-resourced to maximise the impact of a release.

> **[BRETT MURRIHY]:** "The agent's relationship with record labels has always been an important one. This has now intensified more than ever. Where, in the past, artists historically have toured in support of an album release, they are now releasing albums to support the touring. We have monthly meetings with the majority of the major and indie labels because we represent so much of their talent. They want to know what an artist will be doing from a touring perspective to coincide."

For Steve Wade of Select Agency, the role of the agent doesn't start and stop around the artist's album cycle.

> **[STEVE WADE]:** "We work with our artists 52 weeks of the year – 100%. I have artists who haven't released anything all year, but I've had a dozen conversations that year with the artist about where we are at and how they are going. That's the process. When we started, none of our acts had enough profile that they could draw regularly. The big thing for me when we started Select was that I never wanted to think that I had to put an act on the road so I could make income. The second I ever have to think that, then I've done it wrong.

ANDREW WATT

When you pressure an artist to go out and perform when they shouldn't be, it normally ends in disaster. It can be so detrimental to their careers. That old corporate model of sending bands out to pay the bills and line the coffers was something we never wanted to be. We discuss at great length with our acts when and if they should be touring, because we want to have a 10-year plus career out of each act that we develop. Touring at the right times to maintain their status and maximise their earning potential is the aim. Artists and management want to make a decent living and they want to keep challenging themselves and find different markets, and of course we are involved in that process and we research and we do what we can."

The agency landscape in Australia has changed dramatically in the past decade. For most of the '80's and '90's the Australian business was dominated by Premier Harbour, a two-pronged agency business consisting of Premier Artists in Melbourne and the Harbour Agency in Sydney. Some attempts had been made to challenge this dominance over the years, most notably by Zev Eisek's ACE, the Trading Post Agency and Dirty Pool, which was a co-operative of Sydney-based managers seeking to break the stranglehold. All these businesses came and went with varying degrees of success in the market, with some of the people involved in these businesses having ongoing success in other configurations.

The agency landscape had been reasonably stagnant until the turn of the century. Venues would come and go, but the overall market remained much the same. There was always a circuit of pubs and clubs that had been the basis of the great Australian touring ethos and these were supported by the availability of opening spots on tours, college and university shows and the occasional corporate opportunity.

WELCOME TO THE JUNGLE

Steve Wade believes the changes to the live landscape made room for new agencies who were not so familiar with the established way of doing things.

> **[STEVE WADE]:** "I think the accessibility of it came from new players accepting that they have to do things differently. The whole market was based around pubs and clubs and there was one on every corner. There were very few festivals back then, so bands made a great living touring and on the road and our culture was that way. We literally had to start from scratch. We had to invest time and energy into acts that we thought were something special and chip away against the grain. That approach made the way we thought about being an agent completely different. It was less corporate and more quasi-managerial in style. It wasn't just about us booking a show – a lot of these acts didn't have management or they had inexperienced management when we first started so we had to be very hands-on. My philosophy always was that if you are going to be an agent for an artist, you are responsible for their livelihood. If you get it right it's amazing but if you fuck it up, you are left holding the bag. My philosophy is that we have to prove to these acts I'm passionate and I love what they do and then they have to believe in me and get my personality and have trust and faith in that. The agent's real job is to facilitate the opportunities that come your way. There is no magic wand or way to make a band big – you've just got to know when is the right time to place them in the right opportunities and then hopefully their talent and the music they have helps them realise those opportunities and they can go on to further and better things."

Frank Stivala sees the diversity of ways to present music as one of the main drivers for the expansion in the number of agencies in Australia.

ANDREW WATT

[FRANK STIVALA]: "Over the [past] couple of years music has become the flavour of the month and a lot of sponsors are heading toward music. It's not back to where it was in the '80's and early '90's, but it has come through that non-productive spell it went through. For a period of time there was not a lot of creative stuff coming out musically, and there were not a lot of sponsors focusing on music. Music wasn't that fashionable and now it's become fashionable from an advertising and sponsorship point of view. That's feeding the whole industry and helping people grow and creating new acts. That's why there is room for more agencies. We don't necessarily have the time or the expertise to find where that interesting grassroots idea might be, but there are new agents who might find that's their niche. Agents who specialise in those things are great because it broadens the musical landscape of what's out there. There's more diversification with agents."

These days there is a proliferation of well-operated agencies with strong client rosters and this segment of the business is thriving. The scope of what an agent does in Australia is also broadening, with the realisation that all aspects of an artist's career need to be run in accordance with a masterplan for the best outcome. The importance of live revenue for recording artists has been another driver in the rise in the need for great agencies.

Frank Stivala has seen many start-up agencies come and go and agrees that the current crop look likely to be around for the long haul. But he cautions that there is a difference between an agent who understands and can execute the art of the job, and those who are merely bookers.

[FRANK STIVALA]: "A lot of the new agents are not really agents as such; they are bookers. The art of being an agent is trying to negotiate fees and conditions. Just booking a venue and taking a door deal is not being an agent – Blind Freddy, with half a brain could do that. People like Owen Orford and Tony Grace, who have been around a long time are the true agents; many of the others are just bookers. Anyone can put a price tag on a hot act that a festival wants to pay through the nose for, but doing a national tour and trying to get guarantees every night of the week is where the art comes in."

For Brett Murrihy, one of the main reasons he created his Artist Voice agency was his belief that the Australian agency landscape was capable of playing a more respected role than it had been assigned by those outside the industry.

[BRETT MURRIHY]: "One of my main incentives in starting Artist Voice was that I wanted to bring a respectability to what agents do in this country. In America agents are much revered. The press talk about the top agents like Ari Emanuel and Patrick Whitesell as celebrities in their culture, and here agents have been seen as the pariahs of the business. I'm incredibly proud of what an agent does and how we go about it and I'm hopeful that it will be something that young people will forge towards in new careers. There has been a shift in perception with the role and people understand that it's not such a frowned-upon occupation. What we are doing is exciting because we are now not just working within Australia, we are working out touring with New Zealand, Japan, China, South East Asia and India and it is exciting for young agents. You learn a lot from dealing with the different territories."

Murrihy's international vision was vindicated in 2016 when his agency Artist Voice was acquired by huge US based agency William Morris Endeavour. His partner in the agency Matt Gudinski sees this as a natural progression.

ANDREW WATT

> **[MATT GUDINSKI]:** "It was inevitable that William Morris was going to do something in Australia. It surprised a lot of people that one of the biggest entertainment companies in the world saw Australia as such an important territory. It's changed the landscape for breaking acts on a lot of levels. It's certainly created an opportunity for some Australian artists to get more support overseas as well."

Agents now are active sources of A&R in the Australian music scene. Once it was hard to get an agent without having a record deal, because the agent knew it would be hard to get the act many worthwhile gigs without them having a CD in the market and getting radio airplay. Now agents often take on bands without record contracts. The ability for artists to record, release and promote themselves independently means they can be highly attractive propositions for agents long before a label gets involved.

Brett Murrihy points out that this is an international pattern.

> **[BRETT MURRIHY]:** "This is happening the world over in the agency landscape. I think that because of what we do and the increased importance of money from touring, people have become a lot more competitive. In Australia there are a lot of agencies for a market of our size. Because of the way the record business has gone in the [past] five years, you can't afford to sit back and wait to see what they might sign, because if you do that, you might end up missing the boat. The A&R sessions that we have are very intense, and you have to be on things first. The majority of our agents are out six nights a week trying to find the new thing and we are certainly not waiting on anyone else to tell us what is happening any more. Conservatively, 80% of the artists we pick up now don't have labels – and managers are the same. The majority of the bands that we approach don't have either a manager or a label."

WELCOME TO THE JUNGLE

Rob Ziferelli is a leading agent at the United Talent Agency based in Toronto and he also finds that agents now have to get on to new artists a lot quicker than they once did.

> **[ROB ZIFERELLI]:** "There are just so many more agents and everybody is just trying to gobble everything up. There are some agents that have been famously quoted as saying that they are just snapping everything up and then they will see what sticks. The reality is that is part of the fear factor that is out there. We've probably all been in that position – knowing that there are four other agents in the room trying to grab the artist now. I certainly don't think it is healthy but it is becoming more of a necessary evil. But eventually those agents will get found out and I try to live by the rule of "do great work". I hope that's what I do."

The access to information like an artist's social media data and statistics also now comes into play.

> **[ROB ZIFERELLI]:** "It can be helpful but you need to be cautious with it and really scrutinize those numbers. But it is a great thing to have those tools so you can be a bit more scientific in your approach to it. You get feedback from socials that show how excited people might be about an artist in a particular territory, but the analytics are very useful for us. I'm a bit sceptical about streaming service plays because I'm not sure that people are actually 'hearing' the song they might be playing whereas on You Tube they are actually choosing to play that song. The ones that are more active from the user are the ones that I am more responsive to."

Australian agents have tended to operate exclusively within Australia, for obvious reasons. Their role is still largely about live shows and local knowledge of venues, promoters and markets is obviously essential. However, in recent times some agencies have been looking further afield. In the case of Artist Voice (now WME), the push into the Asian market is particularly interesting.

> **[BRETT MURRIHY]:** "In the agency space, we wanted to provide something for domestic artists that was a real pipeline to other territories. From when we started hiring to when we started putting together a roster, I had a real sense of what we wanted to on-sell to other territories. I didn't want to sign things that were only going to work domestically, I was always hopeful that if I was going to sign something it would be of an international standard. I think Empire of The Sun really opened my eyes to what was happening in Asia, Japan and South America – all these new territories that weren't perhaps as locked down as the US and UK landscape. I saw the future of our business for the Australian agencies opening up those territories to our artists to ensure we can make the capital to achieve something meaningful within the space."

In the later chapter on Music Business Education, Brett Murrihy discusses the importance of tertiary education as an entry level to his business. Steve Wade sees being able to understand the idiosyncratic nature of the music business and speak its language as being equally important.

> **[STEVE WADE]:** "You've got to have some kind of connection and understanding of the industry and the people within it. That's what we have tried to foster in our office. Just grabbing someone off the street because they love music and putting them in a chair and giving them four acts to book is absolutely pointless. It's a waste of time and energy and it will pretty much destroy the person sitting in that chair. There is no right or

WELCOME TO THE JUNGLE

wrong in our industry. It's not like carpentry where there is one right way of making a join between that wall and that door – that's not open to interpretation. In our industry there is no black and white – there is so much grey and what separates the best from the worst is how they navigate the grey. There are a lot of things that, if you miscalculate, could have a devastating effect on your artist. For young people who aspire to getting into the agency game, it's about getting into a music company and starting from the ground up – being on the phones, understanding how contracts work, rolling posters up, speaking to people at venues, speaking to other agents. You see those people at gigs and people put a face to your name and you make connections that way. Both my partner Rob G and myself had PAs who want to eventually become agents, and so we exposed them to working with the artists and their management and ticketing and all of that. It means by the time they are ready to cross over they know everybody. They know the managers, so if a manager has a new act they want to represent they have a head start. If you are a young agent and you see a new act and soon all the established agents find out about them, the new agent won't get that band. They won't entrust their band to someone with no history or track record of successful artists and no infrastructures or powerful allies."

Frank Stivala isn't looking for someone carrying a university qualification necessarily; he sees the qualifications as being more inherent, rather than taught.

> **[FRANK STIVALA]:** "What you see is someone who uses their initiative, someone who has the passion and the gift to sell with conviction, someone who can actually close the deal. You see someone that people like and trust and value their opinion and taste. If you are half smart and you've got half an idea and you are streetwise and you are passionate about the music, you

really don't need a university degree. If you have half a brain in maths – without being a genius, as long as you can work out deals, as long as you have the gift of the gab, as long as you have passion and nous, then that's all it requires."

My Path into the Industry

TIM NORTHEAST

"I started by doing a casual bar job while I was at university. I found my way to the Punters Club, and worked my way into a management role there. Matt Everett, who owned the Punters Club, and I decided to go into business together and bought the Corner Hotel. I think a lot of people end up in the industry through a similar path – by just having exposure to it while they are studying and deciding that it is something they enjoy – and then focusing on hospitality as a career. I was doing commerce at the time. Commerce is one of those broad degrees that teach you how to think more than anything else. It helps you to be analytical and structured in your thoughts and it's been a great grounding for me. I think a lot of people in hospitality come from an experience background rather than having actually studied hospitality. Running these sorts of businesses of this size you wear many hats – you are the bean counter, the lawyer, the planning consultant and you have to liaise with lots of bodies. Having exposure to a broad range from having a degree can help you in those situations."

Chapter 15

Promoters

Everybody wants to be a promoter. The idea of touring your favourite band, and having hundreds, thousands or tens of thousands of people turning out to see them, sounds like a dream way to make a living. Well, here's the first tip – if you want to see your favourite band play five times in a week, there are far easier and less stressful ways of doing it that promoting their Australian tour! It would probably be far better for both your health and you bank balance to get on a plane, fly to wherever they might be touring overseas, buy a ticket and a hotel room and enjoy a holiday. At least you know <u>exactly</u> what the holiday will cost and how much you are going to lose!

But even that word of warning won't prevent a significant proportion of readers of this book still being attracted to the business of promotion. And nor should it. Promotion is certainly a risky area of business, but it's also one of the most exciting – when it works. Success as a promoter can come at all levels, from shows in pubs and clubs all the way through to high-stakes concerts at stadiums or multi-day, multi-band festivals.

This chapter focuses more on tour promoters rather than festivals – those are examined in more detail in the next chapter. Though the two types of promotions have a lot in common, they require some significantly different skills and experience.

> **[MICHAEL CHUGG]:** "Festivals are events. They are a specific event and that's totally different from a tour where you are promoting in each city, or at least the cities you choose to tour.

WELCOME TO THE JUNGLE

> A festival will be in one venue and it's a one to three to five-day event that needs a lot of different people involved – site managers and those sorts of people. You might be running campsites and three or four stages. It's really a very different set of issues."

The tour promotion business is a highly complex area, but the basic principles are very simple. Promoting a tour involves finding an artist that you believe people will want to see, calculating how many people you think will buy tickets, at what price, and then determining what the costs are to market that show, stage the tour and then deciding what you can afford to pay that artist to do the shows. If the fee is acceptable to the artist (and their agent and manager), than you may well have a deal. Then you hope that all your estimates prove correct and that the predicted number of people buy the tickets at the price you have set. If they do, you should make a profit.

This description of a promoter's job looks at the role from the point of view of a promoter attempting to make a profit, or at least survive to fight another day and book another tour.

But there is another way of looking at it. A promoter is also another one of those service providers that artists need. An artist needs to tour to build their audience and sustain a career, and the promoter is the service provider that allows them to do this. But where a promoter is different is that they don't charge a fee for their service; rather they are on a risk-return profile that means they make a profit if a tour is a great success (provided they do their budgets correctly) and they don't get paid at all if the tour fails. Even worse they lose their own money if the tour fails. But even a failed tour still involves them proving the same services to the artist that a successful tour does.

Experienced and knowledgeable tour promoters realise that the responsibility to the artist is what helps them build a sustainable business.

[MICHAEL COPPEL]: "Ultimately I think the promoter's responsibility is to maintain, improve, enhance or create an artist career in the market in which they work. My name on a poster does not sell one single ticket; that's why it's in the small print. It's the artist's name in large print that sells the tickets. That artist gives you their career and says you can use their image, notoriety, music, etc, for a limited period of time in return for a substantial financial arrangement. Then you have a responsibility to enhance the value of what they give you. There is no point doing a one-off tour – it's too hard to get the artist to just do a one-off thing. You have to build their career, so the next time they come around the relationship that you have established means you get to do the next tour. It's very important to have that and to remember that artists don't work for promoters: promoters work for artists."

So while the role of the promoter is always painted as that of a high stakes gambler, the reality is that much of the job involves logistics and administration. For Michael Coppel, the biggest challenge is the fact of not knowing what problems any given day will bring. There probably isn't a tour where absolutely everything goes according to plan. Experience will help a promoter deal with the unexpected issues, but the reality is that concert touring involves so many moving parts and unpredictable people that the promoter's job is never as simple as it might appear to the outsider.

[MICHAEL COPPEL]: "To be a promoter you need to wake up every day expecting to have a lot of problems thrown at you. You start every day knowing that you will be putting your flak jacket on and get out and deal with every problem as it comes up, in order to try and get to your strategic objective. You need to have the ability to roll with the punches and to think on your feet and be able to divorce emotion from rationality, so you can avoid getting angry and sort the thing out. You need to

WELCOME TO THE JUNGLE

have a familiarity with different areas – whether it is financial or logistics or whether it is negotiating or whether it's political. You need to be able to interface with government on visas and permits and government authorities that are increasingly taking an interest in the promotion industry from a health and safety point of view, or from a consumer protection point of view, or from some other regulation point of view. It's become very much a multi-skill environment; it's not as straightforward as saying, 'that band could sell some tickets, how do I book them, how do I put the tickets on sale, how do I sell them?' It's a much more multi-faceted business and a much more challenging business as a result."

Promoter Emily York has worked a strong niche via her company Penny Drop. She got experience working with Inertia's touring company Handsome Tours before striking out on her own. She recognises exactly what Michael Coppel is talking about, but she also believes that those challenges are manageable.

[EMILY YORK]: "Yes, it was difficult and it was a huge leap of faith, but it was one of those situations where I knew it was time to do something on my own. That was the driving motivation to do it, and to not worry about all those unknowns. But it was probably a lot easier than I might have imagined. In reality in some ways it was quite effortless, even though I worked harder than ever before; things did fall into place at the same time. It wasn't like starting from scratch, so I guess that was different, because I had years of experience in different guises."

She also seems to understand Coppel's view of the promoter as a service provider in the artist's ongoing career.

[EMILY YORK]: We have been very boutique. I don't want to tour every hot band of the minute. I want to focus on a handful of artists who I see as having very long term careers and really invest in them from beginning to end. There's a lot of satisfaction with going the whole journey with an artist. It's something you don't get to do in Australia very often, because a lot of the time, by the time an artist gets to Australia, they are a lot more established. That's something that I really am into, working with acts from the ground up and I think that our role in this territory is like manager, publicist, label, promoter, agent. They might not have a record deal or they might not have a manager, but we see that they have this incredible talent, so we work with them as a partner within this territory."

Frazer Bourke is another promoter whose company Metropolis Touring has built a niche for itself. He is also intent on building a sustainable business that doesn't necessarily involve a transition to stadium shows and all the complications that come with touring on that scale.

[FRAZER BOURKE]: "My thing is to have a roster of acts that I can tour, like Tim Pittman has with Feel. He's been doing it a long time and he's got acts he tours every two or three years. I just want to have a sustainable amount of income coming in and do it like that. I went to Bruce Springsteen and it just blows my mind the amount of effort that goes into a tour of that magnitude. I'm not sure if that really appeals to me. I'd like to have that sustainable income so I don't have to worry if I want to do a tour that's a bit more risky. If you have those regular tours it means that you are not always having to find new tours all the time. That's the hard situation – having to constantly source new tours. If you can find a roster of tours that make money and you can do those every two or three years, you hopefully end up with a solid base. You've got to hope that if you do the right thing by the artist and you do a good job on the tour and everyone walks away happy then you will keep working with that artist through the course of their career."

WELCOME TO THE JUNGLE

His philosophy isn't all that far removed from that of Chugg or Coppel and it shows that the tour promotion business isn't all about magnitude. However the increasing number of promoters at the small to mid-sized level means that these promoters need to plan further ahead; not to get the acts, but to secure the venues they prefer for the acts they are touring.

> **[FRAZER BOURKE]:** "Trying to get a run is a lot different than it was five years ago. Five years ago you could ring up the Corner Hotel and get a booking in three months' time; now you couldn't do that – everyone has longer lead times now. The key days are still Thursday, Friday and Saturday and there are only so many of those in a year. You've got to plan a lot further out than you used to, to get your run and your routing the way you want it to be, without circumnavigating Australia to get your three or five dates in. Promoters have their venues that they like to use and the good venues are the ones you are happy to keep going back to."

The Australian touring business is different to most international markets. In Australia a single promoter will usually do the whole national tour. In countries with more cities like the US or across Europe, promoters tend to focus on geographic areas. In the US for example, at the small to mid-sized level, there might be one promoter do New England, a different one in Texas and in California and a different one in the North West taking in Seattle and Portland. Cities such as New York, Vegas, Nashville and New Orleans often have promoters that only work in those markets. For artists touring here, the idea of having the same promoter for every show in a country as geographically big as Australia is quite surprising.

> **[MICHAEL CHUGG]:** "It is the unique things here that one promoter does all the territories. In America and Europe there is different promoters for each city or each market or each

country. To do a tour in Europe you are probably dealing with 20 or 30 promoters, certainly in America you are. Here, you get off the plane and you are dealing with one group of people. The acts love it because they get the same high quality care every day of the week."

Breaking In to Tour Promotion

There are basically three ways to break into the tour promotion business.

You can gain experience in one of the established tour promotion companies and work your way into a position where you take an active part in the decision making and thus experience the thrill of the chase and feel the pressure of the risk your company is taking. From there you can consider taking on your own touring projects or making other moves in the industry.

With international companies such as Live Nation having a presence in Australia, international career paths are a realistic possibility.

[**MICHAEL COPPEL**]: "I think there are legitimate international career paths. Certainly in the touring industry in general, there's a lot of Australian tech crew that work overseas. They worked here and got experience working on local and international tours and got offered jobs to work overseas. There are managers, like Roger Davies [Olivia Newton-John, Pink, Cher, Tina Turner], that have gone on to become extraordinarily successful internationally. But I think there is a career path for promoters as well. There is certainly a functional career path within Live Nation, where people in one country can apply for a similar job or another job within the company in another market. There are a few people that have come out of the European company that are working in South East Asia.

WELCOME TO THE JUNGLE

What I've seen is that we are getting a second generation of promoters – not the ones who started the company or who own the company – but the ones who started working for those people. They are the ones who are much more mobile in terms of their career options. You are not going to see Michael Gudinski or Michael Chugg or myself going and working internationally – that's a question of age and family ties and everything else. But now you've got guys coming in, in their 20's and 30's who are much more mobile and don't have commitments that will keep them resident in Australia necessarily. I think a lot of those will make the transition to working internationally."

Alternatively you can transfer skills obtained in one area of the business and re-apply those in the touring world. Two of the leading lights in Michael Gudinski's Frontier Touring Company are Gerard Schlaghecke and Michael Harrison, both of whom served long apprenticeships as senior agents at the Premier and Harbour Agencies, respectively. Their hard-won skills are easily transferable into the tour promotion business.

Others come from less predictable sides of the business. For merchandising guru Brian Taranto, the move into touring was a natural progression.

[BRIAN TARANTO]: "Touring started in 1997 for me when I decided to tour this guy called Tony Joe White. I loved his music. I felt like I'd been at enough shows, I'd been on enough tours, I'd been at all the venues. I just thought I could work it out. I was fortunate enough that the first tour was a huge hit. We added about 10 extra shows and we made about $30,000, even on the crap deal I was on. It was fun to do something I was passionate about and make money from it. So we kept doing it. We came across bands that I had some connection to. The Black Keys is a great story for us. I went to SXSW one year. I read *Rolling Stone* on the way over and there was a great review of their record, so I bought the record. I got to SXSW, went and saw them, loved them and set about trying to get them to tour here. We had them here within about six months and it's just gone from strength to strength, based on developing a great relationship with them. Now they are one of the biggest bands in the world and they stick with me."

Although record companies have shown an increasing interest in the live income of artists in recent years, there does not seem to be a big crossover into tour promotion for people with a record company background. Since leaving Shock Records, company founder David Williams has become involved in touring, but he is one of the few. He acknowledges that there are differences between selling recorded music and selling the live concert experience.

[DAVID WILLIAMS]: "The difference is when you are trying to get someone interested in a particular artist to try and sell them a CD, you would publicise it in a certain way. The way that people discover music has changed and now you are trying to create a profile for a particular artist to create a career to an extent. When you are dealing with touring, you are not trying to sell the new music to people who are on a voyage of discovery; you are trying to sell them a ticket to see an artist that they already like. Trying to convince someone to go and see an artist because you are telling them you think they are really good is a very difficult sale to make. As a record label you are trying to sell music to people who are learning about an artist; as a tour promoter you are trying to sell tickets to people who already like them."

Both Michael Coppel and Michael Chugg share the view that the best training to become a tour promoter is to get your feet wet at a local level and learn from your mistakes. For Coppel it's about learning the value of a ticket dollar as well as the cost of a dollar spent.

WELCOME TO THE JUNGLE

[MICHAEL COPPEL]: "The best promoter in the world is the guy who started working off his own capital and having to protect that capital and increase that capital. It's very true that you have a different attitude when it's your money and when it's someone else's money. If you are working for someone else, it doesn't affect you in the short term if a show doesn't work or a tour doesn't work, or if you have made the wrong decision, then you have a slightly different approach than if it's your money and you can lose your house, or your family's livelihood. So the best guys are the ones that started with their own hundred bucks, thousand bucks, or ten thousand bucks and built it into a business. That's not to denigrate people who are working as employees and not risking their own capital."

[MICHAEL CHUGG]: "We give people internships and try them out, but I've always said to all these youngsters that they find a local band and learn how to promote them. I think starting at a local level is the way to go. You get a background going and if you are any good you will get snapped up. There are limited jobs at promoters businesses. Everybody is pretty lean and mean as far as employing people."

For newer promoters entering the business and hoping to establish themselves, opportunities exist to catch the eye of their bigger counterparts. Promoters like Chugg, Coppel and Gudinski are well aware that having an innate understanding of a particular scene or genre is essential to making it work and they will often establish relationships with younger promoters to assist them moving to the next level – provided the situation is mutually beneficial, of course.

[MICHAEL COPPEL]: "We work with a number of smaller promoters. We are open to do that because my view is that when you start as a young promoter you are one with your audience. As you get older the audience tends to stay the same age, but you get further apart from them and you lose touch with them. You don't actually know them. The best period for any promoter is when he instinctively knows that he wants to see an act live and therefore there will be other people of a like mind who will also want to see that act and you just know in your gut that it will be a successful show. When you get 20, 30, 40 years divorced from that core 15 to 30 year-old audience you don't share the same musical values and you don't share the same social values and the culture has changed around you. It becomes a lot harder to know with any confidence that an act is going to work. When you have a competitive market there is no safety net. You are paying top dollar to get a tour, so you want to be damn sure that other people want to see them in sufficient numbers to get your risk covered. I watch what the younger promoters are doing."

There are a number of roles available with touring companies. Two of the main areas involve logistics and marketing – getting the show on the road and ensuring that there is an audience to see it! There are also important roles behind the scenes in accounting and finance. Touring is a business that relies heavily on the ability to make sense of an Excel spreadsheet! Many of the production roles are filled by contracted tour managers and production managers who are a group of people with highly specialised skills, who generally acquire their skills over a long period of time, through the school of hard knocks. In Australia, names like Jon Pope, Howard Freeman, Nick Marson and a small number of others are legendary, but no one is going to take their jobs straight out of school! You need to earn that status through the school of experience.

In the marketing area there are people who have come from music industry backgrounds, but also those whose marketing skills have been imported from other industries. One of the most interesting elements of the touring business is the diversity of people that make up the workforce. Promotion is an area where there is potential for anyone of any background to built a career.

My Path into the Industry

CHRIS O'BRIEN

"I started off running a punk nightclub, and a gothic nightclub, back in the mid "90s. One was called Sirus, which was a gothic club and we had Oxide that was the punk club. Oxide really took off and was pretty successful for about three years. We had Millencolin, Blink 182, No Fun At All playing there back when they were just breaking into the scene too. Because of that we decided to start a little record label and a booking agency. I was trying my hand at as many different things as I could, just to see where I fitted in and where my actual passion lay. I knew I loved music, but I wasn't sure which direction I wanted to take. I started managing a couple of small local bands at the time, one was Game Over and another was Area 7, playing the Tote and Punters Club and things like that. So I was working with promoters – one was AJ Maddah and there was a guy named Craig from Adelaide, working on all their tours with them back in the mid "90s. The promoting thing and the management thing really stuck with me, so I left the clubs behind then and went full-tilt [into] management. Area 7 took off pretty soon after that and I wound up managing Bodyjar and the Mavis's. I gave up management about seven years ago and went full time with AJ and Chuggi [Michael Chugg]. We left Chuggi after that and started Soundwave in 2003 and went national in 2008."

Chapter 16
Festivals

One of the biggest shifts in the music business in the past couple of decades has been the dominance of festivals in the live music market. As discussed in Chapter 13 on Live Venue Operation, the festival market has had both positive and negative effects on the overall live scene. Festivals have brought hundreds of artists to Australia that otherwise would not have been able to tour here and the concept of the sideshow (when a festival act plays a headline show in addition to its festival appearance) has become an important revenue earner for many live venues. But at the same time some venues feel that festival suck a lot of the money out of the live music market, leaving less money to flow into the venue business. It's also been strongly suggested that artists and managers plan too much of their live activity around festival appearances and neglect regular touring as a result.

The Festival Landscape

In contemporary music, Australia has a rich array of festivals most of which will be familiar to audiences and potential industry personnel – in fact if you are not aware of many of these events, then you perhaps shouldn't be contemplating a career in the Australian music business!

There are festivals that cater for just about any taste and market operating in Australia and yet there are always new events coming on to the scene claiming to offer a point of difference. It's a very volatile and competitive market and it's certainly not a business for the faint-hearted.

WELCOME TO THE JUNGLE

Consider some of the events that have come and gone and in many cases still remain on the festival calendar around Australia: Big Day Out, Splendour in the Grass, Bluesfest, Laneway, Soundwave, Homebake, Stereosonic, Future Music, Woodford Folk Festival, Southbound, Sugar Mountain, Groovin the Moo, Out On The Weekend, Falls, Queenscliff Music Festival, Big Sky Blues and Roots Festival, Port Fairy, Beyond The Valley, Mona Foma, Unify Gathering, Gympie Muster, Apollo Bay, CMC and Tamworth Country Music Festival.

Beyond these are smaller, more music-community type festivals such as Meredith, Golden Plains and Boogie that command a fiercely loyal audience. Then there are the boutique events such as So Frenchie So Chic, Festival of the Sun, Strawberry Fields, The Gum Ball, Sounds of the Suburbs, Let Them Eat Cake, Cherry Rock, The Hills Are Alive, River Boats and others. On top of this are various arts festivals in just about every state that have very significant amounts of music programming such as Womadelaide, Vivid and the Melbourne Festival of the Arts.

Each of these events has it's own point of difference, it's own musical genre and it's own target audience. The reality of the ever-changing festival market is that by the time this edition is published, the landscape will have again changed. The only constant in the festival market is change.

Bluesfest promoter Peter Noble is able to put the discussion about the festival landscape into perspective.

> **[PETER NOBLE]:** "At Big Sound a few years ago they had a panel called – Festivals – Are They the New Pub Rock? And my response to that was, "Is that supposed to mean there is one on every corner?" There are not hundreds of festivals in Australia; there are thousands. They can be everything from very small

or community events right through to the big city-presented festivals like Sydney Festival or the events in the popular music world. There are an awful lot of events – the Australian Jazz Festival is well over 50 years old. So when you make generalised statements about the festival market, you have to look at the market in terms of types of events and who they are marketing toward, and whether those particular areas are over supplying or under-supplying in pure economic terms."

What's interesting is that many of the Australian music business's most high profile promoters such as Michael Gudinski, Michael Chugg, Paul Dainty and Michael Coppel are not the promoters behind the events listed earlier. Admittedly, Chugg does supply many acts to Bluesfest and both he and Coppel have been involved in the festival market to a greater and lesser extent, but on the whole, the promoters of these events are drawn from a different pool of music entrepreneurs. In the case of Live Nation the December 2016 purchase of a majority share in the parent company of the Falls Festival and Splendour in the Grass signified a big step into the Australian festival market. The fact that the existing promoters of those festivals remain in day-to-day operational control of their events seems to reflect the philosophy that Michael Coppel had expressed earlier.

[**MICHAEL COPPEL**]: "I've dabbled in the festival market several times myself and the conclusion I've come to is that a festival is a 365-day-a-year business, not an adjunct to a company that promotes stand-alone shows. You can't allocate staff to do your day-to-day touring as well as the once-a-year event. You need to go into that business and skill it up and resource it as a stand-alone business, because you need to spend three to five years on a festival. No-one gets lucky in Year 1, or if they do it's because the headliner was really strong like Splendour with Coldplay. If that happens you become a festival that is

WELCOME TO THE JUNGLE

dependent on your line-up, not because you have had an organic growth of support, like a Glastonbury or a Coachella or a Roskilde. They are 20-year-plus festivals where you can go on sale (for the next year) the day after the event and sell 50% of your tickets with no line-up in place, but on the expectation from your audience from past experience that you will have a good line-up and that you are going to sell out before the event happens."

The experience that Michael Coppel speaks of – that of a festival being able to sell tickets based purely on the reputation of past events is something that Peter Noble has attained with Bluesfest. He offers such a remarkable feast of talent at his event that you can't help but question how he manages to avoid cutting a few corners, booking a few less acts, spending less money anticipating that the audience won't ever notice the difference.

[PETER NOBLE]: "If I spend $500,000 less, I could put it in my pocket! I am more than aware that we are probably offering more talent per dollar spent than any other event in this country. We are definitely offering a very good array of talent for the price. You are seeing well over a million dollars worth of talent appearing on stage every day. I have had more than one person come to me, including people sniffing around, wanting to buy the event off me, telling me that they think they could present the event for a lot less money! We know that! But if you invest in your artists and your event, then I put it to you that your savings come in two areas – you save on marketing costs but they also come in building your brand. I can sit here a month after the last festival and the next year is 50% sold out, and we are yet to contract one act. The reason for that is that I am giving people a really compelling event. I might spend a bit more on talent, but it comes back in other ways very strongly.

ANDREW WATT

> It's about building that relationship with your customer base. I don't view spending more money that we probably need to as a bad investment. I think it buys you customer loyalty and it puts money in the bank to invest in infrastructure."

With so many events established in the market it's tempting to say that it's an incredibly tough scene to break into, but the facts suggest that new promoters do break into those markets on a regular basis. For many years, industry pundits have been saying that the market is saturated and that the bubble is due to burst and yet most of the existing events appear to have found a niche –in some cases, a very big niche.

Steve Halpin heads Cattleyard Promotions, the promoter of regional touring festival Groovin' the Moo.

> **[STEVE HALPIN]:** We have a niche. We are smaller and so it is easier to sustain and we don't have competition in the regions we go to. We are providing something unique as a festival for young people in regional Australia, outside the capital cities. But it's also an experience for people in the cities to travel to regional Australia. That's been a big part of our growth – more and more people are coming from the cities. The 'road trip" is definitely part of the appeal."

The impact of the huge number of festivals and their effect of sucking a staggering number of potential touring acts out of the market is significant. Where once many of those acts would start small and build an audience in Australia, readying themselves for return tour at a later date, many acts now take the easier and less exposed route of playing festivals. It's not always to their benefit, according to Michael Coppel.

> **[MICHAEL COPPEL]:** "I think it's actually a very negative development from my perspective. When I approach an agent

WELCOME TO THE JUNGLE

about a new act because I think they have a market and I think you can build it, the agent will commonly say that they can only afford to come if we get a festival as an anchor date, because that $50,000 or $100,000 show makes all the difference to the financial benefit of a trip down to Australia. But most of the bands on festivals don't actually benefit from being there. They play in the afternoon to a small group of people in front of their stage, they are over-shadowed and lost in the promotion with 70 or 80 other acts, the sideshows they do are competing with 60 or 70 other sideshows. You get acts that come through and just don't improve their market support by doing the festival route. They just become perpetual festival bands so every two to three years they will be on a festival bill; they never do their own headline shows or a stand-alone tour because they never develop beyond line 5 on the festival ad. I'm a great believer that bands that have lasted and built enduring careers in any market in the world have done grassroots work – they have played the club, they have moved up to the theatre and then moved up to a bigger-sized venue, then the arena and then the stadium. They haven't just come and played festivals three times and disappeared."

Festival Gambling

Dror Erez, the managing director of Totem One Love, the team behind the monster EDM festival Stereosonic, provides a good summary of the risks involved in festival promotion.

[DROR EREZ]: "To be in this industry you have to gamble to a degree, but your gambling can be informed and educated gambling or it can be damn foolhardy gambling. I've seen examples of both. You just need to know that the ones that fuck up have to be a lot smaller than the ones that succeed. That's the key.

ANDREW WATT

It's obviously a very enchanting prospect to select a bunch of your favourite artists, throw them on to a stage and watch the masses roll in the gates to celebrate your brilliant taste in music. It's also a complete fantasy! So much so that it became the plot for a movie called *Wayne's World*. Anyone contemplating a career in festival promotion should see that movie and if you recognise yourself, think of another career! In reality, the ability to operate a successful festival requires two brains operating in unison. The first brain needs to have a brilliant creative flair and the second brain needs to be extraordinarily well organised. Very few people have both. Most successful festival promoters either are a team, or they have a brilliant team behind them.

> **[DROR EREZ]:** "You just need to find the right people to work with. Some of my greatest successes or failures in my life were due to the compatibility or lack of compatibility of the people. When you look at Totem One Love it is a great example of people with different skill sets all coming together. We are all unemployable! We don't like to be told what to do by anyone; we are fiercely independent individuals, but for the greater cause we can come together to make some thing happen. As individuals we are impossible. But when we work together we know when to step back and let the other guy's skills come forward. That's how this industry works, because I don't know anyone who can do it all themselves."

Booking A Festival

The job of programming a festival is part art and part science. There is an incredible amount of instinct involved in finding a line-up that will appeal to the market, but there is a lot of information available to promoters who choose to use it. Aly Ehlinger, who works in festivals for American promoters C3, explains the balance.

WELCOME TO THE JUNGLE

[**ALY EHLINGER**]: "It is both instinct and science. It's instinct finding the right band, but we have a budget and we have to stick with it, and that is science. We are booking so far ahead of time now and we are trying to find those bands that are really going to be as great as their managers and agents say they are. Sometimes we are right and sometimes it doesn't play out the way we think. In the club world it's different, but again it's both science and instinct. You have a lot of different bands routing through and you go off a lot of things, but in smaller venues a lot of it is instinct. Do we think that the crowd is going to buy tickets?"

Richard Moffat has books regional festival Groovin' the Moo and previously has booked events including Parklife and Falls. He believes the biggest challenge of his role is seeing into the future. When booking a festival you are often guessing up to a year ahead what the audience is going to want to see.

[**RICHARD MOFFAT**]: "Festivals are like a snapshot of where the bands are at the time of the year. We tend to book acts that are going to be big for whatever cycle the festival is on. Because bands are getting so big so quickly I'm tending to book a bit later so that we make sure we have the right bands that are getting big on the right cycle. There's no point booking a band 12 months out when people are on to the next one by the time the show rolls around. There are more bands than ever to program, so it's not like we are any chance of running out of bands or options, which is interesting. I'm finding with most of the festivals we have a number of good and viable acts for every spot that our audience already knows and wants to see. It's not like we are finding acts and breaking them at the festival."

[**STEVE HALPIN**]: "At Groovin' The Moo we've never been in the market for the massive headliners that Big Day Out used to aim for, so that takes a lot of the risk out. We focus mainly on

ANDREW WATT

> Australian acts and put a lot of our energy into trying to identify who is coming through and who people might be excited about seeing, rather than having the biggest bands in the world on the line-up."

Part of the art of festival booking is using the new media tools at your disposal to identify the fanbase a band might have. Sophisticated promoters bring social media statistics and analytics into the picture and it's likely that this kind of information will be amplified through the use of advanced streaming services.

> **[ALY EHLINGER]**: "We see it more and more. It's now become something that agents are using as a sales pitch when they used to talk about how many records they might have sold. We use a lot of different tools. I booked a small festival in Bowling Green, Kentucky. It's a very small town about 40 minutes north of Nashville and when we were booking it we were using a lot of cool Facebook tools, where you can actually go in, type in a market and type in a band and you can see how many likes a certain band has in a certain market. Those kinds of things have become a huge tool, especially when you are booking something like that. We had a strategy to book the bands that were just getting big out of Nashville to get the Nashville kids to come up to Bowling Green and for that market Facebook and You Tube was important."

Even the hardest working and most travelled festival bookers are not going to be able to see every act they want to book performing live, so they need to rely on that type of information, and also on the opinions and experience of trusted agents and contacts.

> **[PETER NOBLE]**: "Many artists play Bluesfest that I had not seen play live, but you can gauge from their CV that they are not going to be a dud. It's great to see them, but I am in the US

and UK two or three times a year and in places like Canada. You see as much talent as you can, but you are seeing agents and many of them are great music fans. Most agents don't get to the top in their trade unless they are pretty good at it. You put your ear to the ground. A good agent will let you know about an up-and-coming band. And sometimes you'll listen to the act and sometimes you won't get it. But if you are a good promoter sometimes it's not about you getting it or not getting it, it's about the public getting it. You have to try and decide if it's hype or if it's real."

As the festival business has grown and become more sophisticated, talent booking has taken on another dimension. Not only is it important to have a line-up loaded with great acts for this year's event, but the better bookers are already thinking about the future and building a following for acts that might become staples in later years.

[PETER NOBLE]: "That's fundamental. We do present legendary artists. There are also young acts playing all the time. You've got to be on the ground with new acts. You've got to be on that development side and you've got to be seen as the event that is breaking new talent, because then you are seen as relevant. Some times you can get artists that are already big overseas, but want to come here and open a new market, and their price might be quite reasonable for that reason. You can't be in this game for as long as I have been – nearly 50 years – without developing a pretty good sense of what is going to work. You need to develop contractual skills and things like that, but you have to have ears too. That's what distinguishes the unique events."

On the other side of the fence, agents are also analysing the festival market in Australia. While artists and managers are always anxious to win a place on big festivals, the agents know that this isn't always possible and not always the best options for the act. Some agents recognise that the festival circuit can sometimes only be a short-term gain for an act on their roster.

> **[FRANK STIVALA]:** "For every hundred spots that are available on the festival circuit, there are a thousand acts that want to be on those festivals. The first thing you get from an act when you sign them is 'we want to play Blah Blah Blah Festival'. They think that the agent will just wave the magic wand and you get them on to the festival. Sure, we do have some influence on some of the festivals, but the bottom line is, the act has got to justify itself being on the festival. You've got to have some kind of buzz, some kind of interest to get on a festival. Being a good band isn't enough. The festivals are starting to level themselves out and there's a lot that have fallen by the wayside. It's coming back to survival of the fittest, which will make it more interesting because they won't have as much effect on the local day-to-day scene [by] taking that money out of the marketplace. But festivals have been around for a long time and they will be here for a long time to come and I think there's been a levelling out and it will come to a situation soon where there is enough to be comfortable without being overly saturated."

In terms of local talent Peter Noble sees another problem with artists who throw themselves at every festival that will have them.

> **[PETER NOBLE]:** "There is an awful temptation in Australia, when you get some success to go and play all the events. It takes away that drawing power you have when every appearance is unique and special. You don't blame managers and agents, but they are going for top dollar and they are not giving much exclusivity for it. It's a dangerous practice and the longevity of Australian artists is really damaged as a result. There might be

WELCOME TO THE JUNGLE

too many festivals, but there are also too many bands trying to play all of them."

The other aspect of festival operations is the existence of sideshows. Sideshows occur when festival acts break away from the festival and do smaller headline shows at other venues, either by themselves or with a small bill of other bands from the festival. Soundwave plans its schedule around holding their festival events on weekends allowing the acts to spread out around the country doing mid-week sideshows. Bluesfest utilises the Easter holiday period well, with many acts playing sideshows around the country in and around that week. Splendour and Laneway acts do a similar thing, although in all cases there are some headline acts that are restricted to the festival shows only.

Interestingly, C3's Aly Ehlinger explains the sideshow phenomenon is far stronger in Australia than in America.

> **[ALY EHLINGER]:** "The amount of side shows is different and in the States they are called 'after-shows' and they are definitely under-played. They are an add-on for the fan, more than they are for us. At Lollapolooza there might be 130 bands playing on eight stages so there might be three or four bands playing at the same time that you want to see, so we give them a show afterwards, which also helps the clubs in Chicago. The sideshows are important for bands travelling internationally to make it financially viable to come over and that's something that's more significant here. In America the sideshows are smaller and more intimate and not everybody gets to go to them but its not like the fans are waiting for the sideshows. The major festivals in the US have become an experience and the festivals sell out way in advance of the line-up being announced because they are established

brands. People know that whoever is playing they are going to have a good time. There's 130 bands on – there's gonna be ones you want to see right? It's more than the music now, it's the food and all the activations that are really good that fans want to experience. It's a whole experience within the experience."

Festival Philosophy

Every festival promoter has their own approach to the business. Festival promoters are by necessity visionaries, able to see the big picture, but also realising that a lot of small pieces make up the grand vista. There is no absolutely right or wrong way to create a festival event and clearly the expectations of the target audience for a heavy music festival like Unify Gathering will be very different to those at Bluesfest and will be different again to those at an EDM event. Events aimed at Under 18's are different again.

Splendour in the Grass co-promoter Jessica Ducrou manages to strike the fine balance between art and commerce with her event.

> **[JESS DUCROU]:** "I love my job and I am passionate about it, and I'm still incredibly challenged by it. The money or the commerce is really the by-product of it. My focus is great music and presenting that in any way I can, whether that is switching people on to new stuff, or working with acts that I admire that are already established. I think as an individual and a person you need to have your own barometer of what's acceptable in how you operate and how to hold yourself in your position, and do you want a long career and is your reputation important to you. I guess having that basic understanding of how I wanted to move in the music industry and how I wanted to be represented, combined with my love of music and my interest

WELCOME TO THE JUNGLE

> in art generally, probably is why I work the way I do. I think my arts interest is really about my experience at other events around the world. I'm all for going to other people's shows and watching bands and experiencing what another festival is like. I jump into it boots and all. I understand the experience that everyone is having and to me it's way more than just music. It's getting lost taking a half hour trek into the boondocks at Fuji Rock because there is something great going on at some other stage. That's kind of where my arts interest is about; it's about presenting art in its various forms in a music environment and challenging people who are there to be interested."

The ultimate accolade for a festival is that its tickets sell before the year's artist bill has been announced. That has happened with several events internationally and in Australia several events like Bluesfest have a rusted-on audience that will rely on the event to deliver year in year out sight unseen. There are some other festivals that are approaching that level of loyalty or brand trust, but it's easier said than done.

For Laneway promoter Danny Rogers the importance of getting the vision of the festival right and then delivering on that year in, year out, is even more essential. In his case, the brand that has been created has led his event into uncharted territory – Laneway festivals now occur around Australia, in New Zealand, in Singapore and in 2013 played in Detroit.

> **[DANNY ROGERS]:** "The vision of Laneway is to be a non-headliner festival that is heavily focussed on its programming with a commitment to emerging talent. It sets itself apart from other festivals by being able to understand music trends and being very song-focused. In all markets there were local

promoters who believed that Laneway was the type of event that could travel well as it slowly became a brand that was respected for breaking talent and always being close to the cusp. Over time we have built a clear brand that stands for something and via the programming we've managed to remain relatively unique compared to other festivals. With every expanding market we saw an opportunity that did not exist in that region. We trusted that we had a developing global reputation and with excellent programming we'd have every chance of making it a success. We were also willing to start very small so as to give the event roots and we remained consistent."

The challenges of taking a festival international are enormous and Rogers explains just a few of them.

[**DANNY ROGERS**]: "Patience and respect are essential. I've learnt a ton about each market's love of certain styles of music and each is quite different. Some acts are a phenomenon in certain markets. It's a challenge to be fully across each market like that and the local team are exceptionally on it. In NZ, Singapore and Detroit, there are some amazing radio stations, but nothing compares to the national reach and style of Triple J ... Triple J had been very heavily involved in breaking Laneway bands whereas you definitely have to dig a lot deeper and draw on other methods in, say, Detroit where they simply don't have that one station."

Breaking In Through Festivals

It's clear that the best way to learn how to promote a festival is to work at a lot of them, in various capacities. There is nothing learnt in a classroom that will prepare a promoter for the sheer magnitude of operational and logistical challenges presented by running a festival.

WELCOME TO THE JUNGLE

Sure, festivals can always employ good, experienced people, but these service providers will quickly recognise a competent promoter from a wannabe.

Jessica Ducrou has a meaningful way of looking at this.

> **[JESSICA DUCROU]:** "Even now, if I walk around my festival and there's garbage on the ground, I'll go around and pick up garbage. I don't care. Having a good work ethic and never being above the job put in front of you is important. If I was looking at it now from a 20 year-old's perspective, I would be saying 'work hard, be tenacious and never get above yourself'. Thinking that it's outside your job description or thinking that you have too much knowledge to be doing menial tasks is boring. I find that really boring and I wouldn't work with somebody like that. I work with people who go beyond the call of duty and do what they have to do to get the job done. If you do that and apply yourself, you have a load of potential to go on and do great things."

For Peter Noble there are increasing opportunities to work in the business beyond short-term contracting roles.

> **[PETER NOBLE]:** "There are something like 12 to 14 employees in the company. We are basically a mid-sized business. Outside of that, we have three employees full-time on our site. We made a decision that it was no use building up a staff base for six months because they won't be able to come back the next year. We decided that if we were going to develop skill in our business that we shouldn't develop it to lose it. We've added staff and our touring company has been a growth area. It's grown from a company that toured a few acts because we had to, to a business in its own right.

ANDREW WATT

Because we are not located in Sydney or Melbourne, it has the advantage of attracting people who want a certain lifestyle. Byron Bay is the rural arts capital of Australia, so the well that we can draw on is a deep one. We have a University in Lismore that has event and music training and they are reaching out to us more as well."

My Path into the Industry

FRANK VARRASSO

"I did a BA in leisure studies at university and my very first gig was as an occupational therapist, believe it or not. I did that for about 12 months, hated it and decided to throw that in, move into town and look for work. I started working initially at The Club in Collingwood, working behind the bar. Then a guy named Colin Moss was booking the Club and the Evelyn at the time and I asked him if he wanted some help booking the venue.. That's how I got in touch with *InPress*. Fortuitously *InPress* was looking for someone to sell ads. One thing led to another and I ended up selling most of the rock stuff and doing that I got to meet all the record company people. I'd be out every night, seeing bands and visiting venues etc.

I became interested in what the record labels did from a promotional perspective – getting coverage for all their bands. I was called up by Warner one day and was offered a promotional role in Victoria. I took that and I was there for about three and a half years. At Warner I was offered a number of label manager jobs – East West, Atlantic and Warner, but I didn't want to be a label manager. I loved PR. From there I went over to EMI Victoria and then I was asked to head the PR department, and from there an opportunity came up at Festival Mushroom Records to be the general manager of national promotions and publicity, which I took with glee, because as much as I enjoyed doing publicity, I also wanted to deal with radio. When that company looked like being sold, I took the position of director of national promotions and publicity at Sony BMG. I was with those guys for three and a half years before leaving to start my own business."

Chapter 17

Publicity and Promotion

While the evolution of technology has enabled most artists to make recordings, and the strength of the live scene means most artists are able to gig regularly or tour, that's only part of the battle. There is a danger that, in a market flooded by releases and shows, most artists will be lost in the blast of white noise. So many artists, and their representatives, are fighting for attention and the competition is not confined to the city or country of origin. These days a fan on the other side of the world can easily discover a new artist – if the artist plays their cards right.

The publicist's role is to help an artist's release or performance to gain some traction or currency with potential fans – and this means finding favour with the various media outlets that those fans connect to.

It's one of the first roles that people think of when they contemplate a career in the music business – it's easy to imagine hanging out with rock stars at radio stations and television studios, schmoozing with media personalities and attending to the stars' needs on the red carpet at the ARIAS. And that's exactly what a publicists job is like – around 5% of the time! It's a similar proportion of fantasy to reality, as found in the A&R role.

Nicole Hart, a leading publicist, confirms that it isn't all parties and glamour.

WELCOME TO THE JUNGLE

[NICOLE HART]: "People might be surprised about how hardcore parts of it are and how demanding people can be. You really have to dot your I's and cross your T's and document everything. I don't think you actually realise that until you are in the trenches doing it."

Brian McDonald, whose company RiSH operates in a niche populated by acts that are very serious about their musical bona fides, agrees.

[BRIAN MCDONALD]: "I sometimes think that the problem with the industry is that not enough people care about the music and artist! There are too many people that come into the industry with their marketing or business management degrees and couldn't care less, or they want to earn some cool stripes or hang out with bands. But I really don't care about all that stuff – I'd much rather find someone with passion, drive and ambition, who will turn up on time and work hard for the artist, any day of the week."

Like many other areas of the business, the role of a publicist has become increasingly measurable and accountable. Successful campaigns are measured in column inches, visitation statistics and viewer demographics rather than "the vibe", although there are still intangibles built into the job, such as relationships that a publicist can form between an artist and a media person. The blogger that champions an artist today may be a daily newspaper music editor in a couple of year's time.

For Brian McDonald, clients often evolve from grassroots to mainstream media coverage and for him it's all about knowing how to approach different levels of media.

[BRIAN MCDONALD]: "There are differences between the types of media when dealing with them and you just have to know which mode to switch into and when. With street press, the communication can be a little less formal than when you are dealing with the editor of a metro newspaper's music section. And of course, bringing the message or pitch to those in large mainstream media is obviously a world away from the bloggers, who here in Australia, genuinely seem to be unaffected by PR people. They prefer to discover the music they write about themselves rather than having a publicist shoving something down their throat, so we respect that."

The publicity landscape has changed in the past decade. Up until the '90's, major record companies would have two or three publicists per state and their services would be divided across mainstream and community radio, daily newspapers and street press and the television networks. Towards the end of that era those publicists also started servicing some of the music websites that had started popping up.

Many of the larger independent distributors had publicists on the payroll as well, and even smaller independents often realised that publicity was a necessary role, even if it was one of many hats that the staff at smaller labels would wear.

Now the majors have fewer publicity staff and some of those functions are being out-sourced to independent publicists. There are also many acts not signed to labels that are capable of supporting their own releases and the publicist is an important player on their team, albeit for a period of time based around a release or a tour.

[NICOLE HART]: "There are so many acts that are about level pegging. They are independent; they've funded their own release, they've got a distributor and they have a publicist in place and a record plugger. That has afforded a lot of people opportunities in publicity because those kind of acts are all carving out their own niche in the market and that's really proliferated. They might only sell a relatively small amount of albums, but that beast needs to be fed and so there is opportunity to come in and do that kind of contract work. It's really interesting how those relationships work. A lot of it is coming through the independent sector. The major labels are still a bit protective and don't like to outsource too much, but that may change as the business model changes."

It's worth noting that 'publicity' was generally perceived as different to 'promotions' in the recording industry. The latter role referred largely to radio airplay – the pursuit of playlist additions on the various commercial networks and their stations such as MMM, Fox, 2Day-FM, Nova etc and the regional networks including the Hot-FM and Sea-FM brands. Frank Varrasso is one of the leading radio promotions people in Australia.

[FRANK VARRASSO]: "To me promotion is getting an artist heard on the radio. We all know that radio will spend a lot of money on research. We all know that repetition provides you with an insatiable thirst to hear a song more and more. The more a song is played the more chance there is that people will like it. So it's all about getting radio play and radio exposure. Radio is still paramount. The online element is now really important, but radio is not going away in a hurry. Radio is still the serious catapult to selling serious quantities of CDs."

For a very long time these stations, along with Triple J, were the holy grail of record company promotions people. It was cut-throat business as some of these stations would only add a couple of songs per week and these were always within a very conservative genre range.

[FRANK VARRASSO]: "If you had a continuum – Triple J was always on the left and on the right was Fox and Triple

ANDREW WATT

M. When Nova first came into the market, over 12 years ago they sat comfortably in the middle of that continuum, playing chart hits that Triple M would play, but also the alternative hits that Triple J would play. Then their format changed to CHR – "Chart Hit Radio". So now on the continuum you have Triple J on the left and on the right CHR and in the middle – nobody! So the problem we have now is that Triple J can't play everything and so there are a plethora of bands who cannot get radio airplay. This is where the online thing can come in. If you can generate enough interest online, you might be able to generate interest at commercial radio or Triple J."

[MATT GUDINSKI]: "With three key radio stations pretty much playing the same format and Triple J filling an 'indie' role, it means there's a lot of stuff in the middle that's got no home at radio in Australia. And for the stuff that does fit into the radio formats there's only so many local songs that they are willing to play."

Michael Gudinski regards the constant complaints about commercial radio's lack of support for new music and Australian music to be stating the obvious. He argues that if you wait for radio to be the means of breaking a new artist, then you might be waiting a very long time. Rather, the value of commercial radio is to elevate music that has already built a platform into a higher echelon.

[MICHAEL GUDINSKI]: "When radio comes on board it might take you from being gold to platinum or platinum to triple platinum. If you sit back and whinge and moan about radio it will get you nowhere. It's the same story since I started. It's not better; it's not worse It's the same story. Radio watches iTunes and streaming now. Some commercial radio used to be leaders, but now they are followers. I don't listen to commercial radio to decide what sort of acts we should be signing. Radio is important, but most real artists have to get over halfway there without radio."

His son, Matt has a similar philosophy.

> **[MATT GUDINSKI]:** "It's definitely more challenging because there isn't an easy formula to follow. I find that exciting…but some people might not! There are a lot of ways to expose music but there are still a lot of challenges in the Australian market for an artist trying to get a break."

Part of the publicity role was to build "a story" for the promotions people to use. Being able to tell a radio programmer that an artist had got a great review in a newspaper or a front cover of a street press publication or a mention on Molly Meldrum's segment on *Hey Hey It's Saturday* was supposed to help the programmer allocate one of those precious couple of adds to a song. It rarely had that effect though, as radio relied heavily on a horrible process called "surveying", where listeners were played a few seconds from a song down a phone line to gauge their likelihood of the song causing them to switch stations. For commercial radio, music was just the stuff they used to stop people turning off between adverts. It still is.

Publicity was also an end in itself though. There is inherent value in a good review. Whether or not a good review will be enough to send a reader scurrying out the door to buy an album is debatable, but if the reviewer in question is well regarded and has sufficient credibility, that may carry some weight with certain fans. A feature story gives an artist a chance to expand on their themes and flesh out their audience's understanding of the artist behind the art. Small pieces on social pages or entertainment pages will undoubtedly assist in building awareness of a release or performance, and the perception of an artist's place in the pecking order of attention.

These days, artists and managers have become far more astute about the role of the publicist and how the results of their work can be measured. Many are far more media savvy than in the past. Some are still in need of adjustment.

> **[BRIAN MCDONALD]:** "I do think managers and artists have to get more savvy and have a better understanding of media, that media's target audience or demographic and have a more realistic approach to what is achievable so everyone's expectations are met. A lot of bands want everything upfront; national radio rotation, editorial coverage in the metro newspapers and some just are not ready for that. We've seen some artists and managers try to liaise with media direct, taking a scattergun approach to public relations – firing off a press release aiming at anything with a heartbeat. Or stupidly trying to bully or beg people into giving them airplay and column space, something we never do. At the same time, there are so many pitfalls on many levels when navigating through this industry – there's still some pretty unscrupulous people operating. I've lost count of the times bands have come to us with their woes of paying people thousands of dollars per month with promises to "break you at radio" and that result is rarely obtained. When hiring a publicist to handle media on their behalf, a band or manager should always have an understanding of what they need, then put the brakes on, take their time to speak to people, investigate their options, be realistic about what you can achieve in relation to where they are in their career, at that time. Never rush in to anything, use your time to research, don't be happy with a list of testimonials, ask for references and contact those people direct and get answers."

WELCOME TO THE JUNGLE

Radio promotion internationally has a very mixed reputation. Historically the business has endured several periods of scandal, based around allegations of bribery or payola, with radio stations being paid to play songs. In the US in the late '80s, the process was almost institutionalised, with record labels paying promoters large sums of money for "promotional services" and then turning a blind eye to how it was spent. The promoters would then "assist" the radio stations with funds to help them stage events, or on-air giveaways and magically the songs that the promoters were plugging would be added to that station's playlist. Arguably there was nothing actually wrong with that – the station's listeners would benefit from the expenditure of promotional funds and the record companies would get the airplay they needed to help break new artists. The problem arose when every label realised that they had to play that game to get a song heard and hence the payments to independent promoters weren't able to guarantee success. Eventually the labels (and artists and managers) began to question the value of that form of marketing dollar.

Rev. Moose of Marauder looks at the US position now.

> **[REV. MOOSE]:** "The system in place for how to get an artist on to radio very much involves money, but it doesn't mean that money is going to the programmers who are programming the radio station. Historically that was certainly the case and there are a lot of anecdotes to back that up but you still need to have resources to support it. You need to have a profile for commercial programmers to pay attention to you. Getting that profile requires time and money. When you think about the time you put into your own career building those profile pieces you also realise that the people working for you are also getting paid and they will stop working when they stop getting paid. But are the days of cash in envelopes still happening? I'd like to think they are not."

ANDREW WATT

In Australia, the old form of US radio promotion has never really come into play. The market simply isn't big enough to support it.

> **[FRANK VARRASSO]:** "The main difference is that promotion in the UK and the US has been happening for a long time, whereas here it's a relatively new job in the industry. The US and the UK have a plethora of radio stations and a plethora of artists and a lot of the radio over there is very genre-specific. Given the sheer magnitude of those countries there are a lot of media people to talk to."

The majority of Varrasso's success is based as much in the relationships he has, as much as the music he is working with. And those relationships cannot be created overnight, meaning that radio promotion isn't the easiest world to break into.

> **[FRANK VARRASSO]:** "A relationship can only work if there is a reciprocal relationship. It's give and take – you can't win all the time and it's a compromise. You realise that in this business you may only have a few wins, but those wins are very sweet. You need to be gracious enough to understand that you are going to lose more battles than you win. It's about understanding what the other side is going through and this is where I've been so lucky have worked in media myself, so I knew how media worked and I've learned what triggers they liked and what triggers they didn't like."

Perception is a consideration in the publicity business. Simply doing publicity is enough to placate an artist who is concerned that their career, release or tour may be stagnating. Particularly in less recent times record companies would use the publicist as the "soft landing" for an artist whose release was failing, or in industry vernacular, "stiffing". The publicist would ensure that the artist did enough interviews

WELCOME TO THE JUNGLE

to justify the label's claim that "we did everything we could" to get an album or single away. Artists would often look to see how much publicity their peers at other record labels were getting and this would influence their choice of label or level of satisfaction.

Times have changed though. These days, publicity is result rather than perception driven and this is largely a result of the change in business model used by record companies and touring music promoters. Major labels still have in-house publicists (though not as many of them as in the past) and the bigger tour promoters usually have a salaried publicist in-house. But many labels (including majors) and most tour promoters now use the services of third-party publicists working on a contract or project basis.

Radio promotion is gradually heading in the same direction. Frank Varrasso's client base includes independent artists, but also some major labels who are outsourcing the radio plugging role to him for certain projects, and even some international clients who realise that their song may need a direct focus to get radio support in Australia.

> **[FRANK VARRASSO]:** "Five to seven years ago the major labels went through an acquisition process where they were buying a lot of small indie labels to consolidate their market share. When that happens, it means those labels have more and more releases each week and you can only do so much with the team you have. I decided that outsourcing that role was going to be needed in this country and that's why I went out alone. If you can give an act more time and effort, you can actually get a result."

One of the challenges that emerge from this situation is that publicists don't enjoy the luxury of working with an artist over a long period of time, to slowly and methodically build a profile. Working on a project basis means the publicists is required to deliver maximum impact immediately.

Emily Kelly from Deathproof PR laments the short term approach.

> **[EMILY KELLY]:** "I think establishing a career-long game plan along with an accompanying 'slow build' is the best way to go, but that can only happen when you get the luxury of being on board with an artist permanently and for the long haul. The nature of many campaigns now is that we're hired for the duration of a tour or album, and then we part ways, so you have little choice but to go hard to get the best results for that project. I think the former approach would be a nice one to indulge in with the right artist and right team, but that kind of long-term artist development is not as common as you think."

Frank Varrasso doesn't see streaming services impacting on his traditional territory.

> **[FRANK VARRASSO]:** "It hasn't changed my role at all at this point in time. I dare say, as it becomes more and more popular, it will. Spotify, from a fan's perspective, is fantastic because you can play whatever you want. Those services are for the fans. They cater for a demographic that really enjoys new music in particular, and so the beauty of that is, it generates fans. If you saw a band last night and you loved them, the first thing you would do is source some music on Spotify or You Tube and then you would tell your friends about it."

In the USA Sat Bisla is adamant that radio, in all its forms is still the dominant way to break an artist.

WELCOME TO THE JUNGLE

[SAT BISLA]: "If you look at radio worldwide in most markets it is still the No.1 way to engage audiences, expose music to audiences, drive people to live events and consistently break artists. Is there another platform that can do that?"

For the artist, the publicist is part of a team, or a spoke in the wheel, as John Watson puts it. They work alongside the agent, publisher and digital marketing expert as contributors to the artist's career.

[BRIAN MCDONALD]: "I think all these are equally important in the bigger picture – but not every artist needs all of those things or some don't need all those things at once. A band needs to take the time to educate themselves about the industry, how it works and figure out what they can and can't do for themselves, then set about looking for the right people to fill those gaps. Once that's defined, then engaging third parties and constructing a 'team' should lead to a more effective outcome. Each third party has their field of expertise, experience and varying disciplines, but I don't really see us as having any more or any less value than the booking agent or the publisher. Everyone should know what the other is bringing to the table, then hopefully with everyone on the same page, and the artist's best interest at the forefront, you've got a pretty harmonious working relationship and a dedicated set of people working towards the same, clearly identified goals."

[FRANK VARRASSO]: "Having a song on radio, in isolation, doesn't really amount too much. People might like the song, but in most cases they don't know who it is, where they are from or what they are about. That is where the publicity side comes in, which is predominantly press and on-line. Publicity is about seeing pictures of the artist, reading news about the artist. Publicity is about having the fans connect the dots. Promotion is about creating an awareness of the artist's song or music. Every consulting meeting I have with artists is based around the hub and spokes idea. Someone is going to look after print, someone is going to look after TV, someone is going to look after online/digital and someone is going to have to look after radio. Without having all those spokes in the wheel it's going to be really difficult to cut through. That's the well considered, smart approach."

[NICOLE HART]: "We are one of the pieces of an artist's puzzle and everybody brings attributes to the table to help the artist with whatever it is they are doing. Increasingly we get asked about marketing opportunities now and there is more expectation that publicists can help in a marketing sense – asking us where they should spend marketing or advertising dollars. People defer to us in that area and I think that has changed a lot in recent times – there seems to be less delineation between publicity and marketing. They don't have the big budgets to throw money on TV and you have to use your money effectively, so we are drawn more and more into those conversations as well."

It isn't surprising that many publicists are former employees of major labels, or have at least spent some time in that system. A publicity business is largely built around contacts and relationships and these are best acquired when the power and influence of a major label is behind them. It's certainly a lot easier to achieve some press coverage for a new band when the publicist has major artist access as the carrot to dangle. There's no doubt that many media outlets are willing to assist a publicist on a smaller act in the hope of cultivating a relationship that will pay off with access to a major international.

The challenge for an independent publicist is to maintain that same standard of media relationships without the leverage of bigger artists

WELCOME TO THE JUNGLE

at their disposal or the company credit card to grease the wheels of coverage – although expense account publicity has nowhere near the currency it used to have.

Graham Ashton worked in the major label system prior to setting up his own businesses in the publicity area and views that experience positively.

> **[GRAHAM ASHTON]:** "There are so many things I take from that time. It couldn't be more different today, but at the same time the fundamentals of what we do are still the same. Every project is different and that's what makes it interesting. I learned that you have to look at every project differently and be really nimble with everything you are working with, and don't be too structured because something can change in an instant and it can change your whole approach to whatever you are doing. I remember initially finding that hard to get my head around. I have a reputation for being a bit anal, but the best lesson I ever learned in music was that it doesn't follow any structure. All of the projects and processes you work on need to be very flexible."

Brian McDonald's background in independent labels provided him with a different set of experiences and a different approach to the artists he works with. By definition, an indie label pretty much only signs artists they love and so McDonald never felt like he was working a project because it was a "company priority". Just about every job was a "love job".

> **[BRIAN MCDONALD]:** "Aside from being your own boss and having flexible work hours, one of the most rewarding aspects of the job for me is being able to choose the artists that I want to work with, rather than just have them handed to me with an

'exploit' sticker on it. My background, and the limitations of running an indie label definitely impacted on how I built my business. That made it an affordable option for them, bearing in mind some artists do actually approach you with very little funding. A fixed-price rate card was never going to work so early on and I'd recommend avoiding that approach to any new publicist starting out on their own. A fixed rate service would have probably scared potential customers off and I knew from working at Chatterbox that I was just going to have to build solid working relationships from very early on, that were not solely based around my own pay cheque. That resulted in great word-of-mouth recommendations and repeat business from satisfied clients. Luckily, I was already used to living on the 'indie wage' and prepared to do so for the first few years of being in business as a publicist."

Emily Kelly has a similar experience, and she is always keen to work with artists and managers who have a similar mindset.

[EMILY KELLY]: "We like working with people we know, on artists we understand. The results are always better when you have a comfortable and respectful relationship with the team behind the release, paired with an understanding of their artist and what they need. Our workload obviously plays a massive role in the jobs we choose, as we're really reluctant to overload ourselves and let the work and our reputation suffer as a result. Thankfully we love most of the things we work on. Whether it's literally the artist that we adore, or the crew behind the project or even just the challenge presented, we've really enjoyed just about every job we've taken."

Setting up an independent publicity business is relatively cheap and simple. There is little need for investment in equipment and many of

WELCOME TO THE JUNGLE

those businesses operate from a home office. The majority of work is done by email or phone or at events or media buildings, and very rarely does a publicist's client actually need to visit the publicist's office. As a result there is normally a very small overhead for the business. The biggest costs are normally phone, documents and mail-outs and smart operators should be able to build these costs into a client quote.

For publicists coming out of a corporate environment and into a home office, the sense of isolation can be challenging and it weighs against the convenience and cost benefits of working from home. It's a competitive business, but there is also camaraderie within the ranks of publicists.

> **[NICOLE HART]:** "Everyone occupies their own little space and they've got their own posse of clients that they work really well with. I think there is space enough for everybody and you pick up business that plays to your strengths. I'm acutely aware that we don't have the resources or the horse trading power that we had when we had when we were at a major label. If you want a mailout done, you've got to do it yourself. I still manage all the finances and invoices and chasing payments and you have to be very responsible and astute with all that kind of thing. You need to manage workflow.
>
> You have to make sure you do the right thing by all your existing clients while you are looking for new business, keeping across your relationships with your media. You've got to be really tenacious. You need to have a core of clients that keep you front and centre with the media. You can only foster relationships with media if you have projects that you are talking to them about. So for somebody setting up I'd say that it's really important to have something that keeps your foot in the door with everybody. Otherwise it can be a bit cold and lonely and isolated."

ANDREW WATT

Emily Kelly and Rebecca Reato dealt with the issue of isolation immediately. They started their business Deathproof PR as a two-headed partnership, which has provided them with a diversity of skills to assist their business in operating well.

> **[EMILY KELLY]:** "We would never have done it without a partner and would never do it again without a partner. Thankfully Bec had experience and contacts within radio and television media and my expertise was in print and online, so the combining of the two was pretty important. Also Bec's completed a business degree so she's capable of handling the financial side of the business, while my background in writing lends itself to the more creative side."

As both Nicole Hart and Emily Kelly point out, it should never be forgotten that working as a publicist means operating your own business. Apart from the management activities that involves, it also means the business itself has to be marketed. Smart operators like Deathproof PR have ensured that their business has its own image and profile – a young, funky, indie, edgy aesthetic that seems to attract like-minded clients.

> **[EMILY KELLY]:** "It genuinely wasn't a conscious decision, though it has turned out to be relatively advantageous in retrospect. The 'personality' is just Bec and I being 'idiots' and enjoying our work and the accompanying visual branding is the work of an incredibly talented designer. Those two factors really came together to form an identity for our business that was totally accidental, but kickass nonetheless, in that it did provide us with a little point of difference. I think having some kind of personality associated with your company can result in picking up likeminded clients, so that's an added bonus."

WELCOME TO THE JUNGLE

Breaking into publicity can be a challenging area. The best publicists are naturally those with a great set of media contacts. That isn't easy to achieve – other than by being a publicist! But Graham Ashton believes there are intangibles about a publicist's personality that a potential candidate can't simply acquire.

> **[GRAHAM ASHTON]:** "I think people are born to be publicists. It's about incredible organisational skill and forward planning ability and obviously your communication skills have to be unique. It's a sales job first and foremost, but it's not in the traditional sense. You have to do it in a more subtle way. I think that some people are good at that naturally in their communication skills and I don't know that it's necessarily a learned skill."

Brian McDonald takes a similar view. He respects a job candidate that walks through the door with a degree, but he looks well beyond that also.

> **[BRIAN MCDONALD]:** "I really don't set out looking for anyone with a publicity background or marketing qualification. I was far more open to having someone with a passion for music come on board and the rest we could build over time; at least we would at least be on the same wavelength. I employed a guy who had experience in booking bands, DJing in nightclubs and he'd written and licensed his own electronic music to corporate clients, whilst having interests of seeing live indie bands, skateboarding and music writing. That mix spoke volumes and placed him higher on the scale than those who simply sent in a resume stating what degree they had finished. It's great to have that qualification, don't get me wrong, but don't think that that's all it takes. Some employers out there are actually looking for genuine music lovers to join their team, so my

advice to anyone looking to get into the industry is to highlight even the smallest things that they've done or achieved in relation to their love of music and include it on their resume, no matter how big or small."

For Nicole Hart, a tertiary qualification is likely to become more and more important, even though that's not something she needed when she started.

> **[NICOLE HART]**: "I think it's unique from our era but I'd say that the tide is turning. I think you'll find that the new generation will have tertiary qualifications. I think we were all fortunate to come from a time when you could chase your dream and make things happen, but I think now days in business in general it's just so tough, and so when people are hiring they don't want to make a mistake and they will look at someone with tertiary qualifications and think that the person was able to finish a degree and so they are passionate about what they are doing and that gives them some trust around that. In our day it was more about having the gift of the gab and having really unique extroverted personalities and we were lucky enough that we could get away with that. These days, having a tertiary qualification would give that person an advantage."

Interestingly Emily Kelly – a university graduate in media herself, and in partnership with Bec Reato who has a business degree acknowledges that hands-on experience is still essential in the development of a great publicist.

> **[EMILY KELLY]**: "To be honest, though, I'm not sure that a lot of the qualities that make a good publicist can be learnt in a lecture theatre. For example, things like learning to deal with different, conflicting personalities, agendas, experience

WELCOME TO THE JUNGLE

and 'massaging' them to create an outcome that is mutually beneficial for everyone involved are hard things to teach. It very much comes with experience."

There is a lot more to publicity and promotion than first meets the eye and it's a part of the business where there will always be opportunities for smart, well-organised and passionate young people to make their mark. And if you do break into that world, you could be there to stay.

[FRANK VARRASSO]: "It's a lot of fun. That's why 20 years on I'm still doing it. I love it. Could I make more money doing other things? I'm sure I could. But there is no exhilaration like hearing a song that you plugged get on the radio. There's nothing like it. Even to this day. It sounds bizarre, but it's true."

My path into the industry

ZAC ABROMS

"I never really imagined that I was going to get a job in the music industry. I did media and communication at Swinburne; that was a good course because it gave me a taste of film, television, journalism. I started volunteering at SYN-FM and took an interest in radio, hosting the Australian Music Show and that experience was fantastic. A lot of my friends were starting to pursue music on a professional basis. I'd go to their gigs and observe what was happening and I'd get frustrated at the lack of organisation around some of the things that they were doing. I didn't really know what to do about it, but I had these ideas kicking around in my head.

I went to London and thought that they had it set up better than we did in Melbourne – the way they used social media was excellent. I joined Facebook on that trip, and they were already all over it. When I went back to Melbourne, I went around to various venues and found some guys who just opened a venue called Miss Libertine. They gave me a night that I ran monthly called Clean Young Mess, which was my friends and I choosing bands from Melbourne that we liked, that we would find on My Space or Triple J Unearthed. Everybody got paid, we paid guarantees, the promoter would provide top-notch sound and lights, and everybody got a soundcheck – because those were all the gripes that my friend's bands had. We had good-looking artwork, we used Facebook Groups to start promoting these gigs and even though these were not big name bands, we earned a bit of a reputation for exposing a lot of bands.

Chapter 18

Digital Marketing

If this book had been written a decade ago, this chapter might not have existed. The role of a digital marketing consultant has only been around as long as digital mediums for marketing and distribution of music have been available. It's another example of the technology creating a role that some smart new operators now fulfil.

Digital marketing is a firmly established role with record companies and as with many other jobs formerly part of the record company process, such as A&R, there is now an out-sourcing approach to the function. Increasingly, artists and managers are including a digital marketing person as one of the "spokes in the wheel" that John Watson refers to.

Vanessa Picken's company Comes With Fries is a digital music distribution, consultancy and services company that provides services in online marketing and sales and digital management. She sees her job as being an integral part of an artist's team.

> [VANESSA PICKEN]: "I definitely feel as though we are just one piece of the puzzle. Where we fit within that puzzle is becoming more strategic. We are definitely trying to shift our position within the industry because a lot of people don't even know what 'digital online marketing' actually means. People say 'oh I can post something on Facebook', and we have to explain that's not what we do. The way in which we

WELCOME TO THE JUNGLE

are trying to position our company from a service perspective is that we are a part of the team structure. It's becoming more and more important as people are going independent and creating their own team structure. So we talk to people about building their team and identifying what skills they need on their team and when is the right time to bring someone like ourselves into your release schedule. But I think having a digital music services business as part of your team structure is just imperative."

Picken spent more than five years working within the structure of a major record company – in her case EMI – and regards that experience as invaluable. She came from a background in the corporate world, having worked for Nokia and Westpac in Australia, which was punctuated by a trip to the UK where she had immersed herself in the music scene where bands like Arctic Monkeys and Franz Ferdinand were breaking with the assistance of online platforms.

Her timing, when entering the music industry was probably ideal.

[VANESSA PICKEN]: "I was naïve. Sometimes some of the ideas I put forward were probably a bit too big or too far out of the box at the time, but it was fresh blood coming into the industry. It was when times were a-changing. It was around the time when it was obvious that digital was not going to go away and that there was a shift in the market that wasn't going to go away and people had to take stock of the shift that was happening in consumer habits. It was a leap of faith from the label to not take someone that had come up through the call centre or in music retail or who had been in a band, or who didn't already know someone in the industry. I had no contacts in the industry whatsoever. The music industry is one big happy family, but to not know a single person when I walked into that door was a blessing in disguise because I was saying things on my own merits.

ANDREW WATT

A couple of weeks after I started, I got handed Robbie Williams to label manage and so I was immersed in one of the new deals that hit the music industry. Robbie Williams signed a massive content deal with Sony Ericson, T Mobile and locally Optus. It was all about pre-loading content onto mobile phones and marketing Robbie Williams the artist through technology and the mobile phone. That was relatively unheard of in the music industry, so they really needed someone to come in and understand that music product, technology and marketing could all fit together. That's where they had to rely on my background, because they had no idea about mobile phones and no idea about marketing based around the interaction of a person and content in a mobile phone."

Jackie Krajl is another of the leading players in the digital music marketing field. She too came out of the major label system at Universal, before working in label and artist relations at iTunes Australia and New Zealand. She now runs her own digital consultancy DigiRascal.

For Krajl, the time spent at Universal began with her feeling like an alien although the impact of digital on the business was quickly accepted.

> **[JACKIE KRAJL]**: "I don't think the majors were struggling to come to terms with it, but I do think that it sums it all up that we were called, 'new media', rather than 'digital'. They didn't know how to categorise us, so they just called us 'new'. Back then, 'new media' didn't really impact the bottom line in any significant way. People definitely saw the benefit from the marketing and promotional and editorial point of view, but it was really at its infancy when it came to sales. If the truth be told, sometimes I did feel like I was speaking a different language because I was speaking a new language to them; but it's a language that everyone had to pick up quickly, so I don't think

WELCOME TO THE JUNGLE

there was any struggle. It was like anything new coming into any industry; people had to pedal to keep up."

Zac Abrom has also enjoyed a wild ride. After stints as a live music promoter and with Mark Richardson's Forum 5 Management, Abroms now runs a digital services and management company called Vice Royalty. He's also now heavily involved in programming music conference Face The Music.

[ZAC ABROMS]: "What I brought to it, as the young blood on the team, was social media and online, which was a new game to them; they didn't realise why they needed to have a Facebook or Twitter. I was always bringing innovative technologies to Forum 5 and to our artists. Kimbra became the real poster artist for good social media. We had millions of You Tube views before we signed a record deal and before she was added to Triple J, based on us blogging it on tastemaker blogs in the US and relentlessly emailing people. She took to social networks really naturally.When I started Vice Royalty I was still looking after some of those responsibilities for some of Mark's artists and he would outsource to me on various things and I would still maintain Kimbra's online PR. Even when she signed to Warner they were happy with that arrangement and to keep me sub-contracted to the project, despite them having a great digital department themselves."

Breaking into Digital

So what exactly do digital marketing consultants do? The key is to not get too hung up on the word "digital" and not to forget the word "marketing". While the playing field and the tools have changed drastically in the internet-driven world, it's still much the same process at its core – trying to find ways to put an artist in front of an audience that is likely to enjoy what they are offering. Whether that takes the form of traditional radio airplay, a video on *Rage*, a story in street press, a blog in Brooklyn or a front-page positioning on iTunes, the mission remains the same.

> **[ZAC ABROMS]:** "What I do is all marketing. Sometimes you call it 'digital PR', sometimes it's 'online publicity', but it all falls under the same thing which is taking advantage of the tools available on the web and using the web to your advantage to reach people. It's not at all concerned with product – it's about brand. Bands are brands and we have this enormous array of tools online for you to express your brand and communicate your brand to people. Mostly what I do is educate artists and managers and record labels about what is available and how they can take advantage of it. It's very cost-effective and it has an enormous lifespan compared to radio or print and I really see it as being the future. Radio still has its place and print, although it has declined somewhat recently, still has its place – but digital is usurping a lot of those traditional media and those traditional media are connecting themselves in such a way to work in tandem with digital."

Abroms actually seeks to demystify the process. Part of his reason for this is to avoid his role being treated as some kind of sleight of hand where there's a series of smoke-and-mirrors tricks that a digital music marketer performs that will result in an instantaneous hit record or sold-out tour. He points out that his role involves being able to speak the language of music and music fans just as much as having access to some mystery cache of secret formulae.

> **[ZAC ABROMS]:** "I think we have a lot to learn from each other. I don't have that strictly technological background and everything I know how to use has been self-taught. It always

WELCOME TO THE JUNGLE

impresses me when I work with technical wizards because they can teach me a lot of tricks and tips that I wasn't aware of, but it works the other way as well. Your marketing 'voice' is so important and you need to speak not only a musician's language, but a music fan's language as well. Sometimes I have interns and it is hard to find someone who might be tech savvy and knows how a blog works and can upload a Soundcloud page, or convert a format, but also can be trusted to communicate via email with a very cool tastemaker blogger in Brooklyn that is not going to put them off, or run an artist's Twitter account and sound like the artist. There are a lot of different ways to approach it, and it is a combination of having some tech-savviness and having some of those traditional music journalistic skills and being able to appeal to fans in a way that is not going to seem too commercial. I see the internet as being an important part of tastemaking these days. More than anything now, it is independent blogs, and there is nothing you can do to woo these people other than genuinely get their interest in the band and so when he or she does back your band, it becomes very valuable. Kids are so savvy, they know the difference between seeing a double-page advert for a band and reading about them on some blog in the States – they know that it's super-cool that some band from Sydney is getting big ups from a blog in Portland."

Jackie Krajl is also quick to emphasise that technological awareness can only take you so far in the digital music world. Her advice is if you are going to spend time online researching and perfecting your skills with the latest applications and penetration techniques, do it with the music playing and maintain the passion for music that drives your enthusiasm. It's not a surprising perspective from someone whose first job was working in a record store where most of her wages went back into the cash register.

ANDREW WATT

[JACKIE KRAJL]: "I think it's a combination of all three things – technological awareness, marketing skills and a love of music. From the tech angle, you don't need to necessarily be a total tech geek, but you do have to have a working knowledge of the basics to be able to understand what's out there, what product is being developed and most importantly, what the implications of those will be to the industry at large when these new services and technologies are introduced to the market. You don't necessarily need to know the itty-bitty, nitty-gritty of how something works, but you do need to be able to comprehend its implications to music.

From the marketing side, just as you always get the music in the music business, you also get the business. There are so many products and services always coming out in the digital space, so having the marketing nous to be able to know how to effectively utilise those services and where to leverage them is of great value.

From the music side of things, I think that anyone coming into the industry, regardless of what area they are coming into, will probably have a passion for music. At the end of the day it's the heart and soul of what we all do and without the musicians and what they do we'd all be out of a job in a hurry."

Krajl, Picken and Abroms all completed degrees, although none of them were in computer technology. Picken completed a university business degree, Abroms did media and communication, while Krajl did an arts and communications degree majoring in PR and media studies with a sub-major of social psychology. None of them were afraid of computers though!

[JACKIE KRAJL]: "I always was a little bit of a geek, I won't deny it! Everything I know about computers and technology has either been self-taught through experience, or courtesy

WELCOME TO THE JUNGLE

of my long-suffering brother who is a gun at all that stuff. Computers and technology has always intrigued me and I've never been scared of it. My favorite saying has been 'go in there and try and break it'."

It's almost superfluous to try and understand what the hot buttons are at present in the digital music marketing world, because inevitably there will be new hot buttons by the time anyone reads this book. Such is the life of a digital music consultant, and the ability to stay on top of the latest evolutions in this fast-moving world is what provides the value for their services. It is imperative to their business that excessive time is spent self-educating, so if you are the kind of person who likes to think they know it all, then this part of the industry is not for you.

[JACKIE KRAJL]: "I honestly think it would average out to be an hour a day; just going through reading news stories, reading the newsletters I subscribe to, visiting forums, rumour sites, blogs. It obviously ebbs and flows depending on how much there is out there, but there is always something. I've never woken up in the morning, made a cup of coffee, turned on my computer and had nothing to read! One of the things I've spoken to quite a few managers about is the beauty of them being able to tap into a service like Digirascal. They might not necessarily have seven hours in the week to dedicate to keeping up with all the latest technological developments, but they can pick up the phone and ask someone whose job it is to stay on top of all that."

[VANESSA PICKEN]: "I could do it all day, everyday and then some. I don't have enough hours in the day to read every news piece that comes out, read every development, change and update or new announcement. We need to be able to be strategic, but we need to be able to implement ourselves. So having the capacity to get our hands dirty is a big part of being in this business. We know that most independent artists don't have massive budgets and we have to take that into consideration and that's where learning comes into play. If I have a great concept or marketing idea to apply to a certain artist, I need to know how to implement that and roll out the mechanics myself because they don't necessarily have the team or the budget to pay people to do it. The capacity to learn on the go is so fundamental. It's a constant learning curve. It goes back to that philosophy of business that you have to be sure that you are working <u>on</u> your business as much as you working <u>in</u> your business, and learning is a big part of our business."

It's inevitable that more and more people will follow these leaders into the industry and it clearly is a growth area for people who want to combine their love of music with getting paid to provide an essential service in an online environment, where you are able to work anywhere, anytime.

There's no doubt that the international experience suggests that the world inhabited by these three smart operators is going to continue to evolve.

> **[VANESSA PICKEN]:** "People are coming to it from different angles. There are definitely businesses coming into it from the entertainment realm. There are a lot of digital agencies and digital marketing companies, but they are coming more from entertainment spheres and tapping into music as a natural expansion of their current offering. But then you have a lot of new music companies and even major labels moving into label services, so they are enabling independents who are not signed to the major labels to benefit from those opportunities.

WELCOME TO THE JUNGLE

> I think that Australian artists and managers are quite savvy, They know how to set up a Facebook page and develop a website, so here it's more about a strategic approach of taking them to the next level and cutting through the clutter. We help artists to build a story online that you can take to a radio plugger or a publicist so that you can expand your team from that point. We try to educate artists and managers and the industry as a whole that digital doesn't need to be an afterthought. There's so many facets and services under the banner of digital and they are important to everything from your brand to your positioning, to your live shows, to your fan engagement. It's taken a long time for businesses such as ours to evolve in the market, but it's definitely the right time."

Once someone is educated in the area – and made a commitment that they will keep to stay educated – how do they get a foot in the door? According to Abrom, it's much the same as any other area of the business. You can't just talk a good game; you need to be able to show that you have a real passion for your chosen area and the best way to prove it is to do it. Getting paid is going to be a natural conclusion if a person making a name for themselves in the digital marketing space.

> **[ZAC ABROM]:** "The music industry is a strange business and it takes a long time to get paid doing anything. You have to stick your hand up and show people that you are willing to put in the hard work and the hard yards for free. You have to demonstrate that you can do it with some quality and with some success before it can become a monetised type of thing. My advice is if you want to get into digital PR, definitely have your own blog and maintain it as an example to the kind of people you want to reach. Once you demonstrate that you can do it with some quality, then more bands are going to come to you and you can start looking at charging them and creating a service business out of it."

ANDREW WATT

The Rise of Data

Reaching out to audiences is only one side of the digital marketing side of the new music industry. The digital music revolution also involves understanding how those audiences react and behave. Like many other industries, the analysis of consumer data has been the hot topic of the last couple of years and one of the key areas covered at many music business conferences and events.

Typical of this has been the emergence of international businesses like Next Big Sound, which describes itself in this way: "Launched in 2009, Next Big Sound is the leading provider of online music analytics and insights, tracking hundreds of thousands of artists around the world. As part of Pandora, we deliver powerful analytics tools used by music makers, labels and marketers looking for data and insights about artists and their fans." Projects of Next Big Sound include recommending artists and tracks to brands based on fan preferences and their willingness to relate to brands via their choice of campaign music.

James Overton, the Editor of technology website Innovation Enterprise responded with the following comment when news emerged of Pandora purchasing Next Big Sound.

"The deal follows a number of other similar acquisitions in the sector. Spotify announced in March (of 2015) that it was purchasing Massachusetts-based music data firm The Echo Nest, while Apple purchased media analytics company Semetric, the company behind the Musicmetric music analytics platform, in January (of 2016).

Record companies are increasingly turning to analytics as people listen to more and more music online. Social media and a plethora of new online platforms on which consumers can play music are opening up new avenues to scrape information which reveal a variety of factors that impact on their artist's sales.

WELCOME TO THE JUNGLE

While they may not bring in the same profits that CDs once did, platforms like Spotify provide a far greater insight into listening habits. Whereas previously it was impossible to gather much information past the point of purchase, companies are now able to see how often a song is listened to, when, and by who, giving them the capabilities with which they can predict future hit records.

Analytics is also providing a boon in other areas. Musicmetric focuses on the social media side, garnering customer sentiment from Facebook to Twitter to gauge an artist's popularity, allowing users to gauge which platform they are attracting the most buzz on so that they can be marketed accordingly."

There's no doubt that these high end manoeuvres in the technology world are likely to impact the way music is marketed and consumed and they will certainly help brands engage with artists and consumers in a sophisticated way. It also means that effective digital marketing of music in turn provides the keys to many other doors.

> **[CHARLES CALDAS]:** "If you are clever at social media now and can get 20,000 people to listen to your song, you can work out at what second they stopped listening, how many people added it to a playlist and how many people forwarded it to someone else. All of a sudden that mystery of consumer behaviour is totally unlocked. It means you know who your audience is, where they live, what they ate interested in and how you can build a direct relationship with them in a way you never could."

The applications of music data analysis extend beyond recorded music. In an earlier chapter a festival booker explained how her company uses social media analytics to assist in booking festival line-ups. Australia's Steve Halpin, from Groovin' The Moo, a statistician by profession, also points to the value of that information, albeit with a proviso.

ANDREW WATT

[STEVE HALPIN]: "We can look at our data early on and tell very quickly whether we can expect a sell-out. I do use data a lot to guide our marketing decisions. I think the music industry still has a long way to go in the use of data. It's used in a very naïve way – but that's fine. Music shouldn't be dominated by data. Music is a creative force and you shouldn't plan a festival purely based on data. However the whole world and every aspect of our lives is being measured by data. It's good and bad like most evolutionary things."

My Path into the Industry

ZANDA STROFIELD

Out of school I was actually a carpenter and lopped some fingers off. I wasn't a very good carpenter! So I went into labour hire and recruitment, doing cold calling and getting clients. Within three months I discovered I had the ability to talk to people, and I went from a sales position into a management position and then into directorships. I never went to university at all, but that hands-on experience taught me how to run a business and how to grow a business.

I'm a big fan of music and I have been my whole life. I got pulled into the Red Deer Music Festival, which is a boutique festival just out of Brisbane that holds about 1500 people, because of my background in business and business development – managing the process of developing new businesses and getting the framework of a business right before leaping into something. They were friends of mine and the skills I had were what they were chasing. They needed help developing some more revenue streams and it was a success, increasing turnover by 300-400% in one year. From there I decided to take the leap and do they things I wanted to do. I had Live It Up, the under 18s festival, in my mind for a period of time and when that opportunity came along the time was right to make the leap and get into it. That's how I got started, really."

Chapter 19

Branded Entertainment

The relationship between contemporary music and the corporate world has always been a challenging one – even though the majority of the world's most popular music is itself the product of multi-national corporations. There still remains an inherent belief that music, particularly rock, dance or roots genres such as blues, jazz and soul is the result of more primal instincts and motivations, and the attachment of advertising, sponsorship and commercial motivations to the music somehow sullies its purity and ability to connect with its audience in a meaningful way.

It wasn't that long ago that Neil Young recorded *This Note's For You*, a scathing look at corporate sponsorship of rock music – a song that included the lines "Ain't singin' for Pepsi/Ain't singin' for Coke/I don't sing for nobody/Makes me look like a joke".

Obviously the change in outlook has a lot more layers than a change in the attitudes of one of rock's most unpredictable icons, but it does show that, as has been the case in just about every form of entertainment, the lure of the commercial dollar has led to an evolution of the business.

It's not a sudden phenomenon. Advertisers and sponsors were attracted to the power of music long before Neil Young addressed the issue and there are numerous examples of sponsorships and – what are now known as 'activations' in live and media presentations of music.

WELCOME TO THE JUNGLE

Even in Australia back in the '80s, companies were set up to broker product placements in music videos. Almost two decades ago, the forward-looking Mushroom Group created Mushroom Marketing. That company operated strongly with clients such as NAB, Telstra, Fosters and the Victorian Government. Carl Gardiner was the managing director of Mushroom Marketing, and bought with him almost three decades of matching music and marketing objectives.

> **[CARL GARDINER]:** "I think the cliché I used was that the music led the revolution and therefore in many ways it stood for the antithesis of the top end of town and big business. So the sell-out thing was very strong. You either had to have enormous amounts of money at your disposal – which nobody really had in this marketplace – which would have allowed those concerns to be outweighed by the commercial benefits, or you had to find some very credible angles. As the industry got more accustomed to approaches from the corporate world and people like myself learnt on the job about how to build those relationships, we started to find deals that artists became more comfortable with. And over time, the industry started to notice that artists who did corporate deals didn't damage their image or hurt the relationship they had with their fanbase. It was a learning curve on both sides."

These days, the concept of the band as a brand has become common language in the international music business, and Australia is no exception. There are a number of specialist businesses dealing with corporate and music relationships, while organisations like the Big Day Out and Totem One-Love had sponsorship agencies built into their internal structures.

Carl Gardiner agrees that the music sponsorship industry created some of its own problems.

ANDREW WATT

[CARL GARDINER]: "A lot of people jumped on the music marketing bandwagon who didn't have a lot of experience and there were a lot of bad deals done and a lot of clients got burnt. It gave the music business a reputation for being hard to deal with and having a 'take the money and run' mentality. A lot of corporate decision-makers are conservative by nature. They won't lose their job if they do the same deals that everyone else has been doing, but if they do something radically different like getting involved in rock 'n' roll, they will be a hero if it works and they'll lose their job if it doesn't. But in recent years there's been a lot of research that is actually showing how much more viable entertainment is, relative to more traditional sponsorship options such as sport."

The music business still has to think broadly though. As Leigh Treweek, director of Street Press Australia points out there is still a lot of learn from both sides of the fence – the brands that want to associate themselves with music and the music world that wants to attract brand attention and investment.

[LEIGH TREWEEK]: "We are trying to convince brands and people that want to enter into this market into thinking a bit differently with regards to their approach, and understanding that music fans are incredibly passionate and if you want to play in this space, you have to do it smarter and work with people that actually understand the space. You need to be represented in a way that actually shows you care about the industry and care about music. But brands might look at sponsorship and say "If I sponsor action sports everyone is willing to create video content for me etc. whereas if I sponsor a music festival they might want to put a logo on a stage. No-one will actually get behind my brand". The music business needs to understand that from a brand point of view they are not competing against

WELCOME TO THE JUNGLE

another festival, they are competing against action sports or food or something else."

The Culture of Music and Corporate Sponsorships

Keith Ridgway, whose job in the events industry often finds him as the meeting point between corporate clients and musicians and their representatives, still finds that some corporate clients need to have their hand held when dealing with the music industry; it's an evolving cultural clash.

> **[KEITH RIDGWAY]**: "A lot of people don't understand rock 'n' roll. They don't understand the hours. They don't understand that people may not always be available for an 8.30am breakfast meeting. There has been a shift to a much more professional music business. I look at Brett Murrihy, at Artists Voice and you can see how he's taken the agents' world to a level where you know it's a deadly serious company that you are dealing with."

John Rash operated a business called Brand New Sounds, which has represented businesses such as the Hi-Fi Group and Secret Sounds and has worked with brands such as Jetstar, Red Bull, Ben & Jerry's and CUB among many others. He's now in London in the role of Strategy & Business Development Director for Broadwick Live - owner of a portfolio of over 20 international award winning music, culture & travel festivals.

> **[JOHN RASH]**: "Brands were never really off music. They always wanted to be in music, but two things kept them out. One was that the music industry itself had no desire to let them in there, and so the only way they came in was through specific artists, like Pepsi and Michael Jackson or a Delta Goodrem deal which was a lot of cash for a very obvious transactional

relationship for a very limited time. The music industry didn't want the brands in because they didn't need the revenue and they didn't want tarnish on their creativity.

The second thing was that the music industry was seen as a cowboy frontier and the brands were concerned at the lack of control. The clients want control; they pay for control. If anything happens in the normal commercial media world, the clients control all of it – from when you do it, how much you do it and how much you are going to get. Of course, the music industry is in an uncontrolled state, or at least it has multiple controls – you have publishing, recording companies, managers, promoters and that doesn't bode very well for brands to work with. There was a lot of natural barriers for brands coming in, but then when the digital revolution came along and changed the revenue model in the record industry, opening them up to new revenue sources such as brands, the labels started struggling with exactly the same stuff that advertising world struggled with, which was how to reach the consumer."

LA Based music brand consultancy memBrain is headed by Jennifer Sullivan and creates mutually rewarding and successful partnerships with content creators throughout the world on behalf of Intel, McDonald's, Hasbro, Coty, MillerCoors, Sperry, Keds, Logitech, and other global brand leaders

[JENNIFER SULLIVAN]: "We have tyranny of transparency there is no way to convince somebody of something that is untrue. You cannot create a personality or create a persona using traditional advertising. It reads as false and it doesn't take very much for a consumer or a fan to see right through something that is not authentic. Brands want to work with artists because they are tapping into something that is raw and authentic and emotionally connecting with a consumer. If the

WELCOME TO THE JUNGLE

brand tries to manufacture it, it wouldn't work. With social media and all those other things, we now know that Kanye West isn't actually drinking that Pepsi. You can't fool people like that and that is the sea change that happened."

The clever music brands realise that the sponsorship and marketing business is a two-way street, where their value is enhanced by brand associations rather than having the sponsors as a threat that needs to be controlled (while still extracting their corporate dollars). And in many ways the artists themselves have been insulated from the process as the sponsors and smart operators in the industry have started to make the connections based more around "experiences", rather than direct artist endorsement or involvement. Music is seen as a vehicle for the delivery of a memorable experience rather than the end in itself and hence sponsors are looking more to events and festivals rather than artist relationships.

> **[CARL GARDINER]**: 'There will always be a place for the big brand with the big star, but I believe that tying in a brand on an industry level rather than just to one individual act often has more benefits for the brand. At the end of the day what we are offering a connection with is people's passion for music and for most people that is broader than just one artist. That also gives the artists a bit more comfort because they are not the one act out there on their own. It's a collective endorsement model."

John Rash saw a change in the way brands come to the table already sold on music as the vehicle for their message.

> **[JOHN RASH]**: "When I started in 2005, up to 2009, every single presentation I did needed up to five or six charts answering the question, 'Why music?'. Before we could talk about anything, I had to sell music and explain to whoever I was

presenting to that music offers x, y, z. I had to educate them about what music was and why the hell it was worth talking about. Today you don't have to have a single chart about 'why music?' That's the most radical change. There is no longer an education process about why music is a viable channel; they all know that and they all want it."

Now we are at the point that artists are actually in a position to approach brands on a creative and analytic level.

[JENNIFER SULLIVAN]: "The music has to have the right DNA for the brand you are targeting. Brands look at social media and streams that a song might be getting. Young artists are now on a level playing field in that area. Artists now have the tools to go to a brand and tell them where their fans are and where their music is connecting. That's the way brands think and that's the kind of information they like."

And it doesn't necessarily need to be at the multi-national brand end of the market. Smaller artists can target smaller brands if the DNA is right.

[JENNIFER SULLIVAN]: "All day we have artists coming in telling us about projects they are working on that are interesting related to their music or not and they require funding or they require exposure and at the same time we have brands with products launching or stores opening that need to create friction or some kind of jolt in the marketplace. Sometimes it can be a win-win. Sometimes it might be a song that conveys an emotion and it's just a synch deal and the identity of the artist is secondary. It can be for small artists too. You don't have to wait around for Ford to give you a million dollars to do your music video – you can work with local companies who also have

WELCOME TO THE JUNGLE

money and projects that an artist can tap into if they show they can be brand friendly and willing to come up with ideas."

At an Australian level the relationships between music and brands are gaining importance. Both brands and artists are hungry for alignment and as a result Mushroom are forming a new division to be called Mushroom Creative House that will develop relationships in that space.

> **[MATT GUDINSKI]:** "We've had a lot of different pockets within the group dealing with that area over the years and now we've got a new department that has a dozen people in it that is focussed on not just sponsorship and brand partnership, but things like content creation for third party companies. Five years ago I saw a trend where a lot of brands were pushing towards the music space, but there was still a real reluctance by artists. Now a few years on there wouldn't be a day go by where an artist doesn't ring wanting us to hook them up with a brand to do a show or a product collaboration."

Kim Carter is the director of Rockstar Management, a company formed in 2001 that now works with brands such as Jim Beam, Canadian Club, and Nikon. She realises better than most the need for the owners and promoters of music properties to elevate their understanding of brand motivations. Music, in particular, generates an emotional response because everyone in "brand land" has their own idea of what is hip and happening in the music world. These expectations need to be managed and many brand managers have pre-conceived notions about what the alignment with music will achieve for the brand.

> **[KIM CARTER]:** "Some brands have already defined strategically that music is the route they are going. Somebody will have considered what is right for this brand in terms of reaching a

target audience and what their objective is in reaching that audience. But just because a brand wants to play in music, you still have to try and weed out their motivations. You have to determine whether or not selling someone something in music is actually going to work for them. You have to understand the objectives of the brand. There are a lot of brand managers that want to play in music, but it is completely subjective. They want their brand to be cool or to be associated with something, but it actually has more to do with the brand manager and less to do with the brand. If you really want to make a difference to a brand and have an outcome that is great, you need to get your hands on the documents that say what path a brand should be treading. When a brand says they want to be into music, the first thing I do is try and suss out whether or not the person sitting in front of me is really sure it's the way to go. It's a cluttered space. They have to make the right choices within music. There's a lot to that and a lot of thinking to do before you get to the point of activating a festival or some other music product."

Sometimes the artists are the ones providing the brands with the marketing lessons!

[JENNIFER SULLIVAN]: "Brands are actually looking for that. The best ideas are coming from creative people. I've worked with Will I Am and you will be in a meeting with him and he'll be talking about the future of technology and all these big picture ideas and he has a way of seeing things that brands love. Artists use their brain in a different way and come up with amazing ideas. Those ideas are transferable. He did a Power Point presentation for Coca Cola about reducing their carbon footprint and he told them why the money they were spending on recycling wasn't being done in a cool way."

WELCOME TO THE JUNGLE

The music audiences in today's market are more sophisticated than their earlier counterparts. They are quick to recognise product integration when they see it and brands shouldn't go to too much trouble trying to disguise brand associations as anything they are not. The good news is, the audiences of today welcome brands into their musical experiences.

> **[KIM CARTER]:** "They do get it and they do understand what sponsorship is, they've been raised with it. You are putting blinders on if you think that kids look at an event and don't see the integration, whether it's an event or a festival. If it walks like a duck and quacks like a duck, it's a duck and they see it. There was a time around 2000 or something when we thought we were actually doing something that was subliminal and streamlined and integrated, but if you ask those kids they would say, 'it's sponsorship, but we're OK with it'. It's part of their world. The people who have a problem with 'selling out' or branding in music are older. It's how they have been programmed in their life. The collision between commercialisation and art was coming at them in slow motion years ago; now it's crashed and rolled since then."

Carl Gardiner also advises that the fan can never be the forgotten party in any deal between a sponsor and an artist or event.

> **[CARL GARDINER]:** "One of the principles that I always pushed for with any client that was wanting to get involved with an artist or an event, was that they had to put aside what the benefits were to the promoter or the artist and ask what the benefits were for the fan. If you are able to say to the fan that this opportunity has been created because the sponsors had come in and they've added extra value for the fan, then those sorts of deals are easier to justify for all parties. We've done a lot of deals over the years on that basis."

ANDREW WATT

Breaking in to this side of the music business isn't simple. While enthusiasm and an inherent understanding of music is always helpful – and will help you to know when a deal just won't work for both the creative and the commercial side of the arrangement – it's probably more important now that you are well versed in marketing and business. Gardiner agrees that he spends more time reading marketing trade press than reviews of new albums or interviews with bands.

> **[CARL GARDINER]:** "I'm more focused on where the opportunities lie to build partnerships and relationships. It's more important for me to find the right opportunities to source funding or support and then put the elements together from the music industry. Some people might disagree with this, but I actually think the music industry needs more people that have experience in other industries. We need people that know how to build relationships between our industry and others, and who understand strategic marketing. You don't need to know how every facet of the industry works, but you do need to know people that do know that. I would definitely think that a marketing or communications type degree is useful. Publicity and public relations is also interesting because a lot of the projects we do have a client's PR agency involved, because one thing our industry does do well is to generate a lot of good publicity and media activity."

From Kim Carter's perspective, the opportunities to create a career path in this area of the business go further than just Australia. The language of music and the language of music sponsorship and commercial activations is an international one. The business of music sponsorship definitely offers international career opportunities.

> **[KIM CARTER]:** "I create brand experiences that have a paradigm shift and make a difference to how a consumer looks at a brand and considers a brand, to align with a brand, to

WELCOME TO THE JUNGLE

embrace a brand. From a global standpoint there are an enormous amount of agencies that are out there that are like mine or there are big global agencies that have music specialists. Any agency that does brand strategy will consider music in the scheme of things, so that automatically means that there are international paths. The UK and the US are in front of us and Korea is years ahead in that area. Every market is distinctive and I would encourage anybody to consider working in other countries and look at how things are done. We are in a really small pond here. There is enough work at integration opportunities here and great people to learn from and it's about learning as much as you possibly can and finding great mentors who are prepared to teach you. But what you are trying to do in the finish is work it out for yourself, and pull together as much knowledge as you can to make informed decisions."

My Path into the Industry

MILLIE MILLGATE

"I discovered that this is where I really needed to be was when I was working for Macquarie University Union. I started in their activities department and was involved in all the bands coming through and the programming of the entertainment on campus. That was the mid "90s and from there I moved on to the Annandale and the Hopetoun [hotels], booking those venues and I was simultaneously managing bands the whole time. From there I moved on to Music NSW, although I'd been on the board for a long time. That led me to eventually go to Sounds Australia.

I actually studied a degree in Tourism at the University of Canberra in the public relations and marketing side. I kind of think of that as the way people spend their fun money! I guess even when I was doing tourism, it was always the events side that appealed to me. I was working on the Manly Arts Festival for the Manly Visitation Bureau, and at the time when we had the festival I remember thinking, 'oh, this tourism gig is great', but when I look back it was really being a part of the production and giving opportunities for bands to play live that I was really enjoying. So, if you look at it, it probably looks like a really masterful strategy, but it was definitely not the case. But the fundamentals in terms of marketing and being in a service-based industry – there was a lot in that degree that I probably apply daily, unknowingly."

CHAPTER 20

MERCHANDISE

There's two ways of looking at the merchandise business. Merchandise can be as simple as bands selling t-shirts at shows to raise enough money to pay for petrol to get to the next town. That's a very grassroots perspective. The other way of looking at merchandise is to see it as an essential and rapidly growing revenue stream, a massive opportunity for brand expansion and a litmus test of an artist's penetration into their audience's commercial consciousness.

There's no doubt though, at either level, that merchandise is an important element of the financial mix. For small bands, selling merchandise can literally be the difference between a tour being sustainable or loss-making. At the other extreme, merchandising opportunities represent a lucrative profit centre that often outstrips the core revenue of recording royalties.

These days, there are numerous opportunities for industry newcomers to break into the business via the route of merchandise. It may be as simple as offering to sell merchandise for your favourite band and, by doing that, getting to know their management, or venue management, or catching the eye of a festival promoter.

But it's also a specialist industry now, with many hours being spent on developing brand and band collaborations that lead to custom product being launched in the market place. When Gene Simmons from KISS suggests that through KISS condoms and KISS coffins, the band

WELCOME TO THE JUNGLE

has got you when you are coming and when you are going, he's only half-kidding!

The emotional connection of merchandise shouldn't be overlooked. Fans like to acknowledge and display their support for a band or artist. It's a way of making a tribal statement from dawn to dusk and it's also a way of memorialising an experience. Marketers are constantly searching for vehicles for what's become known as experiential marketing, and in a way, merchandise in an obvious expression of this.

Rowena Crittle operated a Brisbane based merchandiser called Mammoth before joining forces with the British based company Araca Group. She summarises the importance of merchandise well.

> **[ROWENA CRITTLE]:** "The artist to me is a brand and so I am a brand manager. I see my responsibility is for one facet of that brand. I think merchandise is sometimes disjointed from the overall marketing of the artist. When the artist has a new album coming out merchandise has always been a bit of an after-thought whereas I believe it should be considered as part of the original marketing strategy. The merchandise that really connects with fans really tells a story that the artist wants to tell. I see merchandise as being a part of a much bigger picture and it is our responsibility to ensure we understand that brand."

Brian Taranto runs Love Police/ATM, Australia's biggest and most well established music merchandise operation.

> **[BRIAN TARANTO]:** "I call myself the 'rock 'n' roll hotdog seller'. It's more souvenir based – yes the great majority is apparel, but it's more about making a financial commitment to an emotional experience. When I started in the business, merchandisers were treated like shit and I'd like to think in this

country I've gone a long way to helping them be accepted as a part of the touring entourage, and part of the vibe that makes for a good tour. I certainly see myself more in the music industry than the apparel industry; even though our numbers are probably enviable by apparel industry standards, it's an entirely different set of figures that make up the bottom line."

Manager Gregg Donovan comes from a live touring background and, as manager of bands like Grinspoon and Airbourne, he can attest to how important the merchandising revenue stream is to keeping a band on the road.

[GREGG DONOVAN]: "I reckon 80% of our income has come from tickets and merchandise. For Airbourne merch been the most important income stream of all. It can save you from touring and losing money. It is often the only place an artist can make money on the road because the costs are so high. It keeps cashflow going when you are not on the road with your online store. It's really important that you focus on getting it right. If you have the right range you can do really well out there. A lot of people try to be too tricky with merch. The ugly truth with merch is that 'cool' doesn't sell. People like t-shirts that say "I was there". That's why the tour shirt will always sell the best. You try and do a scarf with a little logo in the corner to sell to girls because you think they don't want big logos, and they'll say, 'if I wanted a scarf, I'd go to a fashion store where they have really nice scarves'. If you are a fan of the band you want something that shows you are a fan of the band."

Donovan makes some really valid points. There is a temptation with merchandise to try and get too creative and too clever. It's a conundrum, because everyone from the lead singer, to the manager, to the bloke at the bar has an opinion about what a t-shirt should look like. For career merchandisers this can be frustrating. Like anyone else in

WELCOME TO THE JUNGLE

the business, they have years of experience to draw on in their segment of the industry, but that doesn't stop everyone else suddenly becoming experts!

> **[BRIAN TARANTO]**: "I've been doing this business a long time, and the real trick with merchandising is to let the merchandiser do their job. I don't tell the manager how to manage the band, so if they have contracted me as the merch company they should let me merchandise the band. Certainly there is approval processes to go through, but there is so many people that think they know our job better than we know it ourselves. I have to listen to some guy who manages one band, who thinks they know everything about merchandise when I've probably done eight shows that night all around Australia and New Zealand and grossed half a million dollars. But what would I know?"

Rowena Crittle shares Taranto's view that artists haven't fully realised the potential of merchandise revenue in their business mix.

> **[ROWENA CRITTLE]**: "I think Australian artists are very protective of their brand and the way it is represented. More so in this market as opposed to America, Australian artists are very careful not to push themselves on to their audience and that can be a hindrance in terms of their earning potential and their ability to make money out of their art in the small window they have. At the end of the day it is a business. I do believe in the creative side but merchandise is an opportunity to make a career out of it. Some times we have to sell the idea to artists that it is OK to be proud of what they do with merchandise."

Taranto has an interesting attitude to his industry. He clearly regards his business as being a part of the music industry, rather than say, the 'apparel business' but he's surprised at the lack of recognition it gets from the industry itself.

> **[BRIAN TARANTO]:** "Merchandise is a big part of the financial side on the balance sheet, but I still don't think it is truly being recognised. How many conferences have I been asked to talk at in Australia? There was no mention of merchandising in that "Most Powerful" list they do. I go to SXSW every year and every couple of years there's a minor panel on merchandising, and yet everyone there is walking around in band t-shirts! Tickets and t-shirts are certainly the big revenue earners for a lot of bands and it's certainly not embraced as the commodity it is."

That position seems to be changing. At the 2012 Face the Music Conference, Taranto was joined on a merchandising panel by Adam Jankie, one of the new breed of industry players who completely understands the role of merchandise as part of the revenue model mix. And he's not restricting his thinking to the traditional t-shirts and stubby holders. As the business becomes more sophisticated, Jankie sees great opportunities for smart operators to enter the merchandising business.

> **[ADAM JANKIE]:** "100% there are careers in merchandise. That's a whole other market in itself. Traditional merchandise opens itself up to other things altogether; things that we are starting to explore with our bigger artists outside their own merchandise.
> It's the idea of doing collaborations with existing brands and third-party deals to create third-party product. That requires its own level of specialised skills and expertise. We worked with Casio to do a Bliss n Eso/G Shock collaboration. They are the first Australian artists to do a collaborative watch with Casio.

WELCOME TO THE JUNGLE

We are doing the design through to the whole marketing set-up. We are even doing the contracts for the deal itself, because they had never done anything like this."

That opens up another whole new category of jobs in the music business. Like many other areas there is an opportunity to work your way into a senior role. One night you could be selling t-shirts at a pub, but within a few years you could be heading up a million-dollar merchandising division for a major international artist. It could happen.

Yet strangely, Brian Taranto finds that merchandising is the foot in the door that few people take the opportunity to open.

> **[BRIAN TARANTO]:** "If anyone ever asks me about getting into the merch game, I just say, 'If you are any good come and see me and I'll give you a job'. We don't have many young staff. I give them my phone number and say 'Call me, I'll give you a job', and no one calls! I'm not actively looking for people, but I'd be a lot more encouraged if there was go-getter young kids out there asking for a job."

Getting a job in the business is probably an easier entry point than starting your own business. The merchandise business is capital-intensive. Significant money needs to be invested in stock before revenue can be earned. It's an adage that Taranto often uses, that "you can't download a t-shirt", but equally you can't expect fans to buy a t-shirt if you haven't invested in making that t-shirt physically available. While the costs of international manufacture are now very competitive, there is no substitute for cashflow.

> **[BRIAN TARANTO]:** "The difference between when I started and now is that if you want to get a good quality t-shirt designed and printed at a reasonable price, you don't need to come and

see me. You can just get on the internet and find all that stuff. I will still probably get it done quicker and cheaper than you, but even if you don't know what you are doing you are still going to get the same product. You might get ripped off the first time but you can work that out eventually. So anyone could get one or two bands and start doing t-shirts. But unless you are a smart businessman or you are funded, you get to the point that you won't have the cash to keep it rolling. Let's say your band is playing at the [Sydney] Entertainment Centre level, well, those venues hold on to your money for 10 days. But you still have to get the t-shirts for the rest of the tour. It becomes a cashflow problem."

Internationally, merchandise is a massive business. It's an area of expertise that translates across international boundaries and Taranto's reputation, for example, extends well beyond the Australian border. He has relationships with international companies and artists that support his local business. A lot of it comes down to being pro-active in making yourself known, something that people thinking of breaking into the industry should remember.

[BRIAN TARANTO]: "Love Police ATM merch company represents Bravado, who are the biggest merchandising company in the world. We actually represent a lot of companies over here and we also do direct deals with international acts. We always do all of Jack White's bands direct. We work with different acts that I might meet around the world socially, as a promoter or as a merchandiser. I love doing my international trips. I'm hanging out at a festival having a great time, but I'll walk away from that with one or two tours. I know from my touring experience that you get work done at these shows. You see at the coalface what is going on. You see a band and you look at their merchandise and say, 'your merchandise is terrible'. You'd be surprised how many times I say that to an act and they say, 'yeah, we know, we just can't get it together'. So we step in and help them out."

These days the sale of merchandise is not limited to shows. With businesses like Music Glue providing an on-line platform for artists to sell merchandise there appears to be an increasing importance placed on those branded items.

[MARK MEHARRY]: "Music Glue is a platform for an artist to be a global retailer of anything they want in any way they want to be. They can sell tickets for a Norwegian promoter to a show in Norway bundled with a t-shirt that is sent from a warehouse in the UK, bundled with an MP3 that they can pay their US label for in US dollars, and they can sell that bundle to a kid in Sweden who wants to buy all that in Swedish, on their mobile phone, in Swedish krona."

My Path into the Industry

BERNARD GALBALLY

"I'd worked in outdoor education and had tertiary qualifications in that area. I'd run a business for three years, taking small groups up through the Northern Territory and the Kimberley region. The business used to get a lot of publicity – newspapers, TV shows, all sorts of things and we used to love doing publicity stunts like riding camels through the streets of Melbourne. Then my business partner died in a ballooning accident. I had a friendship with Mario Maccarone who was working with the Bachelors From Prague. Mario and Henry from the band came to me one day and said 'hey, you are really good at making connections and getting things done, how would you like to get involved with the band?. We had no idea about the music industry and we just learned as we went. People say that my background is unusual for the music industry, but the way I look at it, taking a group bushwalking through the Kimberley, with only a map and a compass, is not that different to taking a band and trying to guide them through the music business! We managed the Bachelors for many years, and then Mario had the opportunity, to take over the venue that became the Continental [in Prahran]. They asked me to run that venue and from there I started promoting shows myself. When the Continental closed down, I continued to work as a promoter which went well and from there I segued back into band management and all of a sudden I was managing five acts which is when I met Chris Gough who runs Mana Music. I had a young family and I didn't want to continue in management and Chris suggested I should get into music supervision. I enjoyed it and I think what I've brought into the business is an understanding of it from the artist's point of view."

Chapter 21

INDUSTRY BODIES AND GOVERNMENT

The music industries are largely regarded as a business free from regulation and government infrastructure. Most businesses that operate within the broad area that covers the music industries are privately owned and operated.

Obviously, businesses such as live venues require licenses to operate, and festival and concert promoters are increasingly obliged to abide by OH&S legislation and other forms of regulation such as the *Australian Consumer Law*.

The requirement for record companies to pay mechanical royalties, for example, is enforced by statute and, as we have seen, Acts of Parliament such as the *Copyright Act* 1968 (Cth) are important to the operation of the industry in a number of areas.

However the music business has largely been seen as an industry that does not rely heavily on government support and investment for its survival, and, rightly or wrongly, most music business operators have very low expectations regarding government involvement in their business.

That may be changing, though. Increasingly smart operators in the industry are benefitting from government programs that traditionally appeared to operate exclusively for the benefit of sectors like classical, jazz and indigenous music. Whether that was simply because those sectors were more familiar with the processes of dealing with government, or whether those programs were skewed toward those types of

WELCOME TO THE JUNGLE

applicants, is uncertain. However, in recent years more and more contemporary music applicants are engaging with the government sector.

[JADDAN COMERFORD]: "We work very closely with Australia Council and Austrade. Austrade provide the Export Market Development Grants that are very helpful for touring, but also for a record label exporting our copyrights. We will consistently have at least one artist successfully getting funding from the Australia Council's International Pathways grant that has two rounds a year. Even big acts like The Amity Affliction and Vance Joy or Northlane will still go for those grants because it might mean being able to invest a bit more into the show and making it work or take things to the next level. Things could always be better but I think we do actually get a lot of support from the government. We do everything in-house, but there are very proficient grant writers out there that you can hire to write grant proposals. I think it's quite accessible."

Sounds Australia, set up as a jointly funded initiative of state and federal government and collection societies, has been a great support to numerous Australian artists and the head of Sounds Australia Millie Millgate sees the role of government as important – but only in conjunction with self-starting industry participants.

[MILLIE MILLGATE]: "Government absolutely has a role, but I think it has to be a really healthy mix. I sometimes look at other countries where there is an abundance of support and funding and I do think that breeds a less hungry appetite from the artists themselves. I see them miss opportunities with the attitude of, 'Well, we didn't get the funding so we won't go, we won't make the effort'. I do believe Australians still have the attitude that if they want to go to an event and there is enough buzz and enough serious interest, they will find a way to get there. If we were to ever lose that we are in trouble. I think that government intervention – and I don't like the word 'intervention' and I'd rather consider it a partnership – can be incredibly valuable. An initiative like Sounds Australia is where you really have buy-in from states and federal agencies and from organisations like APRA and PPCA and AMPAL. It's a really unique situation to have that many players all wanting this to work at an export level. That kind of infrastructure can set a base and set templates and platforms and springboards. It's still up to the artists to do their thing but there is strength around what they do and that's essential. It's the same as in elite sport. You could never suggest that those athletes could do it by themselves."

Export Market Development Grants

The Export Market Development Grants (EMDG) scheme is the Australian Government's principal financial assistance program for aspiring and current exporters. The scheme is administered by Austrade and is aimed at encouraging small and medium sized Australian businesses to develop export markets by reimbursing up to 50 per cent of eligible export promotion expenses above a threshold of $15,000. Businesses in the music industry are eligible to participate in this program.

The ability to claim an export grant in the music industry, through intellectual property, revolves around the Export Grant claimant being the owner or exclusive licensee of copyright in either the sound recording or musical work. Additionally ownership of a trademark may allow merchandising rights to be exploited.

Artists can claim an EMDG based on the delivery of entertainment services. Recoupable record label expenditure as tour support, independent promotion and videos, may be eligible in certain circumstances, for a rebate in the hands of the artist.

WELCOME TO THE JUNGLE

The expenditure claimed must directly relate to the intellectual property rights being promoted. Hence an artist may be simultaneously marketing a number of rights through live performances, such as future live performance income, the sale of sound recordings or royalty income from the exploitation of their songs.

Under amendments to the Export Grant Scheme, touring losses of performers and musicians, will potentially qualify for the 50% cash rebate available under the Export Grant Scheme. Previously overseas touring costs only qualified, where a group received no performance income.

The tour losses will be claimable in the following circumstances;

- The loss was incurred primarily to promote future sale of records, the licensing of sound recordings to an overseas record company, or future live performance income.

- The loss was planned i.e. the loss was budgeted for and not incurred through financial mismanagement.

- The entity claiming the Export Grant must control the intellectual property rights (the sound recordings) in overseas markets.

- Where a contribution to a touring loss is claimed by a record company or music publisher, rather than the artist, then if a contribution to touring costs is made, that contribution will qualify provided it is not for accommodation and sustenance. In lieu of accommodation and sustenance, a $200 daily per diem allowance per tour member is allowed by Austrade.

- Apart from accommodation and sustenance, all other touring costs would qualify including production, lights, advertising and transport. Equipment hire qualifies but not equipment purchases. If a van in which a musical group travels overseas is hired, the hire costs will qualify but if a van is purchased and sold at the end of the tour, the costs of purchasing the van or the loss incurred on the sale of the van will not qualify.

Many artists take advantage of the EMDG program – but many do not, even though they might be eligible.

State Government Grants

Each State Government has a grants program that can be accessed by musicians and music industry projects. These vary in size and accessibility.

In Victoria a relatively new initiative is the Music Works Grants provided by Creative Victoria. These Grants are provided in three key areas: Creating Content (effectively recording and creating digital content where new intellectual property is created), Building Capacity (assisting industry stakeholders such as managers, artists, small organisations and industry technicians to offer career development, and to build industry capability) and Connecting to Markets (designed to increase the industry's capacity to connect with new audiences and to take their business to the next level by exploring opportunities and strategies which would usually be outside their reach).

In addition the Music Works program offers quick response grants that provide grants from $1,000 to $5,000 for individuals and $1,000 to $15,000 for groups and organisations to cover immediate opportunities in the Building Capacity and Connecting to Markets Areas of Funding. Many artists seek these grants when they discover they have been accepted into international events such as SxSW or CMJ.

WELCOME TO THE JUNGLE

Under the inspired leadership of Kirsty Rivers and Dean Linguey the Victorian Music Grants program has been perhaps the most effective government grants program to roll out in Australia.

In NSW, Arts NSW has announced the Arts and Cultural Development Program (ACDP) to replace the former Arts Funding Program (AFP), while WA has the Regional & Remote Touring Fund (RRTF). In South Australia ArtsSA provides Artist Development Grants and Industry Development Grants.

Learning From Overseas

There's no doubt we can learn from the experience of both Canada and New Zealand.

> **[JAKE GOLD]:** "Canada has always had the benefit of always having a world view. Our countries are very similar in a lot of ways. We have a population of 30 million people spread out over a huge piece of land like Australia, but we are fortunate enough that we have a market of 300 million just south of us. I can fly from Toronto to New York in an hour. The market from Boston to Washington DC is 80 million people, so I can drive the van to Boston and go down the East Coast and basically go after that population. Like Australia, Canada has benefits from Canadian content rules on radio, and they have programs for funding bands. Canadians have to protect their culture because we have the greatest exporter of Canadian culture in the world sitting right beside us. You guys, because of the distance are still exposed to American culture in a big way, but its not standing right over you like it does for Canada. Americans export their culture everywhere, even more than the British do."

> **[DAVID WILLIAMS]:** "I think Canada and New Zealand are two countries where you can see strong involvement from

government has been incredibly helpful to those industries. New Zealand certainly do punch above their weight, and Canada with the US next door still have some significant successes with their artists. I'd love some level of support in Australia, and maybe I've become a little cynical about the role of government in people's lives generally, but maybe the way that politics has become such a gladiatorial sport, that ultimately there is no votes in supporting what might be seen as a leftist side of the entertainment world."

Veteran festival promoter Peter Noble is another who believes government has a significant role to play based on his international experiences.

[**PETER NOBLE**]: "In Canada they have a $60 million dollar budget to support talent. The reason it's $60 million is that they realise that over-exposure in your own country is a killer of their talent. The money is there to allow Canadian talent to travel beyond the boundaries of their country and build other markets so they don't have to play in their own region five or six times a year and ultimately damage their ability to maintain their audience. It's a great policy that funds travel and accommodation and on-the-ground costs like backline and transport. It allows the act to take something home and to build other markets and learn about overseas marketing and publicity."

Collection Societies

But institutional involvement is not limited to government. There are a number of organisations that have an enormous impact on the music industry that are neither private enterprise nor government departments.

In Chapter 3 we detailed the role and legal basis behind both APRA/AMCOS and the PPCA. APRA (Australian Performing Rights

WELCOME TO THE JUNGLE

Association) and AMCOS (Australian Mechanical Copyright Owners Society) are bodies that have a huge impact on the industry, both at a corporate level and in terms of the livelihoods of individual songwriters and recording artists.

The membership of APRA consists of songwriters and APRA is responsible for the collection of royalties due to those songwriters when their works are publically performed, in all of the many ways that can occur. AMCOS is responsible for the collection of mechanical royalties (those royalties payable when a song is reproduced by way of a sound recording) on behalf of rights owners largely being music publishers and songwriters. The PPCA represents the owners of sound recordings with respect to their performance rights.

A few statistics will point to the significance of these revenue streams. In figures released by APRA/AMCOS in their 2014-15 Year In Review, APRA distributed over $194 million (which has doubled over the last decade) and AMCOS $65.0 million (down 0.8 percent on $65.8 million). The total net distributable revenue was also up 6.9 percent to $262.7 million. Television revenue was up to $79.4 million, from $75.6 million, and public performance up to $65.9 million, from $63.8 million. Revenue from recorded music was down to $12.5 million, from $15.2 million. APRA has over 89,000 members – songwriters, composers and music publishers, while AMCOS has 15,148 members – and 126,000 businesses are licensed to use music.

Brett Cottle, the managing director of APRA/AMCOS, accepts that these organisations have a powerful leadership role in the industry.

[**BRETT COTTLE**]: "I hope we have shown leadership on our side of the industry; that is, the composer and publisher side of the industry. What we have tried to do is handle our rights responsibly and not to over-reach in claims. We've tried to adopt a strong customer service mentality – we want people to want to deal with us, not to hate to deal with us. We want to show people that we are prepared to compromise and to be realistic. All of those things I regard as important leadership roles in this environment of challenge and change. We have also been fortunate enough to do well through the slump because of the enormous diversity across the APRA and AMCOS businesses. We've not had any decline at all in our revenue. The relatively new digital models have meant that AMCOS in particular has collected a lot higher revenue than it ever did in the past. I think the fact that we've done well in a business sense has given us that extra responsibility to show leadership and I hope we've done that."

In many ways the collection societies work at the coalface of the business, especially under the "new" models. As discussed throughout this book, the power may have shifted back towards the creative personnel – recording artists and songwriters, with fewer gatekeepers controlling the exploitation of their works. Accordingly, the organisations that work directly with those creative people and represent their rights and assets – the collection societies – become even more significant than previously.

[BRETT COTTLE]: "I think most companies have to try and distinguish themselves on customer experience and that's what we are trying to do all the time. We are trying to improve the experience of our members in dealing with us; we are trying to improve the experience of our licensees in dealing with us. But by the same token, we do see ourselves very much as a commercial entity. We are here to maximise, in the fairest and most reasonable way, the rewards that writers and publishers get from the use of their property. We are working in an area – public communication and public performance and recording for commercial use – where we are able to enforce compliance and make sure people pay, and the additional responsibility falls on us because in those other areas that have been so impacted by file sharing and unlawful distribution on the internet, our members have suffered tremendous losses. We feel an extra commercial responsibility as well."

The work of the societies continues to evolve. In 2014 they jointly commenced on an initiative called CLEF (Copyright Licensing Enterprise Facility) that will manage their relationships with licensees and improve the speed and frequency of distributions to members as well as proving them with an unprecedented amount of data

The role of APRA and AMCOS means that they are organisations which are quite labour-intensive. There are many people required in these organisations to deal both with their very large membership bases and the myriad external businesses (music licensees) – mainly consumers of music in its various forms that are the, sometimes reluctant, contributors to the societies' revenue streams. Once that revenue is collected, it needs to be distributed among the members and used for their benefit in other ways. Both societies operate generous grant schemes that help their members' professional development. In 2014-15 nearly $1million was allocated to 194 music industry projects. Once you consider exactly how extensive the work of the collection societies is, you will not be surprised at the employment opportunities they offer.

> **[BRETT COTTLE]:** "We probably are the largest employer in the music industry. We have 342 staff. I don't know what the staff at a major label is now, but I'd imagine it is fewer than 100. I don't know what their revenue is these days, but our revenue is over $300 million now for APRA and AMCOS. So we are probably larger than any two labels put together. We would be the largest employer so I think we are an important employment gateway for people in Australia."

ANDREW WATT

In 2014 APRA AMCOS appointed very active representatives in both LA and Nashville in addition to a representative in London to enable members based overseas to be serviced by the societies.

As Cottle suggests, there are significant employment opportunities in the collection societies and many people have launched or developed a career in the music industry from those roles. Under Cottle's leadership, the Australian societies are highly respected and there are few enterprises in the music industry as well versed in current copyright and royalty issues. For example, the societies are on the cutting edge of discussions regarding the revenue flowing from digital delivery mechanisms.

People who have worked successfully at either APRA or AMCOS have experience that is well regarded not just in Australia, but also internationally, albeit with a word of warning.

> **[BRETT COTTLE]:** "We do have some positions overseas. Sometimes some of our technical staff do job exchanges and go and work with our equivalent companies in the States or the UK and I think a CV involving an extensive time at APRA would probably be a very positive thing if you were trying to get a job in the music industry in those countries. But the truth of the matter is that they are all suffering from economic circumstances that are much worse than ours. Many of them are downsizing, including the collection societies internationally."

Even APRA, as one of the industry's most respected organisations, it is not without its critics. APRA operates as a monopoly. There is no other collection society in Australia, and it is able to stand alone because the ACCC (the regulatory body for consumer and competition matters) allows this situation to remain. Like any business in a monopoly situation there is always going to be those who believe that this power is unfairly or inflexibly used. Many licensed venues, for example, believe

WELCOME TO THE JUNGLE

that the fees APRA charge are too high and place an unreasonable burden on their business. Other businesses have expressed concern that APRA operates too inflexibly and is too quick to resort to legal action to collect money that it levies.

APRA has its status reviewed by ACCC and in a 2013 article by Ben Eltham on the Artshub website, it was noted that APRA's monopoly position was not necessarily automatic. Even so, it's hard to imagine a music industry landscape with APRA's role under challenge.

Nevertheless Eltham's article provides food for thought as the following extract suggests:

> *"Collection agencies have a unique exemption under Australian corporate law, which effectively gives them a legal monopoly to collect these royalties. That puts them under the purview of the ACCC. Now, APRA is re-applying for its special authorisation from the ACCC. Without it, the copyright body might fall foul of competition law.*
>
> *Big money is at stake. Along with its sister agency the PPCA, APRA administers the rights for essentially all the music commercially available in Australia. If you want to play a song on a radio station, a CD in a small bar or an iPod in your shop, you need a license from both APRA and the PPCA.*
>
> *Copyright law is fiendishly complex, but in essence it boils down to the legal ability to force ordinary businesses and consumers to pay for the privilege of playing music. Without copyrights, there would be nothing to stop unscrupulous businesses from using music without paying for it, such as in television commercials or on the radio. On the other hand, Australian copyright law also gives collection agencies like APRA powerful incentives to charge high fees to small businesses like bars and nightclubs.*

ANDREW WATT

Negotiation between customers and the big collection agencies can be tense. Both APRA and the PPCA have control over essentially any music that a business might reasonably be able to play, and the agencies have well-resourced legal departments. The PPCA in particular has been a muscular litigant in pursuit of big fee hikes in recent years, such as in its long-running disagreement with the gyms and fitness industry. As a result, several disputes in recent years have ended up before the Federal Court.

In order to keep its monopoly, APRA has to keep re-applying to the ACCC every three years. In previous years, its reputation as the nice guys of the industry has served it well. The agency distributes millions of dollars of royalties to struggling musicians in the form of live performance royalties, which reward small bands and unknown musos throughout the country with cold hard cash every November.

But APRA's money has to come from somewhere, and pubs and clubs in particular have long resented the fees they must pay to APRA simply for booking a live band or putting on a CD. Now that APRA is required to re-apply for its ACCC authorisation, that resentment has boiled over in a slew of angry submissions to the ACCC's review.

Despite these submissions, in 2014, APRA received re-authorisation to continue its activities for another five years. While no organisation of this size will ever please all the stakeholders it's obvious that APRA/AMCOS and the PPCA are extremely positive forces in the Australian music industry and it would be folly for any participant in the industry not to engage with those societies wherever possible.

Industry Peak Bodies

APRA and AMCOS are not the only industry organisations where valuable experience can be gained.

WELCOME TO THE JUNGLE

Most states now have their own industry peak body that represents the industry in that state. While these organisations are not heavily resourced, and hence don't have large numbers of full-time staff, they do provide many opportunities for involvement that, in turn, could lead to job opportunities or project-based positions.

The various state bodies come together under the banner of AMIN, the Australian Music Industry Network. AMIN is stated to exist "to bring together and represent its members, the state and territory music industry associations, and by doing so create a strong network that provides a national platform for the representation of, and the delivery of, projects for the benefit of the contemporary music industry in Australia." AMIN is comprised of state organisations such as Music NSW, Music NT, Music SA, QMusic, WAM, Music Victoria, Music Tasmania and ACT Music.

Music Victoria, is headed by Patrick Donovan, who also serves as the Chair of AMIN.

[PATRICK DONOVAN]: "Music Victoria was incorporated in 2010 and a number of our members are music fans, students and people who aren't musicians and who are not actually in the music industry yet. We've got a large network. We provide professional development workshops each year and we try to ensure that they are not doubling up with the subjects taught in music industry courses. Our mantra is that musicians have to treat their band as a small business and their fans as customers. We actually have had a really good partnership with Small Business Victoria and they put on four or five workshops per year. They basically had their lecturers and their reading material and we found a couple of lecturers that have worked in the music industry so they tailor it that way. That's a good example. There are a lot less labels developing careers than there used to be, so we are providing those skills that perhaps a record label or a manager would have provided in the old days. We are encouraging bands to look at their careers as a sustainable business and if they use all the advice at their disposal, they can have a sustainable career."

In Part 3 of this book it is suggested that attending industry events such as Big Sound or Face the Music is a great way of getting yourself noticed – the mere fact that you are a member of an organisation like Music Victoria sends the message that you are serious about making a career in the industry. Being an active participant in events amplifies that message.

> **[PATRICK DONOVAN]:** "We are often the ones coming up with the ideas and part of the job is trying to find the money to fund the new initiatives. A lot of people who have volunteered for us have ended up getting a job after we have referred them to someone else for work or part-time work. Just being close to the decision-making process is important and you can even have an influence on that. The government is listening, liquor licensing is listening and we are doing the homework and we are able to say what we need to change and why. Imagine going to an underage gig and being able to say, 'I was part of the decision-making process that changed these rules, that allowed this gig to happen'. We do want people to get a bit more active. There are not a lot of paid jobs in music activism, but there are lots of committees and lots of potential to effect change, which will improve the industry and create more opportunities."

AAM

Another industry peak body is the Association of Artist Managers (AAM). Its website describes its role: "The AAM works to expand

WELCOME TO THE JUNGLE

the capacity for artist management in Australia through workshops, sector and skills development opportunities and advocating for and promoting the issues of music managers and their artists. Working with the IMMF, the AAM aims to foster awareness for the importance of copyright for its economic and cultural worth and provide a network for global managers to share information and resources.

AAM have created a Mentor Program allowing young managers to receive guidance from those that are more experienced. Mentors have included John Watson from Eleven Music (Birds of Tokyo, Cold Chisel, Silverchair, Gotye), Gregg Donovan from Wonderlick (Pete Murray, Boy & Bear, Grinspoon, Airbourne, Josh Pyke), Claire Collins from Bossy Music (Art vs Science, D.D Dumbo, Kagu) Andrew Stone from Chugg Music (Shepperd, Megan Washington, The Griswolds, Deep Sea Arcade), Greg Carey from Umbrella Music (Cloud Control, PVT, The Rubens, Elizabeth Rose, Urthboy), and Dan Medland from ie:music (Ladyhawke, Passenger, The Bamboos, Bondi Hipsters, Jack Ladder and the Dreamlanders).

In 2014 the AAM released a Code of Conduct for managers to provide "the utmost ethical, professional and innovative artist management in Australia" to the artists who have trusted them with their careers.

These are the 11 guidelines offered:

- Devote sufficient time to fulfil the agreed responsibilities of management in the interests of the artists as both parties understand them;

- Possess and obtain the knowledge and skills to carry out the required duties of management as agreed and understood with the artists they represent;

ANDREW WATT

- Communicate and negotiate with the artist their responsibilities, obligations, duties and remuneration as a manager of the artist and have those preferably notated in a written agreement;

- Seek support where required and commit to expanding their knowledge base and skills to assist in representing the artist's career with diligence in all phases of the artist's career;

- Operate and conduct their own management business and the artist's business in a professional, transparent, accountable and ethical manner;

- Ensure relevant financial and legal matters are communicated to the artist and where relevant refer the artist to an independent, third party advisor specializing in such financial and legal matters;

- Uphold client confidentiality, ensuring appropriate use of information whilst exercising diligence and duty of care;

- Declare and fully disclose to an artist any conflict of interest whether it is actual perceived or potential, including any income or other consideration earned by the manager directly or indirectly in conjunction with their artists' performance or services;

- Ensure the commission rate agreed with the artist is in line with standard industry norms;

- Be aware of and operate within the parameters of any relevant State and Federal legislative requirements;

- Be culturally aware and act respectfully toward all the nationalities, religious, gender and ethnic groups.

WELCOME TO THE JUNGLE

Live Performance Australia

The live performance industry also has a peak body called Live Performance Australia. Its website states: "LPA is the peak body for Australia's live entertainment and performing arts industry. Established in 1917 and registered as an employers' organisation under the Fair Work (Registered Organisations) Act 2009, LPA's activities centre around three core areas - Workplace Relations, Policy & Strategy and Membership Services & Events.

LPA members work in the live performance sector across all artistic genres, including contemporary and classical music, musicals, theatre, comedy, dance, opera, circus and physical theatre and the body represents producers, venues, promoters, performing arts companies, festivals and industry suppliers such as ticketing companies and technical specialists."

The LPA provides an excellent set of resources for new entrants into the live side of the industry.

ARIA

ARIA (Australian Recording Industry Association) is a representative organisation for record companies with a membership including numerous companies, although there is a perception that its agenda is set by the major labels. In fact ARIA has over 100 members including many smaller labels.

ARIA operates under the leadership of a Board of Directors and CEO Dan Rosen. ARIA maintains a number of committees, including The Copyright Committee, the Finance Committee, the Chart & Marketing Committee and the ARIA Awards/Hall of Fame Committee.

ANDREW WATT

ARIA describes its activities as follows:

- We act as an advocate for the industry, both domestically and internationally

- We support Australian music, and create opportunities to help it be heard

- We play an active role in protecting copyright and the fight against music piracy

- We collect statistical information from members and retailers and compile numerous ARIA Charts with data provided by over 1,100 retailers

- ARIA is a focus for industry opinion and compiler of industry information and views

- ARIA provides in certain cases, a reproduction licensing function for various copyright users

- We stage the highly prestigious annual ARIA Awards

- In conjunction with the Australian Music Retailers Association, (AMRA), we support the voluntary Recorded Music Labelling Code of Practice

- ARIA is the Australian International Standard Recording Code (ISRC) national agency, and allocates the Country and First Owner Codes to members for encoding on all audio and audio-visual recordings, as a method of identification

WELCOME TO THE JUNGLE

- We also help those in the industry who have fallen on hard times, through our support of Support Act Limited, the industry's benevolent fund.

AIR

AIR is an organisation of over 140 independent record labels as well as artists and distributors across the full spectrum of music genres, ranging from small sole traders to some of the biggest independent operations in the country. AIR grew considerably under the leadership of Nick O'Byrne. AIR is administered by a board of directors and management team headed by current General manager Maria Amato. All Board members are elected by the AIR membership and meet on a monthly basis. AIR is a member of the Worldwide Independent Network (WIN), a group of international music associations who collectively advocate for fair, competitive market access for independent music and works closely with Merlin – the global association of independent labels, headed by Charles Caldas who has been extensively quoted throughout this book.

AIR describes its activities as including:

- Information, advice and exclusive member services

- Business development seminars

- Commercial negotiation

- Lobbying and advocacy

- Trade promotion within Australia and internationally

- Assisting access to international markets

My Path Into the Industry

TIM JANES

"I did a marketing degree at university and my first full-time job was selling adverts for *Beat* magazine. I was the bottom of the barrel in sales, doing cafes, bars whatever. It was pretty lousy work, but then they opened up *Beat* in Sydney, so I went up there to be what was called the music editor. It was half editorial, which was fantastic, and half advertising. I did that for a year, in '94 and when I decided to come back to Melbourne I worked for *InPress* as a key accounts manager selling to the promoters and record companies and the indie bands and bookers. It was that job that enabled me to build up a network of contacts, dealing with everyone from bookers to managers to promoters to labels, and it was through meeting a couple of key clients that Shock approached me for a label manger job. It was really from being enthusiastic and interested when I was selling the advertising space that the marketing people at Shock seemed to think I was switched on and knew my local bands. Back then I was looking after AuGoGo and Rubber, so it was bands like Snout, Even, Jon Spencer, Magic Dirt. I also did a few international labels like Matador. That gave me a gauge of how these small indie labels operated and what they needed and that was what I really gravitated to. You were kind of a link person between small indie labels and a big distributor, so I had a foot in each camp and it was a real learning experience to know how small these labels were. From the outside you had no idea just how small those labels were, two and three people. Shock was brilliant in those days, providing a full service option for the first time outside of the major label system."

Chapter 22

Entreprenuerism in the Music Industries

Breaking into, or sustaining a long career in the music industries sometimes means thinking outside the box. Not everyone follows a linear and predictable career path that sees them rising through the ranks of an organisation, or moving between companies to take the next step up the ladder, as is more common in the corporate world. Equally, not everyone can just 'start their own business' in one of the traditional areas such as management and calmly make their way along a rewarding and sustainable career path.

For many people, a career in the music business is an exercise in unpredictability – and that's why they like it! They start off in one area, fuelled by a desire to find work in anything related to music, and find themselves evolving into something they never expected to be doing. There are many examples of those sorts of people in this book.

Personal Entrepreneurism

There's another collection of people who make up an important part of the structure of the music industries, without having any particular job description or permanent role. Don't underestimate the importance of these people; it's their passion and involvement in various projects that gives a city's music industry a lot of its energy. These people tend to work on a "project" basis; they will see something that needs to be done and develop it from an idea. Sometimes the project will evolve into a fully-fledged business and other times not; either

WELCOME TO THE JUNGLE

way, their activities have enriched the overall business and injected something tangible and intangible into it.

Brett Cottle, CEO of APRA/AMCOS has been quoted many times throughout this book, but his observations of the business ring particularly true in this chapter. He has observed an evolution in the business to where it now favors those prepared to take the initiative, rather than those who wait for a job to land in their lap.

> **[BRETT COTTLE]:** "The reality is that it is a difficult time for people entering the industry because there are fewer opportunities to work within corporate hierarchies than there have been in the past – there are fewer major record labels, fewer big publishing companies, but it's a great time for entrepreneurs. It is largely a do-it-yourself kind of business these days and I think if you are tech savvy and you know your way about how the music industry works and you are associated with talented musicians, I think you can do very well in the music industry. But to work for corporates is not the same environment as it was 10, 20 or 30 years ago."

Keith Ridgway has been a manager (of major label artists such as Taxiride), an agent, a studio musician and a studio operator. He's grown and developed artists in an A&R capacity. Most recently he's created a niche in event management where he acts as the link between corporate clients and marketers and the music industry, sourcing artists for events and producing those events to ensure positive creative and business outcomes.

He puts his success in this specialist area down to speaking a lot of languages.

> **[KEITH RIDGWAY]:** "I can speak the language of everybody involved. I can talk to a cameraman, in his language; I can talk to a lighting guy in his language. I'm not a master of any

of these things, but I know enough about what everybody does to have a meaningful conversation with them. In the creation and presentation of a musical event, I can go from A to Z with some level of experience. It's an ever-evolving thing in reality and I do sometimes struggle to define it myself. I've got a reputation for corporate-style events. People ring me wanting ideas for musical entertainment they might be able to have for a certain event and what might be suitable. So I get involved in creating and activating events. I guess I've got a reputation around the country as someone who is able to make things happen in a number of spaces."

There's little doubt that Keith Ridgway is a participant in the music business, but his role doesn't fit in any of the traditional industry job descriptions. It's likely that this is going to be a model that is more common. Put this in the context of the theory put forward by Bertis Downs early in this book – that music is now better described as the "ubiquity industry" - and you can see that people like Ridgway, who can draw all of its disparate elements together, are likely to be in demand.

Mary Mihelakos has had a career that has straddled the music media and the music business. She started as a volunteer at Triple R, then from 1995 to 2005 became the longest-running editor of Melbourne street press publication *Beat*. Around these roles she has been a band manager and a venue booker for prominent venues such as the Evelyn, the Prince of Wales and more recently Yah Yah's. Simultaneously she has been the Sticky Carpet columnist in *The Age* newspaper's music supplement. Somewhere around this she also managed to find the time to found Stage Mothers, run the Aussie BBQ event at SXSW and produce the Leaps and Bounds Festival in the City of Yarra.

Stage Mothers is one of her stand-out achievements and it's a great example of someone seeing the need for something to happen in the industry and taking it upon themselves to make it happen.

WELCOME TO THE JUNGLE

[MARY MIHELAKOS]: "That was a combination of things. It was a knee-jerk reaction. I started going to SXSW in the late '90s and fell in love with it. But I remember a couple of times seeing Australian bands there and being shocked by how little profile they had at the conference. The American bands seemed to be more prepared and they were able to get around the idea that you could only play one showcase by doing unofficial parties. In 2001 an Australian band would go all the way to America and play for 25 minutes in front of no one whereas a band from Dallas would play their 25-minute showcase and then play four more parties that week in front of people that were interested to see them. I went to so many parties and one day I thought, 'I could put on a party!' The next year I went over there and found a venue that I could have for $750 and I put it on my credit card. A guy at Austrade organised some meat for the BBQ and then Glenn Dickie came on and helped stage manage the show and that's how the Aussie BBQ started. The first year we had eight bands and the second year we had 20 bands including Powderfinger and the Drones. Eventually it became three stages and we had 7000 people through the door. It was never about making money. There's been over 300 Australian bands play at the Aussie BBQ. Now it's one of the biggest parties at SXSW in an environment that is so competitive. That is something to be proud of."

It's interesting to note that Keith Ridgway and Mary Mihelakos work at almost opposite ends of the musical spectrum; the former in the area of "commercial' music and liaising between corporate clients and the music business, and the latter in a more alternative/independent sphere, operating in a world that is almost anti-corporate in its positioning. Yet both have built careers based on a very similar principle – knowing who is doing what in their worlds and having a large and reliable contact base and network."

ANDREW WATT

> **[KEITH RIDGWAY]:** "I have a very big network. Early on I realised that I had to make my own position, and so I had to sit down with myself and ask, 'What are you good at?' One of the natural skills that I have is that I'm a very good networker. I have an ability to know a lot of people and get on with them and because of that broad contact with people, I come into contact with a lot of ideas and, in reverse, a lot of ideas come to me. That's the core of what I do. In a lot of ways, it's constantly building stuff out of thin air. The music business is big and different people want to access it for various reasons and they don't know where to go or where to start. For those in the business it seems 'matter-of-fact', but a lot of people outside the industry don't know that. They can find someone via a website, but even when they find them they don't know what to say to that person They just don't know the language and they don't know the deals. They don't know whether they are being ripped off. It's my job to make it a fair market situation for all parties."

Starting your own business and finding your own niche, using the skills you have acquired along the way is also a means to an end – even if you don't know what that end might be. As Mick Newton said right at the beginning of this book, those that do something will get somewhere.

Charles Caldas took the experience he gained at Shock Records and launched his own consulting business – without really knowing who he might be consulting to! Before long he was heading international rights management collective Merlin.

> **[CHARLES CALDAS]:** "I am someone who learnt over the years that one of my key drivers is learning new things and getting challenged by things I don't know about. Towards the end at Shock, the thing that was really exciting me was the digital market, but as we know it took a long time for that to establish in Australia. That curiosity combined with the fact that I felt

WELCOME TO THE JUNGLE

I'd been doing that job for a very long time, naturally led me to do something that I didn't really know about. If I look back on it now there wasn't a masterplan other than knowing that it was time to sever that tie. I left on really good terms and it was an incredible part of my life, but I just knew that if I was going to be happy in a work sense, I was going to have to get challenged in a way that I wasn't being challenged. Then I did what I thought I would never do and what I had an intense fear of, and that was jump out on my own. I started consulting in fields that I actually knew very little about! What allowed me to do that was that over my 16 years at Shock, I was very much a believer that the business relied on its relationships internationally – that was the core of that business."

For Caldas the skills and attitudes that he learned in his very early days still inform his success today.

[CHARLES CALDAS]: "In terms of instilling a work ethic and in terms of understanding what underpins these businesses and what happens on the shop floor, it was really important. Young people now are not going to get a job packing boxes any more, but the equivalent is getting an internship with someone and building the artist's Tumblr profile, or setting up a You Tube channel. I didn't do a business degree. I had no interest or formal trading at all in the business side and I just learnt it as I went, because I had to. A lot of it was instinctive because I was doing something I was passionate about and I understood how all the pieces fit together and what my role in that was. There are a lot of us in this industry who are like that. It's just about following that thing that is driving you and seeing where it goes."

Caldas, Mihelakos and Ridgway all spend significant time working internationally, either on a project basis or by relocating temporarily or permanently. Another who made a similar move in order to establish his own business was Ruuben Van Den Heuval.

> **[RUUBEN VAN DEN HEUVAL]:** "There is a saying that really stuck with me and that is, 'the beginning of wisdom is knowing that you know nothing at all'. If you are comfortable with that idea, then if you really want to progress in this world, go and do something different. Get outside of your comfort zone; go do something in a place that you are not comfortable with; go and make a difference; go and enjoy meeting people and be very committed to who you are and what you do and what you can do to help people. When I moved to Asia and did what I did, the entrance was a little easier. If you got to know people, if you hung out, if you were social and if you know your shit there was great opportunities. The worst thing that can happen is that you can fail. So my advice to people is, if you are sitting in Australia and looking at what is happening in your world and you are relatively confident in what you have done and you have made some mistakes and learnt from them and moved forward and if you have a bit of cash behind you… go do it."

Nick Wallberg came from an advertising and social entrepreneurship background when he started Tram Sessions, a project that involved having musicians play pop-up shows on Melbourne trams. From small beginnings he and his team (Tram Sessions is now led by Ash Hills) have grown the project to the stage that they had 50,000 views a month for the clips generated by the live performances. Artists of the calibre of Paul Kelly, Lanie Lane, Josh Pyke, Xavier Rudd, The Getaway Plan and Lisa Mitchell have been on board and surprised audiences with apparently impromptu performances.

The Tram Sessions team involves around 25 people from photographers, to social media marketers, to web developers, to talent bookers.

WELCOME TO THE JUNGLE

Wallberg tried to place volunteers in positions that are not too time-consuming and he planned around volunteers moving on regularly, without the overall structure suffering.

> **[NICK WALLBERG]:** "The industry is at a stage where you need to try stuff and it's easier to try things with 'a project'. If it works, then you can try to build something. The idea of building a company within music, it's still relatively traditional. Maybe they will do a project within a company to try something, but I don't think Tram Sessions would have worked if we had started by setting up a company and tried to make a profit from it. People would have thought that we did not have an honourable purpose."

For Wallberg it's not about competing with the existing operational businesses, but complementing their roles. When he conceived Tram Sessions, he simply re-examined the connection people have with music and determined how that connection could be refreshed using existing resources. The remarkable aspect of his idea is that all the elements have actually been in place for years – it just took a new set of eyes to see how they could fit together. The music landscape can benefit from new eyes.

> **[NICK WALLBERG]:** "When music originated, it was because someone felt something and they saw a reaction from someone else and so they built on that reaction and it became something to share. What I have found is that if you do a gig at a venue it can be a bit exclusive and not everyone can enjoy these amazing acts – it's too expensive for some or it's inconvenient if you are working or whatever. What we do is bring the music to everyone; we bring the venues to the people rather than vice versa. I think that concept is really cool. It's advanced busking in a way. We want to integrate this in the live music scene in Melbourne

and have chartered events. We've been doing stuff with Yarra Trams for several years, so we understand each other and they trust us. Imagine going around the city and having a concert on a tram and you end up at a live music venue? So instead of competing with a live music venue, we bring people to those venues by literally giving them a musical ride to the front door."

Business Entrepreneurism

While the music industry is presently in a relatively volatile position, the key to understanding the changes in the industry is to see how it has evolved historically, what legal and organisational structures still apply and which of those have been modified by changes in technology or the way people do business.

Illusive Group co-founder Adam Jankie points out that there is nothing magical about the music business that allows success to come any easier than in any other start-up business enterprise.

> **[ADAM JANKIE]:** "If you are deciding to start your own business and do it your own way, whether it's a traditional music business or whether its an online start-up, you need to do your market research first. You need to decide what you are trying to achieve and if you have found a gap and if you are creating a product to suit that gap. Have you thought of the product first and now are you trying to find a gap to put that product in? The first thing to do is to decide if your product is actually feasible and that it's not just born out of emotion. Step away from it and look at it and analyse it properly. If you think it stacks up and would actually work, there's no reason not to actually pursue it. I think there is money there to try and create new businesses in this country from angel investment, grants from the government, both locally and federally. All you need to

WELCOME TO THE JUNGLE

do is be innovative and come up with something that works – whether it's something new altogether, or something that does something better than the existing thing."

Michael Gudinski is quite rightly seen as one of the great entrepreneurial stories of the Australian music business, and indeed a remarkably high percentage of people featured in this book owe at least part of their success to him and businesses he started. But what is less well known is that even Gudinski had periods when his entrepreneurial approach to business left him financially exposed. The important thing, though, is that he learned from these experiences.

[MICHAEL GUDINSKI]: "Credibility is a big thing in this business and it's very easy to muck up… and we all have mucked up. When I had financial trouble with Evans–Gudinski, and in the early Mushroom days and when I was 18 or 19, those times had a really deep effect on me. They made me realise that I was in a business and no matter how hip or cool you were, no matter how much your artists love you – if you can't pay your bills you are shit! It's not something I would like to experience in my 50s or 60s after I had worked all my life. People say 'it must have been tough to run into financial problems when you were young', but I'd rather it happened then, and I learned a lot out of it. You can have dreams, but you are not going to achieve them immediately and you have to be careful not to overcommit yourself. In a lot of things there are steps in a ladder and you have to be prepared to take those steps."

Greg Carey also recognises the importance of following sound business principles, as well as passion for music. His business Umbrella, which he runs with business partner Joel Connolly, is essentially a management business, and some of his best training came from a program run by the Association of Artist Managers.

ANDREW WATT

> **[GREG CAREY]:** "I did a great program through AAM called Control and the main focus of that exercise was to help you realise that while you work for your bands, you also have to think about your actual business. The business side of things was something that we didn't have a strong hold on – things like cashflow, goals, objectives, strategies - and all of that became a focus of our business. We are always doing planning sessions about where we are at and where we are heading. Our main goal is to shape our business to go with the direction of the music industry and become a full service company. It's not that we want to become a label necessarily, or become a publisher necessarily, but we want to be able to do things differently with every artist and use our skill sets to be able to deliver."

The opportunities that exist are immediately apparent to many of the industry's younger movers and shakers. The key, though, is that they look at the music business from a broader perspective than their predecessors.

> **[ADAM JANKIE]:** "The key is that a band is no longer just a band, but they are a brand as well, and any brand just selling a single product will eventually die off and get to a point where your growth stops, you plateau and then you decline. We view it the same way. We put the brand in the centre and start thinking about what a brand can sell and where brand strength is and what revenue streams it can generate. So, yes, there is the music, there's the touring, there's the merchandise, income from third-party licensing, income from endorsements and sponsorships. Artists are becoming highly influential because of social media and some artists are stronger than entire media outlets now."

John Watson is one of the most respected and successful figures in the Australian music business. Watson regards this time as one of

WELCOME TO THE JUNGLE

the most exciting ever for new people entering the industry, precisely because the industry's changes are difficult to adapt to for established players.

> **[JOHN WATSON]** "It's a great time to be entering the music business because many of us who've been in it for decades are generally struggling to adjust to new models and methods. However, if you're already living and thinking in a social media way then you don't need to 'adjust' - you can just get on with it *sans* baggage."

> **[MICHAEL GUDINSKI]**: "I don't mind anyone who has knowledge and experience being around me, but I hate people who talk about 'back then, we could do this or we could do that.' Guess what? The way it is now is the way it is and if you can't handle the change then go into another business."

The experience of fast-rising newer players thriving in the Australia business seems to affirm Watson and Gudinski's view.

> **[JADDAN COMERFORD]** "Everyone has this myth that there is no money in the music industry and that's not true. If people say that you have to diversify or you won't live, it's not true. We expand because we are passionate about providing good services and good solutions and the end result of doing multiple things and doing them well is people like Paul Piticco. He's a ridiculously successful businessman who is up there with other Australian entrepreneurs outside of music."

Johann Ponniah is one of the smartest new operators in the Australian music business, having had enormous success with artists like Violent Soho and DZ Deathrays. His label I Oh You operates under the umbrella of the Mushroom Group.

ANDREW WATT

[JOHANN PONNIAH]: "I can't imagine a time when people get sick of music. The way that they show that they like music might change, so they might not go and buy a CD to show their friends but they will buy a T-shirt or they will go to a live show, and that's their way of showing people what they like. And they will post a link on their Facebook page. With that sort of demand, there is always going to be a way to monetise it, you've just got to think a little bit differently. So perhaps CD sales aren't the easiest thing to get, there are ways if you have a niche audience that you need to get cleverer. I think there is always going to be a way to monetise music."

Yet when all these businesses are examined closely it still remains about connecting the makers of music with consumers, albeit it in a vastly more effective way than the old models – using all the tools at their disposal. Ben Turnbull who founded the Staple Group with Jaddan Comerford and operates touring company Destroy All Lines sees leveraging that connection as the future.

[BEN TURNBULL]: "The key to existing and thriving today is actually to become part of that community because the internet allows you to directly communicate with your consumers. Gone are the days when the only way you could get your message out there was if you could afford expensive ads, or if you had a great team of radio pluggers. Now it is not necessarily about how loud you shout, it about what you are telling people. If you can be consistent and reliable and exist within the community, people are more likely to listen to what you are actually telling them."

[DROR EREZ]: "A big part of it is the culture, the music, the websites. There's a whole generation of people and you have to connect to them and know what they want. So what does it take

WELCOME TO THE JUNGLE

for a young guy to get into our industry? First of all you need to belong to our industry. You can't just say, 'I want to go into this industry', you need to love this style of music, this type of culture and that's how its starts."

Michael Parisi has featured in this book as both a manager and the head of a record label, but his company Michael Parisi Management is also a consultant to other businesses. There are two reasons for this. Firstly, he has the knowledge and experience to provide that advice, but secondly he's aware of the cyclical nature of revenue streams based on an artist's income.

[MICHAEL PARISI]: "Ultimately you are hoping that one of your bands will become a massive success that will help to propel your business, but there will be times when all of the acts on your roster will be off the road or in the studio. I just figured I've been around for 25 years so why not use my years of experience to consult to companies who need that service, whether that is Red Bull or Sound Halo or Westpac or Profile Audio. So we have diversified while we've been waiting for our artists to come to fruition."

This approach echoes the proposition made in this book several times already – that most businesses in the music industry are service providers. For new players in the business, it might be as simple as finding a service that they can deliver well, and then finding someone prepared to pay for it.

PART 3

BREAKING INTO THE MUSIC INDUSTRIES

My Path into the Industry

MARK POSTON

"I was in my final few months of an arts degree at Melbourne Uni and I had one of those 'life' moments. I literally woke up and looked at the alarm clock and my other self said to me, 'Mark you are going to do everything you can to follow this passion and follow this music thing, and if you don't make it, you can know that you tried everything'. I guess I was going down a path towards teaching and I might have ended up doing something in film or media, but my inner self was telling me that my actual dream was to work in music and work with artists and I had to follow that.

I was working in a Brashs record store while I was going to uni and I tried to use every contact I had. I asked the sales reps who used to visit the stores. I became mates with them, and they knew I loved music and they would see me at gigs and they gave me contacts of people to approach at record labels. I sent a resume and within a couple of weeks I had a job at Sony on the sales desk. That was my first gig. Much to my dad's horror at that point I put my degree on hold, grabbed that opportunity and worked my way up. Within three months I had got a promotion and I was looking after a bunch of city stores, like AuGoGo and Central Station and Greville St Records and some of the big suburban stores. I just kept working my way through. I got a job offer at BMG in sales and then in promotions and then I got an offer to work in the marketing team at BMG in Sydney and I knew I should grab that. I knew it would lead me on a good path where I would learn a whole lot. That led to EMI and eventually I got an offer to work in head office in London in the global marketing team in 2005 and that led to me being offered the role of chairman in 2008, when I was ready to come home."

ANDREW WATT

A Job or A Career?

Part 1 of this book surveyed the landscape of the music business and briefly showed some of the key historical turning points and basic concepts that underpin the industry. Part 2 examined many of the roles available to people wanting to be a part of that business and concluded with an examination of both personal and business entrepreneurism.

Part 3 aims to light the path leading to the front door of the industry.

There is no one sure-fire way of getting started and the reality is, different approaches have always worked for different people. It's always going to be that way.

Part 3 considers some of the best approaches to getting started in the business – from formal education, structured internships and volunteering through to working in related fields like the music media or attending industry events and finding and working with mentors. It is likely that the best approach to starting a career in the music business will involve a combination of several of these approaches.

Don't forget the concept of the "unintentional career". Many people interviewed for this book have found themselves working in the music business almost by accident – one thing led to another and the career they intended for themselves was overtaken by a new career trajectory. Their point of entry or "foot-in-the-door" was never planned or structured. Nevertheless, there is still a lot to learn from their experiences – career moves that they made accidently could become a logical blueprint for someone wanting to follow in their footsteps.

However it's viewed, breaking into the music business is hardly an exact science.

WELCOME TO THE JUNGLE

[DAVID WILLIAMS]: "The good thing about the music industry is that you don't need any sort of certificate to work in it. The flipside of that coin is that there are a lot of people in the music industry who have no real knowledge of how business works or how marketing works and they do get by on their wiles. The good thing is you can get into the music industry without knowing anything. The bad thing is there are too many people in the music business who don't know anything!"

Chapter 23
Music Business Education

It wasn't always possible to get a formal education in the music business. For a long time a lot of industry players held the belief that the only school where the music industry could be taught was the infamous school of hard knocks. And while there is a certain amount of truth in that adage, it's also a very narrow view.

Of course there are people in every industry that have the same attitude. Criminal lawyers will tell you that it doesn't matter how many high distinctions you score in your law degree, that won't prepare you for the moment of terror you feel the first time you stand up in front of a judge with your client's liberty on the line. Doctors – whether they are writing their first prescription or performing their first brain surgery – will always pause for a moment and draw on what they have learned in medical school to ensure that a mistake is not made. In both these cases, and in numerous other industries, the industry itself has put structure in place where education is provided alongside on-the-job training, mentorship or practical exercises. Most trades, whether they are plumbers, electricians or chefs combine apprenticeships with education in order to gather the skills and knowledge that make them employable by an industry that cares about the standards it sets. You don't find too many successful practitioners in those industries who simply decided to skip the "education" part of that equation.

Why should the music business be any different?

WELCOME TO THE JUNGLE

Simon Smith was the head of the Entertainment Business Management department at the Melbourne campus of JMC Academy for 10 years, a tertiary institution devoted to creative industries. He now has a similar role at Melbourne Polytechnic. He sees the role of music business education as accelerating, sometimes by many years, the sort of learning that can be achieved in the workplace.

> **[SIMON SMITH]:** "You used to be able to learn on the job, maybe make a few mistakes, get some advice from people who knew more than you, but that was in an era that was much slower. I think doing a course gives people a 10 year head start on people who don't do the course. I understand street smarts, but I think now the winning equation is a skilful, knowledgeable person with street smarts, whereas before street smarts might have been enough to get through. There was less scrutiny then."

While some members of the industry consider music business degrees to be useful, many also look beyond this to broader forms of tertiary education in related fields such as arts, marketing, commerce, law or communications to be just as pertinent.

In his quest to bring greater respect to the business of artist agent, Brett Murrihy set some high standards at Artist Voice (now WMA).

> **[BRETT MURRIHY]:** "Our entry level is a university degree. There are always exceptions to the rule and innovation and entrepreneurial activity are highly regarded, but I really wanted to lift the professionalism of the agency landscape in Australia. What we run is a business turning over millions of dollars and our clients expect professional, innovative and intelligent representation. I think a higher education is a very important part of that 'mail room' experience."

ANDREW WATT

Murrihy's thinking is echoed by Bertis Downs. The R.E.M. lawyer and manager takes a broad approach to higher education. Although he remains an Adjunct Professor in the entertainment law course at the University of Georgia, he sees higher education as having more value than can simply be found in the course materials.

> [BERTIS DOWNS]: "I think higher education is not so much about what you are going to be doing. It's not so much a trade school, it's more about thinking and exposing yourself broadly to things. You might take all kinds of [courses in] languages and anthropology and ancient civilisations that may not have much to do with what you are going to do particularly – although they might – but it's much more about an exposure to ideas, and an exposure to a world of thinking and a way of approaching things. You get out and then you figure out what you are going to do. I'm much more of a throwback to the idea that you get a liberal arts degree and you get communication skills and you get exposed to a broad array of knowledge. Somewhere along the way, you get some ideas of what you want to do."

The American experience is also explained by David Lewis, a recent director of Career and Alumni Services at the McNally Smith College of Music in Minneapolis/St Paul. The conversation with Lewis took place at SXSW where he had a group of students doing work experience and soaking up the information on offer at various panels and seminars.

> [DAVID LEWIS]: "It's something that's a difficult thing to assess, not just in terms of the music industry, but asking 'what is the value of higher education?' period. Much of industry still necessitates a bachelor's degree or more and so we have this difficult scenario that involves young people going through high school, coming up to graduation and saying, 'Well I have

WELCOME TO THE JUNGLE

> to choose to do something, what am I passionate about?'. At that point they are going to move into silos – 'I like accounting and I'm good with numbers'. There is a subset of that that love the arts and music and they say I'm going to go to music business school'. The assumption would be that that is going to lead directly into industry or a career, but to be a creative business person in media or entertainment you don't just graduate and get a job, you graduate and do a ton of different things. [But] if you put up too much of the truth at the front end of the conversation, you burst the balloon. The degree is not the thing that's going to get them the job in the music industry. I think its gotta be this hybrid education model that allows students to get basic skills – accounting, publishing, copyright – and then our job is to help activate them via internships, volunteerism, field trips. Somewhere in there the career identity happens. They realise what part of the industry that they are really interested in."

American lawyer John Strohm was a member of a couple of leading indie bands, Blake Babies and the Lemonheads. He's now a powerful attorney for many of America's fastest-rising bands including the likes of Alabama Shakes. Strohm has seen the music business from the perspective of the musician, but also has worked his way through an arduous law degree to begin his second life in the industry. His viewpoint on American music business education is interesting.

> **[JOHN STROHM]:** "In the States, there are a lot of music business programs in universities and that's good. But I think there is a danger that they are training more people than there are jobs. The people who are the most entrepreneurial and who seem to be the most effective are people who really just dig into the culture and learn from people who are doing it, and who are smart and creative. I'm not necessarily seeing a whole lot of people coming out of these music business programs with

a lot of fresh ideas. The fresh ideas seem to come from watching what works and what fails, people coming out of companies who are seeing first-hand what is wrong with the accepted established models."

The message there is clear. Music business education can be enormously valuable, but knowledge isn't a substitute for innovative thinking. The challenge is to critically analyse what is learned in the classroom and shape a career plan using that knowledge, rather than think the degree is going to do all the heavy lifting.

The Music Business Education Landscape

Diplomas and degrees in the music business are relatively new and they came into vogue long after courses in other areas of the business, such as audio engineering, had become well established. In a way that's understandable. The skills involved in audio engineering are technical skills – they involve the operation of complicated mechanical and/or digital equipment. It's not hard to see why schools would exist to teach people how to operate that equipment, and develop their skills in those areas.

The SAE (School of Audio Engineering) was established in 1976 in Australia and now has campuses literally all around the world. It's a massive business, with a corporate headquarters now based in Switzerland. In some international campuses a degree in Music Business is taught, but not in Australia.

JMC Academy was established in 1982 but their Entertainment Business Management courses were only introduced in 2007. AIM in Sydney and Melbourne and Collarts in Melbourne both have evolving music business courses. There are a number of bachelor degree courses available at Sydney, Melbourne, Brisbane Perth and Hobart and regional higher education campuses. Some institutions like

WELCOME TO THE JUNGLE

Victoria University have their music business subjects housed within a broader Bachelor of Business degree.

Thomas Heymann was the head of the AIM music business course and now is an executive in the music streaming industry. He sees music business education as having great benefits, not just for the students, but also for the industry members who get involved in teaching.

> **[THOMAS HEYMANN]:** "We were very successful at placing students in companies and giving them really fantastic internship opportunities. I put a lot of value on it. I think everyone working in the music industry should work in education somehow, particularly if you do have an academic background. It's a good opportunity to take some time out and learn some more skills. It is a very refreshing and energising experience."

Around Australia there are various TAFE courses offering various certificate-level qualifications that usually combine a number of industry-specific modules with introductory-level business practices subjects. It does pay to remember that most of the businesses in the entertainment industry are small businesses, and an understanding of basic financial management, business structures, OH&S compliance and other areas like that are going to be relevant. These subjects might not sound as exciting as hanging out with rock stars, but hopefully by now anyone reading this book will have worked out that the music business is, first and foremost, a business!

> **[SIMON SMITH]:** "I think the key to it is that it prepares people to enter into a professional business. It *was* a street-smart business where anyone could crawl up out of the gutter and end up being a successful entrepreneur through good luck and determination. Now it's a lot more regulated with responsibilities and legalities. So a Business Principles unit,

for example, is the roadmap through that minefield. If you don't understand that now, you are only going to be as good as your first mistake. It's a global business now so you at least need to understand the fundamentals of the global business. As a manager you used to be able to spend five years working with a band and honing your craft before you got to the point of trying to get a record deal. These days, unknown bands are being scrutinised everywhere a lot quicker and so if you are going to work with a band now, you need to be ready to go at a higher level a lot faster. So the more prepared that someone is to start at a level where they can step up quickly and take those opportunities, the better they will be, because when those opportunities present themselves you've got to be ready to take it. You've got to be able to hit the ground running. Education of this type brings a person up to the level where they can be taken seriously."

There's little doubt that some segments of the industry still have reservations about how much knowledge can be taught in a classroom. Obviously reading a textbook won't provide you with "good ears"; that fabled ability to recognise the next big thing or have a sixth sense of what will make a hit record. But equally any amount of volunteering and getting your hands dirty in a warehouse or loading in a festival won't magically transform you into an A&R genius or a visionary manager or concert promoter. Just as education isn't the sole answer, neither is work experience. In both cases the emphasis should be on the quality of the program or experience.

What an education can provide you with are the tools and knowledge that will help you avoid basic mistakes, and equip you with some of the knowledge you will need to impress those people you deal with. It also shows people that you are serious, committed and capable of finishing something that you started.

WELCOME TO THE JUNGLE

[SIMON SMITH]: "I think what has happened is that there is a radical changing of the guard in the industry and the new guys that are coming in didn't start their careers grubbing around backstage at gigs and nightclubs. For the new breed in the industry, the whole proposition of education is a normal part of their life. Some of the old-school guys don't think there is a lot of benefit in education, because they never had it, but the reality is they are all getting older and evolving out of the industry. The new guys coming in are smart to start with and if you are going to go and work with them you have to be able to compete at that level. For the new guys, they don't even question the value of an education."

[BEN THOMPSON]: "I studied a diploma in Music Business Management in 2000 & 2001. Back then I was told multiple times that you didn't 'study' to get into the music industry. The study gave me a great knowledge of the business side of the music industry which has been a big help over the years. It also gave me the opportunity to get work experience at 3RRR and meet my future employers. I think that peoples perception of studying music business have changed over the years and it is much more widely accepted as a way into the industry now."

The next chapter on interning suggests there is now a narrowing of the difference between on-the-job training and education in the music business. In fact, it's harder to get so-called work experience without an education, because educated candidates have the edge in getting those positions.

[DAVID LEWIS]: "There is a cynicism in the music industry that wants to say that music education is bullshit, but I really think that for a lot of people it's the right thing. They get a degree and they work out what might be for them and what might not be. Then it's about giving them opportunities and options. A bachelor degree is not the end of the world and having a bachelor degree in film or music business doesn't preclude you from doing other things. I work in education and if I didn't have a bachelor's degree I wouldn't be doing that. So it's a delicate dance and to be flippant about it, in the way some industry people are, doesn't take into account that different people learn differently."

Essential Academic Knowledge

As considered in Part 1 of this book, there are certain legal and business concepts that are central to the entertainment business, most notably copyright (and other forms of intellectual property) and the law of contract. The basic contractual principles are not unique to the music or entertainment business – the same principles apply whether the contract relates to a multi-billion dollar enterprise, a transaction at the corner store or a recording or performance contract.

You don't have to learn these principles in a music business course, but you need to learn them somewhere. Equally, the law of copyright didn't evolve exclusively so that record companies and music publishers could manage their relationships with recording artists and songwriters, and those enterprises that want to use the material that the copyright holders create or control. Copyright law could be learned in a completely different environment to the music business and the law remains the same.

What studying copyright and contract as part of a music business course provides is "context"; an appreciation of how those principles apply to the unique circumstances of the music industry.

The area of contract law and copyright can be one where a little knowledge can be dangerous. While a lot of practices in the music business can be learned by talking to more experienced industry members at

WELCOME TO THE JUNGLE

the bar after a gig, the finer details of contracts or copyright issues are probably something that are better gathered in a more formal environment. It's not an area where you can afford to completely trust a 2am expert.

As a lecturer in music business law subjects, as well as a senior music publishing executive, Marianna Annas adopts this philosophy

> **[MARIANNA ANNAS]:** "I tell my students that the skills you learn in the law subjects are not going to equip them to usurp the role of a lawyer. However, you will be able to negotiate from an informed position with a lawyer, you'll be able to read a contract and make sense of it, you'll be able to have a basic copyright knowledge that will enable you to ask the right questions and you'll ideally be in a position where you can minimise your legal expenses because you'll know exactly how to instruct a lawyer."

It's often been said that the worst thing an artist can do when confronted with their first recording or publishing agreement is to take it to a great contract lawyer who is <u>not</u> experienced in the music business. A great contract lawyer will simply apply his or her knowledge to what they see on the printed page and will undoubtedly find a lot wrong with it. An experienced music business lawyer will recognise the way that industry contracts have evolved and won't waste his client's time and money arguing about things that are standard practices in the industry – even if those clauses might offend the lawyer's sensibilities. A client who has knowledge of law as well as an understanding of the industry and its contexts becomes what lawyers like to refer to as "a sophisticated purchaser of legal services".

Having said that, it should also be noted that just because some terms of a contract are in that contract simply because "that's the way it's always done in this industry" doesn't mean that they are necessarily fair or beyond challenge. Sometimes a lawyer who hasn't become conditioned to "standard practices" can be a helpful ally.

Broader Entertainment Business Subjects

There's a lot more to a good music business course than simply studying legal subjects. The better courses offer a curriculum that includes marketing and communications subjects, some subjects in touring and event management and broader studies such as entrepreneurism and international trade and commerce. Not every subject is going to be relevant to every career path, but there is something to be said about understanding the roles and operations of other segments in the industry apart from the one that you personally end up in.

> **[JAIME GOUGH]:** " It really helps to have a grasp of what all facets of the business side of an industry can do for an artist or a songwriter. It's not easy to learn everything about what someone else does because you are still learning about what you do yourself all the time! But we all run into situations where someone in marketing at a label, for example, clearly has no idea what we are doing as a publisher. It's not necessarily their fault – its just that there are so many moving parts."

> **[SCOT CRAWFORD]:** "I think the reason I have survived and progressed through the industry the way I have is that I believe the core of what we do is marketing and promotion. I think that the future of entertainment, whether it is music or visual arts, is based around marketing and promotion. In the digital space you are going to have to fight very hard for awareness to drive people to search for your product, especially if you are an independent artist. With the media changing as much as it is and as quickly as it is, and with us not

WELCOME TO THE JUNGLE

knowing what technology and what people's consumer behaviours are going to be over the next 10 or 15 years – the one stable discipline that is going to be needed is marketing and promotions."

On-Line Study

Tertiary degrees don't necessarily suit a substantial proportion of young artists or industry aspirants because of their geographic location (for example, regional students), time constraints such as work or family commitments, their unsuitability to conventional classroom learning, the nature of content designed to satisfy academic boards rather than essential, practical industry knowledge - not to mention the desire of some people to avoid the burden of HECS debts of over $50,000!

The alternative - learning 'on the job' takes a long time, and involves making expensive mistakes along the way – in fact a recent survey conducted by the Association of Artist Managers found that 91% of Australian music managers primarily learn new skills 'on the job' and over 50% rated their confidence as a manager as average or below average.

In 2016, a company called Music Business Education, headed by the author of this book created an on-line music business course that aims to provide an alternative for people who do not want to do a more formal degree or diploma program.

The course covers the mechanics, business principles and intricacies of the live and recorded music industries through 44 modules in eight streams – foundation, legal & business, recorded music business, music publishing, artist management, live music, marketing and the extended music industry stream.

ANDREW WATT

Due to the flexibility inherent in the model new modules can be added as the needs of industry evolve and emerge. Students can study where they like, when they like on any desktop, tablet or mobile device – and can choose to complete the entire course, or single subjects most relevant to them.

Job Intentions

Whether on-line or in a classroom, it takes a particular mindset to decide to enrol in a music business course. The majority of people coming into those courses don't arrive with knowledge of likely future incomes. There's no doubt that there are easier and more reliable ways of ensuring you'll be able to pay a mortgage in the years ahead.

> [ADAM JANKIE]: "People don't join the music business with the intention of making money after a tertiary education. If you are going to university to earn a degree with the intent of following a career path that is going to make you a guaranteed significant amount of money, then doing music business or event management is probably not the way to go. If you want secure income that goes up relative to inflation, do an accounting degree or a law degree. If you are prepared to trade income for lifestyle and job satisfaction I would say the music business would rank as No. 1 in that regard. It's very unorthodox, it's not just standard 9-5 jobs where you turn up wearing specific attire and sit there doing the same thing all day long. The music business is evolving and changing and you are involved in the musical side of it with the artists, you are going to gigs. You may not get a $5000 bonus, but you trade that off knowing that you've been a part of building something and you feel fulfilment out of being a part of something."

It's the same in the international industry.

WELCOME TO THE JUNGLE

[JOHN STROHM]: "One of the real benefits of the way the industry has shrunk is that it's not a good business to get into if you just want to get obscenely wealthy! It was at one point. You are not getting those people any more. They are doing tech start-ups or something. I'm not saying that it's good that there is less money in the business, but it is good that those people are no longer around. The people at the companies I love working with are obsessive music fans, that's why they do it and that why they build up these companies – cos they fuckin' love it! They put out music they love and they evangelise about it and it works. That's why I have a good law practice, because I paid attention and got involved with artists early in their career. All the artists that are big that I work with now started off as baby artists when I got involved. It's not about trying to steal R.E.M. from Bertis Downs– it's not going to happen. It's about that discovery and being a fan and wanting to encourage it along."

Relationship Building

There's another reason to do a music industry course and it's got nothing to do what happens in the classroom. Like many other businesses, the music business relies heavily on relationships. Paths cross constantly and it helps to have relationships that go back a long way, with people who have a real understanding of what makes each other tick. What better way to build those relationships than by doing a course with a bunch of like-minded people who have ambitions to make their mark in the same industry that you do? Not everyone will become a mover and shaker but over the course of a two or three-year degree you've got a good opportunity to observe who is going places and who is just in it to fill in time. Discussions over a beer after class or at a gig or in the corridor can be invaluable in realising who has particular skills and interests and who might have contacts that will be useful to you somewhere down the track. Of course, the real world is also a fine place to make contacts but – as is the case in a lot of industries – the relationships you build in a tertiary studies environment become some of the strongest of your life.

> **[SIMON SMITH]:** "I think there is a sense of community. Not every student will finish the course and not every one of them will work in the industry, but there is a sense that they are all in it together and the intangible thing is that they think they are part of a community, involved in a course that is exciting and progressive and new and different. The students do take ownership of the opportunity to take this knowledge and then move into the industry."

The tertiary environment is also a great place to get your feet wet in the real-world activities of promotion and event management. Whether they form part of the assessment or are alternatives to it, the resources and environment of a college situation allow people to make their first mistakes without too many catastrophic consequences.

Umbrella's Greg Carey and Joel Connolly formed their business partnership in their heady college days.

> **[JOEL CONNOLLY]:** "Greg and I went to uni together. We went to Bathurst and did this weird, kooky degree called theatre/media that was part of the communications stream. Part of that culture in the degree was that you did a whole lot of extracurricular stuff, like putting on plays or making films. Separately he ran an open-mic night called Fret-Fetish, and he passed that on to me after he left. So we were in a place where you did a whole lot of stuff and organised a whole lot of things on your own. We left university, Greg having graduated before me. We got to talking and accidently started managing bands.

WELCOME TO THE JUNGLE

[GREG CAREY]: "If I was to be assessed on my extracurricular, I was probably better at that than the actual course. It was very much a culture of D.I.Y at uni and it meant we were very creative with budgets, but it taught us that we could do stuff without being a part of a bigger system. I did a lot of community radio stuff at uni as well. Joel and I both separately worked on a uni event called Village Fair that had a 30-year history in Bathurst. It gave us a taste of that kind of thing."

The other benefit of a music business education is that it fast tracks the expansion of your industry vocabulary. The ability to strike up and hold a conversation with an experienced industry person is vital to establishing relationships and often the success of these initial approaches comes down to the ability to sound like you known what you are talking about.

[SIMON SMITH]: "If I handed out a glossary of terms they could probably memorise it, but it's important to also understand it and know the language and what it actually means to people in the industry. That way they could have a conversation with anyone from Michael Gudinski down, and he could think, 'this person knows what they are talking about'. A lot of the businesses in the industry don't have a big workforce and so when they do take someone on, they need someone who just 'gets it'. They need to be able to understand the personality and the character of the industry."

Marianna Annas has some sound advice for people doing music business courses.

[MARIANNA ANNAS]: "Don't underestimate what your lecturers can share with you in terms of skills and knowledge. Don't just rely on them for their contacts and war stories though. You really need to gain knowledge. Go to primary sources wherever possible, rather than secondary sources. You are not going to learn stuff from the blogosphere. A lot of people who are carrying on in the blogosphere don't know what the hell they are talking about, especially about copyright and things like that. The other thing is, don't expect your lecturers to get you a job. You go to an institution to learn stuff, not to find a lecturer who is going to tip you into a job."

In the related area of music supervision, Bernard Galbally sees some obvious advantages in a music business education.

[BERNARD GALBALLY]: "It starts with a keen interest in music and a broad consumption of popular culture, TV shows and films. We have found the people coming out of the music degree courses to be terrific and we've actually employed people from there and found other people jobs in other companies like Warner and Mushroom. To do a music business course is great because they come out understanding copyright and the issues pertaining to copyright."

There is also merit in immersing yourself in external projects while studying. You may find you have less time to maintain a social life <u>and</u> get your study done, but when you can be involved in exciting activity that actually assists your industry experience then there's no reason not to do it.

[NICK WALLBERG]: "Our coordinator at Tram Sessions, who is doing the band booking, was doing a university music business course at the time. For her it is such a big break. At university she learns some things, but with Tram Sessions she could actually go out and apply it. It's redundant to study for three years and then go out and try to apply it, especially in a fast-moving environment, which is what the music industry is at the moment."

Continuing Self Education

The important thing to note about an education in the music business is that it doesn't cease the day you graduate. Any professional in the business will tell you that they never stop learning. Unlike professions such as law or accounting where CPD (continuing professional development) is a formalised annual requirement for maintaining your professional accreditation, ongoing education is (very!) voluntary in the music business. But in such a fast-moving industry, anyone who neglects to keep learning will be fast left behind.

[BILL CULLEN]: "I spend at least half a dozen hours per week self-educating. Naturally I'm a bit of a geek I guess, so I actually enjoy that stuff and I'm not forcing myself to do it. It really intrigues me. Other than music, my second-biggest interest is technology, so I want to know what's going on. I remember hearing about Facebook when you had to be a student at an Ivy League university to get on it. I had a Spotify two-years account early by having a dodgy server address. I feel as a manager that it is really important to see where this stuff is going. I have teenage children, so I find that remarkably helpful to see how they consume music."

[DAN ROSEN]: "I don't know how many email lists I'm on and I'm constantly trawling Facebook and Twitter, every chance I get, because it keeps me in touch with what is going on. I subscribe to quite a few physical periodicals and newspapers and then also constantly feeding myself information online – sometimes even a bit too much! Some days you have a bit more time, some days I put articles aside to read later, sometimes I just skim the headlines of email lists that I subscribe to, and other days something catches your eye and you click through. I think being plugged into a few things is really important."

For Brett Murrihy the self-education process is about bringing the global business onto his desktop.

[BRETT MURRIHY]: "I've always been a massive student of the agent industry. I've been fortunate enough to work with some great agents in Australia, but my heroes were always US agent pioneers like Lew Wasserman, Jules Stein, Mike Ovitz, Stan Kamen, Sue Mengers and modern-day uber-agents like Marc Geiger. I consumed as much information as I could and always watched what was happening from abroad. The US agency landscape going back to vaudevillian days is 120 years old, whereas Australia is just over 30. For our territory I would never pretend to think that we don't have areas that can't be improved upon."

Simon Moor is another who extolls the virtues of ongoing education and he points out that such education is sometimes forced on you by success. It's a good problem to have.

[SIMON MOOR]: "Education is always king in my world, and I believe that you never stop learning. We signed Goyte, for the world excluding ANZ (Australia and New Zealand), and when you have a writer that is as successful in that many territories around the world, you learn a lot and there are a lot of issues you have to deal with. I've had to learn a lot about collection societies around the world; new and evolving income streams such as You Tube. The changing business models and their effect come into sharp focus very quickly, because income is

WELCOME TO THE JUNGLE

sitting everywhere and you have to make sure you are putting in place worlds' best practice for the writer who is due that money.

I tend to spend several hours a week on several different days, reading and learning and educating myself basically. Yes, I believe in university education, and the world dictates that you probably need a university degree to do anything at the moment, however there are some very smart and sharp self-educated people out there. I will take people on face value depending what the role is."

Law and Accounting Qualifications

Professional education – whether it be in law, finance or business, won't just help you when trying to break into the industry, it will also assist you in building your career and getting things done. It's almost like the business professionals in the music business have a secret handshake. Rightly or wrongly, there's no doubt that there is an element of professional respect shown by people in the business.

[MARIANNA ANNAS]: "I think there is a divide there and I think it's unfortunate. Historically, the business was one that you didn't really need any formal skills to break into and that's why so many managers were formerly roadies or even musicians themselves. A lot of the most senior and most powerful people in the business have no formal skills at all. On one hand that's why the business was always known as being unprofessional and shonky and it had a terrible reputation for the type of deals that were being done over the decades. That was largely the result of the lack of formals skills amongst the personnel. When people started entering the business who were formally trained, who had law degrees and finance degrees, that's when the divide started. I say it's unfortunate, because

ANDREW WATT

I think to some extent those people have brought elements of professionalism to the business that didn't exist before, but there's no need for that divide. I think it's almost like a stigma."

Not all people earning law degrees end up being lawyers. Both internationally and in Australia, there are lawyers operating in high places in the music business.

[BERTIS DOWNS]: "Lawyers have to be able to communicate well, they have to have good people skills to be effective and they have to be organised. They have to be able to solve problems. That's a pretty good skills set to have when a band is starting out, trying to figure out how they can make their way in the world and how they can make a career out of this. Some lawyers face a completely different set of problems now in terms of the industry and where it sits early this decade as opposed to early three decades ago when we started. But sure, the things I learned in law school – the way of approaching problems, the way of working through problems with a team of people, the collaboration skills, the communication skills – have been handy when it comes to managing a band."

[BRETT COTTLE]: "I was a law graduate with not much clue, really, about what I wanted to do. I felt that I didn't want to practise as a lawyer or solicitor. I'd done my articles of clerkship and it hadn't really enamoured me to that kind of life. I was fortunate to see the job of APRA Legal Officer advertised on a notice board at the University of Sydney. It was the old story of being in the right place at the right time. As it happened, the management of APRA at the time felt that they didn't want anyone who had a particularly successful degree, they wanted someone who was going to stay with them and not use the position as a springboard into the profession. I was a child of the

WELCOME TO THE JUNGLE

'60s and music was everything to me. I was completely obsessed with music and I was very passionate about going to gigs and I spent every spare dollar on records, so it suited me down to the ground. I became APRA's first legal officer in 1977."

Accounting qualifications don't hurt either, as tour promoter Frazer Bourke explains.

[**FRAZER BOURKE**]: "I did an accountancy degree and I used to be an accountant. As much as the last thing I wanted to be was an accountant, to have a knowledge of numbers and be able to understand spreadsheets is absolutely essential to this, because if you get the numbers wrong it can really hurt you. But outside of that, I would say you learn a lot more by doing it hands-on than by studying theoretical stuff that doesn't have that much grounding in the real world. You would be better to spend two or three years learning how to do spreadsheets."

So the question isn't whether you should get an education in the music business, but rather what form that education should take. The opportunities range from degree and even masters courses at serious academic institutions in Australia and overseas, all the way through to sitting in front of YouTube watching interviews with prominent industry players. Both approaches to education have something to recommend them.

It's worth noting that it's never too late to commence a formal education process.

[**SCOT CRAWFORD**]: "Coming back and studying at the age of 35 was extremely important and the most I've got out of education in my life. People get stuck in their own little world, but in reality there is so much more going on around them. I

ANDREW WATT

found going back and doing post-graduate study gave me more confidence because I realised that the skills I learned in this industry are transferable and that I really did know what I was doing. I was able to qualify those things in an adult education environment and talk to other people in other industries and do projects with other people in other industries, and it gave me the sense that everything I had done actually had a value."

My Path into the Industry

GRAHAM ASHTON

"I was completely invested in surfing as a kid. I was a competitive surfer and worked in a surf shop and I felt that was going to be my career path and I would somehow make a living in that industry. I'd always loved Radio Birdman and Hoodoo Gurus and the Sunnyboys and all those Australian rock bands that were part of the surf scene, and then a mate of mine gave me a compilation cassette of American hardcore bands like Husker Du and the Minutemen and Black Flag and Bad Brains and those kind of bands.

Within 24 hours everything changed. I started a band, started a club, a label and threw everything into it, shaved my head and away I went. Twenty-five years later I'm doing much the same thing, really. If I had been any good at being in a band that's what I'd still be doing, but I wasn't any good at it and I found it was better for everybody if I did my work on the other side of the stage.

"My best mate was a guy called John Zucco who was working at Polygram Records in Brisbane, and he got a transfer to Sydney. He got me an interview to work on the sales desk that, in those days, was a call centre. The state manager at the time gave me a crack at it and I haven't done a day's work since that wasn't music related."

Chapter 24

Internships & Work Experience

Whether someone is enrolled in a music business course, studying independently, or they are approaching the industry from a different angle, one of the key steps they will take is getting some work experience. Very few industry players, if any, walk straight into a highly-paid position. In fact it's rare to find anyone whose first work in the industry has been anything but voluntary; whether it be volunteering at a festival, working in street press or community radio or television, organising the school social or helping a band of school friends.

When this work experience takes the form of a structured, formalised, and possibly even supervised arrangement, it goes by the name "internship".

Australia has been slow to embrace the concept of internships, not just in the music business, but in business generally. The idea of working for nothing hasn't been ingrained into the Australian culture and there has always been a suspicion attached to employers who offer "work experience", with many students and/or their parents thinking that it is somehow akin to a free labour scam. The Australian working culture suggests if you are going to do part-time work while you are studying it should be paid work – even if that means taking a lowly-paid job in a supermarket or at a fast-food outlet.

It can be a misguided notion. Those who are serious about breaking into the industry take every opportunity they can to get exposure to

WELCOME TO THE JUNGLE

the business and people in the industry. There is no harm in taking lowly work in a job somehow related to the music business, even if it feels like it's below the ambitions that person has.

> **[BILL CULLEN]:** "What I say to young managers who are worried about how they are going to make a living is, if you are determined to become a manager, rather than packing shelves in a supermarket, go and sell merchandise or pull beers at a pub that is a music venue, sign up with a loaders' agency and lug PAs at gigs – anything to immerse yourself in the business. If you want to be a manager, make sure you are doing something every day that is about pursuing that path."

So while a paid job of any type is ideal, an industry aspirant should always be willing to take an opportunity to advance themselves, even if there isn't a pay cheque attached. Of course, some work experience opportunities do no more than help the young person gain a degree in coffee making, and others receive an advanced diploma in photocopying, but even in that situation there is something to be learned from reading the pages you are copying!

Other internship opportunities really are the golden key and do lead to full-time employment.

> **[MICHAEL GUDINSKI]:** "It's not an easy road, but it's all about somehow getting yourself in a position where you are learning. If you've got enough dedication and you believe in yourself, then you'll do it. Some of the best people I have ever got have been out of work experience. David Geffen and Elliott Roberts started in the mail room at William Morris. There are at least half a dozen people in the Mushroom building that started doing work experience and they are in good jobs now. If you want it, you have to find some way, somehow to get in with people – but don't get in with the wrong people."

ANDREW WATT

The international culture of interning is much more engrained as an essential part of the education process. The American experience suggests that interning often takes place after a student has completed a university degree, as well as during that process. There is far less of an assumption that once you have a degree, the next step should be to take paid employment, even if it means doing something totally unconnected to either your degree or your career ambitions.

Aly Ehlinger is a talent booker for Texas-based concert giants C3, the company behind festival such as Lollapolooza and Austin City Limits. A lot of her friends think she has the best job in the world and it started from an intern position.

> **[ALY EHLINGER]:** "The intern culture is very different over in America. In Australia it seems to be mostly about getting school credit. But it's something you do before you graduate in America, and a lot of the people that get hired at C3 start off interning. The intern program at C3 is mostly about students looking to learn and make contacts in the business, but we have had interns who might have been booking clubs in their own state and came over to learn in their summer break."

Minneapolis-based music educator David Lewis has seen many internships bear fruit for his students.

> **[DAVID LEWIS]:** "I think internships are the lifeblood of helping a student determine if a certain path is right for them. It's totally essential and I wish we required it for every student. I think we have a great culture for internships in the Twin Cities. There are lots of small companies who want help, but they also care about helping a student learn through the process. The question for students is always, 'do I have time to do an internship with all the other work I am doing?' Ultimately it ends up being a really defining experience. On the mentor's end, once they have an

WELCOME TO THE JUNGLE

intern for the first time, they typically come back and want more interns because they are really happy with the experience."

As Lewis points out, the intern-employer relationship can be a positive for both parties. But a lot of that depends on managing expectations. An intern who is going to sit around and wait to be told what to do has the potential to become an annoyance for an employer who is probably already busy enough running their business. But equally, the intern can't expect to walk in and take over the business either! It's a fine line. For employers, it's all very well to expect an extra pair of hands that you don't have to pay for, but it can't be a one-way street. The intern must have a positive experience also and come out of it more knowledgeable than they went in.

[NICK O'BYRNE]: "One of the issues for an employer taking an intern is to work out how helpful they will be against how much time they are going to take. You invest time in an intern, teaching them stuff, and so you want an intern that 'gets it' and starts finding their own work to do. You want them to come up to you and say, 'hey, have you thought of servicing these people and would you like me to research that?' After they finish every task, you can't sit there for 10 minutes thinking about what they can do next. We had a strong culture of interns at when I was at AIR. We had a few rotating. They come in one day a week and do stuff and we always try to give value back to them, because I do understand that they are working for nothing. Outside of a reference and a few perks they don't get a helluva lot. I think that culture is growing"

Street Press Australia runs a strong intern program and Leigh Treweek is very conscious of it having to be a successful two-way street.

[LEIGH TREWEEK]: "You learn a little bit about everything. Even though we are a media organisation you do learn about how the entire industry works. You might get a feel for an area and decide that it's an area you want to go into. We are getting better at it. It's very hard to find good staff these days and to find people who want to work across all facets of the business. It opens their eyes to what it's really like working in the industry. People think its glamorous but at the end of the day a lot of it is sitting in front of a computer like you do in any other job. I support intern programs but I also think its imperative that the company that's doing it ensures that the interns are getting a lot out of it."

There's no doubt that the intern culture is beginning to evolve in Australia and it seems to work well when operating in conjunction with music business studies. Most educators agree that the two paths are completely complementary.

[SIMON SMITH]: "Most education courses are "applied" courses, not theoretical courses. If someone is interested in the Copyright and Publishing unit, then they need to try and do work experience at APRA or make the tea at Mushroom Music. As much as you can learn in the classroom, you still have to understand the tone and the mood of the industry and the environment. That's what glues it together. Students also need to understand the demeanour of the business. You will get so much more out of the unit and greater outcomes from the course if you are simultaneously applying it somewhere. I don't emphasise work experience for first-year students because there is a lot of transitioning they have to do. There are kids that haven't studied a lot, kids that might have dropped out of high school, kids that might already be working a job. I try to make them focus on the course. Once they finish the first year, over that summer they should be out volunteering and getting their hands dirty."

WELCOME TO THE JUNGLE

In fact, the level of education available now has changed the nature or work experience in this country. There is a difference between "work experience" and "internship" and the quality of candidates is lifting the bar all around.

> **[PATRICK DONOVAN]:** "People are so busy that they don't want to sit there and explain what they do. That's work experience rather than internship. Even with internships, a lot of companies think they are too busy or it will take too long to explain the process and they put it in the too-hard basket. A lot of music companies in Victoria are micro-businesses with a small number of staff who are all really busy. What we are trying to let the businesses know is that that there are students with lots of skills, and try to improve their understanding of the level of skill and expertise. The students coming out of tertiary courses have a really high level of skill. It is difficult if you don't study a course now. In the old days they thought that study was a joke, but now there are so many students coming out with really good knowledge that it's hard to get an internship without that kind of knowledge."

Even in the upper echelons of the industry, the question of internship is gathering some momentum and it's to be expected that more and more positions will become available in the future. Dan Rosen's international experience has shown him the value of internships.

> **[DAN ROSEN]:** "I used it a lot in America. It's an interesting question; people are wary because they are not getting paid, but you are getting credible experience for a couple of months and often you get a position at that company, or when you go for another job, you are able to say you worked at a credible company for three months. I think it's a fantastic system and I'd love to see how it could work in Australia a bit better."

ANDREW WATT

The larger music industry operations are also embracing internships as a method of recruiting and staff development. Denis Handlin, promotes a strong internship and mentorship culture at Sony Music.

> **[DENIS HANDLIN]:** "At Sony Music we run an intern program and actively mentor and support staff. We also encourage and support new ideas and initiatives through special rewards and acknowledgment. A real highlight for me is being able to mentor and develop talented people who I know will make a difference to the business. In the past few years alone we have provided over 100 intern positions, of which 30 have gone on to full-time roles with us. I meet with the interns and staff regularly to hear their views and spur their confidence to contribute creative ideas and value-add to the business. I was fortunate enough to start in the warehouse and work in sales, promo and marketing and ultimately head the company and now be the president of the Asia region. I had great mentors who taught me about the people, artist relations and the whole gamut of our business."

While completing a formal course of study will show potential employers that you have the ability to finish a challenge that you started, the willingness to work for nothing shows them that you have a passion for the industry and a willingness to put your time and energy where your mouth is.

People notice and soon word will get around about the intern who has what it takes to make it in the industry. You may not get a job with the employer where you did an internship, but you may get a job based on a recommendation from that person, or someone they work with. There are plenty of examples of that happening.

> **[BONNIE DALTON]:** "I really like to give people the opportunity to get involved in this business whenever I can because

WELCOME TO THE JUNGLE

they might be great, and more great people working in music will always be a positive thing. As much as possible I try and help the really good ones find a job to go on to. I'm not into the idea of free labour in the shape of endless 'internships', but it's not always possible to create a paid role, even if that person's excellent. Networks are really important and people rely on those trusted sources, so you can only recommend people that you know will be a huge asset to whoever you're suggesting them to, which is why having actually worked with a person is a key factor. It's definitely worth interning if you're motivated and keen, because you never know what will come of it. Case in point: one year I was complaining to a Canadian booking agent at SXSW that my intern/assistant was leaving me to move to Canada. As luck would have it, his assistant had just been promoted and he hired mine then and there!"

[STEVE WADE]: "The people who have had the most success are the ones that have been willing to come down and intern for nothing, learn as much as they can, meet as many people as they can and keep popping up. My PA was suggested to me by one of my artist's managers. She'd done work experience for them, she'd gone on the road and done merch. She was working another job at the time, not in the industry, but she had done volunteer work for several people in the industry and when I asked them about her, they told me she was fantastic. It was one of the best decisions I've ever made but she made it easy because she had done all the groundwork herself. By doing merchandise, she ended up knowing the managers of those bands and they thought she was great and everyone is inter-connected. The real key is to keep throwing your hat in the ring for as many skill sets as you possibly can, because you are not ever going to be just one thing in the music industry."

ANDREW WATT

[**DAVID WILLIAMS**]: "The way I've run my businesses is to throw people in the deep end and see if they can swim. I will give people something to do and if they can't do it, I'll give them something else to do and if they can't do that then I'll know they can't do it. I'm looking for people who have initiative. I'm looking for people who will get on the phone and try to make it happen. If you can't make it happen, that's fine, but if you won't try to make it happen then you are of no use to me whatsoever. I've always tried to run my business as if I was hiring a lot of different entrepreneurs. I want people to go create something themselves. I want them to have an idea and tell me the idea and I can say, 'go make it happen'. The people who don't have an ideas and who just want me to tell them what to do are not going to go anywhere for me. I look at the bastard spawn of Shock, scattered throughout the industry and I think they have done incredibly well because they were forced to become entrepreneurs in the first place."

Interning certainly is a great way to get the foot in the door of the industry, but again enthusiasm needs to be balanced with a healthy dose of realism. Is it as easy as calling up Paul Piticco or Michael Gudinski and offering yourself up as an intern? After all, you are willing to work for free so why wouldn't they welcome you to their inner sanctum? Obviously it's not as easy as that, and increasingly, organisations have a structured process for internship applications, to help them manage the applications they receive.

It pays to show a real understanding of the organisation you are applying to.

[**CHARLES CALDAS**]: "If you see an organisation that appeals to you, you should always write to them. You just don't know what that will lead to. I had a woman who worked in our office

WELCOME TO THE JUNGLE

doing a lot of the distribution of statements. It's not a sexy job. I hired her because I got emails from her over five or six months – not saying, 'I'm the greatest person on earth, hire me and I'll make you rich'. She would send me a paper she wrote at uni about digital music, or offer to do some filing, or comment on something about us she may have seen in the press. After a few of these emails I realised that she was actually paying attention and so when it came time to find someone, she was only an email away. She worked part-time for three weeks and then I gave her a full-time job. Be selective and careful about who you write to, but do it. The thing that we are using more is graduates from the University of Westminster music business course and when we have a need for temporary, short-term, intern-type positions, I look in those sorts of areas, because those people are obviously interested enough to be doing those kind of courses. For us it becomes very easy. Then it only takes a meeting for us to work out if they think they are going to come into a glamorous, digital world, or if they are willing to sit there and enter 400 pieces of data into a spreadsheet."

As Caldas suggests, it also helps to have realistic expectations. Kim Carter sees some generational change in the notions of work experience in her part of the industry.

[KIM CARTER]: "I will look at taking an intern if they are enrolled and doing something from a study perspective. Whenever we are hiring, we always say that we are looking for a Gen X trapped inside a Gen Y body. In my experience I've found that it's hard to find people in their 20's who are prepared to earn their place. They want to be given the accolade and then earn it, as opposed to earning the accolade. It makes me resistant to teach people and pass on knowledge. An intern has to realise that I am giving them something that will make them money. I want people to be respectful and want to learn.

ANDREW WATT

Ambition is great, but humility is really important. As a Gen X, my peers were paid rubbish and we worked till 10 o'clock at night and we were grateful because we learnt a lot. So my advice is 'be grateful'; don't be an upstart and think you know everything. You've been given two ears and one mouth, and you've got to recognise that the people giving you advice and information have done the hard yards and worked hard for what they know and are willing to share it with you. If you want to learn from anyone, you have to be prepared to sweat a little bit."

Richard Moffat, festival and venue talent booker agrees.

[RICHARD MOFFAT]: "I did a lot of jobs in music before I was paid a wage. I come across a lot of people who whinge about work conditions, but that never occurred to me when I was first booking bands. I'm not suggesting that people should be exploited, but all I cared about when I first started working in music was that I could make people money, and it was only after I knew that I was making people money that I expected to get paid. I don't think I was all that weird for thinking that."

There are many ways of opening the door to an internship. One of the best ones is to attend a conference like Face the Music or Big Sound, because the mere fact that a person is there will show a prospective employer that they are serious about the music business. Asking a question at a panel, or politely approaching a speaker after the panel has concluded, will get someone noticed in a positive way. Most industry people are approachable in these circumstances, provided the newcomer shows some patience. Having a question prepared that shows a person actually listened to what the speaker might have been saying will encourage a real engagement. If that question prompts a reaction that indicates the speaker appreciated the thought put into it, perhaps then would be a good time to request an email address to follow up. Chances are a good reaction will result. Everyone was young and inexperienced once!

WELCOME TO THE JUNGLE

[MILLIE MILLGATE]: "Compared to other countries, the people in the music industry in Australia work very well together. As much as you might think that everyone is in it for themselves, we really are quite unique when it comes to giving people a leg up and taking time out for others, certainly those that are starting out. When Sounds Australia was being set up, I don't think I realised what kind of intangible benefit it would bring in the international space. There is a real camaraderie and a real sense that together we can knock down these doors and bring everyone through. There is this serious teamwork and I get a little bit cheerleader-like about it when it comes to that kind of thing, but it is amazing to see. There are so many capable and inspiring and passionate young managers and they are all working together."

It's the old story – be persistent, but not annoying. Short polite emails, preferably that show some awareness of the business you are applying to will help. Opening with "Congratulations on having the No.1 album on the ARIA chart last week…" will always be welcomed – assuming it is true! It's not a bad idea to mention something that you might have done recently to further your experience also. "I recently spent a couple of days as a volunteer at Falls Festival and I think that will help me bring something to your business" is a reasonable attention-grabber.

[DAVID WILLIAMS]: "Firstly you've got to work out which area you might be interested in and then you've got to work out how to get into that industry somehow. There are a lot of people who want to be part of the industry, but one of the frustrations I have is that they don't know what that means. Getting involved and doing an internship is one way. I've had interns come in and after six weeks say, 'I actually don't think this is what I want to do'. That's cool. People want to get in because of the glamour – personally I don't see it as a glamorous world. If you get caught up in that, then you are in the wrong industry. The industry doesn't want people who are looking for that. I don't have a golden answer for those people who want to be involved. If every person who wanted to be a part of the music industry went for an internship right now, then I don't think there is enough internships available for them all."

[JADDAN COMERFORD]: "We have our eye on people, we attend shows and see bands, but we also see people and talk to people. We mostly reply to emails from people asking for advice; we will invite them in for a meeting if we feel their passion for what we are doing. So there are lots of ways to get noticed by us. At the same time we are bloody busy, so sometimes things do go under the radar!"

Sometimes it's as simple as being in the right place at the right time.

[KEITH RIDGWAY]: "There was this girl who had moved into town from the country. I just kept seeing her everywhere. Every time I saw her she was talking to all these people I know. She'd been in Melbourne four months and she was already talking to people and getting to know people. She clearly had a natural ability to move in this world. I found out that she was studying PR and wanted to get into the music space. I had a three-month event we were working on and so she came on board for that time and she was able to learn a lot doing that. So I think you can recognise people fairly quickly. You can see that passion and that ability to move in the space."

Joel Connolly and Greg Carey have had great success with the intern policy at their company Umbrella, and it seems likely that their model is the way that entry point into the business is going to evolve, with the relationship being a strongly flowing two-way street.

[JOEL CONNOLLY]: "We have an intern program and the things we recognise instantly in someone is if they are

WELCOME TO THE JUNGLE

pro-active and are passionate about music. It sounds so simple, but we look for really good common sense. I don't think the music industry is rocket science. You've got to be savvy, but it's not like we are curing cancer. You would be surprised how much of it is about using real common sense. So when we see someone who doesn't mind taking some action and making a move to work for us, and that they are willing to do it for free, we take notice. That's how we started, by doing things for free."

A word of caution is necessary. There have been some internships that have not turned out well for either the interns or the businesses offering them. A couple of these matters have ended up in court pursuant to the Fair Work Act. This follows the international experience. The first push against unpaid internships started in Europe. In the United States, media companies including Hearst Magazines, Fox Searchlight Pictures, Gawker, Condo Nast and Warner Music have faced lawsuits over unpaid internships.

The United States Labor Department has developed a test to decide when interns should be paid including examining whether the internship focuses on training and whether the intern does the work of a regular employee. In France, employers must offer interns payment after two months.

In Australia short, fully supervised unpaid work trials to test a job applicant's skill are legal, as are college-backed, short-term student placements where students gain course credits for a term of work.

Volunteering

There is a difference between gaining an internship and volunteering. The latter tends to be event-based and the former is more in the realm of medium to long-term work experience. Volunteering has its merit. In a lot of cases the benefits are short term. Volunteering at a festival will usually result in someone working a couple of shifts and being able to enjoy the rest of the festival for free. Depending on what job is allocated, a volunteer may see a lot of music or no music at all. Either way it's not a bad deal if you don't feel like paying for a ticket!

But there can be a lot more to volunteering. It can be a stepping stone to an internship, or at the very least it can get someone noticed and have their name and face on the radar of someone that might be able to help them along the way, if not today, then somewhere down the line.

> **[PATRICK DONOVAN]:** "The people that stand out are the ones who are willing to volunteer. You can't have a sense of entitlement. Everyone wants to work in music and it's a fun industry to work in, but it's the ones who actually volunteer and do things that get noticed. We have some students that volunteer and work with us on some projects in their holidays and I say to everyone that volunteers, 'it will lead to something'. It's very cut-throat to get one of those hot jobs that come up from time to time and you have to do everything you can to get noticed. You've got to volunteer, you've got to attend gigs which is where you meet people. You've got to be really hungry. And you've got to be versatile. A lot of the people on our student committee are involved in different things – they are in a band, or they book a night somewhere. They are multi-skilled. It's the people you do see out at forums and you see them applying for grants or doing programs."

Some organisations take their volunteer culture very seriously and put a lot of time into making it a worthwhile experience for both the volunteer and the event. When Chris O'Brien was at Soundwave (he's now at Destroy All Lines), he was a big supporter of volunteers.

> **[CHRIS O'BRIEN]:** "Most of the people that came through the Soundwave doors started off as volunteers. We tried to

WELCOME TO THE JUNGLE

> impart that knowledge to as many young kids as we possibly can. Put your hand up and volunteer. You might go through that system for two or three years, but if you shine enough and catch our eye, there will always be opportunities. We had numerous employees come through that have been volunteers. My last mentee was on the road with us for two years and she learnt an incredible amount and it helped her no end. She's got a full-time job in the industry. They got themselves around Australia and show their passion and commitment to being in the industry and people see that."

Volunteering isn't about confining yourself to a particular genre of music, or to shows where only a person's favourite bands are playing. It's a lesson that many people in the industry, particularly in the live music industry, know well. They don't just work when they like the music – that's for a fan, not a professional. A volunteer could just as easily make a good contact behind the scenes at a Wiggles show as at the Black Keys!

> **[SIMON SMITH]:** "The most critical thing that comes into it is the networking. Sometimes they say, 'oh but I don't want to volunteer at such-and-such an event, it's too daggy'. What I explain to them is that there will be someone working on that event that also works on the Falls Festival or Splendour. They need to meet that person and be the one that impresses that person, so that next time when they are looking for someone it's you that they call. That's a huge part of it."

A volunteer position will also expose the volunteer to the realities of event operation. There is a lot of information that can be gained that you might be able to apply to a smaller-scale event.

> **[CHRIS O'BRIEN]:** "We had a high level of training that we put volunteers through. We had a lot of meetings before the event itself so we can walk them through exactly what we expected of

them, whether they are crowd care or working at the gate. As much as the word 'volunteer' has a negative connotation about it, we took it extremely seriously and pass that on to the kids as well. Essentially they are ambassadors for the event when they are doing it. If you are a volunteer at the gates, you are the first thing people see when they come to the festival. The volunteers need to be knowledgeable, they need to know where everything is on the grounds; they need to be able to answer questions. It's a serious role and we put a helluva lot of work into it. What we find the kids take out of it is a sense of belonging to the event. That's why we had so many repeat volunteers every year, because they gain a lot of experience, but we treated them well. If they want to take the next step by touring with the festival on a national basis, we allowed them. We had probably 13 kids travelling nationally with the event. It was good for us too, because it meant we had the same people in the same roles roll around, and the knowledge they get is huge, even if they only do it for one or two years. We gave them references and assisted in getting them roles in the industry where we can."

There are volunteers who simply sleepwalk through the position, hoping to remain unnoticed and see as many bands as they can, and there are those who make something of it and get noticed for all the right reasons. How does a volunteer land in the latter group?

[CHRIS O'BRIEN]: "Attention to detail was a big one for us, for starters. So is punctuality and turning up to meetings on time. They need to have a willingness to learn. They are the three biggest things. Once we see that someone is punctual and they value the role they have been given and they are passionate about it, we look at that and say, 'OK, if you are willing to do that for an unpaid role, and throw everything into it, what would you be willing to do for a paid role?' They are the things that caught our eye straight away."

My Path into the Industry

BONNIE DALTON

"It was somewhat unconventional I suppose – but then that is usually the way with music managers isn't it? My general management skills and experience came initially from managing cinemas through university, where I studied arts. I find I also draw on a lot of other skills that I then developed while working for the cinema chain's innovation, IT and international operations departments once I'd finishing studying. The music side came about when I 'dropped out', so to speak, and worked in a pub in Lorne for a summer and happened to become good friends with the Falls Festival crew who are all based down there. I started working at the festival casually each summer and after moving back to Melbourne and working on film festivals for two years at ACMI, a full-time role came up at the Falls Festival, so I took it.

At the time, they were also managing local band the Vasco Era and part of my role became day-to-day/assistant management of the band. I loved working on the festival, but found that I preferred the artist management side of things and soon after I left the Falls Festival (and took the Vasco Era with me), a producer friend of mine introduced me to a band called Little Red – and I managed them through the release of two albums. About the same time, I started working with Danny Rogers' assistant managing Gotye and Clare Bowditch and in various roles for the St Jerome's Laneway Festival. We've worked together ever since on the festival side and he was really supportive when I started my own management company, Minnow & Co, three years ago. Minnow & Co now manages Little Red, Husky, the Vasco Era and New Gods."

Chapter 25
Industry Events

The last chapter briefly mentioned the value of industry events and conferences as a great way to make contacts that could lead to internships or even jobs. This chapter delves a little deeper into that world. There are multiple reasons for attending music industry conferences and only one of those reasons is that they are a lot of fun!

There is a multitude of events and conferences around the world and they are not confined to the music industry. The conference industry is a massive business and there's a lot of money to be made in that world if you get in at the pointy end of it. But in this chapter we are concerned more with the experience a person can have by attending a conference rather than running it.

In Australia there are a number of annual conferences that have varying degrees of importance. Very few people need to go to every conference, every year. In Victoria, **Face the Music** (operated by The Push) is the main event targeted at both entry-level players and established professionals. On top of this, events such as Melbourne Music Week have their own program of education and information-based events separate to the Face the Music conference. **Big Sound** in Brisbane is the biggest event of its type in Australia and has a strong platform of artist showcases as well as a very well programmed schedule of panels and seminars. The three-day event also includes some high profile guest speakers, both national and international. Perth has the **WAM** conference that attracts some good national and international speakers in conjunction with the WAMi Awards.

WELCOME TO THE JUNGLE

Intune is the premier music conference for musicians and music industry in the Northern Territory. Held annually in either Darwin or Alice Springs it attracts leading music industry identities for masterclasses, workshops, networking opportunities, panels and showcases of the best bands from the Northern Territory.

There's no shortage of opportunities to meet industry people across Australia and most industry players get to at least one of these events every year.

For Vanessa Picken, the best part about attending conferences is the expansion of horizons that inevitably occurs.

> **[VANESSA PICKEN]:** "There's so many amazing conferences and events that are held now, and events that allow you to be in one place and tap into the knowledge bank that is available to you. SXSW is one of the drivers in that knowledge base. I've been going to SXSW for five years and I really immerse myself into that world. It makes you hungrier to do better within your craft, whether it be interactive, film or music. In Australia, Big Sound is a phenomenal event that everyone should attend. Hearing what people have to say and their opinions is definitely one part, but it's also about forming your own opinion about how you apply it."

There's real value in attending these conferences when you are starting out in the industry, far beyond the actual information that you will hear from panels and speakers.

> **[ADAM JANKIE]:** "It's more likely that someone who comes up to me at Face the Music and asks for a position, will get it over someone who just sends an email, because being at Face the Music shows that they have actively gone out to pursue

something. They are not just sitting behind a computer looking up email addresses of every music company in Australia. Going to a conference shows that they actually believe they are going to pursue the music industry as a career path. I see all sorts of people all the time like that and we do take them on for work experience and internships."

Graham Ashton programmed Big Sound for several years and was a key part of building it into an essential industry event. He has some tips on how to go about your conference participation.

[GRAHAM ASHTON]: "The first time I ever went to one of those events was SxSW about nine years ago. I had no idea what I was doing and I had nearly 20 years of music industry experience behind me. Whichever one you choose to do, the first time you go, just go for fun and have an open mind, treat it as a learning experience and don't put pressure on consequence. It doesn't matter how experienced you are, the first time you go to one of those events it just flies by you."

And what should someone try to avoid at such an event?

[GRAHAM ASHTON]: My biggest 'don't', is that, in those hours between midnight and dawn don't talk about business, talk about music. If you have made a connection with somebody after those hours and they want to talk business, suggest that you have a beer or have a dance and make a meeting to talk business in a professional way the next day or whenever. The amount of times I've seen really good people have ridiculous business-type arguments and take their work into those after-midnight hours is crazy. As far as 'dos', it's about listening, pacing yourself and finding the energy to be the first one there in the morning and still be going strong into the evening. You

WELCOME TO THE JUNGLE

really need to go into those things with a sense of what you are trying to achieve out of it and make sure you put your energy into that as well."

For Ashton, the value of these events for established industry people is to stop for a moment and get a perspective on where the industry is at, away from the daily pressure of running their business. For newcomers to the industry it becomes a great time to approach industry people because they should hopefully be a little more relaxed than if they had been in their office.

> **[GRAHAM ASHTON]:** "Nowadays Big Sound is the one place where the lion's share of the Australian music community are in the one place at the one time and instead of just reacting to emails all day and that kind of stuff, you actually have the opportunity to sit down and talk to people and listen to people and come up with ideas – and to be inspired more than anything. To me, the idea is to walk out of it and be re-energised to fight another year."

Music Victoria head Patrick Donovan also thinks that events like Face the Music have great value.

> **[PATRICK DONOVAN]:** "There's no excuse for not being at Face the Music. Apart from anything else it's cheap! The reason they should be going is that the experienced people in the industry really want to pass on their knowledge. It's in their interests if there is a wiser, more switched-on music industry. The artists deserve that. So you should go along, attend as many panels as you can, ask questions, talk to the speakers afterwards. Maybe you'll have a great idea for a panel next year. There's a lot of networking done around that time. It's free information, basically."

ANDREW WATT

Keith Ridgway, whose networking skills have been the core of his career in the industry, agrees that building relationships is an essential element of finding your place. He subscribes to the theory that who you know adds a vital layer to what you know.

> **[KEITH RIDGWAY]:** "You would like to think that you can do it on your own merits and everybody can build a career based only on being good at what they do. That would be the politically correct thing to say. But the reality is that everyone in the music industry is always helping someone. Yes, it's a glamorous industry and people want to be around it and want things from it, and people are constantly ringing you and wanting you to do things for them. When that happens you think, 'well, I may as well be doing things for people I know, or half know, rather than complete strangers!' There will be times that you can give an opportunity to somebody – and it needs to be somebody that has the skills – but it's more likely to be somebody that you might have met a couple of times, or who somebody else has recommended."

On an international level, the biggest event among Australian industry members is SXSW, the massive music, film and interactive conference held in Austin Tx, every March. There are a number of ways of looking at SXSW. First and foremost, it is tremendous fun and it would be hard to go there and not have a good time.

However, it can be a daunting and somewhat overwhelming experience and a newcomer needs to go into it with realistic expectations. Many people recommend not even going to SXSW unless you feel you have mastered Face the Music or preferably Big Sound. Otherwise, it will be like attempting to drive a Ferrari before you can control a Commodore. The result is likely to be a very disheartening and expensive accident.

WELCOME TO THE JUNGLE

Graham Ashton's advice regarding Big Sound can also be applied to SXSW – the first time you go, don't have any expectations, targets or essential outcomes. It probably takes at least one year to get your bearings, find out what areas and activities interest you the most, and master the art of transport, travel, accommodation, queuing, networking and timetabling. A newcomer should simply let the whole event wash over them and land where the wave decides to drop them off. It may sound like an expensive experiment to embark on without any expectations of an outcome, but it's likely to be an investment in greater returns on your second attempt.

Obviously there is a difference when you are going in connection with a showcasing band, as their manager or even as a band member. The expense of travel and accommodation is multiplied for a band, and often they will only get one shot at being an invited showcasing artist. In that situation, there needs to be a return on that investment, if not immediately, then in the future. For that reason, a smart manager will be making a return to SXSW when their band is first showcasing, not making their maiden voyage.

> **[MILLIE MILLGATE]:** "The absolute rule and our mantra is, 'go before you show'. The investment that a standard four-piece band would make to go to Austin for SXSW is likely to be around $20,000 and that's a big hit. To get the lay of the land and get a feel for what the event is about is so important. If you come the year before, you can still do a considerable amount of networking, you are included in all our activities and events and you will be really well prepared. When you look at the managers that have done that and self- managed artists that have do that, the results are tenfold compared to those that are just trying their luck. I think that applies to Big Sound now, too. If you think that might be a really good springboard for you, then go one year and find out the types of things that happen and understand what it's about."

My Path into the Industry

MARY MIHELAKOS

"I was a lucky kid because there wasn't too much competition for your attention then. You watched TV and you listened to rock 'n' roll. That kind of shapes your taste and tunes your ears. I became really, really obsessed with music. I was really into Australian music even before I knew what indie rock meant. I was watching every single music video show and taping everything on the VCR when I was 10 years old. Even as a kid, I remember thinking, 'I want to do what Molly Meldrum does'. It wasn't even a choice; I just didn't feel like I had any other options.

I started listening to Triple R and then volunteering when I was 13, doing the Radiothon and I started going in there most days after school and during holidays. I didn't have that much ambition to be on air, but I just liked being around there. So my obsessions with music and the media collided. I'd compile the Gig Guide and so I'd ring up venues and talk to them to get their gig listings. So it was easy for me to network at that age, without having to actually go to the pubs. After a while I just started managing bands and doing publicity for a venue called the Sarah Sands. I started doing media studies at Swinburne and as soon as I got in there I started writing for the school newspaper and running the radio station and then became the activities chair. I started managing a band called the Earthmen, and when you start managing bands, that's when you really start to meet people and that led to me booking the Evelyn. Everything else flowed from there, really."

Chapter 26

Music Media

There are two types of people that work in the music media. Those who work in the music media because they genuinely want to work in the music media, and those who are using it (deliberately or unconsciously) as a stepping stone into the music business. There's an old adage that says, 'if you can't do it, you can always write or talk about it' and that has been used many times with respect to music journalists and DJs.

It's a little unfair. Not every music writer is a failed musician, and in fact some of the best music journalists cannot play a note, by choice. Equally there are many people in radio – well, public or community radio – that are passionate and well-informed music fans that don't actually suffer from rock star envy.

There are many music media people who have no desire to be anything other than great music media people – writers like **Jeff Jenkins, the late Ed Nimmervoll, Martin Jones** and **Bernard Zuel**, broadcasters like **Stephen Walker, Brian Wise, Karen Leng** and many others are great journalists who sometimes chose to direct their talents towards music, such as **Chris Johnston.** None of these people have ever tried to start a label, manage a band or get a job at a record company.

On the other hand several of the best managers and label people in this country came from a background of music journalism – namely **John O'Donnell** (who rose to be head of EMI Australia and

WELCOME TO THE JUNGLE

co-manages Cold Chisel), **John Watson** (who features throughout this book as one of the best managers and label heads this country has produced) and **Michael Parisi**, one of the best A&R people of the past 20 years and a former street press writer and advertising salesman. Others such as **Ed St. John**, the highly respected **Tim Janes** and **Frank Varrasso** all came through street press and into the major or independent label system. One of Australia's almost legendary music writers **Stuart Coupe** has, for more than a decade, operated the Laughing Outlaw label, a critically acclaimed indie that is beloved by the artists on the label. Even music industry lawyers like **Brett Oaten** and **David Vodicka** have a street press past, even though Vodicka didn't write so much about music as comic books! **James Young**, the high-profile proprietor of the Cherry Bar, came through street press and Triple R (where he did a long-time program with Vodicka and was also a Breakfaster and Program Director), prior to a stint in the advertising world. **Patrick Donovan**, now the head of Music Victoria, came directly to that role from his position as a music journalist at *The Age*. **Steve Cross** who co-owns hugely respected music label Remote Control, tells some great stories of interviewing artists on his Triple R radio show, while Damien Slevison is a highly regarded A&R Manager at Liberation.

Music Media Landscape

The music media in Australia has both consumer and industry elements. Consumer media is targeted at music fans and includes press, radio and television, while industry media is forms of media seeking to connect and inform members of the industry, and those interested in it, about the news and issues of the day.

Prominent media company Street Press Australia works in both areas, and as such is probably a part of both the media and music industries. Leigh Treweek is the director of that company.

ANDREW WATT

[LEIGH TREWEEK]: "I think we see ourselves as a bit of everything in a sense. We see ourselves as part of the music industry – I think we play a pretty important role in the music industry for both up-and-coming artists but also developing the next generation of journalists and the next generation of industry professionals. But more and more from a media company point of view we are moving more towards being a content creation company looking at ways to create quality content that can be read by more and more people and used in a better way. In our case, people working here see themselves as part of the music industry. We are listening to new music everyday. We have Spotify playing in the background where we are listening to new releases daily. I think that's important. At the core we very much hire people that are passionate about music. We look at their education and what they want to do but also we recognise that a lot of our staff wont have a full journalism degree, but are great writers and are equally as good as someone with those qualifications."

Mary Mihelakos has worked extensively in the music media and also in venues and in management and she sees the two aspects of her career blurring regularly.

[MARY MIHELAKOS]: "Even though I did study journalism, I don't consider myself to be a journalist at all. I'm comfortable saying I have good taste in music and I've followed my own thoughts about music and so I'd be comfortable being described as a 'tastemaker' or something like that. I do go out to see bands six or seven nights a week, always have, always will. While I've never referred to myself as a journalist, I have referred to myself as a music writer, or a band booker or a promoter. So I think I work in the music industry, rather than the media industry."

WELCOME TO THE JUNGLE

So, is building a reputation in the music media still a viable means of breaking into the business side of the music industry? Michael Parisi launched his music business career by being poached from his job selling advertising at Melbourne street-press magazine I*nPress*.

> **[MICHAEL PARISI]:** "That's absolutely still a viable way to break in. My first A&R job was actually while I was at *InPress*. Neil Bradbury was paying me $250 a week to go scouting for him for Chrysalis Records. He rang me out of the blue because I was the guy writing single reviews for *InPress*! That wouldn't happen now but it's still a great place to get noticed. More importantly, these days, is possibly having a blog. We were street press natives, now these guys are digital natives. It's a very important breeding ground. I know for a fact that certain labels have A&R scouts who do nothing but sit online."

Street Press Australia sees being in touch with – in fact, 'immersed in' – the industry side of music as an essential part of it's activity.

> **[LEIGH TREWEEK]:** "Being very much a music industry news chasing organisation that is important to us. As free press it means that a strong music industry means a strong Street Press Australia. We need our staff to understand what the industry is going through and how we can work to have a strong industry, because we feed and make our money off a strong industry, whether that's touring or record sales or venues. We are very much about our staff understanding those issues. When they are researching stories they are needing to ask "What is the changing face of the industry" because that effects our business directly. It's important for us to gather that knowledge and feed that knowledge back to those companies operating in the industry."

ANDREW WATT

There's no doubt that music media can be and end in itself – and a completely legitimate one at that, but its also a means to and end.

> **[LEIGH TREWEEK]:** "Within our area of media we are a stepping stone into bigger and better things. With our growth we have been able to hold onto staff a lot longer and give them better opportunities but obviously we are still a breeding ground for other areas; whether it be working for other industry based companies or whether it be moving into media companies or ad agencies."

Richard Moffat also puts public radio in perspective. He regards music media work as akin to volunteerism, as discussed in the previous chapter. For him it's just about expanding your contact base and breadth of experience.

> **[RICHARD MOFFAT]:** "I always tell people that volunteering at things that care about the culture of music or creativity or whatever never has anything negative about it. I did a show on Triple R for years and being around a non-profit that supports creative people, you learn so much stuff just by being in that space and in that environment. I always encourage people to do that."

Having a presence in music media almost necessitates that a person will be seen at industry events and their name will come up when opportunities arise.

Cath Haridy wasn't even looking for a job at a record label, when her work at Triple R provided her with one.

> **[CATH HARIDY]:** "When I was volunteering at Triple R, I actually applied for the assistant programming manager's job

WELCOME TO THE JUNGLE

and I got down to being one of the last two candidates for that position, but I didn't quite make it. Michael Parisi was looking for an assistant to help him in A&R at Warners and James Young from Triple R suggested me, knowing I had almost got the [Triple R job]."

Tim Janes, who also rose through the ranks in both editorial and advertising in street press, thinks that the pathway he took may be a little different these days.

[TIM JANES]: "I can't give you any examples like there was 10 or 15 years ago. You think of John Watson and John O'Donnell and Ed St. John, and all these people had been journalists. These days the equivalent of writing for street press is running a blog on punk rock, and I think those people would be great A&R sources, whether that's a full-time job or maybe a scouting position. Those people are closest to the scene, so I think the media is still a good way to come through, but the format of that media has changed compared to 10 or 15 years ago."

James Young was a rock culture columnist at *InPress* and a leading broadcaster at Triple R, rising to be program director. Interestingly, as the holder of a law degree, Young has little time for the role of the classroom – and he puts enormous value in music media as a kick-off point.

[JAMES YOUNG]: "I see street press, including online, and community radio as THE PATH into the music business - that, and being in a band or being involved with a live music venue. You don't learn about the music biz in books, you learn about it by 'being in it'."

My Path Into the Industry

CATH HARIDY

"I had a journalism background; I studied it at RMIT. My passion was in music, but it was also in media and print journalism. So I got to marry the two passions I had by contributing and volunteering at *InPress* and at Triple R. The connections I made through those two mediums were invaluable in terms of me then progressing through to get a job at a record label. A lot of it was hard work on my behalf, but I also had the opportunities presented to me at the right times that I was able to capitalise on. I think it's really important to create opportunities for yourself or to put yourself in situations that give you opportunities to then progress.

"I knew early on that I wasn't the greatest musician in the world and was never going to be. I had tried through my school years to learn various instruments, for a while with the idea of eventually wanting to be a performer. Early on I made the conscious decision that I was never going to be comfortable in that role and that I was way better suited to be a conduit for creative people and help translate for creative people by being the business end of their business. I really enjoy that end of the process, I find it really interesting and I see it as a really valuable part of the artist's career."

Chapter 27

Mentors

The music industry is particularly well suited to the concept of mentorship. It's an industry where advancement does not rely on a process of moving up the ranks of a hierarchal structure, where promotions within the organisation are the normal road to improved salary or conditions. Obviously in more corporate environments, such as multinational record companies, there are some roles that do work on a promotion-type system, but generally progress in the music business is based on wits, self-promotion, relationships and success – which tends to breed success. Thus there is no textbook (including this one!) that will provide a step-by-step guide on how to develop a career. That also means that there are no real safety nets built into a person's career path. There's no "three-warning" system or checks and balances that will minimise the impact of any possible mistakes.

In these circumstances, finding mentors that will help avoid career derailing mistakes – or at least help make the key decisions that affect a person's career and that of the artists they work with – are vital. There are very few music industry success stories that don't point to someone who may have saved their skin at some early point in their career.

One simple definition of mentorship is that a mentor is a more experienced (typically older) professional in your field who offers you career guidance, advice and assistance from a real world point-of-view. That definition will work well for this chapter. While the music business changes rapidly that doesn't mean that there isn't something to learn

WELCOME TO THE JUNGLE

from more experienced members of the industry. Fortunately the music industry seems to be populated by people who don't mind sharing their experience and knowledge. Nearly 100 of them contributed to this book.

Mentorship relationships can be formal or informal. In Victoria, the Push operates a formal mentorship program through FReeZA that has had some great success. As described on its website, this program gives a number of young people great opportunities every year.

"The FReeZA Mentoring Program is funded by The Victorian Government and presented by The Push. It offers young Victorians aged 18 – 25 years the opportunity to be teamed up with an established music industry professional to gain advice, get hands-on training and experience, and learn more about the career opportunities that exist within the industry.

The program includes one-on-one mentoring, tailored Master Classes, networking and skills development opportunities. Mentoring is offered in five music industry streams:

- Event Management

- Marketing and Publicity

- Technical Production

- Music Business

- Performance"

The Push/FReeZA mentorships match young up-and-coming people with some great mentors including industry professionals. The program includes one-on-one time with the mentors, some group activities and masterclasses and skill development sessions and run for 20 weeks.

In addition The Push now runs Squad, a mentoring program for woman performers aged 18 – 25 year in Victoria which offers young women the opportunity to be teamed up with an established music industry professional to gain industry advice and support on their career development as performers.

The program will include one-on-one mentoring, tailored master classes, networking and skills development opportunities as well as a special intensive development weekend where participants will work on craft and career with a range of experts.

> **[CHRIS O'BRIEN]:** "I'm part of the mentor program at the Push and have been for years. I think it's an outstanding program. I tell the same thing to all the kids that are coming through. Just volunteer and try as many things as you possibly can. Volunteer at booking agents and management companies and record labels and you'll know what you like. You only have to spend a couple of weeks with these people and you'll know whether you like it or not. If you don't it's no big deal, you'll eventually find something that's the right fit for you."

There are other approaches to mentorship. Highly respected artist Clare Bowditch took matters into her own hands and established the Big Hearted Business Conference. The idea behind the conference was to help entrepreneurs in the creative industries to learn to manage the demands of business, creativity, real life, relationships, ambition and the desire to make a difference – all in one day! The definition that Bowditch used for a creative entrepreneur certainly

WELCOME TO THE JUNGLE

includes many people embarking on a career in the music business: "A Creative Entrepreneur is anyone wanting to build a business based on their creative skills or ideas. That means everyone from bloggers and musicians to graphic/fashion designers, actors, filmmakers, artists, creative small-business owners, and right-brain creatives of any kind who want to build a successful business based on their creativity."

In an earlier chapter, the Release program for the mentoring and development of skills for independent label owners was considered.

Also very highly regarded is the Seed Fund, a program established by John Butler and his wife Danielle Caruana, which provide grants to arts practitioners and artists. In particular the Seed runs an annual workshop that mentors young managers and allows them to develop valuable networks. Numerous emerging managers have benefitted from the program since its inception in 2006.

While these sorts of mentorship programs and events are invaluable, most mentorship relationships are not as formally structured. The majority of these relationships simply emerge from the less experienced person having the smarts to reach out and ask a question. Those questions rarely go unanswered.

Management, in particular, is an area where advice is often needed and freely given. As a manager rarely has a big corporate structure to support them, advice needs to come from other managers rather than people within the younger manager's own organisation – because usually they don't have an "organization".

> **[GREGG DONOVAN]:** "I wouldn't have a business working as well as it is today, if it wasn't for a handful of people, a couple of them being really good managers who gave me advice,

being John Watson and Michael McMartin (Hoodoo Gurus). Those two guys have been amazing to me. I've literally been able to call them up in my darkest moments and John will have a genius solution and Michael will have a really logical solution."

Cath Haridy has a similar story when asked about the importance of mentors to her career.

[CATH HARIDY]: "Absolutely integral. The people I met along the way I consider to be mentors and very good friends as well. I consider them teachers in the classic sense of being in school when you have your favourite teachers who really inspire you to move forward and be better at what you do. There have been people – and there still are people – in my career that I see that way. Michael Parisi is one very important person because he gave me the opportunity to move and rise and change and learn, within an A&R role, within a record label. I learned a lot of useful, wonderful ways of thinking from him. Linda Bosidis from Mushroom Music was really important to me as well, and still is. She was very generous with her time, very kind and very open to introducing me to a lot of contacts she had and being very inclusive in a lot of things she was doing and with people she was working with."

One of the ways to achieve a mentor relationship is to observe a business that you like and tell them! Industry people are naturally drawn to younger players who have taken the trouble to actually look at their business and appreciate what they see. It's not just rock stars that appreciate having fans.

[JOHANN PONNIAH]: "Jaddan Comerford especially was a huge help to me and so was Jai who used to run Below Par

WELCOME TO THE JUNGLE

Records. I used to email him when I was 14 years old, asking him how to put on shows and he took the time out of his day to talk me through it. I grew up in Sydney and when I moved down to Melbourne Jaddan was a really pivotal person who gave me a lot of advice. Now we are all doing what we are doing and it works well that we are all quite supportive. Australia is too far away from the rest of the world for us to waste time being competitive."

You take your mentors where you can find them – even if it's at the bar! Brisbane festival promoter Zanda Strofield received some valuable guidance from someone he originally met by chance; albeit by being at the right place at the right time.

[ZANDA STROFIELD]: "I do talk to James Dein who is the CEO of the Gympie Muster; he's been a bit of a mentor and a good sounding board for me. The Gympie Muster is a big show – they do 15,000 people a day over five days. He's a mate now, but I actually met him at the industry bar at Splendour. He's someone that I do talk to."

Internationally, the importance of mentorship is just as powerful. For music industry lawyer and former artist John Strohm, the transition he made from the stage to the desk had a lot to do with having experienced professionals he could turn to. Strohm is now the lawyer for important artists such as Alabama Shakes and Ben Kweller.

[JOHN STROHM]: Bertis Downs, for example, has been a great mentor to me. These are the guys that I call. Coming up, I didn't work with entertainment lawyers, and I had to just find my way and I relied very heavily on people who were out there doing it, calling them up and saying, 'hey, this is what I'm trying to do'. I definitely pay it forward. I get a lot of those calls and I take them very seriously. There are some people who want to get into entertainment law for very suspect reasons, but if it's someone who is coming into it because they've been an artist, or they love music or music makers, then that's exactly the sort of people that should be doing this."

My Path into the Industry

MICHAEL PARISI

"I started my music career with *InPress* in a couple of roles, selling advertising and helping out with editorial. I went from *InPress* to Warner in a Victorian Promotions role, which was a fantastic experience. I was thrown in the deep end. Carmel Nunan, who was going to be my boss, went to Sydney to be national promotions manager a week after I started. So I was left with Victoria. I left there to run a new label called Imago, under John Woodruff, who was my first real mentor. Again I was thrown in the deep end. The day after I started there, Woody went overseas for three months to work on the Baby Animals record. BMG stopped the funding for Imago about 18 months after I started there.

"Then Warner got me back to do what they called 'artist development', which really meant I was to work on all the acts that they didn't understand! I was in charge of things like Snoop Dog, Dr.Dre, Nine Inch Nails and Marilyn Manson – which was a fantastic experience because that was the kind of music I was into. It was when the alternative scene was really exploding, post-Nirvana and Jane's Addiction. That involved a lot of travel because I had to travel with those artists whenever they were in Australia, making sure that promotion was working. Because I was travelling so much I was seeing a lot of local bands and I started suggesting bands to Mark Pope who was head of A&R. I fell into A&R that way. He eventually told me that I should go ahead and sign one of these bands and have it as a side-project to my artist development role. He let me sign Regurgitator and from there it was the Superjesus and then the Whitlams and all of a sudden I was in A&R."

Chapter 28

Conclusion

It should be obvious by now that there are an enormous opportunities available to develop a career in the music business in Australia. It may appear daunting, and reading the stories of many of the people featured in this book may make new players think that the competition is intense. However, their stories should also make it clear that successful music industry careers can start from just about anywhere. There is no single right or wrong way to make the grade.

Future Leaders

The international recorded music business has seen incredible business careers evolve, with names such as David Geffen, Jimmy Iovine, Doug Morris and Clive Davis being among the most celebrated in the entire entertainment sphere. And there's no reason why more careers of that type cannot still be possible in the future.

> **[DENIS HANDLIN]:** "I believe the opportunity still exists for the next Doug Morris or Clive Davis to come through and shine in our industry. The characteristics will be the same – a mix of passion, instinct and creativity, intelligence, relationship skills, experience, application, hard work and the ability to lead people. I love a quote from Doug Morris – 'I get into trouble because I'll say that nothing has changed in the whole industry since I started. What hasn't changed is you need a hit.

WELCOME TO THE JUNGLE

What has changed? We distribute music differently, and we sell music differently. Big deal'."

David Williams offers an interesting perspective when considering the likely emergence of new industry leaders. He points out that it's not exactly like the Olympics where you enter the race and hope to win.

> **[DAVID WILLIAMS]:** "There are not 30 potential industry leaders standing at the starting line waiting for someone to fire the gun. They are going to come one at a time and they are going to come through organisations that are already there. There are young people building businesses in the same way the previous and current industry leaders built their businesses. They saw that there was a possibility and went for it. It's great to be able to work in an industry that you really enjoy, but the industry has to be your life. It's not a 9-5 job. You have to be out there all the time. If you are out there and working and creating awareness of what you are working on, then you start to build. It doesn't always work, but if you stick to it you can make it work. I won't say, 'if you believe you can make it happen', because sometimes even if you believe, it won't happen, but if you are going to have that attitude in the first place then it certainly won't happen."

Colin Daniels from Inertia takes a more aggressive view about the opportunities currently on offer in the business. He thinks that the emergence of the new breed was overdue.

> **[COLIN DANIELS]:** "I don't think we had forward-thinking leadership in the late 1990s and early 2000s. The recorded music industry was declining at a rapid rate, people were getting fired and artists were getting dropped. It wasn't a happy industry to be in. Artists were complaining about their

record companies. The media was predicting the demise of the industry. We made a lot of strategic errors and the industry has paid for it. There has been little investment in the future of the industry by record companies. We always need young smart people who want to be in the industry for 20 or 30 years to ensure that we still have an industry to work in in the future."

In the live music side of the business, Michael Coppel believes that similar opportunities exist in his field. He also considers the time is ripe for new leaders to emerge.

[**MICHAEL COPPEL**]: "I think there is a generation of promoters that missed out in Australia. I think we are one of the few markets in the world, along with Japan, where for about 20 years no new promoters came along. There should have been young guys coming along kicking my arse, and Gudinski's arse and Chugg's arse. You shouldn't have 60-year-old guys at the top of the tree. In the past 10 years there have been so many new promoters come along and it will be those that take the industry forward. No matter how much Chuggi and Gudinski want to keep going and die with their boots on, there will be a point where they become irrelevant. We won't be driving the industry. Some of the younger guys are coming out of the culture of the audience that they are selling to. They understand it, they are familiar with it, they are a part of it and their instincts are fashioned by being familiar with the area in which they are working. That's the key to being a promoter; you are the one guy in the crowd that sticks his head up and looks around and thinks, 'I could get this 1000 or 10,000 people to come to a show because I know what they want to see, even though they may not know it yet themselves'."

WELCOME TO THE JUNGLE

The Next Generation

Even some of the current shining stars of the industry realise that the next generation will always be ready to come through.

> **[JADDAN COMERFORD]:** "We talk about it all the time. Somebody made a comment about an older person reaching out to somebody here and they made the joke that they were trying to stay relevant. And I said, 'don't make that joke, we're going to have to do that soon!' We're already doing it. We've got 19-year-old staff and 15-year-old work experience kids. You can't go out every night of the week. You need to have a new generation and you need to look after them. I think a lot of old companies retained a lot of staff through fear, the fear of not being able to work somewhere else, whereas we retain our staff based on really good performance incentives and empowering people to actually make their own decisions and drive their own careers."

Comerford and UNFD put their money where their mouth is. During his Big Sound 2016 keynote speech, Comerford announced The Unified Grant, comprised of five $5000 grants to help passionate young creatives who work in the music industry.

Grants like this are incredibly generous and helpful but no-one should wait for such an offer to be made. Rewards like that generally come to self-starters anyway.

> **[EMILY YORK]:** "I don't think it's this impenetrable thing and I don't think that people should be deterred from getting involved in music, because it's a very vibrant scene, and it's actually such a great time for the next generation beyond me to come up. I think it's a really great time for them because

they will be discovering bands that they go out and see on a Wednesday night at 11 o'clock when I'm probably asleep. It's one of those unfortunate things, that the moment you feel like you get what's going on and you have hit your stride, to a point that's when it's nearly over and it's time to shuffle off and let someone else take over."

For Michael Gudinski, who has been at the top of the tree for so long, some of the best advice for those following him is to put a value of the experience you can gain, and don't get ahead of yourself.

[MICHAEL GUDINSKI]: "It's easy on the way up, but it's very important how you treat people when you are going up. But there are a lot of people who go up, go down just as fast and if you mistreat people on the way up, it's a lot harder coming down, and then it's a lot harder to get back up again. Nothing beats a bit of experience. It's very easy to write a lot of people off, because they are older or because they are not the most savvy in new technology. I never have been and have never claimed to be, but I was smart enough to give my people the money to build the best live touring site in the country – even if I couldn't operate it myself for the first 10 years we had it! You can't beat experience – for every 10 young guys coming up, there will only be one or two that will make it. You will see people that you might not have heard of for a few years, but then the good ones will always come back with a great act. It's when you can have more than one life on the business side of things then you have achieved something."

The First Steps

In his role programming Big Sound Graham Ashton saw numerous people taking their first tentative steps in the industry. Some

WELCOME TO THE JUNGLE

of them have ended up working for him in his business Footstomp Music Services. When asked about his approach when looking for new employees, he tells a story that should be heartening to anyone hoping to break into the business.

> **[GRAHAM ASHTON]:** "It's very clear for me now. I haven't done any interviews for jobs; I've just found people by seeing them around. I do a lot of workshops for young people aspiring to be part of the music industry and I see the same people coming back again and I'll see them at gigs and I just see something in people. The best way I can describe the people I want to work with is that they are not at all interested in the glamour of the music industry and all that kind of stuff, they are just interested in the music of the music industry. There's a girl called Renee Brown that I saw at one of these workshops and she had two black eyes. I said, 'what happened to your head, mate?' And she said, 'I was in the front row at the Living End and I was in the mosh and I got kicked in the head'. I said, 'you're hired!' That was the job interview. She was 18 or 19 at the time. We'd be working with some of her favourite bands and in her publicity role she'd have to go backstage and work with the bands. I'd see her go from the front row moshing with the best of them to going backstage and be completely professional and not starstruck at all. It was just the music that she cared about, not the bullshit. If we have a philosophy about the sort of people we work with, then that's the philosophy."

Michael Gudinski emphasises how important the first steps in a career will be. He has a theory that several people in this book have endorsed. It's probably applicable to a lot of industries but none more so that the music business, where there is no one correct way of doing things. There are even more wrong ways!

ANDREW WATT

[**MICHAEL GUDINSKI**]: "I've found with a lot of people that the first couple of bosses they have had have been very influential on them. That's where you pick up the right and wrong way of doing things. I've seen people and I've looked back in time and seen their first couple of bosses and they have been the wrong people. You have to knock those habits out and that's hard to do once those habits are there. To get in with the right person, you are better off working for nothing than getting paid working for the wrong person. Some of the best people in the music business – and its been that way for a long time – are fans. They have grown up with it, they know what they think and so long as you are willing to work on different music, coming to it by being a fan is hugely beneficial. They want to know more about it, they'll go out on their own accord to listen to stuff and they want to hear new stuff. In any office you need to make your own impact.

When I see someone who comes in with a resume and they've been at six places in two or three years that bothers me. Whether you are working at a major or an indie you've got to work out within a few years of being in the business where you are heading to. Some people are happy never to make bundles of money, but to work on music they love and they make sacrifices for that."

Even within a single organisation you can start in one role and end up doing something completely different. And if you only have one skill, you might end up doing something completely different again – outside the music industry!

[**ADAM JANKIE**]: "People do need to start multi-tasking, because if someone is dedicated to a single job, their position could become obsolete a week later and then they are redundant if they can't do anything else or don't understand anything

WELCOME TO THE JUNGLE

else. Specific to the Illusive companies, there are some staff that are dedicated to specific businesses, but for the most part, staff cross multiple areas. They may start in one position, but they will end up doing a lot more and taking on a lot more."

Gregg Donovan suggests that the knowledge of how all the pieces fit together is important.

[GREGG DONOVAN]: "I've spoken to marketing managers at record companies who have zero idea how publishing works. In other industries I'm sure there are people who understand every facet of their business. There are a lot of executives in our business who have a simple understanding of one piece of the pie and it's constantly surprising to me and it's bad for the industry. We need the next generation of kids coming through to know about all of this and to start thinking about it all coming together from an artist-friendly point of view. If we are able to keep the artists earning money and making a living so they can keep doing this, we are going to have a healthier scene for all of us."

The importance of finding your niche by trial and error has emerged several times in this book and this sometimes means that people have several false starts in their career. History sometimes records these people as the ones with the game-changing ideas.

[CHARLES CALDAS]: "I'm still a firm believer that if you truly have a passion for something and if you have a work ethic you can make it. I know that is a very old-fashioned thing to say, but if someone has that level of passion and commitment and is willing to actively put in the work to put themselves into a field, then they will work it out eventually. But the way the market is now, it has a different set of opportunities and a different set of entry points and it probably rewards entrepreneurship a bit more. I'm a firm believer that any of these organisations need a mix of people, from educated, disciplined business backgrounds, to the maverick mad person who might come up with the killer idea that will make the business what it could be."

This can easily occur in a smaller market like Australia. Internationally, some of the big moves have come from countries other than the traditional US or UK and Australia could just as easily be an incubator for new initiatives.

[THOMAS HEYMANN]: "What is particularly exciting about this industry is that if you have entrepreneur skills and talent, there isn't a better industry in which to hone those skills. Students are not sure that they are going to get a job, but you are not sure of getting a job if you study brain surgery or if you are in the finance sector. If you go to Europe you will see that there are people and economies that are really, really struggling. There are great opportunities in Australia in the service industry and great opportunities to start your career here. And from here you can go to other markets and then if you prove yourself overseas and you want to come back you become highly employable."

Self Starters

A constant theme through the book has been that music isn't the sort of business that will work for anyone expecting to have a career handed to them on a plate. It certainly favours self-starters and those who are prepared to make mistakes and learn from them. It also favors people who have no choice but to be in the industry.

[KEITH RIDGWAY]: "To get into this business, you are going to have to be someone who has the courage of their convictions. It is a business full of big egos and people who are very

WELCOME TO THE JUNGLE

opinionated and will elbow you out of the way. You have to stand your ground. I've realised that I am in this business, whether I make money or I don't make money. I'm in this business because this is who I am. That's the kind of person who can survive in this business; someone for whom being in this business reflects who they are fundamentally. Real musicians get up in the morning and write a song because it's what they do and who they are. It's the same with people who are in the industry. It's not just what they do, it's who they are."

It's also important not to get caught up in the hype of the business. Hopefully anyone reading this book will have worked that out by now, but Steve Wade offers a reality check.

[STEVE WADE]: "My advice would be to never think of yourself as more important than the artists you want to work with. For me it's always about the fact that I get out of bed and think to myself, 'wow, I get to work with Boy & Bear'. I'm a part of their team. Regardless of what success you have and what goals you kick, we are only able to have a job because people sacrifice a whole lot of stuff and have the talent to produce amazing music. Sometimes the allure of working in the music industry obscures those things. If you are thinking 'oh, I want to be backstage', or 'I want to earn lots of money', if any of those things creep in above you feeling privileged to work with talented people, then you have it around the wrong way."

Mary Mihelakos also has some strong advice.

[MARY MIHELAKOS]: "Never compromise yourself. Never lose that passion and whatever you do, do something that you feel good about. Forget what other people think. There is no one you could bring to me whose opinion matters more to me than my own. I would never find myself doing something I didn't want to be doing. There are a lot more options these days and the industry has grown. Volunteer, because a lot of the best stuff is the stuff where there isn't money! I think I got a reputation for being a hard worker that has followed me. Now I've got a reputation for being a trashbag, but that's OK!"

It's almost impossible to put a value on the work done by the likes of Mihelakos in the music business; people who are driven by a passion for music and a drive to get things done. Even without particular qualifications, people like that are unique to the music business and could be role models for others to follow. Richard Moffat recognises this when discussing his hometown of Melbourne, but he could be talking about any great music city.

> **[RICHARD MOFFAT]:** "The reason for that is that we have all these crazy, obsessive music people who are not business people. They are just salt-of-the-earth music people who run this town even though they are not connected to the business of anything, really. I'd put those people on the door of any show in a heartbeat because they are so much a part of the fabric of why everything works here. I think we are privileged to be in a town fuelled by community radio and by a really good community of people that understands the value of music and creative people."

Deathproof PR's Emily Kelly expresses some concern that the raw enthusiasm for doing the basics seems to be lacking in some newcomers. It's a strong warning to new players that if you expect too much too soon, it's obvious to established people in the business.

> **[EMILY KELLY]:** "We can't help but compare the young students with ourselves at the same age/situation and we're

WELCOME TO THE JUNGLE

sometimes surprised at the lack of enthusiasm. Bec and I both recall being giddy at even being in the same room as a mailout. If we had to wrap CDs that were going to *Beat* magazine or *Rolling Stone*, we were beside ourselves with our newfound proximity to cool music magazines. That kind of attitude is not as apparent anymore. Or maybe we were just massive dorks! We appreciate a person with passion who can get excited about new music because that's the thing that's going to sustain them through the boring bits."

Final Words of Advice

ARIA's Dan Rosen speaks for many industry people when he suggests that the best way of getting started, is simply by getting started.

[DAN ROSEN]: "I think the key is to get a start wherever you can. Don't wait for the perfect job to come along – just start somewhere. You meet a lot of people who you think might be at the top of the game, but they have all come through various doors. It's about getting your foot in the door and once you are in, proving yourself. It's about being patient, but then working hard and proving yourself. You have to learn an enormous amount and find good people to align yourself with and if you are passionate about it and follow that approach, you will end up finding your right niche within the industry."

[GRAEME ASHTON]: "When I managed to get a start in the music industry, it was almost impossible for people in the business not to notice me, because I was at every gig; wherever they went, I was sniffing around. I was working on doors and being an all rounder. In those days it was 'start your own fanzine' now it's 'start your own blog'. In those days you would get a part-time job at a record store. That's obviously a lot harder these days, but now it's about working the door at a venue or something like that. It's about being incredibly visible and learning as much as you can. I still think you have to swallow your pride for a couple of years and do the shit jobs for next to nothing and do them well, honestly and passionately and your opportunities will arise from there. That's a bit of an old-school way of looking at things, but that's certainly the type of people I'd be hiring."

[**JAKE GOLD**]: "I've been saying for a long time that if you don't commit to 10 years of any one thing then you can't be successful. You need 10 years to gain respect in your chosen field. If you want to have relationships with people, they don't want to invest in someone who is not going to be around tomorrow. That's a really important piece of information that everyone's got to understand. Ten years is what you need for people to say you are a lifer. Before you hit 10 years you are not really in the business, you are *trying* to be in the business."

[**MARK POSTON**]: "You've got to make your own path. If you are good at what you do and you are true to yourself and true to the music and true to the artists you work with, then that will carry you through. None of that other stuff should get in your way. For me, the more diversity the better and the more creative and more crazy the better. I'd honestly be happy to come into work and see people dancing on top of their desks and going crazy. Something that happened in the past 10 years, with all the doom and gloom while we were searching for the new model in music, it lost a bit of its creativity and craziness. We have to remember that we are working with artists and they actually respond to imagination and creativity and energy. You need that more than ever to get through now."

[**JOHN WATSON**]: "I never set out to 'build a career' and I'd almost be a little suspicious of those who do. I just set out

WELCOME TO THE JUNGLE

to find a way to make a living somehow from being around music because I truly loved it and found it exciting. I never knew there was such a thing as networking – I was just making friends with people who were equally obsessed with music. However, in hindsight, those relationships I forged through my twenties have turned out to be the bedrock for my entire career. My advice to young people starting in the business is therefore really simple – always deliver more than you promised to deliver, before you promised to deliver it. Bite off more than you can chew and chew like hell – volunteer for public radio, write a blog, manage your friend's band, work the door at your local venue. Do anything and everything that allows you to gain experience and meet people. Read lots and ask lots of questions. Don't be afraid to make mistakes, but try not to make the same mistake twice. Through all of it, remember that your reputation is either your biggest asset in business or your biggest liability, so treat it accordingly."

Interviewees

Michael Newton is the director of Roundhouse Entertainment, the company behind the A Day On The Green events having previously been a booking agent at Premier Artists.

Paul Gildea has been a 25 year member of Icehouse, played lead guitar for James Reyne, Rick Price, Daryl Braithwaite, operated his own production studio, managed acts such as Motor Ace, Michael Paynter and Stonefield and heads the music business program at the Melbourne campus of AIM.

Michael Gudinski is probably the Australian music industry's only genuine household name and as the founder of the Mushroom Group of companies his interests include record labels, agencies, venues, touring companies, management, merchandise, media, marketing, film and television.

Luke O'Sullivan is the former Managing Director of the Hi-Fi Group, the operator of Hi-Fi live music venues in Melbourne, Sydney and Brisbane.

Colin Daniels has been the Managing Director of music distribution and services company Inertia since 2007 and is on the board of global rights agency, Merlin.

Charles Caldas is the CEO of Merlin, a global rights agency representing the world's most important collective of independent music rights with members including the world's leading independent labels. An Australian, Charles was formerly CEO of Shock Records, Australia's

WELCOME TO THE JUNGLE

largest and highest-profile independent music company and has been on the boards of ARIA, AIR and WIN.

Carl Gardiner has been proactively developing relationships and creating music initiatives with prominent Australian brands, marketers and Government for over thirty years as an executive with Mushroom Marketing.

Allen Bargfrede is Executive Director, Rethink Music, an Associate Professor, Berklee College of Music and the Co-Author of the book Music Law in the Digital Age,

Vanessa Picken has been at the coalface of digital music for the last six years working at EMI Australia before launching her own business in 2011, a digital agency called Comes With Fries.

Mark Poston was Head of Capitol Records at EMI Australia before a stint as Managing Director of Parlophone Australia and Warner Bros. Records Australia.

John Watson is the owner and President of both John Watson Management and the label, Eleven: a music company. Over the last 15 years every artist on the JWM and Eleven rosters has enjoyed either gold or multi-platinum success and the companies have helped four separate artists achieve gold certifications in the United States.

Sat Bisla runs LA based artist development and consultancy business A&R Worldwide and the MusExpo Conference.

Leigh Treweek is the Director of Street Press Australia, the publisher of a network of street press titles in Sydney, Melbourne, Perth and Brisbane and on-line destinations including The Music.

ANDREW WATT

Rev. Moose runs a New York based marketing and promotions company, Marauder.

Pixie Weyand is the owner of iconic Brisbane venue, The Zoo as well as industry favorite café Lost Boys and is the founder of the forthcoming Feed Music project

Peter Leak is one of the world's best-credentialed managers currently operating his management business under the umbrella of Red Light Management, one of the most powerful management businesses in the world.

Todd Rundgren is a legendary American musician, songwriter, recording artist and record producer and was one of the first rock artists to explore the possibilities of video production and internet distribution.

Gregg Donovan had his own artist management company with Stuart MacQueen called Wonderlick Entertainment currently overseeing the management of Boy & Bear, Airbourne, Grinspoon, Josh Pyke, Max & Bianca, Marvin Priest, Jackson McLaren, Tim Hart and The Paper Kites.

Joel Connolly is co-director of music company Umbrella with Greg Carey (see separate entry). Predominately an artist management company they look after the careers of Australian bands, Belles Will Ring, Cloud Control, Fishing, The Rubens (Aust/NZ) & Urthboy.

Greg Carey is co-director of music company Umbrella with Joel Connolly (see separate entry). Predominately an artist management company they look after the careers of Australian bands, Belles Will Ring, Cloud Control, Fishing, The Rubens (Aust/NZ) & Urthboy.

WELCOME TO THE JUNGLE

Richie McNeill was Managing Director of Festivals, Touring and New Business of Totem OneLove Group, the promoters of Stereosonic and Creamfields. Richie has well over a quarter century of experience in EDM and is one of Australia's pioneers of the genre.

Dror Erez is the Managing Director of Totem OneLove Group Pty Ltd the promoters of Stereosonic and Creamfields.

Nathan McLay has been an active in the Australian electronic music scene for close to ten years, both as a DJ and as founder of internationally respected record label Future Classic, an indie music company encompassing artist management, record label, music publishing, booking & touring.

Denis Handlin is CEO of Sony Music Entertainment Australia & New Zealand and President, Asia. He has been with the company since 1970 and leading it since 1984. Denis is also the long-time Chairman of ARIA.

Simon Moor opened the Australian office for Kobalt Music Group and is now currently the Managing Director for Kobalt Music Publishing Australia and is responsible for working with Kobalt's international roster of writers and artists as well as the growing local roster.

Marianna Annas is Head of ABC Music Publishing. An experienced music lawyer and formerly at Simpsons Solicitors, Marianna has also held senior legal and business affairs roles at major record labels and music publishers.

David Williams launched Shock Records in 1988, quickly becoming Australia's largest independent recorded music company and now operates a music company active in licensing, A&R, touring, label representation, digital services, CD, vinyl & DVD, distribution, marketing and publicity.

ANDREW WATT

Ruth Barlow is Head of Live at the Beggars Group based in the UK.

Jaime Gough is the head of music publisher Native Tongue

Dan Rosen is the CEO of ARIA (the Australian Recording Industry Association).

Brett Cottle has been the Chief Executive of Australasian Performing Right Association (APRA) since 1990, and of the Australasian Mechanical Copyright Owners Society (AMCOS) since 1997.

Mark Meharry is the founder of UK based music retail platform Music Glue.

Steve Halpin is the head of Cattleyard, the promoters of the Groovin' The Moo regional touring festival.

Susan Cotchin operates International Royalties Rescue, a neighboring rights management company.

Jackie Krajl has been operating in the digital side of the Australian music industry for 10 years and now spends her time working with clients across the industry on digital strategies, project management, content creation and digital distribution plans with her company Digi Rascal.

Thomas Heymann is an executive at music streaming service Pandora and prior to that role was head of Deezer for Australian and New Zealand.

Michael Parisi operates his own record label (Wunderkind – a joint venture with Michael Gudinski) and a Music Management and Consultancy Company and also helps major companies like Soundhalo, Red Bull, Gucci and NAB with their music strategies.

WELCOME TO THE JUNGLE

Ruuben van den Heuvel has been a senior international business executive with leading multi-national companies including Sony Music, Nokia, NewsCorp and most recently Google in Asia, Europe & Australia.

Rowena Crittle heads the Australian arm of music merchandising business The Araca Group

Bill Cullen is the managing director and founder of One Louder Entertainment – providing management to End Of Fashion, Paul Kelly, Sarah Blasko, Kate Miller-Heidke and Seeker Lover Keeper. He is also a Director of the PPCA, an APRA ambassador and a founding director of the Association of Artist Managers.

Bertis Downs is best known as the lawyer and de facto manager for R.E.M. throughout their career.

Bernard Galbally is the General Manager of Mana Music Australia. Mana Music has been licensing music for the Film and Television industry for over 20 years. Bernard is in charge of commercials and premium licensing and he also looks after overseas catalogue management.

Jaddan Comerford is a Melbourne based music entrepreneur who formed the Staple Group with Ben Turnbull (see separate entry) a Melbourne based collection of music businesses and in 2014 established We Are Unified (aka UNFD) a diverse music company housing labels, management and publishing interests

Ben Turnbull was the joint founder of The Staple Group with Jadden Comerford (see separate listing) having been the promoter behind iconic alternative club nights. He owns Destroy All Lines Touring which works in partnership with Chugg Entertainment.

ANDREW WATT

Terry Blamey is best known for having successfully managed the worldwide career of Kylie Minogue for over 25 years.

Adam Jankie is the co-founder (with Matt Gudinski) and Chief Operations Officer of the Illusive Entertainment Group and now has a senior role in the Mushroom Group of which Illusive forms a part.

Johann Ponniah created Melbourne music company I OH YOU in late 2009 and has also extended to function as a record label that releases DZ Deathrays, Snakadaktal, Bleeding Knees Club and Violent Soho, while also promoting tours for international acts.

Ian James has been the Managing Director of Mushroom Music since 1986 and is Chairman of the Australasian Mechanical Copyright Owners Society Limited, Deputy Chairman of the Australasian Performing Right Association and a Director of the Australasian Music Publishers Association Limited.

Nick O'Byrne was General Manager of the Australian Independent Record Labels Association (AIR) for several years and was appointed to the position of Executive Programmer of Big Sound for 2014 while maintaining a very successful management business himself that looks after artists including Courtney Barnett.

Paul Piticco managed the career of Powderfinger, later forming Secret Service Artist Management in the late 1990's and expanding the management roster. In 2001 Paul created Dew Process, an independent record label and is also Co-Producer of Splendour in The Grass and national touring company Secret Sounds.

Michael Coppel has been one of Australia's most prominent concert promoters for over thirty years and built an incredible touring

WELCOME TO THE JUNGLE

business under his own banner before having that business acquired by global live concert giant Live Nation in 2012. Michael now heads Live Nation's Australian operation.

Dave Faulkner is the lead singer and major songwriter for legendary Australian rock band Hoodoo Gurus, who have had numerous successful albums and tours over a thirty-year career.

Millie Millgate is the Export Music Producer at Sounds Australia promoting Australian musical repertoire to the world at events such as MIDEM, SXSW, The Great Escape, CMJ Music Marathon, Music Matters, Americana, Folk Alliance International and Canadian Music Week.

Ben Thompson was the director of the Venue Collective, an independent venue booking operation that booked multiple Australian live music venues and he continues to book a number of venues.

Frank Stivala is the Managing Director of booking agency Premier Artists and plays a role at Frontier Touring while also operating venues in Melbourne.

Richard Moffat heads Way Over There an independent music programming business representing local venues and national Australian music festivals including Falls Festival, Southbound Festival, Groovin' the Moo and Parklife.

Tim Northeast is co-owner and operator of a number of venues including the Corner Hotel, the Northcote Social Club and the Newtown Social Club in Sydney.

Brian Lizotte and his wife Jo set up their first Lizotte's restaurant on the Central Coast of New South Wales. This has been followed by two more venues that combine great music with great food.

ANDREW WATT

Emily York is the founder and director of touring company Penny Drop located in Melbourne. They provide bands with full service Australian tours with partners in New Zealand and Asia.

Michael Chugg is one of the truly legendary figures in the Australian music business. After co-founding The Frontier Touring Company in the mid 1970s, in 2000 Michael went out on his own and founded Chugg Entertainment, from there going on to garner a reputation both internationally and locally as one of Australia's most prominent rock promoters.

Frank Cotela is a director of Totem One Love. Credited with changing the aesthetic face of dance music culture in Australia, Frank has worked behind the scenes on some of the country's most successful and prolific EDM brands for over 30 years.

Jessica Ducrou established Village Sounds as a booking agency to represent her then large roster of notable Australian acts, before going on to create the Splendour in the Grass festival As well as her festival promotion role, Jessica continues to expand her domestic booking agency Village Sounds and also operates Secret Sounds, an international touring company in partnership with Paul Piticco from Secret Service

Sophie Miles founded Mistletone an independent label and touring company, in 2006 with her husband Ash. Mistletone has grown into a thriving indie touring and events company and much-respected label with a catalogue of over 65 titles and since 2006, Mistletone has promoted over 50 tours.

Joe Alexander runs independent record label Bedroom Sucks

Julia Wilson operates prolific indie record label Rice Is Nice

Mark Dodds is an A&R and Australian Music Manager at Inertia and operates their touring company Handsome Tours.

WELCOME TO THE JUNGLE

Tim Janes heads a Universal Label Services arm in Australia called Caroline Label Services and has also served on the AIR Board.

Harvey Saward is joint owner of record company Remote Control (with Steve Cross) that includes an impressive local and international roster and PR services.

Andy Kelly is one third of Winterman & Goldstein Management, Ivy League Records and Ivy League Music Publishing (along with Pete Lusty and Andy Cassell) working with The Vines, Jet, Empire Of The Sun, Lanie Lane, Youth Group, Something For Kate, Paul Dempsey and The Mess Hall.

Zac Abroms operates Viceroyalty, Artist Management & Music Publicity specializing in Online PR, Branding and Content Production and is the co-prorammer of music conference, Face The Music

Danny Rogers heads Lunatic Entertainment, an artist management and touring company representing Gotye, The Temper Trap and CHVRCHES with offices in Sydney and London. Danny is also co-founder of St. Jerome's Laneway Festival.

Bonnie Dalton is an artist manager for clients such as Little Red, Husky and Ali Barter & Oscar Dawson. In the past Bonnie has also been the Artist Logistics Manager at The Falls Festival and a producer at Laneway Festival.

Steve Kilbey is the lead singer, bass player and songwriter for The Church, one of Australia's longest running and most respected bands.

Benji Rogers is CEO and co-founder of Pledge Music, a crowdfunding based business which helps artists use digital technology to

ANDREW WATT

create financially rewarding direct-to-fan relationships with offices in London, New York, Los Angeles, Boston and Melbourne.

Frank Varrasso started radio promotion and publicity company Varrasso PR in January 2009 working across radio, television and print.

Peter Foley operates The Caravan Music Club and Memo Music Hall.

Catherine Haridy is an artist manger for Eskimo Joe, Jebediah, Adalita and Bob Evans and a number of music producers and is also a currently Chairman of the Association of Artist Managers, an APRA Ambassador and is s board member on the Community Broadcasting Foundation,

Craig Hawker is the Head of A&R / Creative of Sony/ATV Music Publishing Australia.

Kim Green is a freelance Music Supervisor (owner operator of Music Licensing Pty Ltd) specialising in music licensing for film, TV and theatre worldwide.

Jess Beston is Director and Founder of Tiny Monster, a boutique music business specialising in Artist Management for The Trouble With Templeton and Holy Holy, and A&R/Management Consulting.

Jake Gold is Director and CEO of Toronto-based management company, The Management Trust and has been awarded 'Manager of the Year' three times by the Canadian Music Industry and was also synonymous with Canadian Idol, after his appearance on the judging panel for six seasons.

Rae Harvey has been artist manger for The Living End since 1997 and in the last eight years also started managing artists including Children Collide, Gyroscope, 360 and PEZ.

WELCOME TO THE JUNGLE

Brett Murrihy is a booking agent and CEO of Artist Voice, a full service talent agency based in Sydney, a company that recently became part of the William Morris global agency business.

Jon Perring has been the co-owner of venues including Bar Open, Pony, Yah Yah's and The Tote Hotel in Melbourne and is a participant in the Live Music Taskforce and a former member of City of Yarra Arts Advisory Committee.

James Young is the proprietor of the Cherry Bar and Yah Yah's and the marketing business Cherry Rock.

Mary Mihelakos writes Sticky Carpet, a weekly column in The Age, and has booked live music venues including Yah Yahs and The Prince, while also establishing a music festival for the City of Yarra in Melbourne and starting Stage Mothers with Glenn Dickie.

Stephen Wade is owner and booking agent at Select Music, a major talent agency.

Rob Zaferelli is a senior talent agent for United Talent Agency based in Toronto, Canada

Fraser Bourke is a tour promoter specializing in alternative music and less commercial artists through his company Metropolis Touring.

Brian Taranto started Love Police, a company and brand that has gone on to be a multi-faceted business producing merchandise, graphic design, concert and tour promoting and book publishing.

Peter Noble is sole Festival Director and owner of Australia's Bluesfest.

Aly Ehlinger is a Talent Buyer at giant concert promoter C3 Presents in Austin, TX. C3 creates, books, markets, and produces live experiences,

ANDREW WATT

concerts, and events including Austin City Limits, Lollapalooza, and more than 1000 shows nationwide.

Nicole Hart is a music industry publicist with over 20 years experience operating her own company Revolutions Per Minute since 2006 where she devises and manages media, publicity and radio campaigns for a variety of clients.

Brian McDonald operates RiSH Publicity with a roster that has included numerous international and local acts and events.

Emily Kelly started Music PR company Deathproof PR with Bec Reato working with local acts at a grassroots level as well as collaborating with major labels and promoters on international releases and tours.

Graeme Ashton operates Footstomp Music, a music services company specialising in artist, project, event management and artist mentoring and was the Executive programmer for BIGSOUND until 2013.

Matt Gudinski now sits aside his father Michael at the helm of the country's biggest independent music and entertainment group which includes almost two dozen music and entertainment entities including the likes of Frontier Touring, Liberation Music, Ivy League, Mushroom Music Publishing and Love Police ATM.

Keith Ridgway is the director of a music and events company called A-Live Events having been an artist manager and booking agent.

John Rash has been the head of brand and music agency Brand New Sounds founded in 2010 and now works in London with a brand management agency.

WELCOME TO THE JUNGLE

Kim Carter is Executive Partner and Strategic Director at streetwise marketing agency Rockstar Management working with multiple youth and entertainment brands for the last 12 years.

Jennifer Sullivan is the President of memBrain, a strategic entertainment consulting firm based in Los Angeles.

Patrick Donovan is the CEO of Music Victoria, the peak body for contemporary music, in Victoria. This followed a 15 year career at the Age Newspaper, where he was chief music writer for 12 years.

Nick Wallberg founded Tram Sessions a not-for-profit enterprise providing public access to musicians by operating gigs on Melbourne trams.

Simon Smith is head of the Entertainment Business Management department at the Melbourne campus of JMC Academy having previously been a booking agent and musician.

David Lewis has been the Director of Career Services for McNally Smith College of Music in Minneapolis, USA.

John Strohm was formerly a musician with bands such as the Lemonheads and Blake Babies before launching a career in music and entertainment law in Nashville USA.

Scot Crawford has over 20 years experience in entertainment marketing and currently represents Pledge Music in Australia and is the manager of artists including James Reyne and Palace Of The King.

Chris O'Brien is the General Manager of Destroy All Lines Touring. Chris is also an active participant in the mentor program operated by The Push and also has an artist management business.

Index

123 Agency 106
360 Deal 137-140
Adam Jankie 139, 145, 150-151, 156-157, 209, 216, 311, 407, 443-444, 445, 465, 496-497, 525-526
Ahmet Ertegun 257
AJ Maddah 122, 334
Allen Bargfrede 49-50, 54, 80-81, 198, 240
Aly Ehlinger 341-343, 346-347, 479
Amanda Palmer 165
Amazon 12, 56, 83-84
Amy Schmidt 94, 97
Andrew McManus 113
Andy Cassell 130
Andy Kelly 130, 151-152, 181, 193, 260, 265-266, 279
Andrew Stafford 93
Ann Gibson XIX
Apple 4, 6, 12, 41-42, 46-47, 55
AAM 85, 284, 427-429, 445
ABC Music 34, 62
AC-DC 42
AIR 85, 211, 214, 225, 432
AMCOS 65-66
AMIN 227, 426

AMPAL 85, 415
AMRA 28
APRA/AMCOS 16-17, 44, 66-68, 77-78, 85-87, 91, 102, 157, 415, 419-425, 436, 473
ARIA 28, 35, 38, 85, 149, 431-432
Ari Emanuel 316
Artfacts 28, 44-45
Artist Voice 107
Australian Institute of Music XV 457, 458

Beats 54
Ben Eltham 424
Ben Thompson 306, 460
Ben Turnbull 144, 447
Benji Rogers 166-171, 277
Berklee 49
Bernard Galbally 245, 246, 247, 248, 412, 469
Bernard Zuel 43
Bertis Downs 58-59, 90, 243, 289, 455, 466, 473, 516
Big Day Out 120, 122, 128
Big Sound 336, 427, 487, 495-497, 523
Bill Cullen 57, 107, 176, 225, 268, 270-271, 272, 470, 478

WELCOME TO THE JUNGLE

Black Keys 6, 115, 135, 330
Bluesfest 113, 120, 121, 122, 336
BMG 41, 60
Bonnie Dalton 182, 276, 278, 283, 287, 483-484, 494
Bono 49
Brett Cottle 44, 87, 175, 420-423, 436, 473-474
Brett Murrihy 106, 146, 173, 186, 291, 312, 316, 317, 319, 454, 471
Brian Lizotte 108, 294
Brian McDonald 354-355, 358, 364, 366-367, 370
Brian Taranto 330, 405-405, 406, 407, 408-410

C3 128
Carl Gardiner 10, 173, 390-391, 394, 398, 399
Cath Haridy 199-200, 253, 269, 283-285, 507-508, 510, 515
Charles Caldas 2, 7, 12, 52, 56, 79, 81, 185-186, 213, 229, 386, 439-440, 485-486, 526-527
Chris O'Brien 334, 491-493, 513
Claire Bowditch 513-514
Clinton Walker 92
Clive Davis 519
Coca Cola 148
Collarts 457
Cooking Vinyl 155
Colin Daniels 6, 8, 12, 13, 20, 38, 50, 115, 133, 184-185, 197, 230, 520

Coran Capshaw IX, 141, 148, 290
Craig Hawker 20, 241, 242-243, 256-257, 260, 261
Creative Victoria 417

Damian Costin 106
Damien Cunningham 92
Daniel Ek 48-49, 147
Danielle Caruana 514
Dan Rosen 35, 85, 149-150, 202, 470, 482, 530
Danny Rogers 122, 175-176, 186, 348-349
Dave Faulkner 94-97
David Geffen 478, 519
David Lewis 455-456, 460-461, 479-480
David Vodicka 214-215, 504
David Williams 2, 34, 116, 153-154, 229-231, 331, 418-419, 452, 485, 488-489, 520
Dean Linguey 418
Denis Handlin 32, 138, 192, 201-202, 203, 204-205, 483
Dror Erez 32, 123-124, 340-341, 447-448
Doug Morris 519
Duran Duran 74

Eleven 14
Elliot Roberts 478
EMDG 415-417
Emily Kelly 363, 367, 369, 371-372, 529-531

ANDREW WATT

Emily York 110, 135, 172, 326-327, 522-523

Facebook 27, 30, 50, 119, 134, 386, 447
Face The Music 378, 427, 487, 495
Fair Music Project 49
Frank Cotela 123-124
Frank Sinatra 36
Frank Stivala 104-106, 302, 310, 315-316, 321, 345
Frank Varrasso 307, 352, 356-357, 361-363, 364-365, 372, 504
Frazer Bourke 308, 327-328, 474
Future Classic 133, 151, 218, 221

Gary Van Egmond 113
Gene Simmons 403
Gerard Schlaghecke 330
Google 4, 12, 51, 56, 154
Graham Ashton 366, 370, 476, 497-498, 523-524, 530-531
Guy Orseary IX, 148-149
Greg Carey 30-31, 445, 468
Gregg Donovan 26, 143, 193, 253-254, 283, 287-288, 405, 514-515, 526
Groovin' The Moo 105, 339, 342

Harbour Agency 106, 142, 146, 313
Harvey Saward 180, 215, 218, 226-227
Howard Freeman 333

Ian James 77-78, 232, 239, 242, 243, 281
IFPI 45
Inertia 6, 115, 229, 520
Instagram 27
iTunes 42, 45-46, 74-76, 83, 148
Irving Azoff 126

Jacqui Krajl 45-46, 51, 377-378, 380-382
Jaddan Comerford 13, 144, 145, 178-179, 209, 211, 215-216, 222, 262, 281-282, 414, 446, 489, 515, 522
Jake Gold 264, 285-286, 418, 531
Jaime Gough 234, 237, 242, 463
James Dein 516
James Overton 385
James Packer 55
James Young 299, 504, 508
Jay Brown 142
Jay Z 56, 142
Jennifer Sullivan 393-394, 395, 397
Jerome Barazio 175
Jess Beston 190, 193, 252, 258
Jessica Ducrou 88, 113, 132, 143, 347-348, 350
Jim Griffin 90
Jimmy Iovine 54, 519
JMC Academy 454, 457
Joe Alexander 209, 210, 220, 224
Joel Connolly 30, 153, 467, 489-490
Johann Ponniah 250, 447, 515-516
John Butler 514

WELCOME TO THE JUNGLE

John Kalodner 256
John O'Donnell 20
John Rash 392-393, 394
John Strohm 456-457, 466, 516-517
John Wardle 91-92
John Watson 14, 29, 143, 176, 181-182, 196-197, 204, 270, 274-275, 445-446, 531-532
John Woodruff 518
Jon Perring 298, 306
Jon Pope 333
Julia Wilson 179, 209, 210, 212, 221-222, 223-224

Karlheinz Brandenberg 40
Keith Ridgway 392, 436-437, 439, 489, 499, 527-528
Kim Carter 396-397, 398, 399-400, 486-487
Kim Green 244-245, 245-246, 247, 248, 249
Kirsty Rivers 418
Kobalt Music Group 33, 77, 236
Kylie Minogue 65

Lance Whitney 84
Laneway 121-122, 175-176
Lars Ulrich 38
Leigh Treweek 391-392, 480-481, 504-505, 506-507
Lee M Bass 55
Len Blavatnik 55
Linda Bosidis 241

Live Music Office 92, 104
Live Music and Performance Taskforce 102
Live Nation 89, 113, 125-127, 148, 329
Live Performance Australia 15-16, 90, 430
Love Police 115, 142
Luke O'Sullivan 5, 118, 297, 300

Matthew Burke 94, 97
Matt Gudinski 3, 8, 31, 106, 150, 180, 216, 228, 316-317, 357, 358, 396
Matthew Guy 100
Marc Geiger 106-107
Mark Dodds 209, 219, 255, 258
Mark Poston 11, 136-137, 185, 203-204, 450, 531
Mark Meharry 159-161, 410
Marianna Annas 34, 61-62, 234-235, 238, 230-240, 462, 468-469, 472-473
Martin Elbourne XVIII, 102-103
Martin Mills IX, 139, 215
Mary Mihelakos 304-305, 437-438, 502, 505, 528-529
Michael Browning 92
Michael Chugg 91-92, 109, 110, 112, 114, 117, 122, 131, 135, 302-303, 323-324, 328, 330, 332, 337, 521
Michael Coppel 89-91, 109, 110-111, 112, 114, 120-121, 124, 127, 131,

133-134, 325-326, 328, 332-333, 337-338, 339-340, 521
Michael Gudinski IX, 3, 91, 109, 110, 112, 123, 131, 142, 196, 202, 227, 266-267, 330, 337, 357-358, 444, 446, 478, 521, 523, 524-525
Michael Harrison 91, 330
Michael Jackson 235-236
Michael McMartin 515
Michael Newton XII, XIII, XIX, 119, 174
Michael Parisi 138-139, 202-203, 209, 211, 212, 220, 226, 254-255, 257, 259, 261-262, 277, 448, 504, 506, 515, 518
Michael Rapino 113, 127
Millie Millgate 97, 101, 125, 177, 307, 402, 414-415, 500
Mistletone 9, 115, 132, 213, 217
Molly Meldrum 4, 358
Mushroom Group of Companies 3, 10, 77, 123, 131, 142, 214, 228, 390
Music Business Education 464-465
Music Glue 159-161, 410
Music Matters 84

National Live Music Office 91
Nathan McLay 133, 151, 209, 218, 221
Napster 38-41, 46
Neil Bradbury 506

Neil Young 389
Next Big Sound 385
Nick Marson 333
Nick O'Byrne 166, 208-209, 211, 220-221, 225, 480
Nick Wallberg 441-443, 469-470
Nicole Hart 200-201, 353-354, 355-356, 365, 368, 371

One Music 67

Pandora 6, 46-47, 385
Patrick Donovan 193, 426-427, 482, 491, 498
Patrick Whitesell 316
Paul Dainty 109,112, 337
Paul Gildea XIV, XV, 193, 275
Paul Piticco 113, 143-144, 176, 179, 209, 212-213, 217, 223, 268, 271, 290
Penny Drop 110, 135, 326
Peter Karpin 241
Peter Foley 292, 295
Peter Leak 18-19, 183-184, 224-225, 272-273, 279, 280, 282
Peter Noble 113, 336, 338-339, 343-344, 345, 350-351, 419
Phil Dwyer 61
Pixie Weyand 109, 295, 299
Pledge Music 166-171
PPCA 17, 66-68, 415
Premier Artists 104, 105, 142, 313

WELCOME TO THE JUNGLE

Rae Harvey 273, 289
RIAA 39, 41-42
Red Bull 148, 157
Red Light Management 18, 141, 280, 282
R.E.M. 58
Renee Brown 524
Rene Ritchie 55
Rethink Music 49
Rev Moose 177-178, 360
Richard Kingsmill 5
Richard Moffat 105, 118, 172, 303-306, 487, 507, 529
Richie McNeill 31, 121, 124-125
Robert Levine 9
Rob Ziferelli 183, 318-319
Roc Nation 142
Roundhouse Entertainment 119
Rowena Crittle 404, 406
Ruth Barlow 140-141, 159
Ruuben van den Heuval 51, 186-187, 198-199, 441

SAE 457
Sat Bisla 13-14, 19, 161, 178, 182-183, 363-364
Scooter Braun IX, 148, 183
Scot Crawford 166, 193, 206, 463-464, 474-475
Scott Borchetta 48
Select 106, 312
Shawn Fanning 39
Shock 7, 34, 116, 229

Simon Moor 33, 77 236-238, 471-472
Simon Smith 193, 454, 458-459, 460, 467, 468, 481, 492
SLAM 99-100
Sony Music 35
Sophie Miles 9, 132-133, 209, 213-214, 218
Sounds Australia 101, 177, 415
Soundwave 122
Splendour In The Grass 121
Spotify 6, 7, 45-46, 53, 56, 58, 149, 385
Stereosonic 124
Steve Halpin 339, 342-343, 386-387
Steve Kilbey 164
Steve Wade 213, 312-313, 314, 319-320, 484, 528
Stevie Van Zandt
Stuart Coupe 3, 110, 117
Susan Cotchin 68
SXSW 6, 8, 158, 176, 307, 484, 499-500

Taylor Swift 48
Ted Cohen 57
Terry Blamey 267, 273-274
Tim Janes 134-135, 434, 504, 508
Tim Northeast 108, 294, 296, 297-298, 300-301, 322
Todd Rundgren 25, 43
Tony Grace 146
The Push 512-513
Thomas Edison 22-23

ANDREW WATT

Thomas Heymann 47, 458, 527
Totem One Love 31, 123, 340-341, 390
Trent Reznor 54
Troy Carter IX, 148-149, 183
Triple J 5
Tunecore 75
Twitter 27

Umbrella 30, 42
UNFD 13, 117, 144, 209, 215, 262, 281
Universal 35, 196

Vanessa Picken 10, 152-153, 375, 376-377, 382-384, 496

Vevo 155-
Victor Willis 73
Village Sounds 106

Warner 35, 42
Warren Zanes
Willard Ahditz 33
WME 106-107, 316, 454

You Tube 11, 27, 30, 50, 77, 119, 141, 154, 157-158, 183, 262, 474

Zac Abroms 374, 378-381, 384
Zanda Strofield 388, 516

About the Author

Andrew Watt is a lawyer, writer and educator. The holder of law and economics degrees from Monash University and a Master of Arts (Creative Enterprise) from Deakin University, Andrew has had a long career in the entertainment and music industries, including roles as an entertainment lawyer, street press publisher (founder of InPress), band manager, music publishing executive, television producer and venue owner.

Andrew currently lectures at a number of Music Business Programs in Melbourne Australia and has created an on-line music business course at www.musicbusinesseducation.com.au

www.ingramcontent.com/pod-product-compliance
Lightning Source LLC
Chambersburg PA
CBHW070522090426
42735CB00013B/2856